Policing across the World

Policing across the World

Issues for the Twenty-first Century

R.I. Mawby

First published in 1999 by UCL Press

UCL Press Limited
1 Gunpowder Square
London EC4A 3DE
UK

Distributed in North America by

Garland Publishing
19 Union Square West
New York
NY10003–3382
USA

363.2

The name of University College London (UCL) is a registered trade mark used by UCL
Press with the consent of the owner.

British Library Cataloguing-in-Publication Data
A CIP catalogue record for this book is available from the British Library.

Library of Congress Cataloging-in-Publication Data are available

ISBN: 1–85728–488–7 HB
      1–85728–489–5 PB

Typeset by Graphicraft Limited, Hong Kong.
Printed by T.J. International, Padstow, UK.

Contents

Notes on Contributors

Rob Mawby is Professor of Criminology and Criminal Justice at the University of Plymouth. After receiving his doctorate from the University of Sheffield he lectured at Leeds and Bradford before moving to Plymouth in 1980. He is the author of numerous books and articles on the criminal justice system, especially policing and victimology, and much of his recent work has a cross-national dimension. Books include *Comparative Policing Issues: British and American Experience in Comparative Perspective* (1990, London: Routledge) and (with Sandra Walklate) *Critical Victimology* (1994, London: Sage). He has recently completed directing a CEU and Nuffield funded project comparing police response to victims in England, Germany, Poland, the Czech Republic and Hungary.

David Bayley is Dean and Professor in the School of Criminal Justice, State University of New York at Albany. He has been acknowledged as an expert on comparative policing since the publication of *Police and Political Development in India* in 1969, followed by *Forces of Order: Police Behaviour in Japan and the United States* in 1976, which was reprinted in modified form in 1991. His extensive research and publications cover a broad spectrum of policing systems and are well illustrated in his latest book, *Police for the Future* (1994, New York: Oxford University Press).

Monica den Boer is currently Senior Lecturer in Justice and Home Affairs at the European Institute of Public Administration in Maastricht. Since receiving her doctorate from the European University Institute in Florence in 1990 she has worked on an ESRC funded project on European police co-operation at the University of Edinburgh and was subsequently seconded from the Netherlands Institute for the Study of Criminality and Law Enforcement to the Dutch Parliamentary Enquiry on Special Police Methods. She has published widely on policing in Europe, including co-authoring *Policing across National Boundaries* (1994, London: Pinter) and *Policing Europe: Theory, Law and Practice* (1995, Oxford: Clarendon Press).

Mike Brogden is Professor and Director of the Institute of Criminology and Criminal Justice at the Queen's University of Belfast. He has published extensively on policing issues, most recently with a comparative dimension. His numerous books include, most recently, *Policing for a New South Africa* (1993, London: Routledge) in conjunction with Clifford Shearing.

Jennifer Brown has recently moved to the Department of Psychology at the University of Surrey. Since receiving her PhD from the University of Surrey she has worked as Research Manager for the Hampshire Constabulary and Principal Lecturer in Criminology and Police Studies in the Institute of Police and Criminological Studies at the University of Portsmouth. Her research interests and publications include stress among police officers and the role of policewomen.

Bankole Cole is Senior Lecturer in Criminology in the Department of Law, University of Lincolnshire and Humberside. Having graduated from Lagos University, Nigeria, he completed his MA and PhD at Keele University. His research interests include comparative criminal justice, particularly regarding the developing world, and his publications cover youth justice, police power and court processes in Nigeria and the UK. He is currently working on a Home Office funded project on policing and drugs in rural Humberside.

Anita Hazenberg was a Dutch police officer before becoming Director of the European Network of Policewomen. Based in Amersfoort, the Netherlands, she is currently active in promoting support for policewomen in post-communist societies.

Les Johnston is Professor of Criminology and Head of the Criminology Section at the University of Teesside. He has research and teaching interests in public, commercial and civil policing, the politics of law and order, criminal justice policy and social theory and the state. His publications include *The Rebirth of Private Policing* (1992, London: Routledge), *The British Police in Transition* (1997, London: Longman) and (with Clifford Shearing and Philip Stenning) *Governing Diversity: Explorations in Policing* (1997, London: Routledge).

Frank Leishman has recently moved from the Institute of Police and Criminological Studies at the University of Portsmouth to become Principal Lecturer in Criminology at the Southampton Institute. A former police officer, he left the service to live, work and, later, study in Japan. On the basis of this experience he has written a number of papers on Anglo-Japanese policing issues and is also co-author (with Barry Loveday and Stephen Savage) of *Core Issues in Policing* (1996, London: Longman).

Barry Loveday is Principal Lecturer and Co-ordinator of External Relations in the Institute of Police and Criminological Studies at the University of Portsmouth. He has published extensively on policing issues and is a specialist on police accountability, and is also co-author (with Frank Leishman and Stephen Savage) of *Core Issues in Policing* (1996, London: Longman).

Carol Ormiston formerly worked for Amnesty International and the London Metropolitan Police. Her interest in the role of women in policing was strengthened when she was seconded to the European Network of Police Women.

Louise Shelley is Professor in the Department of Justice, Law and Society and the School of International Service of the American University. A long-time specialist on crime in the Soviet Union, she is currently running a joint Russian–American project, funded by the MacArthur Foundation, to establish crime study centres in Russia. Her most recent book is *Policing Soviet Society: the Evolution of State Control* (1996, Routledge: London), and she is also co-editor of *Demokratizatsiya* and *Trends in Organized Crime*.

P.A.J. Waddington is Professor of Sociology at the University of Reading. He has published extensively on all aspects of policing and especially on armed and public order policing. He is the author of *The Strong Arm of the Law* (1991, Oxford: Clarendon), *Calling the Police* (1993, Aldershot: Avebury) and *Liberty and Order: Public Order Policing in a Capital City* (1994, London: UCL Press). In 1992 he conducted an official inquiry into the policing of the Boipatong massacre in South Africa, under the auspices of the Goldstone Commission.

List of Abbreviations

ACPO	Association of Chief Police Officers
ARV	Armed Response Vehicles
ASU	Active Service Units
BIDS	Business Improvement Districts
BKA	Bundeskriminalamt: Germany's international crime unit
CBO	Centraal Bureau Opsporingen: Belgium's central bureau of investigations
CCTV	Closed-Circuit Television
CDR	Comites de Defensade de la Revolucion: one of Cuba's state security systems
CID	Criminal Investigation Department
CPO	Community Police Officer
CPS	Crown Prosecution Services
CRI	Centrale Recherche Informatiedienst: the national criminal intelligence service of The Netherlands
CTCH	Chilean Workers Confederation
DEA	Drug Enforcement Agency
DKGfSWA	Deutsche Kolonialesellschaft fur Sud-west Afrika
DPF	Departmento de Policia Federal: the federal police of Brazil
DSE	Deparmentot de Seguridad del Estado: the Cuban secret police
DVU	Domestic Violence Unit
EC	European Community
ENP	European Network of Policewomen
EU	European Union
FASP	French autonomous federation of police unions
FBI	Federal Bureau of Investigation
GIA	Groupe Interforce Antiterroriste: Belgium's anti-terrorist group
GNP	Gross National Product

GSO	Groupe de Surveillance et d'Observation: Belgian surveillance and undercover police unit
GfdK	Gesellschaft fur Deutsche Kolonisation
HMIC	Her Majesty's Inspectorate of Constabulary
IACP	International Association of Chief Police Officers
ICS	International Crime Survey
INCIS	Integrated National Criminal Intelligence System
IRT	Dutch inter-regional crime squad
JP	Justice of the Peace
KGB	USSR secret police
KLPD	Korps Landelijke Politiediensten: Dutch 26th police force with national competences
LPA	Local Police Authority
LEAA	Law Enforcement Assistance Administration: US funding programme
LKA	Landerskriminalamter: Germany's national crime unit
LRT	Landelijk Rechercheteam: Dutch national crime squad
MVD	Russian Ministry of Internal Affairs
NCIS	Integrated National Criminal Intelligence System
NHS	National Health Service
NPA	Japan's national police agency
NWMP	Northwest Mounted Police Force
NUM	National Union of Mineworkers
NWS	Neighbourhood Watch Scheme
ODA	Overseas Development Administration
OM	Openbaar Ministerie: the public prosecution service of The Netherlands
PANI	Police Authority in Northern Ireland
PIRA	Provisional Irish Republican Army
POSA	Peloton voor Observatie, Schaduwing en Arresatie
RCID	Regional Criminal Intelligence Department
RCMP	Royal Canadian Mounted Police
RIC	Royal Irish Constabulary
RUC	Royal Ulster Constabulary
SAP	South African Police
SAS	Special Air Services
SIE	Special Intervention Team
SIRENE	Supplementary Information Request at the National Entry
SIS	Secret Intelligence Service
SWAT	Special Weapon and Tactics
UCLAF	Unité de Coordination de la Lutte Anti-Fraude
UNCJIN	United Nations Criminal Justice Information Network
UN	United Nations
USCP	Union de Syndicat Categoriels de la Police: French police union

PART 1

An Introduction to Comparative Policing

Introduction

While an international comparative element is central to many disciplines within the social sciences, it is only recently that it has become a significant feature of police studies. This raises at least three questions: just what are international studies of the police; why should an international perspective be so important; and if it is important why has it received so little attention until now?

David Bayley is unquestionably the pioneer of international police studies. In chapter one he acknowledges the lack of interest among his US colleagues on comparative analysis and then argues persuasively that, in contrast, international studies are an essential part of any academic discipline, including criminal justice and policing. He identifies four major benefits of cross-national study: extending knowledge of alternative possibilities; developing more powerful insights into human behaviour; increasing the likelihood of successful reform; and gaining perspectives on ourselves as human beings.

The enthusiasm with which Bayley pursues his mission is evident and it is indeed arguable that he understates the difficulties involved in international research. Mawby's chapter identifies four problems that regularly arise; first the availability of valid, reliable and detailed data; second, the fact that definitions vary between countries in ways that are not always easily identified and controlled; third is the practical 'impossibility of becoming an expert on everywhere'; finally the basis on which to compare and categorize is often complex. Before this, however, Mawby distinguishes between practitioners and policy-makers and academics in their contribution to international analysis and in the latter case identifies six approaches to the subject. Broadly these fall into three groups: those that consider policing across a range of societies, whether focusing on similarities, differences or both; those that concern international or multinational agencies or what Bayley terms 'transnational processes'; and those that focus on particular issues in policing and address them comparatively.

Parts 2 and 3 of this book focus on two of these. In Part 2 policing in a range of developed and developing societies is considered. Then in Part 3 a number of key issues in policing are addressed from a comparative perspective.

CHAPTER 1

Policing: the World Stage

DAVID H. BAYLEY

Introduction

The comparative study of the police is viewed as an exotic frill in the professional study of criminal justice. It is a marginal enterprise thought to be difficult, if not impossible, to do and yielding little of value. This invidious position stems from the fact that 'comparative' has been made synonymous in academic circles with 'foreign'. Foreign experience is not considered central to any discipline I know, with the possible exception of history. Thus the major academic disciplines have sub-sections entitled comparative economics, comparative sociology, comparative political science, and now comparative criminal justice, all devoted to the study of things abroad. Doubts about the usefulness of foreign study arise from the fact that international differences are perceived to be so great as to bear no relation to one's own national or local experience. 'You can't compare those countries,' one frequently hears, 'they're too different.' So comparative study is dismissed as an excuse for international travel; a luxury that serious social scientists leave to dilettantes.

The purpose of this chapter is to show that these views about comparative study, in this case about the police, are the result of muddled thinking. Comparative study is thoroughly mainstream in any significant intellectual way; it can indeed be done successfully, and there are substantial reasons for doing so.

The Centrality of Comparison

The association of 'comparison' with 'foreign' creates the impression that comparative study is a choice that social science has. One may be mainstream and noncomparative or idiosyncratic and comparative. This is nonsense. All science is comparative in the sense of depending upon analysis of multiple cases. Science is the systematic

3

observation of many instances of a phenomenon. In western intellectual life, comparative study hasn't been problematic since Francis Bacon (1561–1626). The comparative study of criminal justice institutions is neither epistemologically nor methodologically pathbreaking. To call the international study of any social phenomenon 'comparative' marginalizes the concept of comparison and confuses understanding of what is needed for scientific inquiry.

The comparative, meaning foreign, study of criminal justice raises no difficulties in principle from the scientific study of anything. It is not inherently more difficult to study police forces on both sides of the Atlantic Ocean than on both sides of the Hudson River or more difficult across the Belgium–France border than the Texas–Arkansas border. Large bodies of water are not a more serious bar to comparative study than small ones. Nor are international boundaries more so than intrastate boundaries. Yet comparing the police of Los Angeles and New York City or of Kent and Northumbria seems entirely natural, while comparing Kent with New York City or Bombay with Sydney is regarded as peculiar and problematic.

'Comparative study' is a misnomer. Because all science is comparative, 'comparative' should not be used to denote a subfield of any discipline. Instead, it would be more accurate and intelligent to refer to the *international* study of social phenomenon. What distinguishes the various 'comparative' subfields is not comparison but political geography, that is, whether the cases to be analyzed occur within a single country or several.

Some may object to 'international' as the right substitute for 'comparative' because 'international' can refer to processes that occur within several nation-states or processes that are undertaken by nation-states or supranational institutions across international boundaries. With respect to police, for example, would 'international policing' cover the study of police forces in several nations or activities of the FBI internationally, or the growth of collaboration among police forces in Europe, or even UN Peacekeeping in Bosnia? In other disciplines, 'comparative studies' has meant the former, with 'international studies' referring to the study of transnational processes.

If one must distinguish research by the geopolitical location of the cases studied, then my preference is to talk about studies being international (or cross-national), referring to analysis of instances from different countries, and transnational, referring to activities which cross borders. It would make sense to have courses designed as either 'international' or 'transnational' criminal justice, and to have corresponding sections of scholarly professional organizations. This is much better than lumping both together clumsily into the category of 'comparative'.

Part of the reluctance to study criminal justice, or anything else, internationally arises out of the perception that differences among phenomena are so great that analysis is impossible. Anyone who lectures about international criminal justice has had the frustrating experience of someone in the audience rising to ask, 'How can you compare Japan and the United States? They are so different.' The assumption seems to be that national boundaries impose discontinuities in human experience, qualitative differences, that make it impossible to understand what is going on, let alone to learn something that might be useful at home. There are indeed differences in human experience across national boundaries. But so there are across the boundaries of any social unit – families, neighbourhoods, cities, provinces, and regions. The degree of difference is precisely the point. If we were all alike, then social science could rely on single case-studies. Whether differences are so great as to bar informative analysis is a matter that can only be determined by looking. To argue against international study because differences may be beyond our understanding assumes a conclusion that can only be proven by undertaking the very sort of study that is being questioned. Maybe some beings are beyond our ken, like the Klingons of *Star Trek*, but we will never know until we make the effort to find out.

This argument against international study is not only intellectually silly, it is disturbing morally because it elevates parochialism to the level of scientific principle. It assumes without examination that we are unique, unlike anyone else, certainly unlike foreigners. This conceit is sadly universal. Social science must firmly resist this sort of us–them chauvinism. It is unfortunate that a willingness to challenge this conceit even among social scientists is considered a dubious activity. The point is that international comparative study in social science raises no new epistemological or methodological problems. Whether broadening the scope of study can be useful intellectually as well as in terms of policy cannot be predicted in advance. The proof of the pudding is in the eating. Science may fail, but we won't know until we try. This is as true of the international study of criminal justice as it is of any systematic empirical inquiry into human behaviour.

Although there are no reasons in principle against undertaking cross-national studies of criminal justice, there are certainly practical ones. The most obvious are language, access, and expense. Once again, however, the degree to which such conditions are limiting cannot be determined in advance. They depend on the nature of the topic to be studied, the venue chosen for study, and the methodology of research. One should not assume that such barriers are insurmountable, although in some places they will be, or even that they are greater than similar obstacles at home. Colloquial language skills, for example, are not needed in all research. A great deal of useful research can be done from statistical sources or from material readily translated. Foreign collaborators can serve as interpreters as well as informants. Being 'one of us' is not essential to all research, nor is it necessarily easier to achieve at home. It may be easier for a white American to do research on the police in Britain than on the police of Washington, DC. Similarly, access may sometimes be easier to obtain abroad than at home, even in the area of policing. Foreign scholars are less threatening politically because they come and go; they do not stay around to teach, write, and give interviews. Moreover, it is flattering to be studied by a foreigner, who may also be easier to influence than a local scholar. Expense surely does rise the farther one goes to study, except in that dwindling number of countries where the cost of living is actually lower than at home. Altogether, language, access, and cost are generally greater obstacles to research abroad than at home, but they vary case by case. Some may wonder why I don't mention expertise, in the sense of knowledge about local history and circumstances, as an additional practical impediment to foreign study. It certainly can be. Taking on new countries multiplies the background work that must be done, a problem that does not generally arise when increasing the size of domestic samples. For each new country, one has to do a cram course in history, politics, law, economics, social structure, and culture – all matters that are common knowledge for people raised locally. At the same time, there are some advantages to being able to look at things uninstructed by common opinion. I have often argued that international colloquia featuring a variety of national case-studies are done by the wrong people. Invariably, local nationals are asked to do the case-study of their own country. It might be more insightful instead if foreigners did the local case-study, on the argument that they might see things that locals miss, things that are so commonly experienced as to be unremarkable. While not every-one has de Tocqueville's gifts for quick and insightful study of a foreign country, his example should be followed more often than it is. Furthermore, the amount of local knowledge that is needed to understand something is itself an empirical question. While some is undoubtedly needed, it is not necessary to 'go native'. It depends once again on the question asked, the place studied, and the methodology adopted. However, because the advantages of not having local knowledge are unpredictable, I am not suggesting that one be deliberately ignorant, simply that lifelong immersion is not necessary.

The Benefits of Comparison

Having established that international study of criminal justice institutions may en-counter difficulties of practice but none of principle, is it worth doing? Are there benefits to expanding the generality of cases covered, especially over international borders? In my opinion, there are four substantial benefits from cross-national study of criminal justice. They are (1) extending knowledge of alternative possibilities; (2) developing more powerful insights into human behaviour; (3) increasing the likelihood of successful reform; and (4) gaining perspective on ourselves as human beings. I shall discuss each of these with particular reference to policing.

(1) Extending knowledge of possibilities

There is a tendency to assume that the way things are is the way things must be. More exactly, that what one has experienced is the way things must be. The fact is that there are all sorts of variations in the way criminal justice is organized and con-ducted. Without international study, it is impossible to know whether local practice is in the mainstream or is an outlier in some regard. There may be more possibil-ities than local experience would suggest. In addition, without international study it is easy to believe that local practice is not only inevitable but best. International study may suggest better ways to build the criminal justice mousetrap. The 185 nation-states in the world constitute a vast living laboratory of naturally occurring experiments in criminal justice systems and policies. With respect to policing spe-cifically, countries vary enormously in national structures, mechanisms for achiev-ing accountability, weapons and the use of force, role of women, organization and

6

training for crowd-control, dependence on technology, deployment of operational personnel, standards of recruitment, nature and length of training, levels of remuneration, public regard, acceptance of the rule of law, separation from the military, styles of management, relations among ranks, and morale. If thoughtfully analyzed, this wealth of variation in police structures and practices can be used by police forces when they confront a new problem or find that their customary policies are not working. Instead of reinventing the wheel, they can study the practices of other countries that have tried something different and determine whether these practices work better than what is being questioned at home. Unfortunately, few countries systematically canvass foreign police experience when grappling with local problems. Despite widespread operational interests in policing, the United States, for example, does very little to encourage the study of foreign police practices. It generally acts as if foreign practice was irrelevant, even though it freely recommends its own practices to other countries. The National Institute of Justice, the research arm of the federal Department of Justice, has expressly avoided funding foreign study, in part out of fear that the Congress will accuse it of 'junketeering'. Ironically, junketeering is a matter about which the US Congress is expert. On the other hand, Japan systematically enquires about foreign practices and sends young officers abroad expressly for that purpose. Since the Meiji Restoration over a hundred years ago, Japan has studied foreign experience whenever a new problem arises or it perceives the need for reform. European countries, including Ireland and the United Kingdom, occupy a middle position with respect to their readiness to study foreign experience. Because of the variety of experience in Europe and the proximity of countries to one another, the operational needs of law enforcement have forced co-operation and the development of informed liaison. Knowledge of policing methods and criminal justice processes has increased sharply in recent years as a result of the movement toward European Union. The agreements signed at Trevi in 1975 were the galvanizing event as far as policing was concerned (Fijnaut 1987).

At the present time, it is not easy to find out about foreign police practices. Information about policing globally is not routinely collected in reference volumes or databanks. Although several helpful reference works have been published in the last few years, international information is still superficial and patchy in coverage (Andrade 1985, Kurian 1989, Fairchild 1993, Terrill 1995). The United Nations is now beginning to make country information available through its United Nations Criminal Justice Information Network (UNCJIN) located at the School of Criminal Justice, State University of New York, Albany, NY. Most questions about foreign police practice, however, still require contact with whatever countries the researcher is interested in. Embassies are not particularly helpful, tending to view policing as a sensitive matter and generally not having information about police ready-to-hand. Trying to work through embassies to construct an informative sample of global experience is an uncertain and tedious process. For many topics, therefore, the only alternative is to develop local informants in foreign countries or visit the countries personally. These processes are costly and time-consuming.

The upshot is that answering even simple questions about worldwide policing at the moment is difficult and likely to require original research. The same is true

7

for almost any topic in criminal justice generally. In order to take advantage of the national laboratories in criminal justice and policing that exist around the world, investment needs to be made in developing ongoing, systematic inventorying of criminal justice practices. Without such inventories, neither academic researchers nor practitioners will be able to look for alternatives to their own local problems. Worldwide description is an essential first step toward the long-term goal of learning about what may work better. As a result of the paucity of up-to-date information about policing worldwide, there have been few attempts to develop generalizations about the range of variation in police practice, even about fairly straightforward, uncontroversial matters, such as degrees of centralization/decentralization, ratios of police to population, proportions of personnel assigned to different ranks, proportions of personnel assigned to different functions, qualifications for recruitment, and programmes of training.

(2) Developing more powerful insights into human behaviour

Analytically, two questions may be asked about policing: first, what effect is it having on society, and, second, what effect is society having on the police. The former is the question most often asked by practitioners and policy-makers; the latter tends to be the concern of social scientists. International study is necessary both for understanding what works in criminal justice, as we saw above, and to explain why different sorts of criminal justice practices come about. Social scientists want to explain variations in human institutions, among them approaches to crime, justice, and policing. Expanding the range of examples increases the generality, and hence the power, of theories. Since the institutions of criminal justice are the constructs of governments, and in the last two centuries the governments of nation-states, any theory of criminal justice institutions, including the police, must include more than one country. Not to do so constricts the scientific study of policing to what are essentially case studies.

This explains why there is so little genuine theory explaining criminal justice institutions: in their marginalization of international comparison, scholars have been unable to see patterns of systematic variation. Describing the range of variation in a phenomena is the first step in developing explanations for it. Historians have been way ahead of social scientists in developing insights into the development of criminal justice practices because their discipline forces them to observe changes over time. Criminal justice specialists by neglecting history as well as international comparison have virtually guaranteed that they will be unable to understand what they are studying. At the present time, we know hardly anything about the factors that shape the character of policing. Indeed, the question is hardly ever asked. As a result, the explanations offered tend to be simplistic: such as 'historical reasons' or 'people get the government they deserve'. It is really quite surprising how little is known about the factors that shape policing. For example, does the character of government affect policing, especially whether government is democratic or authoritarian? The answer seems to be yes and no, depending on the feature of policing being examined. One of the first lessons, by the way, that international study teaches is that policing is not all of a piece. Police and policing are complex variables. Moreover, the connections among their varied features is virtually unexplored. We simply don't know what features of policing go together and which may be incorporated into any policing package. With respect to the character of government, here are some probable patterns of impact. Democracies undoubtedly constrict the ability of police to affect political life more than authoritarian regimes. Although authoritarian governments probably have more centralized police systems, many democratic countries are centralized systems too (for example, France, Italy, and Sweden). Democratic countries have more mechanisms for making the police accountable, with the accountability being to the general public as well as to government. Furthermore, police in democratic countries are undoubtedly more responsive to the disaggregate needs of citizens, as opposed to the needs of regimes, than they are in authoritarian countries.

What effect does economic development have on the police? Richer nations have more police per capita, but it is unclear whether they invest more in technology and less in personnel. Policing seems to be labour-intensive to almost the same degree in every country. The police of richer nations may devote more time to the non-criminal needs of their populations. At the same time, clear-up rates may be unaffected by economic development. It is far from clear how economic development effects the sharing of the responsibility for policing, meaning the crime-prevention and social discipline, between government and communities. Is informal social control over behaviour greater or less in developed countries? Are communities more or less willing to shoulder responsibility for preventing indiscipline in developed or underdeveloped countries? It is interesting that worldwide attention to 'community policing' originated in developed countries. This may not be because less developed countries didn't have it, but because they hadn't thought to call it by a new name. National culture may also play a role in determining the nature of policing. Countries where personal identity is submerged in group membership, such as Japan and China, may emphasize informal involvement of the police in community life more than individualistic countries. On the other hand, the use of force by police is probably not tied to culture. And what of corruption? Can that be tied to culture, and if so to what features? Or is corruption its own culture, having more to do with economics than general sets of cultural values.

There may also be structural factors that underlie variations in policing, the sorts of variables that sociologists focus on. For example, one can make strong a priori arguments that conflict is more likely between police and the public in countries with heterogeneous populations; that rural localities will emphasize community policing more than urban ones; that the more educated a population becomes the more demanding it will be for police service, especially with respect to non-criminal problems; and that industrialization will increase specialization within police organizations and the professionalization of management. International research using countries as units of analysis must be undertaken if genuine theories of criminal justice are to be developed. Until that happens, explanations will be lacking in generality as well as insight.

(3) Increasing the chances for successful reform

Understanding the factors associated with differences in policing is not simply an academic exercise. It is essential if the deliberate reform of public institutions, sometimes called planned change, is to be successful. In order to build a better mousetrap, one must not only obtain the plans but determine whether it can be built with the tools at home. By examining the correlates of police practice abroad, one can determine the conditions that are likely to facilitate or inhibit particular reforms. In other words, research internationally shows whether foreign practice may be successfully imported. My own research suggests that the exportability of foreign practice varies according to the feature being considered. For example, the structure of policing within countries – the number of forces, their autonomy, and co-ordination – are rooted in deep historical traditions and cannot be changed apart from foreign occupation. Technology, on the other hand, is readily transferable, as are scientific procedures of both management and forensic analysis (Bayley 1995).

The point is that the exportability of any practice must be determined by international analysis and ultimately by trial and error. I believe that the possibilities are much greater than is generally imagined. Nations have been learning about policing from one another for hundreds of years, across significant divides of economic development, political character, and cultural diversity (Bayley 1975, 1985). One clear indication of this is the complex and vital connections still maintained between European countries and their former colonies. In my own experience, Japanese koban – neighbourhood police posts – were dismissed by American police in the 1970s as costly and impractical based on limited experience with storefront stations. Two decades later neighbourhood police offices are springing up throughout major cities in the US. Similarly, the Japanese practice of calling at each residence once or twice a year seemed unthinkable given American suspicion of government intrusion into private life. However, experiments with 'house visits' in Houston, TX, and Newark, NJ, in the mid-1980s showed that they were not resented and had a greater effect on the fear of crime than the other interventions tried (newsletters, neighbourhood police offices, and victim follow-ups) (Sherman 1986). There is an enormous hunger for humane, face-to-face policing in the United States. Culture is no bar to house-visits by police. The real obstacle is the reluctance of police to get out of patrol cars and do it. International differences are rarely dichotomous – wholly one way or another. Instead, practices lie along continua with many gradations. People share to varying degrees the ways of others. Moreover, in the hurly-burly of daily life, such differences tend to drift toward a middle-position, defying the dichotomies so beloved of social scientists. This proposition may be tested with respect to police institutions. I suspect we will be surprised at the permeability of international boundaries to police borrowing.

(4) Gaining perspective on ourselves

Extending knowledge of possibilities, developing explanations, and raising the likelihood of successful reform are practical reasons for studying policing internationally.

We learn from it so as to improve our own practices. But there is another reason, less demonstrable but every bit as important. Through the study of foreign experience we learn who we are as human beings. International study provides a mirror in which we can see ourselves reflected against the backdrop of others, and it thereby helps us to discover who we are and who we are not. Self-discovery of this sort is a chastening experience because we discover the limits to what we may become and of the experiences we may comfortably share.

From my own experience in international study of the police, I have discovered that Americans tolerate implicit social rules less well than Japanese. Americans are less proper, less restrained, more casual, perhaps less considerate. They are also less ceremonious. On the other hand, they are more orderly than Indians or Italians in public places. Like the English, Americans are more comfortable when crowds are organized and queues are naturally formed. Americans are also more suspicious of government than Japanese, and probably more so than Europeans. In this they are much more like Indians. Americans value privacy more than Indians but invade others' private space more readily with their eyes than Japanese. Americans, like most Westerners, prefer wheat to rice and coffee to green tea. Americans are punctual like Germans and do not tolerate ambiguity in communication like South Asians. Americans stress informality but do not as a result develop more friendships. Compared with most Asians, written rules are more important to Americans than interpersonal undertakings. Finally, although Americans are more impatient than Japanese or Chinese with the social status quo, they are more sceptical that individuals can change for the better. As a rule, therefore, Americans prefer 'just desserts', predictability, and equality over rehabilitation, discretion, and individuation.

International study teaches that other people may be good and beautiful despite being different. With respect to criminal justice, societies that are organized in very different ways may provide equal measures of justice and order. One society neither monopolizes nor exhausts the potentialities for virtue.

Conclusion

Policing should be examined on the world stage to determine what might be done to improve its performance and to understand the requirements of such improvement. International study is necessary, in other words, for the scientific insight that policy-making requires. Such study is not problematic theoretically or methodologically. All that is at issue between international study and mainstream social science is whether the cases to be analyzed should be expanded across the artificial boundaries of politics or the irrelevant ones of geography. Police may also be regarded as a village that can be studied, as anthropologists do, in order to understand foreign people and in so doing ourselves as well. A global perspective transforms the study of the police from an applied, technical speciality into an undertaking that enables us to understand more fully essential elements of government and the human condition.

Bibliography

Andrade, J. 1985. *World police and paramilitary forces*. New York: Stockton Press.

Bayley, D.H. 1975. The police and political development in Europe. In *The formation of national states in Europe*, C. Tilly & G. Almond (eds). Princeton, NJ: Princeton University Press.

Bayley, D.H. 1985. *Patterns of policing*. New Brunswick, NJ: Rutgers University Press.

Bayley, D.H. 1995. A foreign policy for democratic policing. *Policing and Society* 5 (2), 79–94.

Fairchild, E. 1993. *Comparative criminal justice systems*. Belmont, CA: Wadsworth Publishing Co.

Fijnaut, C. 1987. The institutionalization of criminal investigation in Western Europe. In *Police co-operation in Europe*, C.J.C.F. Fijnaut & R.H. Hermans (eds). Netherlands, Lochem: Van den Brink.

Kurian, G.T. 1989. *World encyclopedia of police and penal systems*. New York: Facts on File.

Sherman, L.W. 1986. Policing communities: what works? In *Communities and crime*, A. Reiss, Jr. & Michael Tonry (eds) 343–86. Chicago: University of Chicago Press.

Terrill, R.J. 1995. *World criminal justice systems: a survey*. Cincinnati, OH: Anderson Publishing Co.

CHAPTER 2

Approaches to Comparative Analysis: the Impossibility of Becoming an Expert on Everywhere

R.I. MAWBY

Introduction

Until comparatively recently, most of the writing – and indeed research – on policing had focused on the situation in England and Wales and the United States. In the latter country there was a reluctance to look outside to policing in other societies while in Britain writers, without – until the 1980s – an established 'home grown' literature, tended to transport US material across the Atlantic without concern that internal (to the police) and external (socio-political) factors may be so different as to make simplistic comparisons hazardous. Even now British writers tend to ignore the fact that the police systems of Scotland, Northern Ireland and the Channel Islands are quite distinct and that when we talk or write about 'our own' police we really are limiting ourselves to England and Wales.

This lack of an international comparative dimension is surprising. The social sciences, and sociology in particular, were developed by a number of theorists who used social conditions in different societies as the starting point from which to explain the differences they identified and used such explanations to develop more extensive theoretical arguments. What these writers were doing, in essence, was to identify variations in social conditions and social institutions and use the comparative method as a means of explanation. Much the same advantages might be attributed to an international perspective on policing. First, a review of policing in other societies gives us a broader perspective; it helps us appreciate that the policing arrangements we have for example in England and Wales are not the only option, that in other societies, many similar to our own, the police are organized differently, held accountable to greater or lesser extents or in different ways, and expected to carry out a variety of different responsibilities. In this context it is notable that the Posen (1994) inquiry into core policing tasks, allegedly set up to allow the government to recommend the hiving off and privatization of marginal tasks that the modern police cannot be expected to fulfil, has pointedly ignored evidence from other societies where police functions and roles are often even more extensive.

Having set the scene and identified points of similarity or difference, researchers may then want to explain why police systems, or specific features of policing, have developed differently in different societies. For example, the fact that in Scotland the police have traditionally been accountable to the procurator fiscal, whose responsibilities cover prosecution decisions, while in England and Wales it was not until the 1980s that a (even then more diluted) prosecution service was established, may be explained in terms of the influence of France on the Scottish legal system. Which of course raises the question as to why the French and English systems are so different. So, having attempted to explain the differences between two societies, we may wish to extend the explanation and argue that different types of society, measured in terms of socio-political factors, economic development, culture, etc., produce different policing arrangements.

This raises the notion of change which is central to many discussions about policing in an international context. Change can be identified on a number of levels. On a macro level, for example, we might wish to consider how far the widespread political changes taking place in Central and Eastern Europe will lead to changes within the police. On a micro level, in contrast, we might consider how successful was the import of US innovations in neighbourhood watch or community policing into England, or how feasible it is to translate such initiatives into other societies – for example from continental Europe, post-communist societies or former colonial societies – with more markedly different policing traditions. In this context it is not surprising that many of the early attempts at international comparison of policing were written by practitioners and administrators. Raymond Fosdick, for example, who worked as an administrator with the New York police department, toured Europe at the beginning of the twentieth century. His text, published in 1915 and subsequently reissued (Fosdick 1969), uses his discussions with senior police in a number of countries as the basis for the development of a classification of police systems, contrasting systems of continental Europe with those of England and Wales and the US. Not surprisingly, his work is somewhat superficial, but it was unrivalled for over 40 years.

Interestingly, a later attempt to classify police systems was provided by another practitioner, this time a British colonial administrator, Sir Charles Jeffries. Based on his practical experience in different parts of the British Empire, Jeffries (1952) identified a specific type of police system, the colonial model, which he argued was created for Ireland and proved so successful that it was passed on, in modified form, as Britain's empire expanded. Practitioners are still involved in international comparisons. Senior police officers on the gravy train of study visits have been required to write reports and articles summarizing their experiences (Alderson 1981, Finch 1984) while recent changes in Central and Eastern Europe have also invited response from western police forces (Interpol 1992, 1994). However, more of these recent contributions have been made by academics. International policing research has become an essential ingredient of the developing police studies discipline.

The Academic Contribution

Most of the contributions of academics may, for convenience, be assigned to one or other of six categories. First a number of writers have focused on policing in one particular country. Of course, such material is not necessarily comparative, and when British or American academics are writing about their own countries it often appears as quite the opposite. However where these academics are writing about non-Anglo-American countries and aiming for a wider audience, it is almost inevitable that they, at least implicitly, draw comparisons between policing in the nation under discussion and policing elsewhere. This is generally true where the author is writing about his/her own system; it is almost inevitable where outsiders describe and analyse police systems elsewhere. For example, in Japan Ames (1981) and especially Bayley (1976) draw comparisons with the US, while a more recent Japanese researcher, Miyazawa (1992), reassessing his material for an English-speaking audience, makes quite explicit comparisons with Anglo-Saxon police systems. Similarly Morrison's (1985) account of the Royal Canadian Mounted Police assesses its development in the context of both the British (Colonial) and US traditions and Stead (1957, 1983) draws on his British experiences in describing the French system.

A second approach is to draw comparisons between two or more countries. Some of the early work of this sort was historical: for example both Miller (1977) and Emsley (1983) consider the emergence of the modern police, the first comparing London and New York, the second France and England. Rather differently, others have noted the similarities and differences between countries that might be 'grouped' as examples of one policing system. For example, following Fosdick, Bayley (1975) compared the police systems of a number of European countries and subsequently (Bayley 1979) contrasted these with the United States. The similarities and differences between colonial police systems have been the subject of detailed scrutiny in two volumes edited by Anderson & Killingray (1991; 1992). Similarly, while Brady's (1982) work on China makes few direct comparisons with other countries, in a separate article (Brady 1981) he contrasts the police of China and Cuba. More recently, Lee (1990) draws an interesting comparison between Japan and South Korea. Many of these studies, particularly where rather more countries are included, are based on secondary data although some, including Banton's (1964) pioneering comparison of the US and Scottish systems, rely heavily upon direct personal observation. In contrast, the use of other forms of primary data is less common; for example interviews with the police or surveys tapping public perspectives on the police are rare and tend to be confined to specific issues in policing (see below).

A third approach, that is perhaps a variant on this, is what we might term the global perspective. Here primary or secondary material may be drawn from a number of countries to illustrate similarities in policing structures and functions or the issues facing the police. In an earlier work, Bayley (1985) combined this approach with the one described above. On the one hand, he contrasted aspects of policing such as whether or not the police were organized on a national basis as a centralized institution or on a local level. On the other hand, he identified what he saw as the key features of modern police systems – public, specialized and professional – and argued that in contemporary society similarities between nations were more notable than differences. In his most recent work, Bayley (1994) focuses almost exclusively on the similarities between police systems. Based on research in Australia, England, Canada, Japan and the US he argues that the police face a common set of problems related to their roles and sets out various 'agendas for change'.

A fourth category of international comparison is where authors draw links between countries by focusing on international or multinational agencies. One recent example is Anderson's (1989) study of Interpol. Another, perhaps currently 'flavour of the month' among British academics, concerns the co-operative arrangements that have been negotiated – at governmental, ministerial or agency level – within the European Community (Benyon et al. 1993, Hebenton & Thomas 1995, King 1995).

A fifth category includes studies where policing issues are covered as part of wider international surveys. The most obvious example here is the international crime survey (ICS) which has been conducted twice to date, in 1989 and 1993. The first ICS concentrated on western industrial societies, although Japan and cities from Indonesia and Poland were also included (van Dijk, Mayhew & Killias 1990). The second ICS covered many of the same countries but also incorporated some post-communist societies and cities in developing societies from Africa, Asia and South America (del Frate, Zvekic & van Dijk 1993). While essentially a victim survey, the ICS covers both victims' experiences of police response to their crime and public perceptions of the police. Inevitably the range of questions here is limited. However it includes the extent to which crimes are reported to the police and the basis for victims' decisions, victims' levels of satisfaction with police response and public feelings about the way the police control crime. Interestingly, its data have rarely been utilized by policing specialists, which is unfortunate since some of the findings are surprising. For example the Japanese police, generally assessed by police researchers in a positive light, are according to the ICS viewed somewhat more negatively by the Japanese public, compared to the results from western societies!

Finally, international comparative analysis may be based on issues or concerns pertinent to policing, where a review of the situation in different countries is attempted. By focusing down in this way it is perhaps easier to draw direct comparisons and to make policy recommendations. On the other hand, while more detailed studies of nations' police systems may locate these in a wider socio-political and cultural context, there is the danger that in focusing upon one particular aspect of policing the extent to which it is shaped by wider circumstances in any particular country is lost. It is also notable that while in theory primary research may be more feasible at this level, most analyses of policing issues tend to be based on secondary data. In the context of public order policing for example this is true of both Roach & Thomandeck's (1985) edited collection on European systems and Brewer et al.'s (1988) worldwide review. It is also the case that certain issues have received more attention than others and that, with notable exceptions, much of the attention has been directed at a small pool of western industrial societies, core among them the US, Canada and England. Thus while community policing has received particular attention from both academics and practitioners, much of the emphasis has been Anglo–American (Rosenbaum 1994) with Israel (Friedman 1992) and Australia

(Chappell & Wilson 1989) thrown in for good measure and Japan treated as a special case (Bayley 1976, Moriyama 1992, Thornton & Endo 1992).

The Problems with International Analysis

While research based on these alternative approaches is becoming more and more common, the fact that much of it is so recent in origin owes much to the intrinsic difficulties of undertaking international police research. At least four difficulties can be identified. These relate to the problems of data, definition, expert fallibility and comparative method itself.

First let us consider the problems concerning available data. While in England and Wales, if we want to carry out an analysis of policing we may draw on a number of primary and secondary sources, these sources are not necessarily available in other countries. Of course, crime statistics, annual reports by the police and other political/parliamentary documentation may be available in most western industrial societies. They may very well be accessible too! However even the basic data may be more difficult to come by in less developed societies. And until recently even crime statistics were inaccessible in most socialist societies. Yet these sources are only the starting point for any serious academic analysis of policing. Consider how adequate it would be to base an analysis of the English police on records of this type, without any review of the multitude of research studies carried out over the last 30 years. Moreover, since most international researchers lack the resources to carry out their own research, secondary data may be all that is available. As a result, much comparative research is, essentially, a critical review of secondary data from different countries, where the data may be difficult to check, constructed in different ways in the different countries, only partially available etc.

One attempt to rectify data deficiencies is through original research. Extensive observational research is, of course, a viable option where the focus is on one country – possibly compared with one's own and where language does not present an insurmountable barrier. Bayley's (1976) Japanese research remains perhaps the best example of this kind where the researcher was heavily reliant upon an interpreter. Other forms of data collection, for example using postal questionnaires or personal interviews, are less common, and – as for example where Walker & Kratcoski (1991) attempt to compare police subculture in England and North America – may be open to criticism that such subjects are almost impossible to research using such methodologies! Research using both primary and secondary data analysis does, moreover, run into further difficulties.

A second, and related problem, concerns the question of definition. It is well established that definitions of crime vary between societies. So do definitions of police and policework. Researchers then are in a difficult position, where they are often not comparing like with like, or indeed may be unaware of any differences which do exist. Take for example the apparently simple question of the numbers of police in society. Should we compare numbers to population, or crime rates, or compare spending on the police with GNP, spending on other public services, or what? And does it make any sense then to say that, for example, Germany has a higher rate of police than England, if the German police have a greater number of responsibilities? Or, if we are interested in the gender balance, a superficial reading of Israeli police data might show us that there are relatively more policewomen in that country, while a closer review of how the police is defined shows us that traffic wardens (predominantly female) are counted as police in Israel but not in England and Wales.

The problem with definitions of concepts used in comparative analysis has been made forcefully by Hill (1995) in a critique of the extent of paramilitarism in the English police. Comparing the stances of Waddington (1987) and Jefferson (1987) she argues that much of the difference between their perspectives emanates from the fact that they adopt different definitions of paramilitarism. Her own, that paramilitary forces are those that 'act in support of, or in lieu of, full-time active or reserve armed forces' (Hill 1995: 453) is much more exclusive and allows her to conclude that there is no paramilitary police system in England. Yet if we consider the extent to which the police exhibit paramilitary or militaristic qualities, defined across a range of criteria including for example armaments, training elements, uniform, rank structure, tactical deployment, formal links with the armed services, personnel transfer between police and armed services, ministerial responsibility, disciplinary code and living arrangements we may conclude that while the English police exhibit less of these qualities than the police of, say, France or Italy, there have been marked shifts in recent years.

Equally, the concept of centralization, that is whether policing is organized nationally or locally, is contentious. In an international context Bayley (1976, 1985) and Ames (1981) disagree on the extent to which the Japanese police are centralized. In England, there has been considerable debate over the apparent growth of centralizing tendencies in policing (Reiner 1991, 1992), yet many outside commentators (Bayley 1985, Hunter 1990) consider the English police to be locally-based. Clearly there is no one unified national police force in England. However central government influence is extensive and has been expanding. A definition that placed more emphasis on the extent of central government involvement in local force policy and less on the existence of a unified structure might lead to the conclusion that the English police system is no more – and no less – decentralized than the apparently national Swedish system (Akermo 1986) or the contentious Japanese system (see Leishman, this volume).

These problems described so far are not insurmountable. We may be able to carry out research in different countries to supplement secondary sources, and we can untangle definitional problems. However there are a number of problems associated with being an expert on a country, or countries, other than one's own, which incorporate practical difficulties of access to material, language barriers, time etc. but also include the near-impossibility of becoming an outside expert, a goal that is even less attainable as we increase the number of countries studied.

Let us take two examples to illustrate this. First is the controversy surrounding the analysis of the Swiss system carried out by an American (Clinard 1978) and a Danish academic (Balvig 1988). In his earlier work Clinard (1978) had argued that Switzerland is one of a small number of highly industrialized societies with low crime rates. Criticizing this, Balvig (1988), on the basis of a month's work in Switzerland, argued that the crime rate in Switzerland was not particularly low, but that in an attempt to present a 'Snow White image' the Swiss criminal justice system was geared towards hiding the true extent of crime. This analysis was, in turn, criticized by a Swiss criminologist:

> Comparative research in criminology is difficult and time consuming, this is not a field designed for quick and easy studies. The most difficult task may be to overcome language barriers, either by learning foreign languages or by relying on hired staff and/or the views of experts . . . Balvig was thus not eager to listen to whatever Swiss experts might have been able to tell him, but unfortunately he did not care about learning Switzerland's languages either. The result is a series of misrepresentations . . . since it is impossible to point to all the inaccuracies in a review, the reader may be warned that the sections on statistics, on self-report studies, on immigration policy and the status of foreigners, on white-collar crime, and on the role played by the media are seriously flawed (Killias 1989: 301).

Of course, it is easy to dismiss such dangers and argue that Balvig's study was severely flawed methodologically due to his own inadequacies as a researcher. However outside researchers with considerably stronger academic credentials are not immune to some degree of criticism from 'insiders'. So for example in the first English language book published on the Japanese police, Miyazawa (1992) argues that Bayley (1976) was presented with the public image of the Japanese police, the facade or *tatemae* rather than the reality, the *honne*. His own research thus demonstrates how police intimidation of suspects, corruption and illegal practices are not only common features of the Japanese police, but that the police occupational culture and a conservative legal system actually facilitate such practices.

A rather different difficulty with carrying out international research is endemic to the comparative method itself. That is, if we are going to draw comparisons between systems or then go on to explain differences in policing, on what basis should we be making comparisons? On one level, we might distinguish according to a typology of police systems. I have already referred to a continental model and a colonial model of policing and these, and others, are discussed in more detail in Part 2 later. But we might also want to relate these to other, more general, ways of classifying societies. For example, following Cole *et al.* (1981) we might make a distinction according to a country's legal tradition. Or we might wish to use a political typology, comparing perhaps capitalist democracies, socialist societies, right-wing dictatorships etc. However, as research on China illustrates, there are marked differences between urban/industrial and rural/industrializing socialist societies (for a social policy example see Deacon 1983) so we may feel that level of development or urbanization is a crucial component of any categorization. Perhaps inevitably then, while there is no 'right' way of classifying societies, within a range of permutations we may wish to limit comparisons to those that are feasible; in other words not try to compare police systems in totally different societies but instead compare the situation in societies that have some similarities and some differences. Thus the student who compares policing in say, China and Germany, may find that the differences are so great as to eliminate any potential benefits.

Definitions of Policing

We have already identified definitional issues as a key problem in comparative research. Equally we have noted that our understanding of the key issues in policing may be blinkered if we concentrate exclusively on Anglo–American police systems and assume that this is 'what policing is all about'. Indeed the word police, derived from the Greek *politeia*, originally applied to the general instruments of government and the police of the Roman Empire and later seventeenth century Europe were charged with a far wider mandate than we would recognize as policing today.

The blinkered view of policing is illustrated in Cain's (1979) review of police research at the time, where she noted that while numerous academics wrote about the police few defined it. She subsequently defined the police in terms of its key practice, 'maintaining the order which those who sustain them define as proper' (Cain 1979: 158). While the definitions offered by others such as Bayley (1985: 7) differ in part from this, most incorporate three elements: (a) Function: policing centres on, but does not exclusively involve, the maintenance of order and the regulation of norms; (b) Structure: policing is carried out by specific individuals, organized so as to fulfil these functions; (c) Legitimacy: underpinning this structure or organization is the overseeing of the police by some 'political' authority. Using this threefold distinction, Mawby (1990) argues that different police systems may be compared according to the precise nature of the function, structure and legitimacy of the police. That is, while the police are charged with the maintenance of order, in some societies they are predominantly concerned with quelling political unrest, in some they incorporate a range of administrative responsibilities, while in others they are associated with various welfare tasks. Similarly, the structure and organization of the police varies, for example in terms of whether they are a local or national body, whether they incorporate militaristic features etc. Finally, the extent to which the police are held accountable, and the source of their legitimacy, differs between societies.

Such an approach is controversial because it uses a definition of policing as a variable in order to compare the police in different societies. Precisely for this reason it also has its advantages. When members of the public travel abroad and confront police from other countries, they take with them a common sense notion of what 'the police' is, and will generally be able to identify overseas police according to that common sense definition. On the other hand, they will frequently draw distinctions between the police of their own society and these 'other' police. Teasing out the similarities and the differences between police systems in different societies, explaining the differences, drawing examples of good practice that might be introduced elsewhere, and learning from experiences of bad practices; these are the key features of international policing studies. While the difficulties surrounding such endeavours may be considerable, the potential benefits make the challenge worthwhile.

Bibliography

Akermo, K.E. 1986. Organisational changes and remodelling of the Swedish police. *Canadian Police College Journal* **10.4**, 245–63.

Alderson, J.C. 1981. Hong Kong, Tokyo, Peking: three police systems observed. *Police Studies* **3.4**, 3–12.

Ames, W.L. 1981. *Police and community in Japan*. Berkeley: University of California Press.

Anderson, M. 1989. *Policing the world*. Oxford: Clarendon Press.

Anderson, D.M. & D. Killingray 1991. *Policing the Empire*. Manchester: Manchester University Press.

Anderson, D.M. & D. Killingray 1992. *Policing and decolonisation*. Manchester: Manchester University Press.

Balvig, F. 1988. *The snow-white image: the hidden reality of crime in Switzerland*. Oslo: Norwegian University Press.

Banton, M. 1964. *The policeman in the community*. London: Tavistock.

Bayley, D.H. 1975. The police and political development in Europe. In *The formation of nation states in Europe*, C. Tilly (ed.). Princetown: Princetown University Press.

Bayley, D.H. 1976. *Forces of order: police behaviour in Japan and the United States*. Berkeley: University of California Press.

Bayley, D.H. 1979. Police function, structure and control in Western Europe and North America. In *Crime and justice: an annual review of research*, N. Morris & M. Tonry (eds). Chicago: University of Chicago Press.

Bayley, D.M. 1985. *Patterns of policing: a comparative international analysis*. New Brunswick: Rutgers University Press.

Bayley, D.M. 1994. *Police for the future*. New York: Oxford University Press.

Benyon, J., L. Turnbull, A. Willis, R. Woodward & A. Beck 1993. *Police cooperation in Europe: an investigation*. Leicester: University of Leicester, Centre for the Study of Public Order.

Brady, J.P. 1981. The transformation of justice under socialism: the contrasting experiences of Cuba and China. *The Insurgent Sociologist* **10**, 5–24.

Brady, J.P. 1982. *Justice and politics in peoples' China: legal order as continuing revolution*. New York: Academic.

Brewer, J.D., A. Guelke, J. Mume, E. Moxon-Browne & R. Wilford 1988. *The police, public order and the state*. London: Macmillan.

Cain, M. 1979. Trends in the sociology of policework. *International Journal of the Sociology of Law* **7**, 143–67.

Chappell, D. & P. Wilson 1989. *Australian policing: contemporary issues*. London: Butterworths.

Clinard, M.B. 1978. *Cities with little crime: the case of Switzerland*. Cambridge: Cambridge University Press.

Cole, G.F., S.J. Frankowski & M.G. Gertz 1981 (eds). *Major criminal justice systems: a comparative study*. Beverley Hills: Sage.

Deacon, B. 1983. *Social policy and socialism*. London: Pluto.

Dijk, J.J.M. van, P. Mayhew, M. Killias 1990. *Experiences of crime across the world*. Deventer, Netherlands: Kluwer.

Emsley, C. 1983. *Policing and its context 1750–1870*. London: Macmillan.

Finch, R.J. 1984. An inscrutable force. *Police Review*, 10 February, 274–75.

Fosdick, R.B. 1969. *European police systems*. Montelair: Patterson Smith.

Frate, A.A. del, U. Zvekic, J.J.M. van Dijk 1993. *Understanding crime: experiences of crime and crime control*. Rome: UNICRI.

Friedman, R.R. 1992. *Community policing: comparative perspectives and prospects*. London: Harvester Wheatsheaf.

Hebenton, B. & T. Thomas 1995. *Policing Europe: cooperation, conflict and control*. Basingstoke: Macmillan.

Hill, A. 1995. Militant tendencies: paramilitarism in the British police. *British Journal of Criminology*, **35**, 450–58.

Hunter, R.D. 1990. Three models of policing, *Police Studies* **13**, 118–24.

Interpol 1992. Poland's painful transition to democratic policing. *Police*, April, 28–30.

Interpol 1994. Slovenia. *Police*, February, 24–5.

Jefferson, T. 1987. Beyond paramilitarism. *British Journal of Criminology* **27**, 47–53.

Jeffries, S.C. 1952. *The colonial police*. London: Max Parrish.

Killias, M. 1989. Review of The Snow White Image. *British Journal of Criminology* **29.3**, 300–3.

King, M. 1995. Police cooperation and border controls in a 'new' Europe. In *Social change, crime and the police*, L. Shelley & J. Vigh (eds). Chur, Switzerland: Harwood Academic.

Lee, S.Y. 1990. Morning calm, rising sun: character and policing in South Korea and in Japan. *Police Studies* **13.3**, 91–110.

Mawby, R.I. 1990. *Comparative policing issues: the British and American experience in international perspective*. London: Routledge/Unwin.

Miller, W.R. 1977. *Cops and bobbies: police authority in New York and London, 1830–1870*. Chicago: University of Chicago Press.

Miyazawa, C.P. 1992. *Policing in Japan: a study on making crime*. New York: SUNY Press.

Moriyama, T. 1992. Community policing in Japan: formal and informal aspects. Paper to International Symposium on Community Policing, Heidelberg, Germany.

Morrison, W.R. 1985. *Showing the flag: the mounted police and Canadian sovereignty in the north, 1894–1925*. Vancouver: University of British Columbia Press.

Posen, I. 1994. What is policing? *Police Review*, 11 February, 14–15.

Reiner, R. 1991. *Chief Constables*. Oxford: Oxford University Press.

Reiner, R. 1992. *The politics of the police*. Brighton: Wheatsheaf.

Roach, J. & J. Thomaneck 1985 (eds). *Police and public in Europe*. London: Croom-Helm.

Rosenbaum, D.P. 1994 (ed.). *The challenge of community policing*. Thousand Oaks, Calif.: Sage.

Stead, P.J 1957. *The police of Paris*. London: Staples.

Stead, P.J. 1983. *The police of France*. London: Macmillan.

Thornton, R.Y. & K. Endo 1992. *Preventing crime in America and Japan: a comparative study*. Armonk, New York: M.E. Sharpe, Inc.

Waddington, P.A.J. 1987. Towards paramilitarism? Dilemmas in policing civil disaster. *British Journal of Criminology* **27**, 37–46.

Walker, D.B. & P.C. Kratcoski 1991. A cross cultural comparison of police in the United States, Canada and England. Paper presented to annual conference of Law and Society Association, Amsterdam.

PART 2

Police Systems Across the World

Introduction

This section considers the police systems of a wide range of countries world-wide. However, rather than focus on an – inevitably – limited number of individual countries, each chapter takes as its subject countries that may arguably be classified together.

In Chapter 3 Rob Mawby compares the development of the modern police in Britain, the USA and Canada. While possibly the subject of more research and more texts than the rest of the world together, much of the work here has been a-comparative. That is, there is an implicit assumption that essentially the police systems in these countries are the same. In contrast, Mawby argues, not only are there marked differences between Britain and North America, but within Britain there are also considerable variations, with the police systems of Scotland, Northern Ireland and the Channel Islands quite distinctive.

As already noted, discussions of an alleged continental European policing system have a long history, Indeed, debates over the desirability of police reorganization in England and Wales were often prefaced with critiques of the European 'way'. Fosdick's (1969) account of continental police at the beginning of the twentieth century is the first of many attempts to identify key characteristics of the police systems of continental Europe (see for example Bayley 1975, ibid. 1979, Fijnaut 1990, Mawby 1990, ibid. 1992). In terms of the dimensions described earlier, Mawby (1990) argues that continental police systems may be characterized as (i) structurally more centralized and militaristic (ii) functionally putting more emphasis on political and administrative tasks (iii) in terms of legitimacy, being more closely tied to government and less accountable to either public or law. Nevertheless, there are marked variations between countries (Mawby 1992). For example the Dutch system was not excessively centralized and recent changes make it more akin to England and Wales (Interpol 1992) and while the Swedish police were amalgamated into a national body in 1965 efforts were taken at that stage to ensure the continuance of local accountability structures (Akermo 1986). Moreover while the French, Italian and Spanish police may traditionally be identified most fully with the model, in each case the maintenance of at least two police forces allowed governments to ensure that no one institution achieved too much power. Overall, though there are marked differences between the police of England and Wales and their counterparts from the continent, there are then also considerable differences between the nations of continental Europe (Mawby 1992).

In Chapter 4 Monica den Boer argues that co-operation between European nations has contributed to a convergence of police systems. Using the examples of Belgium, England and Wales, Germany and the Netherlands she argues that centralized pressures have been evident in all four countries, especially concerning more serious offences and 'high policing', which has correspondingly increased in importance. Thus while subsidiarity appears to be a common principle within nations it is generally restricted to routine police work. Changes in the political regimes in Central and Eastern Europe have predicated changes in policing, at least partly because the 'old' police were so closely tied to the communist regimes. However as Rudas' (1977) account of the Hungarian police illustrates, to a large extent the soviet-model of policing was based on the system common in Europe before the communist takeover. Similarly Kowalewski (1981) acknowledges the link between the police system created by the early Bolshevik government and its Tsarist predecessor, and accounts for much of the difference between the Soviet Union and China in terms of the social and political conditions preceding and underpinning their revolutions. The link between Central/Eastern and Western Europe is also important in terms of how the police of post-communist societies will change. Political alliances with the West, through Interpol and possible EC membership, will draw post-communist societies closer to the West, and especially closer to Western Europe.

Under the soviet system, Eastern Bloc countries' police systems shared a number of features: a centralized and militaristic uniformed police subordinate to the even more centralized secret police; an emphasis upon political order rather than conventional crime; and a close link between police and party with minimal public or legal accountability, in practice if not always in theory. The changes currently being undertaken – for example through demilitarization and depoliticization of the police and lustration policies – coincide with rising public concern over crime and financial constraints on public services (Fogel 1994, Mawby, et al. 1997). In Chapter 5 Louise Shelley reviews the situation.

The other police system that has been consistently recognized in the literature is the colonial model. In many respects it corresponds to the continental model – not surprising given that much of the administrative and legal structure of European states was based on earlier Roman institutions, where the Romans were themselves colonists. It is also important to remember this, since it reminds us that the British were not the only colonists! However, while the French transported their centralized, militaristic policing structure across their empire, the British government allegedly created a different type of policing for its empire, one that was more appropriate for the control of a subjugated population. The model it used was the one first established for Ireland (Tobias 1977) where the police could not rely on public consent. Again using Mawby's (1990) model, colonial police may be characterized as (i) structurally more centralized and militaristic; for example armed and living as units in barracks (ii) functionally giving more priority to public order tasks, but also having a number of administrative responsibilities (iii) deriving their legitimacy from their colonial masters rather than the indigenous population.

In Chapter 5 Shelley notes that policing in Central/Eastern Europe incorporated many of the characteristics of colonial policy, given the dominance of the Soviet Union. A fuller discussion of colonial policing is, however, the subject of Chapter 6 where Bankole Cole assesses the emergence of colonial policing. He introduces systematically for the first time material from colonial powers other than the British. Distinguishing between policing in settlement and pacified colonies, and in the latter between the European settlement areas and the protectorates, he agrees that in the protectorates the needs of economic imperialism required a politically controlled paramilitary force prioritizing public order. Noting that its legacy is to be found in post-colonial societies, he questions the extent to which its influence is evident in conservative Britain.

Another example, which at first glance seems rather different, is Japan, perhaps the most extensively researched of all police systems outside England and North America. With its low crime rate Japan has become the envy of many Western societies, and while policing is only one aspect of this it is pertinent to consider how far Japan's police system contributes to its apparent tranquillity. Compared with Anglo–American policing, perhaps the most notable features of the Japanese police surround their functions, which embrace a range of welfare responsibilities, and the structure of the police, with police firmly located within their communities. However, as Ames (1981) has noted, this does not mean – as Bayley (1976) implied – that the police are locally accountable. Mirroring Japanese society, the police are a centralized organization and cultural definitions of authority and duty mean that the police are not a publicly accountable organization. Recently Leishman (1994) has provided an interpretation midway between those of Ames and Bayley, and pointed out, for example, that in reality the Japanese police may be no more (or less) centralized than the police of England and Wales. Nevertheless the fact that the police operate within a culture that has been moulded by Confucianism, Buddhism and Taoism, where duty and obligation are central and rights subordinate, suggest both that social control in Japan is more problematic than Bayley for one implies (see also Miyazawa 1992) and that Japan's police may share many characteristics with its geographical and cultural neighbours. These links, not surprisingly, were reinforced during Japanese military occupation of many of its neighbours prior to or during World War II. So, for example, China may be viewed as a society whose police has been shaped by both socialist principles and Asian culture, and Hong Kong similarly may evidence features of Asian and colonial influence. Singapore is another example of a police system which appears to combine a community-orientation with tight central control (Austin 1987) and while Lee's more recent comparison of Japan and South Korea emphasizes the differences, he also notes that 'both forces are natural, hierarchical, authoritarian – respected and feared by the vast majority; opposed, even hated, by politically progressive minorities' (Lee 1990: 91).

In Chapter 7 Frank Leishman, a British researcher on the Japanese police who, like Ames, is a Japanese linguist, pulls together the now somewhat dated studies of the Japanese police in a review that incorporates more contemporary analysis and questions the extent of similarity between the Japanese system and that of its neighbours. Offering a typology of policing according to democratic, authoritarian and communitarian principles (of police systems and societies), he argues that while Japan shares with its East Asian neighbours elements of authoritarianism and communitarianism, it differs in also embodying democratic features. Nevertheless his review is optimistic and he concludes that ongoing changes in Eastern societies are likely to result in more democratic political and policing systems.

Inevitably Part 2 can provide only a broad sweep of policing systems across the globe and there are areas and socio-political systems missing from the list. What we have attempted to do here is to assess the extent of similarities and differences between police systems in different countries or groupings and to aid in an understanding of the relationship between policing and the wider context within which it takes place. Part 3 then focuses on specific issues that confront the police in different societies.

Bibliography

Akermo, K.E. 1986. Organisational changes and remodelling of the Swedish police. *Canadian Police College Journal* **10**, 245–63.

Ames, W.L. 1981. *Police and community in Japan*. Berkeley, Calif.: University of California Press.

Austin, W.T. 1987. Crime and custom in an orderly society: the Singapore prototype. *Criminology* **25**, 279–94.

Bayley, D.H. 1975. The police and political developments in Europe. In *The formation of nation states in Europe*, C. Tilley (ed.). Princetown: Princetown University Press.

Bayley, D.H. 1976. *Forces of order: police behaviour in Japan and the United States*. Berkeley, Calif.: University of California Press.

Bayley, D.H. 1979. Police function, structure and control in Western Europe and North America: comparative historical studies. In *Crime and justice: an annual review of research*, N. Morris & M. Tonry (eds). Chicago: University of Chicago Press.

Fijnaut, C.F.C.F. 1990. The police and the public in Western Europe: a precarious comparison. *Police Review* **63**, 337–45.

Fogel, D. 1994. *Policing in Central and Eastern Europe*. Helsinki: HEUNI.

Fosdick, R.B. 1969. *European police systems*. Montelair, NJ: Patterson Smith.

Interpol 1992. Netherlands, *Police*, November, 20–1.

Kowalewski, D. 1981. China and the Soviet Union: a comparative model for analysis. *Studies in Comparative Communism* **14**, 279–306.

Lee, S.Y. 1990. Morning calm, rising sun: national character and policing in South Korea and in Japan. *Police Studies* **13**, 91–110.

Leishman, F. 1994. Under Western eyes: perspectives in policing and society in Japan. *Policing and Society* **4**, 35–51.

Mawby, R.I. 1990. *Comparative policing issues: the British and American experience in international perspective*. London: Routledge.

Mawby, R.I. 1992. Comparative police systems: searching for a continental model. In *Criminal justice: theory and practice*, K. Bottomley, T. Fowles, R. Reiner (eds). London: British Society of Criminology/ISTD.

Mawby, R.I., Z. Ostrihanska, D. Wojcik. 1997. Police response to crime: the perceptions of victims from two Polish cities. *Policing and Society*, 7, 235–52.

Miyazawa, S. 1992. *Policing in Japan: a study on making crime*. New York: State University of New York Press.

Rudas, G. 1977. The changing role, responsibilities and activities of the police in a developed society. *International Review of Criminal Policy* 33, 11–16.

Tobias, J.J. 1977. The British colonial police: an alternative police style. In *Pioneers in policing*, P.J. Stead (ed.). Maidenhead: Patterson Smith.

CHAPTER 3

Variations on a Theme: the Development of Professional Police in the British Isles and North America

R.I. MAWBY

Introduction

At first sight, the introduction of a section on policing systems in different societies with a chapter on the police of the British Isles, USA and Canada seems to make sense. After all, this is the alleged 'Anglo-American' policing tradition that has been contrasted with policing systems elsewhere. Moreover the Canadian system (directly) and the US system (indirectly) developed from the Anglo-Saxon tradition. It is also notable that much of the research from Britain and North America has been non-comparative, with the assumption that conclusions from one society can be readily applied elsewhere, and while Banton's (1964) pioneering comparison is an exception to this practice, it is perhaps the exception that proves the rule. On the other hand, from the beginning differences have been recognized. For example while the traditional 'British bobby' and the determined 'Mounty' provide perhaps unique examples of a fusion of law-enforcement and national identity, the mythology is markedly different. It is however a positive image, unlike that associated with the US police who, as Das (1986) plaintively observes, have regularly been compared unfavourably with their overseas equivalents. Indeed, US commentators have, since Fosdick (1920: 3) described the police as 'perhaps the most pronounced failure of all our unhappy municipal history', almost universally considered police systems elsewhere as better than their own.

One of the most common criticisms of the US police is their diversity, expressed in terms of lack of co-ordination. However while the argument that the US does not have a police system, but rather any number of police structures, is plausible, it must equally be recognized that Canada has at least two systems, provincial or metropolitan police and the Royal Canadian Mounted Police (RCMP), while the police systems of Scotland, Northern Ireland, the Isle of Man and the Channel

Islands are markedly different from that of England and Wales. It is not, then, just a matter of comparing the British Isles, Canada and the US: internal differences are in some cases just as extreme.

Accepting that, this chapter follows the historical development of the police. In the following section policing is traced back to its Anglo-Saxon roots. Then the emergence of the modern police and subsequent developments are considered, first for the British Isles, then for North America.

Early Forms of Policing

The British Isles

Policing in Saxon England was based at the local kinship and community level. Groups of families belonged to a tithing, corporately responsible for controlling the behaviour of its members. Tithings were themselves grouped into hundreds, under the aegis of the hundredman who was directly responsible to the shire-reeve, or sheriff (Critchley 1978). The invasion of the Normans in 1066 inevitably led to an increased emphasis on central control. However, rather than dismantle the entire system, the Normans restructured it as the system of frankpledge. The office of constable was created as the local representative of central government and co-ordinated the work of the sheriffs who imposed the law through their own courts. Thus while, as Stead (1985) observes, the emphasis on local, unpaid officials was distinct from the Roman practice of deploying paid state officers, it did combine local involvement with a more centralized system of control (Brogden et al. 1988). However, as the Normans became more integrated into their conquered communities, much of the central control lapsed and the manor, with its manorial court, became the key institution for social control. At the same time, the term 'constable' became more widely and variously used, with local part-time, unpaid constables a world away in status from the head constable of the shire.

Two pieces of legislation then moulded the policing system for the next 400 years: the Statute of Winchester (1285) and the Justices of the Peace Act (1361) (Critchley 1978). The Statute of Winchester rationalized and extended the administration of law and order in a number of respects. It confirmed the place of the part-time constable as the hub of the system but established – for the growing townships – the system of 'watch and ward', through which all able-bodied townsmen were required to take turns to guard the town during the hours of darkness. The re-establishment of the Saxon custom of hue and cry, provided a further level of community support for the constable. While the Statute of Winchester provided the structure for everyday policing, the Justices of the Peace Act was arguably more important since it re-established the institutions of social control that linked local law-enforcement with central government. The new justices (JPs), usually high status lords of the manor, became responsible for local law-enforcement on behalf of the crown. The parish constables, appointed annually as the JPs' agents, while the most significant of the locally appointed officials, thus lost status to the justices who presided over the local courts and, through their constables, combined crime control with civic responsibilities such as the supervision of tax collection. By the sixteenth century, the role of constable had been transformed from that of a respected local representative to that of a dogsbody, and those who could afford to do so avoided serving as constable by paying a deputy to do the work on their behalf. In the meantime the justices, as part of the strong English feudal system, operated the local law-enforcement system on behalf of the monarch and provided the balance between central and local control that the French system, with a more divided aristocracy, was unable to do (Stead 1983).

However, while the 'team' of justices and constables provided an adequate basis for the enforcement of law and order in rural areas, it proved inadequate in industrial and more urbanized communities. The additional problems of policing the growing townships had been acknowledged through the establishment of the nightwatch, but by the seventeenth century this was clearly inadequate, and a variety of alternative arrangements were established that extensively modified the concept of community responsibility. For example, problems of industrial unrest in the eighteenth century caused the government to attempt to enforce community responsibility through the 1715 Riot Act and the confirmation of the system of hue and cry in new legislation in 1735 (Critchley 1978: 29). At roughly the same time, the yeomanry (Mather 1959) and the Special Constabulary (Gill & Mawby 1990) provided reliable middle class support in the face of working class protest.

Alternatively, between the 1740s and 1850s a number of middle class communities established street patrols to protect their neighbourhoods, and while some of these were effectively self-policing arrangements it became common for local people to get together and hire street patrols (Shubert 1981). Private policing was also encouraged by the operation of a bounty principle whereby 'thief-takers' received a percentage of any stolen property recovered (Ascoli 1979, Radzinowicz 1956a). Large scale private companies similarly formed their own private forces, perhaps the best known being the Thames River Police which was initially funded by the West India Merchants (Radzinowicz 1956a, Stead 1985). Individual victims, meanwhile, routinely engaged in 'self-policing' whereby they took upon themselves the responsibility for prosecuting their protagonists (Brogden et al. 1988).

In many respects, these early forms of policing were reproduced throughout the British Isles. However, there were differences. In Jersey, for example, a parish-based system of control centring on the key figures of lay-magistrates (Jurats) and constables was in evidence by the fifteenth century, although their control remained at parish level and constables became more significant local political figures, day-to-day law enforcement being delegated to centeniers, vingteniers and constables' officers, all of whom – like the constables and jurats – were periodically elected and retained their status and power within the local community (Le Herissier 1973). In Scotland, early forms of locally administered policing were similar to in England. However, from the fourteenth to the sixteenth centuries conflict with England and closer links with continental Europe resulted in the emergence of a distinct system. Most notably, while justices never attained the power of their English equivalents, sheriffs established themselves as the key local figures, and their staff, including the procurators fiscal, played a significant role in the system (Gordon 1980, Stead 1985). Consequently, constables and town guards operated in similar ways to their equivalent in England and Wales, but they did so within a somewhat different administrative structure that subsequently underpinned the form of the new police.

Even more so than in Scotland, the concept of community self-policing in Ireland was unrealistic in the light of the need to impose English control in a colonial context. By the eighteenth century a number of baronial police forces existed that enabled the Protestant minority to maintain control over the Catholic peasantry, and it is perhaps unsurprising that it was in Ireland that the first paid police was established.

What then of early forms of policing in North America?

Early forms of policing in the USA and Canada

Major colonization of North America began in the seventeenth century with British and other European settlements along the East Coast of America. Generally, English common law traditions were adopted, with the emphasis placed upon victims shouldering responsibility for 'their' crimes (Gittler 1984, Steinberg 1989). However in some areas where other migrant groups predominated, local policing arrangements took on elements of other cultures, although these were eventually superseded:

> As early as 1636 a night watch was established in Boston and thereafter hardly an important settlement existed in New England that did not have, in addition to its military guard, a few uniformed watchmen. In New York the Schout and Rattle Watch of the Dutch Colonists were superseded by the Constables' Watch of the English require, and the complete English system of local government, including a High Constable, sub-constables and watchmen, was imposed . . . (Fosdick 1920: 59).

Similarly in Canada, the urban developments of the East coast were the first to establish policing arrangements, partly as a means of controlling the growing population, partly as a protection against the external threat of the indigenous population. Areas of French settlement adopted police structures from their homeland, and the most powerful landowners appointed themselves as magistrates and formed night militia, whose tasks included law-enforcement, fire protection and a guard against Indian attack (Kelly & Kelly 1976, Whittingham 1981). In British Canada unpaid constables were first appointed in Newfoundland in 1729 and problems caused by sailors provoked the governor of Halifax to introduce a similar system in 1749. In Upper Canada (later Ontario), high county constables were appointed in 1793, whose responsibility included the organization in their districts of unpaid night-watchmen (Kelly & Kelly 1976). In both the US and Canada, these early policing initiatives centred on the townships, and on the frontier vigilantism flourished, more spontaneous and more independent of what 'government' existed (Brown 1969). Nevertheless, in some situations powerful landowners were able to establish early 'police' systems to facilitate their control of their workers. For example Reichel (1988) describes the slave patrols of the late seventeenth century South as militia units organized by the slave owners to discourage revolt and round up runaways. Thus while in theory

North America might have been the land of opportunity and the land of the free, in practice community-based law-enforcement institutions operated within a system of power and privilege that enabled property-owners to control workers, slave owners to regulate slaves, and settlers to protect themselves against the indigenous Indian population.

The Emergence of a Public Police

The new police

While on continental Europe public police systems were well established by the seventeenth century (Bowden 1978, Chapman 1970, Emsley 1983, Stead 1983), Anglo-American policing was essentially private, non-specialized and non-professional until the nineteenth century, and indeed in England the 'invidious' continental system was cited in arguments against the introduction of a paid police (Radzinowicz 1948, ibid. 1956b). The modern Anglo-American police systems that emerged then in the nineteenth century have been characterized by Bayley (1985) as public, specialized and professional organizations. The reasons for their emergence have been the subject of considerable discussion (Brogden *et al.* 1988, Emsley 1996, Reiner 1992). On the one hand, orthodox police histories have tended to see the emergence of the new police as evolution, an inevitable progression to meet the problems of urban industrial society that the 'old' police was failing to address. On the other hand, radicals have argued that the new police were appropriate forms of control within capitalist societies where traditional forms of social control had broken down yet order, predictability and continuity were crucial to the smooth running of *gesellschaft* societies. In between, revisionists argue that the 'new' police reflected both the needs of newly industrialized and urbanized societies and the forms of organization most appropriate to such settings. In this context it is clear that just as the social conditions in Britain and North America in which the new police emerged varied markedly, so the resultant police systems also varied. Thus while Bayley (1985) could rightly draw out similarities between 'new' police systems, equally differences are evident both within and between Britain and North America.

England and Wales

In England, attempts to create a police force for London in 1785 were rejected. However, given the specific problems of policing in Ireland, the Bill was reformulated as the Dublin Police Act of 1786 (Radzinowicz 1956b). A national, centralized force was then established in Ireland in 1814 and subsequently modified in 1822 and 1836. However unlike in England, where there was concern that no police should be created as an arm of central government, in Ireland the model was one of a centralized, militaristic force, dominated by Irish Protestants and English recruits, that was directly answerable to the government in Westminster (Palmer 1988, Tobias 1977).

In England, despite the advocacy of key reformers such as Bentham, Chadwick and Colquhoun and parliamentary committees in 1816, 1818 and 1822, there was considerable opposition to reform. Eventually, though, a further Select Committee in 1828 paved the way for the 1829 Metropolitan Police Act, operating throughout the capital except in the City of London and headed by two commissioners, Charles Rowan and Richard Mayne (Critchley 1978, Emsley 1996, Hart 1951). Given the controversial nature of the new police, two policies were implemented from the first that crucially established the nature of the English police. First, in contrast to the French system, the police were uniformed and an emphasis placed upon preventive patrolling; indeed it was not until 1842 that plain clothes detectives were appointed, and no CID existed until 1878. Second, and combined with this high visibility feature, was that of minimal powers: the emphasis placed on the police as operating with public consent and close to the community, epitomized in the concept of police as 'citizens in uniform' with few powers additional to those enjoyed by the general public.

A further feature of this model was that of the police as highly accountable (Reiner 1995). However, although the police were recruited from the working class, in other respects they were deliberately distanced from the public. For example they were consciously recruited from outside the London area, and indeed the number of agricultural labourers joining the Metropolitan police was notable, and they were directly accountable to the commissioners, with no suggestion of local community accountability.

Once the Metropolitan Police Force was established and gradually became accepted, it was argued that similar policing arrangements should be adopted elsewhere. Given that crime was recognized as an urban phenomenon, it seemed to make sense to concentrate next on other cities. The Municipal Corporations Act (1835) thus allowed large boroughs to establish their own paid police forces under the control of Watch Committees comprised of local councillors and magistrates. This was followed by the County Police Act (1839) that allowed counties to establish police forces, in this case controlled by JPs. By the mid-nineteenth century a number of towns and counties had used the new legislation to form their own forces, in some cases provoked by local crime, in others by labour unrest, most notably from the Chartist movement. There was, none the less, considerable opposition to the introduction of a unified structure and the abolition of small, local forces (Emsley 1996). However the County and Borough Police Act (1856) made the establishment of paid police forces compulsory and required the Home Office to contribute a quarter of their costs.

With the establishment of local forces throughout England and Wales, the following 80 years saw further consolidation of the police and an extension of central government influence over the ways in which individual forces developed. This extension of Home Office control, a bitter pill for the local elite of councillors and magistrates to swallow, was sweetened by the decision, in 1874, to increase the central grant to 50 per cent. One example of Home Office influence was pressure to limit the range of non-crime roles the police performed, a restriction reluctantly conceded by local government keen to 'get value for money' from the police, especially in low crime areas (Emsley 1996, Steedman 1984). Another was persistent pressure to restrict the number of small autonomous forces. Thus the Local Government Act (1888) abolished independent forces in towns with less than 10,000 population – resulting in a drop in the number of forces from 231 in 1880 to 183 in 1889 – and throughout the 1920s and 1930s the Home Office attempted, unsuccessfully, to raise the minimum population or number of officers in a police force area (Critchley 1978).

Let us then take stock and assess the ways in which the English system of policing developed up to 1940, distinguishing between the function, structure and legitimacy of the new police.

In terms of functions, it was clearly the policy of both government and senior management to focus on the police role in crime control, most especially crime prevention through uniformed patrol, while at the same time cultivating the image of the police as also fulfilling a welfare and service order role. As Donajgrodski (1977) notes, this early emphasis upon service helped legitimate the police before a sceptical, and sometimes hostile, public. While, as already noted, the Home Office was concerned that the role should not be extended too far, particularly by making the police (local) government administrators in the way that many continental and colonial forces were, it was clearly important to establish the police as a service rather than a force. This was of immediate concern because the police, in many cases supported by the Special Constabulary, were also used to control public disorder, especially labour disputes (Gill & Mawby 1990, Weinberger 1991). Self-evidently the role of the police incorporated political aspects; equally the image portrayed was of an agency combining the prevention of crime with a welfare mandate.

What then of the structure of the new police? As already noted, successive Acts through the nineteenth century resulted in three types of police force: the London Metropolitan Police, county forces and borough police. While the Home Office acted to curb the proliferation of small borough forces, the advantage of the new policing arrangement was the balance between central and local government. Whereas under the old system the justices acted as local overseers of crime-control but were, through the feudal system, intimately tied to central government, so within the new police JPs – and to a lesser extent local councillors – were the local representatives of central governments, where a combination of common interests and central grant funding ensured that despite local variations a degree of conformity existed that was perhaps unique within a localized system.

This interpretation of local control is particularly notable in the context of police legitimacy. In no sense were local forces subject to populist control or accountable to their local communities. Rather, the new policing structure reconfirmed the power of local elites that had epitomized the old system. This is illustrated in Wall's (1998) analysis of the relationship between chief officers and these local elites in the period. Wall distinguishes between country and borough forces. In the former, chief constables were appointed by the police authorities, with the approval of the Home Secretary. These chief constables tended to be younger sons of local landlords, frequently with military backgrounds, who were appointed to represent local elites and then left to get on with the job. In contrast, power within the boroughs was vested in the watch committee and the chief officer was initially an agent of this committee. However, because in practice watch committees were unable to manage policing on a day-to-day basis, the authority for managing the force was, by default, delegated to chief officers. While force amalgamations meant that borough chief officers gained in status and responsibility, Wall (1998) argues that, compared with the county chiefs, they were essentially trusted employees of the watch committees, and it was not until the 1940s that the Home Office was able to exert influence over chief officer appointments and begin to establish a more co-ordinated policy that levelled-out differences between county and borough forces.

Developments elsewhere in the British Isles

In Scotland the role of procurator fiscal was preserved as 'modern' police forces were established in the largest cities between 1800 and 1824 (Gordon 1980). Some degree of national harmonization was introduced between 1833 and 1850 and the creation of the Scottish Office in 1885 enabled the new civil service to operate in a similar way to the Home Office for England and Wales. As in England and Wales pressures were put on smaller forces to amalgamate, although there were still 33 separate forces in 1964. The procurator fiscal, operating with a more proact-ive mandate than the subsequently formed Crown Prosecution Service in England and Wales, and indeed more akin to prosecutors in many continental countries, remained perhaps the most notable point of contrast between England and Wales and Scotland. Elsewhere in the British Isles, however, more distinctive policing arrangements were created.

As already noted, policing in Ireland was initially established as a force of colo-nial occupation. The Irish Constabulary sought its legitimacy from Westminster, rather than within Ireland, and in effect operated as a highly centralized, armed, militaristic force of occupation. Its recruits, many of whom were English and with army backgrounds, lived in barracks, and were responsible for maintaining order on behalf of the British government. Nevertheless, by the beginning of the twentieth century the generally peaceful situation in the province, combined with government policy, meant that while the RIC (Royal Irish Constabulary) remained armed and controlled by Protestants and (ultimately) London (Enloe 1980), it was coming to be seen as an indigenous force, recruiting from and maintaining close contacts with the local population (Brewer 1989).

Following partition in 1920 and the continuance of Northern Ireland as a part of the UK, a new force, the Royal Ulster Constabulary (RUC) was created in the North, initially comprising 3,000 men, drawn primarily from the RIC and the Ulster Special Constabulary (USC), and ideally composed of one third Catholics and two thirds Protestants. However, Catholic membership never exceeded 22 per cent, fell to 17 per cent by the late 1920s and was about 10 per cent by the 1960s, and this, allied to the direct control of the force by the Protestant Unionist government, the important role of the Ulster Special Constabulary (USC) as a Protestant public order police reserve (Mapstone 1994), the open and accepted involvement of the police in Protestant pressure groups, and the creation in 1922 of sweeping legal powers (under the Minister of Home Affairs), clearly established the police as an agency of state control (Brewer *et al.* 1988).

In the Channel Isles the power balance was entirely different and the resultant policing developments distinctive. For while part of the British Isles since the Norman Conquest of 1066, the islands' geographical position closer to France than mainland Britain gave them each a considerable degree of political leverage. This is well illustrated if we consider the situation on Jersey, the largest of the islands. As already noted, a community-based system of policing, essentially controlled by local elites, was well established in Jersey by the nineteenth century. It first attracted the attention of the British government in the 1840s when a series of scandals, allegedly emanating from the use of the police to control political minorities, provoked a Houses of Parliament (1847) inquiry. This uncovered a number of idiosyncrasies that were cause for concern. Policing, essentially closely enmeshed within the local political system, had helped maintain a tightly controlled island on which sectional interests superseded the rule of law. However, while the inquiry recommended the establishment of an island-wide paid police, the enmeshing of police and politics meant that Jersey government was in fact being invited to relinquish its policing powers. Given the extent of local political autonomy it not surprisingly declined this invitation and, as a compromise, instituted a small, relatively powerless paid police in the capital, St Helier. The voluntary system, subsequently known as the Honorary Police, continued to provide the main police presence until 1951 when an island-wide paid force was established, and even then the States Police was restricted in its involvement outside St Helier. Thus while in Ireland and Scotland the 'new' police that emerged in the nineteenth century varied to a greater or lesser extent from the English prototype, in Jersey the 'old' police continued as an important institution of social control until well into the post-war era.

The emergence of public police in Canada

In many ways, the circumstances in which paid police systems developed in Canada and the USA were similar. For example, in both countries the majority of the early settlers lived in townships on the East coast, and modern police forces first featured in these townships. The key difference, however, was the relationship held with the British government. While the USA had attained independence in 1788, before the establishment of paid police in Britain, Canada's independence was ratified in the North America Act (1867). Before then, early policing was directly influenced by the British government; afterwards, as part of the British Empire, Canada continued to be subject to British influence.

Of course, this influence was considerably diluted in Quebec province, where paid police forces were established in the 1830s and 1840s and, within the federal government structure, maintained their French influence (Chapman 1978, Kelly & Kelly 1976). In British Canada, though, paid town forces were established at a similar time to England: York (later renamed Toronto) being the first in 1835. The Municipal

Institutions of Upper Canada Act (1858) then authorized towns and cities to establish their own forces under police boards. However, of perhaps greater significance during the nineteenth century was the policing of the vast, underpopulated areas of rural Canada, where control of the Indian and Inuit populations and protection of the territory from foreign incursions required distinctive forms of policing. The first indication of this came from British Columbia in the 1850s when the discovery of gold and subsequent migration from the US led the colonial authorities to request British support, which came in the form of a sub-inspector from the Irish constabulary who established a colonial style police force (Chapman 1978). This became the first provincial force in 1866. The following year brought the British North America Act which made provinces responsible for their own justice administration and this led to other provincial forces being established. The Newfoundland force was formed in 1871, for example, it too being modelled on the Royal Irish Constabulary (Kelly & Kelly 1976).

It was, however, a federal force that became the linchpin for colonial-style policing in Canada. Created as a mounted force to maintain order among construction workers on the Welland and St Lawrence canals and to quell political unrest in Montreal (Kelly & Kelly 1976, Statistics Canada 1986), this force was named the Northwest Mounted Police Force (NWMP) in 1873 and became responsible for enforcing the law in the central plains, the Yukon and Northwest Territories (Morrison 1985).

This centrally co-ordinated but mobile force was seen as ideal for exerting order across the vast territories of Canada, whose sheer scale made law-enforcement, public administration, and the assertion of sovereignty, difficult. The form it took, however, was very different from the police of England and Wales:

> The Mounted Police were, in a certain sense, the Canadian equivalent of those forces of imperialism – the British Army, the Royal Irish Constabulary, and the various colonial police forces – which brought British law and civil administration to the wild corners of the Empire. The difference in the Canadian case was that the colonial power was in Ottawa rather than in London. As agents of this central power, the police imposed on the Canadian north a system largely alien to it, a system which originated elsewhere, in a different culture, and which was designed not to express the aspirations of the north, but to control it (Morrison 1985: 2).

The NWMP extended its influence in the early twentieth century, taking on security and counter-espionage services during the first world war and, in 1919, helping to break the Winnipeg general strike (Horrall 1980). In 1920 it was renamed the Royal Canadian Mounted Police (RCMP) and continued to expand, on the one hand taking on additional responsibilities from federal government, on the other hand extending its services in the provinces. By the 1930s it provided police services in the Yukon and North West Territories and for six of the ten provinces; in the post-war period it assumed provincial policing responsibilities in two further provinces and established a foothold in urban policing (Chapman 1978).

The emergence of public police in the USA

While the Canadian policing systems were strongly influenced by British examples, policing and law-enforcement in the USA emerged in the aftermath of the struggle for independence and concern that control from Westminster should not be substituted by control from Washington:

> The individual states were not willing to turn over complete authority to the federal government, and they stringently guarded their rights to govern themselves within the parameters of the Constitution and to enact and enforce their own laws (Sweatman & Cross 1989: 11).

An appreciation of early policing arrangements thus has to take account of differences according to the areas being policed – urban, rural and state – but also the extent to which local distinctions – such as the French influence in New Orleans (Emsley 1983) – resulted in local idiosyncrasies.

The first examples of paid police forces were found in the cities, where perceived threats to public order were apparently a crucial factor (Lane 1992). City administrators therefore looked elsewhere – initially to England and subsequently to other American cities – for ideas about how to respond to the problems (Monkkonen 1981). The first modern force, established in New York in 1844, for example, was in many respects modelled on the London police (Miller 1977, Richardson 1970). Then in the 1850s new forces were established in a number of cities, including Boston, Philadelphia, Chicago, New Orleans and Cincinnati (Fosdick 1920, Lane 1967) which built on the New York experience.

As in England, local government interests dictated that these early police carried out a wide variety of administrative and service tasks, rather than concentrating solely on law-enforcement (Fosdick 1920: 211–15, Monkkonen 1981, Smith 1940). As Fogelson (1977: 16) notes:

> In the absence of other specialised public bureaucracies, the authorities found the temptation almost irresistible to transform the police departments into catchall health, welfare and law-enforcement agencies. Hence the police cleared the streets and inspected boilers in New York, distributed supplies to the poor in Baltimore, accommodated the homeless in Philadelphia, investigated vegetable markets in St Louis, operated emergency ambulances in Boston . . .

In other respects, US city police were markedly different from their English cousins. For example, they were issued with firearms, but only reluctantly donned uniforms (Lane 1992, Miller 1977), the latter being rejected initially as 'Un-American', 'undemocratic' and symbolic of the (British) military (Fosdick 1920: 70). Perhaps the most notable distinctions, however, surrounded the community-base for US city police, expressed in terms of recruitment policies, police corruption and control of the police. For example, unlike the English police US city police were specifically recruited from their local communities. Miller (1977) describes how the police in New York were not only local residents; they were recruited from within the districts they were assigned to police, and efforts were made to ensure that they were representative of the ethnic composition of those areas. Moreover such local residency requirements continued well into the twentieth century (Fogelson 1977: Chapter 5, Smith 1940: 162).

However the fact that police officers were closely identified with their precincts and the power structure at that local level meant that corruption was an endemic feature of city police and that attempts to 'clean up' the police at force level were generally unsuccessful, with police chiefs wielding less influence than precinct commanders and, ultimately, local power elites (Fogelson 1977). The Lexow Committee of 1895, which exposed corruption and political manipulation in New York, was one of many critiques of urban policing systems, demonstrating not merely the extensiveness of corruption but also the impotence of local government to eliminate it. The extent to which corruption was a feature of the political manipulation of the police is illustrated in the way in which control over the police was exercised. Whether the police were controlled by a single commissioner or board of commissioners, the fact that such appointments were temporary and subject – directly or otherwise – to political influence, meant that police policies were a political football. On one level this was reflected 'in the conflict between the (usually Democrat controlled) city and the (often Republican controlled) state' (Miller 1977). On another level it meant that a change of political control meant not merely a change in police policy, or senior personnel, but also perhaps widespread sackings with the department. Fosdick (1920: 272) for example, cites the aftermath of a Democratic victory in Kansas in 1913 when 170 out of 200 Republicans were dismissed from the Police, and quotes a police chief of a city in Pennsylvania describing his career shifts between 1893 and 1920:

> I was first appointed chief of police in this city in 1893, and served in that capacity for two years . . . A political change occurred and I worked as superintendent for a private detective agency for six years. I was then re-appointed chief of police, serving for six years, when I was again thrown out by a turn of the political wheel. I was again appointed in 1912 and have been on the job since (quoted in Fosdick 1920: 257).

In rural areas, political influence on policing was even more direct. The offices of sheriff and constable, adopted from the English system, were maintained but with popular elections substituting for the control of colonial governors (Smith 1940: 79–125). While constables continued as part-time local officials and dropped most of their crime-related work, sheriffs became paid officials responsible for law-enforcement as well as various administrative duties such as tax collection, with their income largely derived from the fees and fines they collected.

In the rural areas and the large cities police politics was to some extent linked to populist politics, but the development of state police forces reflects political domination rather than populist control. The first state force, the Texas Rangers, was formed in 1835 under the direction of the military to operate as a patrol along the border with Mexico. More general state forces, however, were established to enforce unpopular laws where local, partisan, police could not be trusted. The Massachusetts force, for example, was created in 1865 with a mandate to eliminate commercial vice (Smith 1940). The establishment of the Pennsylvanian force in 1905, however, heralded a new wave of state forces designed to 'crush disorders, whether industrial or otherwise, which arose in the foreign-filled districts of the state' (Reppetto 1978: 130). The Pennsylvanian State Police was a military force, modelled on the RIC and the Philippine Constabulary. Similarly the New Jersey State Police was described by Reppetto as a jingoistic military unit, headed by a colonel with senior officers recruited from the armed services.

This plethora of policing arrangements developed in the nineteenth and early twentieth century without any central direction. Federal law enforcement agencies, with notable exceptions such as the Postal Inspection Service, are of relatively recent origin (Geller and Morris 1992). Indeed the lack of a public national police force meant that on occasions national private police systems were used by central government (Morn 1982, see also Johnston in this volume). Early attempts to co-ordinate policing activities were taken on by the International Association of Chiefs of Police which established a national clearing house for criminal identification records in 1896 and initiated a uniform crime reporting system in 1927. Those responsibilities were subsequently transferred to the Bureau of Investigation, which was renamed the Federal Bureau of Investigation (FBI) and also established a voluntary fingerprint bank and forensic laboratory (Smith 1940: chapter 8). The creation of the FBI was not however uncontroversial and President Roosevelt formed the Bureau by executive order in 1908, having failed to convince Congress of the need for a federal law enforcement agency (Ungar 1975).

Thus while in Canada, British colonial policing provided an alternative to local urban policing systems that resulted in the creation of the RCMP as a national, though not monopolistic, public police agency, reaction against colonial dominance in the US created an atmosphere of suspicion towards central control. In consequence, the police systems that developed differed considerably from one another, and while – particularly at state level – colonial-type forces could be identified, they illustrate the creation of different forms of policing in response to different local conditions rather than any shift towards a national system.

Contemporary Anglo-American Police Systems

England, Wales and Scotland

What then of the police in Britain and North America today? Given the different ways in which the modern police developed, are such differences maintained or can we detect a convergence in police systems as transitional influences are strengthened? With regard to the British Isles it is perhaps most convenient to start with England and Wales and Scotland, where differences are minimal, and then note the different situations in Northern Ireland and the Channel Islands. As has already been noted, the police of England and Wales inherited a broad mandate to provide a service to the public that was wider than an exclusive emphasis on crime control and public order maintenance. To some extent this has been maintained. On the one hand, emphasis on services for consumers and Force Charters provide indications of political reaffirmation of such policies (Bunt & Mawby 1994). On the other hand, early research on police time-allocations (Martin & Wilson 1969) and public calls to the police (Punch & Naylor 1973) suggested that only a minority of police time is spent dealing with crime.

However, as in the USA, increased technology and the replacement of foot patrols with mobile patrols was seen as shifting the emphasis of the police from community service to reactive crime fighting. The Accrington experiment in the 1960s, whereby a balance between beat offices and rapid/response specialist back-up was sought (Home Office 1966), was generally considered a failure. Moreover, unlike in the USA, advocates of community policing were in a minority within the senior police management, with many chief constables distancing themselves from the outspoken views of John Alderson (1979, 1981) in Devon and Cornwall. While the Brixton disorders in April 1981 and subsequent riots in other major cities were at least partially provoked by aggressive policing methods, and the Scarman (1981) inquiry advocated a 'return' to community policing, the impact of the report on accountability structures (see below) seems to have been more profound than its impact upon police styles and roles. Significantly, zero tolerance policing, with its more assertive and control oriented message, seems to have struck a chord in recent years (Dennis 1997).

Other research has indicated that an increasing number of public-initiated police contacts are crime-related, especially in inner-city areas (Jones, MacLean & Young 1986, Shapland & Vagg 1988, Skogan 1990) and in a time of stretched resources many have argued that police duties should be more closely restricted to crime-work. This was the dominant message behind the setting up of the Posen (1994) inquiry into core policing tasks, which, despite denials, was envisaged as clearing the way towards the privatization of alleged 'peripheral' policework (Hoddinott 1994, Howe 1994, Judge 1994). While the conclusions of the inquiry fell short of recommendations to promote wholesale change (Home Office 1995) the debate itself signalled a marked shift in thinking about the English police, during which a number of 'sacred cows' were declared profane (Reiner 1994).

However while this debate has centred attention on the balance between crime-fighting and service roles for the police, perhaps the most notable shift in emphasis on police functions emanates from the role of the police under a Thatcher government, particularly in the early 1980s, where police were clearly used to enforce government policies, notably in breaking the power of the unions, best illustrated in the confrontations during the miners' strike (Fine & Millar 1985). While clearly the English police, despite the power of the myth, have never been divorced from politics, the role of the police in these industrial disputes reaffirmed the police role in the maintenance of the status quo – through the maintenance of public order – and left a legacy which still affects police–public relations in the mining areas.

Industrial disputes and urban protests in the 1980s also bequeathed dramatic changes in the structure of the police. True, the 'average' police officer patrols armed only with a truncheon, albeit a longer and heavier one than in the past. However CS spray guns are currently being tested in a number of forces and recent years have seen considerable pressure from within the ranks to issue firearms on a routine basis (McKenzie 1996, see also Waddington in this volume). All forces include officers trained and qualified to use firearms, and many deploy armed response teams (Jefferson 1990). Back-up squads, normally used in public order situations, specially trained and issued with riot gear, operate as paramilitary units and provide a high profile range of policing light years from the cosy Dixon of Dock Green imagery of 1950s Britain. Thus while the police of England, Wales and Scotland remain among a minority in international terms who do not routinely carry firearms, armed police are becoming a more common sight on the mainland and the question of arming the police is perhaps more openly debated than ever before (McKenzie 1996, Pead 1991).

A further key question regarding the structure of the police relates to the balance between local and central control and organization of policing. As already noted, Home Office influence towards consistency was evident through the latter half of the nineteenth century, but at the outbreak of World War II there remained nearly 200 separate local forces. These were reduced in the immediate post-war period to about 130 and, principally due to the Royal Commission on the Police (1962) and the subsequent (1964) Police Act, this number was significantly reduced to 43 by the mid 1970s, with the number of forces in Scotland similarly reduced, in this case to eight (Stead 1985: 136–40). The Royal Commission identified the protection of local police forces' autonomy through the institution of the tripartite structure of accountability: individual chief constables, police authorities, and central government. However, it is widely accepted that local government influence on policing has been muted. Indeed, the 1962 Royal Commission, in clarifying the intended relationship between chief constables and police authorities, accepted that the latter's influence should be merely advisory (Spencer 1985). Moreover, a series of recent developments have further strengthened the role of central government (Loveday 1995, see also Loveday in this volume). These include the role of the National Reporting Centre, notably during the miners' strike, as a mechanism for providing a co-ordination of police planning and policy implementation; the increased influence of central bodies, such as the Audit Commission and Her Majesty's Inspectorate of Constabulary (HMIC), on local forces' policies and practices; the creation of the National Crime Intelligence Service; the expanding role of central government, through the national police training college at Bramshill (Reiner 1991), in the approval and training of senior officers; and, with the 1994 Police and Magistrates Courts Act, the introduction of central government direct influence on the appointment of a significant minority of Police Authority members (Loveday 1996).

The balance between central and local control over policing clearly impinges upon the nature of police accountability and legitimacy. Police legitimacy is, it is alleged, derived from the law and public consent. In a legal context, civil law may be used to claim damages against police organizations, though not against individual officers. The 1984 Police and Criminal Evidence Act, moreover, strengthened legal controls over police powers, with regulations of police procedures and practices that had previously been the subject of common law being brought together and more clearly presented (Reiner 1992). Accountability to the public is more ambiguous.

On the one hand it may reflect indirect accountability through the medium of elected politicians, at local or national level. On the other hand it may imply direct accountability to the citizens 'in general'. While, as already noted, it was not local communities, but local elites, that controlled the police in their formative years, there is clear evidence that the rise of central government influence has undermined local influence on policing. Nevertheless, following the Scarman (1981) Report, opportunities for local scrutiny of policing operations – if not policy – have been strengthened in at least two ways, with the introduction of police consultative committees (Morgan 1992) and lay visitors schemes whereby designated members of the local community routinely visit prisoners remanded in police cells (Hall and Morgan 1993). These attempts to allay public concern by providing public access to local police management and by providing 'independent' scrutiny of police stations have been bolstered more recently by incorporating police services in the Citizen's Charter (Audit Commission 1994), encouraging forces to produce their own force Charters, and by urging forces to routinely carry out 'consumer' surveys (Bunt & Mawby 1994). While in many ways this enhances local peoples' say in policing matters, it signals a shift from seeing legitimacy in terms of citizens' rights to a position where the citizen is replaced by the consumer. The question thus becomes one of which members of the public rate as consumers, with a say in policing issues. The indications are that victims, not suspects, are designated consumers of police services. In this case, police legitimacy must be contextualized in terms of 'legitimacy in the eyes of victims' rather than the wider public.

Northern Ireland

While there is no denying the changes that have taken place in mainland Britain, the contrasts with the situation in Northern Ireland remain stark. Equally, while there are considerable area variations in the nature of policing within the province (Brewer and Magee 1991), the changing nature of the public order situation means that police policies have been subject to considerable change. This is illustrated in discussions, at the time of writing, over the ideal police system for the future. It is further illustrated in recent history.

Although policing patterns have their roots in Irish colonial history, the current situation can be traced to the escalating public order crisis of the late 1960s. These provoked the despatch of British troops to the province and a series of inquiries – the Cameron Commission, the Scarman Tribunal and the Hunt Committee – into the role of the police in the disturbances. As a result, an attempt was made to civilianize the police, by giving the army primary responsibility for maintaining order, disarming the police, disbanding many of the features of the 1922 Special Powers Act, establishing a Police Authority[1] to distance police from government, and introducing a complaints system. In effect, many of these changes were short-lived: by 1971 the police were rearmed, internment introduced, and the Diplock Committee recommendations were to lead, in the 1973 (Emergency Provisions) Act to wider powers of arrest, special rules of evidence, and trial without jury for terrorism offences. Direct rule from Westminster, introduced in 1972, gave the British government full responsibility for security and ultimately led to a further reversal of policy when in 1975 the police were again accorded primary responsibility for maintaining public order (Brewer *et al.* 1988, Enloe 1980, Jackson and Doran 1995, Weitzer 1985).

The paramilitary nature of policing since the mid-1970s, described by Weitzer (1985: 48) as the core feature of policework, 'shaping virtually every aspect of the RUC's activity', is reflected in the high casualty rate among police, army and civilians and illustrated in the hardware routine to policing:

> Indicative of their military image, the police ride in armoured Landrovers, wear bullet-proof flak jackets, patrol in a combat-ready style, and operate out of fortress-like police stations. Units are equipped with the latest high-powered weapons and all officers are now trained in riot control and counter-insurgency tactics. The RUC operates the largest computerized surveillance system of any force in the United Kingdom (Weitzer 1985: 48).

Clearly the legitimacy of the police of Northern Ireland was conceived in Westminster and fostered out, at the time of partition, to the Ulster government. Controversies over the treatment of suspects in custody, most prevalent in the late 1970s, over alleged shoot-to-kill policies, the subject of the abortive Stalker inquiry in the mid-1980s, and over the special legal conditions that apply in the province, have led to allegations that the police operate outside the rule of law and that the law is either conducive to police malpractice or impotent in the face of it. Public opinion surveys in the North clearly reveal that the legitimacy of the police is rated very differently by Protestants and Catholics (Brewer *et al.* 1988: 74–5; Weitzer 1985: 50–1).

However it is difficult to envisage locally-based legitimacy of the police throughout the North while it remains a divided society, and it seems more feasible to see the law, rather than the people, as the basis for legitimacy. In this respect, there is at least some evidence that the police have distanced themselves from the Protestant camp, especially since the signing of the Anglo-Irish Agreement in 1985, partly due to the role of the Police Authority, partly to the willingness of recent Chief Constables to maintain their control of operational decision making (Brewer *et al.* 1988). In a sense, this combination of militaristic features with autonomy and professionalism parallels earlier developments in the USA. It is, however, widely acknowledged that with a centralized, armed, militaristic, and public-order focused police, Northern Ireland's system is quite distinctive within the British Isles. Even though Brewer and Magee (1991) have argued that routine and public order policing are interwoven and that the former shares many features with that in the UK and indeed elsewhere, Northern Ireland represents one extreme in the British Isles. This may be contrasted with the other extreme, the rather less well-researched police systems of the Channel Islands.

Jersey

With a population of about 80,000, Jersey is the largest of the Channel Islands. Like its neighbour, Guernsey, its system depends very heavily on parochial officials and

States politicians who are elected and, for the most part, unpaid. However there the similarities end. Thus, while an island-wide paid police was introduced to Guernsey in 1914 and continued after World War I, as already noted on Jersey it was not until 1951 that an island force was established and even then there were restrictions on its involvement outside St Helier. Many of these were removed in the 1974 Police Force (Jersey) Law which provides the basis for the current system. However, unlike elsewhere in the UK, the volunteer, community-based police system remains a significant feature. This can be illustrated in a number of ways. First, in terms of their numeric significance, volunteers outnumber paid police; in 1996 there were 283 Honorary Police compared with 242 members of the States Police. Second, in terms of structure, the Honorary Police is quite a separate entity, and while normally under the control of the Attorney General is essentially controlled within each parish. Third, in terms of the law, the States Police are obliged to inform the parish centeniers, themselves senior members of the Honorary Police, when they are called to incidents within the parish; centeniers act as magistrates for minor crime and prosecutors in the magistrates courts; and the legal powers of centeniers (regarding charge, bail, and search without warrant) exceed those of the regular police. Fourth, in terms of accountability, the regular force is accountable to a political committee on which the Honorary Police influence is considerable. Finally, in terms of community-orientation, Honorary Police are based in the parish halls, using marked cars paid for by local taxation, whilst the involvement of the States Police in communities out-side St Helier has been restricted, making it more of a reactive force (Clothier 1996, Gill and Mawby 1990, States of Jersey Police 1997). Jersey provides an example of small island police systems within the British Isles. There the community has a more continuous tradition of involvement in the policing process, and thus provides a contrast with forces in mainland Britain. Nevertheless, the way policing developed was also somewhat different from its neighbour, Guernsey, which has had a paid island-wide police force since 1914. On Jersey, the island police is a more recent development and the continuance of the voluntary police has restricted the role of the public police. This example, therefore, helps to illustrate the variety of police systems still existing within the British Isles.

Contemporary Canadian policing

Underpinning the structure of policing in Canada today is the 1867 constitution, modified in 1982, which established a federal government structure with consider-able autonomy delegated to the provinces. On one level this means that policing within each province is a matter for local government to decide, with the result that policing is a combination of metropolitan and provincial forces, with in some cases amalgamations creating police forces covering a number of towns and cities. On the other hand, the federal police, the RCMP, provides three sets of services that impinge on this local blueprint. First, it serves as a federal police force with national responsibilities throughout the country. Second, it maintains the responsibilities for policing the Yukon and North West Territories. Third, it can be contracted to provide police services at provincial and municipal level, should local governments so wish. And since these services are subsidized there are considerable advantages to local governments subcontracting their policing responsibilities to the RCMP. Consequently while in Ontario and Quebec the RCMP's responsibilities are confined to national legislation and policing is provided by metropolitan and – to a lesser extent – provincial forces, elsewhere the RCMP has a substantial foothold. In seven provinces it monopolizes provincial policing, the exception being Newfoundland and Labrador where a local provincial force exists alongside it. Moreover, it also provides substantial metropolitan police services in Newfoundland and Labrador and British Columbia and some services within the other six provinces. Nevertheless, because of the population concentration in Ontario and Quebec, the RCMP only accounted for 27 per cent of the public police in the mid-1980s (Statistics Canada 1986).

In essence then, Canada today has at least two policing systems. In Ontario and Quebec, and in many municipalities elsewhere, policing is provided locally, by provincial government, municipal government or an amalgamation of municipalities. In such cases the role of the police, with an emphasis upon crime-control and order-maintenance (Ericson 1981; ibid. 1982) and recent debates concerning community policing and service aspects of policework (Braiden 1991, Murphy 1988), parallels discussion in Britain and the US. Local accountability, through a variety of police boards and commissions (Hann et al. 1985; Stenning 1981) similarly reflects much of the debate elsewhere over unrepresentativeness of membership. On the other hand, the RCMP, with its traditional order-maintenance emphasis and its involvement in a wide range of administrative responsibilities (Dion 1982; Morrison 1985; Weller 1981), appears as a more remote and more militaristic alternative and it is interesting that reviews of community policing largely ignore the RCMP (Murphy 1988; for a somewhat generalized overview see Leighton 1994). Moreover with its centralized structure it is clear that local accountability has traditionally been restricted, even where its relationship is a contractual one (Weller 1981), although recently it has established citizens' advisory councils (Bayley 1994: 105).

Given these marked variations between the RCMP and local policing systems, it is perhaps surprising that there is no established body of comparative analysis of policing within Canada. None the less, criticism of the role played by the RCMP in political policing and in the repression of minority interests (Taylor 1986, Weller 1981) are a reminder of concerns voiced in the USA over the spectre of a national police apparatus.

The US scene

What then of the US police? How is the present situation moulded by earlier developments? In terms of functions it is commonly agreed that the police of the United States moved away from their original broad welfare mandate and concentrated more on the crime fighting role. To a large extent this is associated with moves to reform the community-based early police with their roots in local politics by creating a more 'professional' police, where professionalism is located at the organizational rather than the individual level and becomes bound in with militarism

(Fogelson 1977, Walker 1977). This shift, which Walker (1977) illustrates through the changing priorities during the career of August Vollmer in the inter-war period and William Parker in Los Angeles in the 1950s, is also evidenced in emerging imagery in Hoover's FBI, as the US was introduced to the 'war against crime' (Walker 1992).

However while some commentators, like McKenzie and Gallagher (1989), see this as a linear development, there is considerable evidence that the police have either maintained or re-established a wider mandate. On the one hand, a variety of studies from the 1960s onwards demonstrates that routine policework involves providing a myriad of services for the public and that 'dealing with crime' is only a small part of the patrolling officer's workload (Meyer 1974, Reiss 1971, Wilson 1968, Wilson & Kelling 1983), leading Cummings et al. (1965) to describe the police as 'philosopher, guide and friend'. More recently Bayley in a comparison of policing in industrial societies, recognizes that the US police, like their contemporaries abroad, spend little of their time preventing crime and more of it 'restoring order and providing general assistance' (Bayley 1994: 18–19). On the other hand, many researchers suggest that while there was a shift from the welfare focus of the 'political era' of policing to a crime focus during the 'reform era', there has been a swing back towards a wider mandate as US policing has entered the 'community problem solving era' (Kelling & Moore 1988). As in England, this change of heart is to a certain extent associated with a recognition that more sophisticated technology had distanced the police from their publics, although in the US research also questioned the effectiveness of rapid response (Spellman and Brown 1984). However it was also promoted by the problems of the 1960s, with both the President's Crime Commission (1967) and the National Advisory Commission on Civil Disorder (1968) recognizing that in moving to more professional forces city police had lost support in the local communities. Community policing thus became identified with a move away from scientific management and excessive bureaucracy (Goldstein 1987, ibid. 1990, Trojanowicz and Bucqueroux 1990). Structural changes towards decentralization, the introduction of foot patrols, closer links with community groups etc. (Angell 1971, Germann 1969), were thus paralleled by an emphasis upon problem-solving over crime control, the latter being recognized as a symptom of community problems rather than their cause (Eck & Spelman 1987, Goldstein 1987, Rosenbaum 1994) (see also Brogden in this volume).

> 'Community Policing' could arguably be called the new orthodoxy of law enforcement in the United States. It has become an increasingly popular alternative to what many police administrators perceive as the failure of traditional policing to deal effectively with street crime, especially crimes of 'violence and drug trafficking' (Sadd and Grinc 1996: 2).

While community policing programmes come under a variety of names (Cordner 1994, Sadd and Grinc 1996) and differ in emphasis and definition (Bayley 1989, Skogan 1995), they have received widespread endorsement from police management from large metropolitan departments, to departments serving smaller towns (Maguire et al. 1997, Moore 1992, Sadd and Grinc 1996, Trojanowicz 1994). In a national survey of 1,606 municipal and county police and sheriff's departments, Wycoff

(1995) noted that police chiefs and sheriffs overwhelmingly endorsed the notion of community policing, despite being somewhat unclear about what precisely it entailed! Nevertheless, the assumption that community policing currently dominates the policing philosophy must be treated with some scepticism. Thus, Sadd and Grinc (1996) report that police officers frequently resisted such developments and whilst Lurigio and Skogan (1994) and McElroy *et al.* (1993) discovered that community policing served to increase police job satisfaction, the former also found that police officers approved of more emphasis on policing non-crime problems, but at the same time were hostile towards increased foot patrols and generally sceptical about the effectiveness of community policing. In a survey of police administrators, Zhao and Thurman (1997) also note that crime control is still prioritized over service functions.

These points are underlined by recent emphasis on zero tolerance policing, a US development that has found favour in the UK (Dennis 1997). Here again the initial starting point is a critique of past failures in policing strategies and the need to focus on non-crime problems. However, rather than seeing these as underlying pressures that result in offending behaviour, advocates of zero tolerance policing view such 'allegedly' minor incidents as indicative of the fact that the police 'have lost control of the streets'. The message is thus that by taking such incidents seriously the police can re-establish order and control and enhance the quality of life for the law-abiding majority. While such policies, as in the New York Police Department, may be described as community policing and incorporate many elements of community policing (principally decentralized control and community and multi-agency partnerships) there is an unequivocal renewed emphasis on order-maintenence and control. Thus Kelling and Coles (1996), in an advocacy of zero tolerance policing, emphasize 'aggressive order maintenance' as the appropriate police response to the problems of the inner city. They subsequently note:

> With some exceptions, advocates of community policing generally have been reluctant to emphasize the crime control capabilities of community policing or order-maintenance activities, emphasizing instead broader concepts like quality of life, fear reduction, and problem solving (Kelling and Coles 1996: 164).

However, unlike community policing, which appears to have gained widespread acceptance in a variety of police departments, zero tolerance policing seems to have been targeted at larger city departments. This point is important, since policing styles, police functions and priorities, and indeed, public expectations of appropriate policework, vary between different areas (Flanagan 1985, Meagher 1985, Weisheit *et al.* 1995, Zhao and Thurman 1997).

Despite recent exceptions, much of the research evidence is based on studies of urban, especially 'big city' police, and little research has been conducted on rural forces (Maguire *et al.* 1997, Reiss 1992, Weisheit *et al.* 1995). Nevertheless:

> At its core, policing in the United States consists of a large number of politically autonomous police organizations with overlapping jurisdictions (Reiss 1992: 55).

There are, in fact, six levels of law-enforcement organization: federal, state, county, city, rural and 'special district' (Reiss 1992, Sweatman & Cross 1989, Walker 1992). At the federal level, while no agency has responsibility for policing in general, some 50 agencies have specialist nationwide law-enforcement responsibilities and are authorized to conduct searches, carry firearms and make arrests (Geller and Morris 1992, Sweatman & Cross 1989). Of these perhaps the best known are the FBI (Ungar 1975) and the DEA (Drug Enforcement Agency) (Dickson 1968). The former is responsible to the Attorney General and deals with crimes that transcend state boundaries, principally pornography, racketeering, bank robbery, white collar crime and terrorism. Overall about 10 per cent of police are based in federal government agencies (Maguire & Pastore 1994: 26). The FBI and the US Customs Service, each with about 10,000 officers with the authority to carry firearms, are the largest of these (Reaves 1996). The second level of law enforcement is the State. Almost all states have their own police force, with some 10 per cent of police based at this level (Maguire and Pastore 1994: 26 & 46). While most state forces deal with crime in general, some specialize in traffic duties (Sweatman & Cross 1989). The largest state force is the California State Highway Patrol with some 6,000 sworn officers.[2] State forces are commonly accountable to State Governors.

The third level of law enforcement is the county. Most of the 3,000 or so counties in the US have their own police departments, headed by a sheriff elected to run the department for two to four years, who is in turn accountable to the county administrators (Sweatman & Cross 1989). Most sheriffs' departments are also responsible for jails and court security, but are less likely than other generic departments to cover traffic related issues (Reaves and Smith 1993). In 1992 some 124,000 sworn officers were employed at county level, more than double those in state forces (Maguire & Pastore 1994: 40). The largest county force is the Los Angeles County Sheriff's Department, with about 8,000 sworn officers.[3]

The fourth level of law enforcement, and the one that has received the most attention from researchers, is the city. There are about 1,000 separate urban forces (Sweatman & Cross 1989) with about one fifth of all police officers employed in the 25 largest cities (Bayley 1994: 90). The largest force is New York City with about 27,000 officers (Maguire & Pastore 1994: 50).

The fifth level of law enforcement operates at the rural level in the small towns. There are, possibly, 15,000 such forces, most employing very few staff (Sweatman & Cross 1989). Galliher et al. (1975), for example, in a survey of police departments serving communities with under 50,000 people, found that 87 per cent of such departments in one state operated in communities of under 5,000 population and employed an average of only two officers.

Finally, separate police forces may be located in 'special districts', providing the police services to particular institutions and/or geographical areas like parks, university campuses and military bases (Ostrom et al. 1978, Walker 1992.) For example, Reaves and Goldberg (1995), in a recent national survey, found that three quarters of college and university campuses used sworn police officers with the rest relying on non-sworn security officers.

Reaves (1990) estimates that in 1990 there were about 17,000 separate police departments, including some 3,100 sheriff's departments. Most, approximately 14,000, served areas with populations of under 50,000. In a later survey of local police departments (excluding sheriff's departments), the same author noted that 38 departments employed over 1,000 sworn officers each whilst at the other extreme 6,400 employed fewer than 10 officers (Reaves 1993). However, only one in 19 local police officers worked in departments with less than 10 sworn officers, about 60 per cent in departments with at least 100 and 33 per cent in departments with over 1,000. That is, whereas the typical police department in the United States is a small town one, the typical police officer works for a big city department (Walker 1992).

It is scarcely surprising, given the extent of variation, that police standards also differ considerably. Manpower levels differ markedly, with the largest cities spending more per capita and having more police per population (Maguire & Pastore 1994: 52). This may be neither surprising nor contentious, however there is no central restraint on minimum policing levels. It is also notable that salaries are highest in the largest cities (ibid.: 56) and that training standards vary between forces (Walker 1992). The fragmented nature of policing is further illustrated by the difficulty of transferring from one police department to another (ibid.). Clearly also many police jurisdictions overlap. New York, for example, with the largest city force, is also serviced by five county forces which have jurisdiction in different parts of the city (Sweatman & Cross 1989).

But does such a level of variation bring with it inefficiency and a duplication of services? There is some evidence to suggest otherwise. For example, small departments appear no less effective and may have higher clear-up rates than their big-city counterparts (Cordner 1989, Gyimah-Brempong 1987). Further, in an early study of police agencies in 80 medium sized metropolitan areas, Ostrom *et al.* (1978) argued that duplication of services was not common. Focusing on patrol, traffic control and criminal investigation, they argued that relationships between the myriad of agencies could be best described in terms of co-ordination and alternation (that is where different agencies provided similar services at different times, in different locations, or to different client groups). Moreover small forces, that might be considered inefficient or lacking in specialist skills, routinely subcontracted out services to their larger neighbours. In conclusion, the authors argue that diversity should not be equated with fragmentation. Others, however, are less convinced (Hunter 1990, Reiss 1992). For example, while Loveday (in this volume) argues that the FBI has provided some central co-ordination of local police departments, Geller and Morris (1992) point out that although relationships between federal and local agencies have improved, rivalry between federal (and between local?) agencies continues. Reiss (1992) also notes that efforts to improve co-ordination, through amalgamations or subcontracting arrangements, have been limited.

While the 'fragmented' nature of US policing is contestable, the infinite variety of agencies involved in the policing process is clearly not. This variety is equally reflected in the extent to which police organizations are accountable, and to whom they are accountable. Thus police chiefs, notably county sheriffs, may be elected and thereby directly accountable, or they may be political or internal appointments accountable to mayors or police boards. The extent of corruption associated with the early police led reformers away from a politically accountable police. Reformers like Fosdick and Vollmer favoured the London Metropolitan Police model whereby police were internally accountable and politics was (allegedly) distanced from police management (Reppetto 1978). Thus Fogelson (1977) argues that attempts during the 1970s to decentralize police organizations, encourage citizen participation and break down professional barriers, and hold the police externally accountable, failed because of fears of a return to earlier levels of corruption. Similarly, while emphasis on community policing and problem-oriented policing incorporates elements of local accountability and decentralization of command units (Kelling & Moore 1988), such attempts are circumscribed (Mawby 1990).

The very different relationship that exists between police and local government in England and the USA is illustrated in Ruchelman's (1974) study of police politics in New York, Philadelphia and Chicago in the 1960s. Ruchelman argues that the balance of power between police chief and mayor varied between the three cities: in New York it was characterized as a 'war' between two strong personalities, in Philadelphia the police had, for all intents and purposes, 'co-opted' the mayor; in Chicago the mayor controlled the police. One lesson from Ruchelman's study is clearly that the police are not necessarily closely tied to the political process; another is that past experiences of police controlled by local politicians may be repeated in certain circumstances, with Chicago a stark illustration of the fragile boundary between police and politics. A third re-emphasizes the variety of policing forms, such that clear differences exist even between the police forces of the largest cities.

Summary and Conclusions

This chapter has, of necessity, included a broad sweep of the police systems of the British Isles and North America. Clearly a number of issues, such as increased civilization, the expansion of private policing, community involvement, and the growing numbers of female police officers, have been excluded, although many of these issues are debated elsewhere in this volume.

Two conflicting perceptions set the scene for subsequent discussions. On the one hand, there is a widely held assumption that an Anglo-American tradition exists and that consequently the police of Britain and North America are distinctly different from systems elsewhere in the world. On the other hand, American commentators in particular have identified differences between the US and 'British' police. In considering these perspectives, two issues are of particular importance. The first is the relevance of history to an understanding of current practices. While the US and Canadian police were born of the British legal tradition, local circumstances at the time of police development modelled different police forces in different ways. For example, in Canada the colonial tradition drew an early distinction between English and Canadian police philosophies; in the USA the aftermath of independence fed a hostility towards central control and a suspicion of federal structures. Second, though, while in the USA, this led to a fragmented policing system that exists to this day, and in Canada to a distinction between the Federal Royal Canadian Mounted Police and more localized police systems, it is dangerous to ignore diversity within the British Isles. Thus policing in Scotland is different in a number of respects from policing in England and Wales, and Northern Ireland, itself part of the colonial inheritance, is even more distinctive. Equally, some details have been included here of the small Channel Island of Jersey that, while part of the British Isles, evidences a form of policing that is perhaps unique.

That said, there are still considerable differences between the British, US, and Canadian police. For example, the British police (with the exception of Northern Ireland) are not routinely issued with firearms; they are less diverse and more subject to central control; and traditionally local political influence has been less evident. On the other hand, there are considerable similarities. Thus there is little evidence that the role and functions of the police are markedly different, and numerous policing initiatives, such as neighbourhood watch (Bennett 1987) and more recently zero tolerance, have been introduced to Britain from the USA. This raises two questions of wider relevance to the comparative study of policing. First, are the differences between police forces within the British Isles, Canada and the USA as great or greater than differences between the three? The evidence from this chapter suggests that this is at least arguable. Second, are the differences between the British Isles, Canada and the USA greater than those between the so-called Anglo-American tradition and other police systems? This second question can only be answered by following a more detailed review of policing elsewhere in the world.

Notes

1. The Police Authority in Northern Ireland does, however, differ in its composition from those of England and Wales, with its members being direct political appointees selected as representative of the population.
2. See *Census: state and local law enforcement agencies* (http://www.ncjrs.org/txtfiles/census.txt).
3. Ibid.

Bibliography

Alderson, J. 1979. *Policing freedom*. Plymouth: MacDonald and Evans.

Alderson, J. 1981. *Submission to Scarman: the case for community policing*.

Angell, J. 1971. Towards an alternative to the classic police organizational arrangement: a democratic model, *Criminology* **8**, 185–206.

Ascoli, D. 1979. *The Queen's peace: the origins and development of the Metropolitan police, 1829–1979*. London: Hamish Hamilton.

Audit Commission 1994. *Staying on course: the second year of the Citizen's Charter indicators*. London: Audit Commission.

Banton, M. 1964. *The policeman in the community*. New York: Basic Books.

Bayley, D.H. 1985. *Patterns of policing: a comparative international analysis*. New Brunswick: Rutgers University Press.

Bayley, D.H. 1989. Community policing in Australia. In *Australian policing: contemporary issues*, D. Chappell, P. Wilson (eds), 64–82. London: Butterworths.

Bayley, D.H. 1994. *Police for the future*. New York: Oxford University Press.

Bennett, T. 1987. Neighbourhood watch: principles and practices. In *Policing Britain*, R.I. Mawby (ed.), 31–51. Plymouth: Plymouth Polytechnic.

Braiden, C. 1991. Ownership 2: who washes a rented car? Unpublished paper.

Brewer, J.D. 1989. Max Weber and the Royal Irish Constabulary: a note on class and status, *British Journal of Sociology* **40**, 82–97.

Brewer, J.D., A. Guelke, J. Hume, E. Moxon-Browne, R.Wilford 1988. *The police, public order and the state*. London: Macmillan.

Brewer, J.D. & K. Magee 1991. *Inside the RUC*. Oxford: Clarendon Press.

Brogden, M., T. Jefferson, S. Walklate 1988. *Introducing policework*. London: Unwin Hyman.

Bowden, T. 1978. *Beyond the limits of the law*. Harmondsworth: Penguin.

Brown, R.M. 1969. The American vigilante tradition. In *The history of violence in America*, H.D. Graham & T.R. Gurr (eds), 154–225. New York: Praeger.

Bunt, P. & R.I. Mawby 1994. Quality of policing, *Public Policy Review* **2.3**, 58–60.

Chapman, B. 1970. *Police state*. London: Pall Mall Press.

Chapman, B. 1978. The Canadian police: a survey. *Police Studies* **1.1**, 62–72.

Clothier, C. 1996. *Report of the independent review body on police services in Jersey*. St Helier, Jersey: States of Jersey.

Cole, G.F., S.J. Frankowski, M.G. Gertz (eds) 1987. *Major criminal justice systems: a comparative study*. Beverley Hills, Calif.: Sage.

Cordner, G.W. 1989. Police agency size and investigative effectiveness, *Journal of Criminal Justice* **17**, 145–55.

Cordner, G. 1994. *Neighborhood-oriented policing in rural communities: a program planning guide*. BJA monograph (http://www.ncjrs.org/ txtfiles/neio.txt).

Critchley, T.A. 1978. *The history of police in England and Wales*. London: Constable.

Cummings, E. *et al*. 1965. Policeman as philosopher, guide and friend, *Social Problems* **12**, 276.

Das, D.K. 1986. The image of American police in comparative literature. *Police Journal LVIX*, 265–78.

Dickson, D.T. 1968. Bureaucracy and morality: an organizational perspective as a moral crusade. *Social Problems* **16**, 143–56.

Dennis, N. (ed.) 1997. *Zero tolerance: policing a free society*. London: IEA Health and Welfare Unit.

Dion, R. 1982. *Crimes of the secret police*. Montreal: Black Rose Books.

Donajgrodski, A.P. (ed.) 1977. *Social control in the nineteenth century*. London: Croom Helm.

Eck, J.E. & W. Spelman 1987. 'Who ya gonna call?' The police as problem-busters, *Crime and Delinquency* **33**, 31–52.

Emsley, C. 1983. *Policing and its context, 1750–1870*. London: Macmillan.

Emsley, C. 1996. *The English police: a political and social history*. London: Longman.

Enloe, C.H. 1980. *Police, military and ethnicity: foundations of state power*. London: Transaction Books.

Ericson, R.V. 1981. *Making crime: a study of detective work*. Toronto: Butterworth.

Ericson, R.V. 1982. *Reproducing order: a study of police patrol work*. Toronto: University of Toronto Press.

Fine, B. & R. Millar (eds) 1985. *Policing the miners' strike*. London: Lawrence and Wishart.

Flanagan, T.J. 1985. Consumer perspectives on police operational strategy, *Journal of Police Science and Administration* **13**, 10–21.

Fogelson, R.M. 1977. *Big-city police*. Cambridge, Mass: Harvard University Press.

Fosdick, F.B. 1920. *American police systems*. New York: The Century Co.

Galliher, J., L.P. Donavan, D.L. Adams 1975. Small-town police: trouble, tasks, and publics, *Journal of Police Science and Administration* **3**, 19–28.

Geller, W.A. & N. Morris 1992. Relations between federal and local police. In *Modern policing*, M. Tonry, N. Morris (eds), 99–158. Chicago: University of Chicago Press (Crime and Justice, volume 15).

Germann, A.C. 1969. Community policing: an assessment, *Journal of Criminal Law, Criminology and Police Science* **60**, 89–96.

Gill, M.L. & R.I. Mawby 1990. *A Special Constable: a study of the police reserve*. Aldershot: Avebury.

Gittler, J. 1984. Expanding the role of the victim in a criminal action: an overview of issues and problems. *Pepperdine Law Review* **11**, 117–82.

Goldstein, H. 1977. *Policing in a free society*. Cambridge, MA: Ballinger.

Goldstein, H. 1987. Towards community-oriented policing: potential, basic requirements, and threshold questions, *Crime and Delinquency* **33**, 6–30.

Goldstein, H. 1990. *Problem-oriented policing*. New York: McGraw-Hill.

Gordon, P. 1980. *Policing Scotland*. Glasgow: Scottish Council for Civil Liberties.

Gyimah-Brempong, K. 1987. Economies of scale in municipal police departments: the case of Florida, *Review of Economics and Statistics* **69**, 352–6.

Hall, C. & R. Morgan 1993. *Lay visitors to police stations*: an update. Bristol: University of Bristol Centre for Criminal Justice.

Hann, R.G., J.H. McGinnis, P.C. Stenning, A.S. Farson 1985. Municipal police governance and accountability in Canada: an empirical study, *Canadian Police College Journal* **9.1**, 1–85.

Hart, J.M. 1951. *The British police*. London: Allen and Unwin.

Heininger, B.L. & J. Urbanek, 1983. Civilisation of the American police: 1970–1980, *Journal of Police Science and Administration* **11**, 200–5.

Hoddinott, J. 1994. Core questions, *Police Review*, 5 August, 20–2.

Home Office 1966. *Report of the Working Party on Operational Efficiency and Management*. London: HMSO.

Home Office 1995. *Review of police core and ancillary tasks*. London: HMSO.

Horrall, S.W. 1980. The Royal North-West Mounted Police and labour unrest in Western Canada. *Canadian Historical Review* **16**, 169–90.

Howe, S. 1994. Hidden agenda, *Police Review*, 4 March, 20–1.

Hunter, R.D. 1990. Three models of policing. *Police Studies* **13**, 118–24.

Jackson, J. & S. Doran 1995. *Judge without jury: Diplock trials in the adversarial system*. Oxford: Clarendon Press.

Jefferson, T. 1990. *The case against paramilitary policing*. Milton Keynes: Open University Press.

Jones, T., B. MacLean, J. Young 1986. *The Islington crime survey*. Gower: Aldershot.

Judge, T. 1994. Gnawing at the core, *Police*, July, 12.

Kelling, G.L. & C.M. Coles 1996. *Fixing broken windows: restoring order and reducing crime in our communities*. New York: Free Press (Martin Kessler Books).

Kelling, G.L. & M.H. Moore 1988. The evolving strategy of policing. *Perspectives on Policing*. Washington DC: US Department of Justice.

Kelly, W. & N. Kelly 1976. *Policing in Canada.* Toronto: Macmillan.

Lane, R. 1967. *Policing the city: Boston 1822–1885.* Cambridge, Mass.: Harvard University Press.

Lane, R. 1992. Urban police and crime in nineteenth century America. In Tonry & Morris (eds) op cit, 1–50.

Leighton, B.N. 1994. Community policing in Canada: an overview of experience and evaluations. In *The Challenge of Community Policing,* D.P. Rosenbaum (ed.), 209–23. Thousand Oaks, Calif.: Sage.

Le Herissier, R.G. 1973. *The development of the government of Jersey, 1771–1972.* St Helier, Jersey: States Printers.

Loveday, B. 1995. Reforming the police: from local service to police state? *The Political Quarterly* **66**, 141–56.

Loveday, B. 1996. Business as usual? the new Police Authorities and the Police and Magistrates' Courts Act, *Local Government Studies* **22**, 22–39.

Lurigio, A.J. & W.G. Skogan 1994. Winning the hearts and minds of police officers: an assessment of staff perceptions of community policing in Chicago, *Crime and Delinquency* **40**, 315–33.

Maguire, E.R., J.B. Kuhns, C.D. Uchida, S.M. Cox 1997. Patterns of community policing in nonurban America, *Journal of Research in Crime and Delinquency* **34**, 368–94.

Maguire, K. & A.L. Pastore 1994. *Sourcebook of criminal justice statistics – 1994.* Washington, D.C.: U.S. Department of Justice.

Mapstone, R. 1994. *Policing in a divided society: a study of part-time policing in Northern Ireland.* London: Avebury.

Mather, F.C. 1959. *Public order in the age of the Chartists.* Manchester: Manchester University Press.

Martin, J.P. & G. Wilson 1969. *The police: a study in manpower.* London: Heinemann.

Mawby, R.I. 1990. *Comparative policing issues: the British and American system in international perspective.* London: Unwin Hyman.

McElroy, J., C. Cosgrove, S. Sadd 1993. *Community policing: CPOP in New York.* Newbury Park, Calif.: Sage.

McKenzie, I. 1996. Violent encounters: force and deadly force in British policing. In *Core issues in policing,* F. Leishman, B. Loveday, S.P. Savage (eds), 131–46. London: Longman.

McKenzie, I.K. & G.P. Gallagher 1989. *Behind the uniform: policing in Britain and America.* Heel Hepstead: Harvester Wheatsheaf.

Meagher, M.S. 1985. Police patrol styles: how pervasive is community variation? *Journal of Police Science and Administration* **13**, 36–45.

Meyer, J. 1974. Patterns of reporting non-criminal incidents to the police. *Criminology* **12**.

Miller, W.R. 1977. *Cops and bobbies: police authority in New York and London, 1830–1870.* Chicago: University of Chicago Press.

Monkkonen, E. 1981. *Police in urban America, 1860–1920.* Cambridge, Mass.: Cambridge University Press.

Moore, M.H. 1992. Problem solving and community policing. In Tonry & Morris (eds) op cit, 99–158.

Moore, M.H., R.C. Trojanowicz, G.L. Kelling 1988. *Crime and policing. Perspectives on policing.* Washington, DC: US Department of Justice.

Morgan, R. 1992. Talking about policing. In *Unravelling criminal justice,* D. Downes (ed.), 165–83. London: Macmillan.

Morn, F. 1982. *'The eye that never sleeps': a history of the Pinkerton National Detective Agency.* Bloomington: Indiana University Press.

Morrison, W.R. 1985. *Showing the flag: the mounted police and Canadian sovereignty in the North, 1894–1925.* Vancouver: University of British Columbia Press.

Murphy, C. 1988. Community problems, problem communities, and community policing in Toronto, *Journal of Research in Crime and Delinquency* **25**, 392–410.

Ostrom, E., R.B. Parks, G.P. Whitaker 1978. *Patterns of metropolitan policing.* Cambridge, Mass: Ballinger.

Palmer, S.H. 1988. *Police and protest in England and Ireland, 1780–1850.* New York: Cambridge University Press.

Pead, D. 1991. Firearms poll reveals a divided service, *Police Review*, 4 January, 16–17.

Posen, I. 1994. What is policing? *Police Review*, 11 February, 14–15.

Punch, M. & T. Naylor 1973. The police: a social service, *New Society* 24, 554, 358–61.

Radzinowicz, L. 1948. *A history of English criminal law and its administration from 1750, volume 1: the movement for reform.* London: Stevens & Sons Ltd.

Radzinowicz, L. 1956a. *A history of English criminal law and its administration from 1750, volume 2: the clash between private initiative and public interest in the enforcement of law.* London: Stevens & Sons Ltd.

Radzinowicz, L. 1956b. *A history of English criminal law and its administration from 1750, volume 3: cross currents in the movement for reform of the police.* London: Stevens & Sons Ltd.

Reaves, B.A. 1990. State and local police departments, 1990. Washington, DC: Bureau of Justice Statistics Bulletin.

Reaves, B.A. 1993. Local police departments 1993. U.S. Department of Justice (http://www.ncjrs.org/txtfiles/164617.txt)

Reaves, B.A. 1996. Federal law enforcement officers, 1996. U.S. Department of Justice (http://www.ncjrs.org/txtfiles/lpd93.txt).

Reaves, B.A., A.L. Goldberg 1995. Campus law enforcement agencies, 1995. NCJ 161137 (http://www.ncjrs.org/cle95.htm).

Reaves, B.A., P.Z. Smith 1993. Sheriff's Departments 1993. U.S. Department of Justice (http://www.ncjrs.org/txtfiles/sd93.txt).

Reichel, P.L. 1988. Southern shore patrols as a transitional police type. *American Journal of Police* **7** (2), 51–77.

Reiner, R. 1991. *Chief constables.* Oxford: Oxford University Press.

Reiner, R. 1992. *The politics of the police.* London: Harvester Wheatsheaf.

Reiner, R. 1994. What should the police be doing? *Policing* **10**, 151–7.

Reiner, R. 1995. Myth vs modernity: reality and unreality in the English model of policing. In *Comparisons in policing: an international perspective*, J-P Brodeur (ed.), 16–48. Aldershot: Avebury.

Reiss, A.J. 1992. Police organization in the twentieth century. In Tonry & Morris (eds) op cit, 52–97.

Reiss, A.J. 1971. *Police and public.* New Haven: Yale University Press.

Reppetto, T.A. 1978. *The blue parade.* New York: Free Press.

Richardson, J.F. 1970. *The New York police: Colonial times to 1901.* New York: Oxford University Press.

Rosenbaum, D.P. (ed.) 1994. *The challenge of community policing.* Thousand Oaks, Calif.: Sage.

Ruchelman, L. 1974. *Police politics: a comparative study of three cities.* Cambridge, Mass.: Ballinger.

Sadd, S. & R.M. Grinc 1996. Implementation challenges in community policing. NIJ Research in Brief (http://www.ncjrs.org/txtfiles/implcp.txt).

Scarman, Lord 1981. *The Brixton disorders*. London: HMSO (Cmnd 8427).

Shapland, J. & J. Vagg 1988. *Policing by the public*. London: Routledge.

Shubert, A. 1981. Private initiative in law enforcement: Associations for the Prosecution of Felons, 1744–1856. In *Policing and punishment in nineteenth century Britain*, V. Bailey (ed.), 25–41. London: Croom Helm.

Skogan, W.G. 1990. The police and public in England and Wales: a British Crime Survey report. London: Home Office (HORS no 117).

Skogan, W.G. 1995. Community policing in the United States. In Brodeur (ed.) op cit, 86–111.

Smith, B. 1940. *Police systems in the United States*. New York: Harper & Bros.

Spelman, W. & D. Brown 1984. *Calling the police: citizen reporting of serious crime*. Washington DC: U.S. Government Printing Office.

Spencer, S. 1985. The eclipse of the Police Authority. In Fine & Millar (eds) op cit, 34–53.

States of Jersey Police 1997. Annual report 1996. St Hellier, Jersey: States of Jersey Police.

Statistics Canada 1986. *Policing in Canada*. Ottawa: Canadian Centre for Justice Statistics.

Stead, P.J. 1983. *The police of France*. London: Macmillan.

Stead, P.J. 1985. *The police of Britain*. London: Macmillan.

Steedman, C. 1984. *Policing the Victorian community: the formation of English provincial police forces, 1856–80*. London: Routledge.

Steinberg, A. 1989. *The transformation of criminal justice: Philadelphia, 1800–1880*. Chapel Hill: University of North Carolina Press.

Stenning, P.C. 1981. The role of police boards and commissions as institutions of municipal police governance. In *Organizational police deviance*, C.D. Shearing (ed.), 49–82. Toronto: Butterworths.

Sweatman, B. & A. Cross 1989. The police in the United States. *CJ International* **5.1**, 11–18.

Taylor, I. 1986. Martyrdom and surveillance: ideological and social practices of police in Canada in the 1980s, *Crime and Social Justice* **26**, 60–78.

Tobias, J.J. 1977. The British colonial police: an alternative police style. In *Pioneers in policing*, P.J. Stead (ed.), 241–61. Maidenhead: Patterson Smith.

Trojanowicz, R. 1994. *Community policing: a survey of police departments in the United States*. Washington DC: U.S. Department of Justice.

Trojanowicz, R. & B. Bucqueroux 1990. *Community policing: a contemporary perspective*. Cincinnati, Ohio: Anderson.

Ungar, S. 1975. *The FBI*. Boston: Little/Brown.

Vollmer, A. 1971. *The police and modern society*. Montclair, New Jersey: Patterson Smith.

Walker, S. 1977. *A critical history of police reform*. Lexington, Mass.: Lexington.

Walker, S. 1992. *The police in America: an introduction* (second edn). New York: McGraw-Hill.

Wall, D. 1998. *The chief constables of England and Wales: the socio-legal history of a criminal justice elite*. Aldershot: Ashgate.

Weinberger, B. 1991. *Keeping the peace? Policing strikes in Britain, 1906–1926*. Oxford: Berg.

Weisheit, R.A., L.E. Wells, D.N. Falcone 1995. Crime and policing in rural and small-town America: an overview of the issues. NIJ Research Report (http://www.ncjrs.org/txtfiles/crimepol.txt).

Weitzer, R. 1985. Policing a divided society: obstacles to normalization in Northern Ireland, *Social Problems* **33**, 41–55.

Weller, G.R. 1981. Politics and the police: the case of the Royal Canadian Mounted Police. Paper presented at Annual Conference of Political Studies Association, Hull, England.

Whittingham, M.D. 1981. The evolution of the public police . . . a social history. *Canadian Police Chief* (June), 27–9 & (October), 67–70.

Wilson, J.Q. 1968. *Varieties of police behaviour: the management of law and order in eight communities*. Cambridge, Mass.: Harvard University Press.

Wilson, J.Q. & G.L. Kelling 1983. Broken windows, *Atlantic Monthly*, March, 29–38.

Wycoff, M.A. 1995. Community policing strategies. NIJ Research Preview (http://www.ncjrs. org/txtfiles/cpstrat.txt).

Zhao, J., Q.C. Thurman 1997. Community policing: where are we now? *Crime and Delinquency* **43**, 345–57.

CHAPTER 4

Internationalization: a Challenge to Police Organizations in Europe[1]

M.G.W. DEN BOER

Introduction

Policing is back on the political agenda in most of the 15 Member States of the European Union (EU). The internationalization of internal security seems to have sent a new wave through the management and organization of law enforcement. First, there is crime itself. European states have come to recognize common patterns in their crime statistics, such as its growth, its scale, and its consequences for society as a whole (Horn & Cozijnsen 1995: 1). Second, the explanation of crime is now more than ever related to supra-national causes, such as the relaxation of internal border controls, the cross-frontier mobility of criminals and the global character of crime-enterprises. Law enforcement organizations, mostly the producers of these analyses, react to internationalization of internal security in different ways. They tend to adapt the scale of their organization to the seriousness of the crime, and they seek to improve their efficiency by adopting innovative managerial strategies. In this process, police organizations monitor the latest developments in befriended and neighbouring countries and 'borrow' features which they consider to be resourceful in their fight against crime problems. This demonstrates how internationalization of criminality influences the development of national law enforcement, but it also demonstrates that, conversely, cross-border 'law enforcement shopping' encourages the internationalization of policing. It goes without doubt that processes of internationalization and cross-fertilization tend to iron out some of the remaining differences between the Anglo-Saxon and continental policing systems.

This chapter analyses the impact of internationalization on the structures of police organizations in some EU Member States. I will argue that although the internationalization of crime and law enforcement has resulted in more centralization generally, regionalization and local policing have not lost ground. On the contrary, law enforcement initiatives have been developed integrally, and local policing may have benefited from the revival of political interest for law enforcement and integrated criminal justice programmes. Subsequently, I will argue that emphasizing structural differences between continental and Anglo-Saxon policing is no longer justified apart from in genealogical terms (Mawby 1990: 32): the central directive character that used to be characteristic for most continental policing systems has become more diffuse due to a growing emphasis on locally and regionally determined intervention, and the decentralized character of the English and Welsh police organization is challenged by a reinforcement of the position of the Home Secretary and the introduction of performance tables. Finally, I will deal with cross-border co-operation initiatives between law enforcement organizations. There I will argue that bilateral and multilateral co-operation produces more effective contacts than the centrally directed co-operation within the framework of the EU. In particular, topical co-operation related to specific investigations and the pooling of information about police management and law enforcement methods tend to be very much valued by professionals, and have positive effects on the approximation of police systems.

The Impact of Internationalization on the Structure of Police Organizations

The architects of law enforcement organizations at the national level have become more perceptive to external factors. Developments within the European Union, such as the creation of the European Drugs Unit (generally called 'Europol'), can stimulate centralization tendencies within the national police organization (Boek 1995: 308, Hoogenboom 1994: 331, Walker 1994b: 27–30). Walker (1996: 265) illustrates this by saying that the '. . . Trevi meeting at The Hague in December 1991 determined that national satellite units were prerequisite to the establishment of Europol.' Along comparable lines it was agreed that in order to improve the smoothness of the judicial co-operation between the Schengen countries,[2] each Schengen partner would institute a national SIRENE-bureau[3] (responsible for the import and verification of data loaded in the Schengen Information System). In some Schengen countries, such as Belgium and The Netherlands, the improvement of the mutual legal assistance structure was given an impulse by the installation of a national prosecutor (or magistrate), who has, among other responsibilities, a task to monitor and supervise cross-border pursuits, observations and controlled deliveries taking place on the national territory (de Hert 1997). These measures thus parallelled the increasingly international character of cross-border law enforcement operations and the need for better national accountability structures. The 'decree' issued by Trevi and the agreement reached by the Schengen countries provided an extra impulse to the national governments to create national units. As such, the drive for more European integration should be regarded as a timely, potent and credible rationale for the creation of central bodies within national law enforcement organizations (Buruma 1990).

The internationalization of crime and law enforcement also created a new set of problems, mostly related to the trespassing on national sovereignty. The 'Americanization' of police methods and strategies in West European states led to the unsolicited import of American undercover agents and to unsupervised interventions no central authority could account for (Nadelmann 1993). Also neighbouring European countries [. . .] released their agents provocateurs on the territory of the other where they acted in accordance with the rules of their own law, but not always with those of the guest country. As such, undercover agents from abroad have been known to commit punishable acts on foreign territory, provoke suspects-to-be into committing crimes and produce a subterraneous labyrinth of [. . .] contacts and businesses (Fijnaut & Marx 1995). This situation, in turn, easily gives rise to diplomatic conflicts between the countries involved. In addition, the complex tapestry of formal and informal assistance and co-operation agreements becomes counter-productive as investigations undertaken by the authorities in two different police districts sometimes overlap and/or compete: police authorities for instance may well run the same informer without knowing it from one another.[4] The need for improved control, accountability and transparency therefore has not only existed at the international, diplomatic level, but also at that of the regional and national level of EU Member States (Walker 1997, Van den Wyngaert 1997). Centralization efforts within the police organization are as such situated at the intersection of interior and exterior demands. An analysis of recent developments in the police organizations of some EU Member States provides some illustration of these centralization efforts, particularly with regard to the fight against international organized crime and the employment of covert police tactics.

Belgium

Although the basic model that underlies the policing system in Belgium is hierarchical, the system is fragmented as a result of historical evolution (De Cock 1992: 3). There are three police forces in Belgium: the Gendarmerie, the Judicial Police and the Municipal Police. Through this structural division runs the distinction between administrative and judicial policing. In 1987, Team Consult (1987: 109) established the existence of 612 forces: one Gendarmerie, with national competence; 598 municipal police forces which are competent on the territory of the municipality; and 22 squads of the Judicial Police, which, like the Gendarmerie, have a national competence, but depend on 26 magistrates. The three forces negotiate together with the chief prosecutor and local government in the so-called *vijfhoeksoverleg* (pentagon consultation).

Some centralization was established within the Judicial Police: in 1988, a 23d brigade or National Squad was created in the face of growing serious crime, such as drug-trafficking. Within the National Squad, a special unit for surveillance and undercover policing methods was created in 1987, which is called the *Groupe de Surveillance et d'Observation* (GSO) (Rambach 1993: 42). Other important reforms took place within the Judicial Police to improve international co-ordination of criminal investigation activities. A *Commissariat Général* was created after the Royal Decree of 2 September 1991; this institution centralized the international co-ordination of policing tasks that resulted from the ratification of international

(UN) Conventions. The National Squad of the Judicial Police is also one of the *Commissariat Général*'s responsibilities. This unit functions as a national pool of information and expertise and can be utilized by the local police forces (De Cock 1992: 31).

The Gendarmerie is also responsible for the investigation of organized crime, which is mainly conducted by its Central Bureau of Investigations (*Centraal Bureau Opsporingen* or CBO). The *Peloton voor Observatie, Schaduwing en Arrestatie* (POSA) is subdivided into four regions and a Special Intervention Team (SIE) (Rambach 1993: 43).

The fragmentation of the Belgian police system has been countered by a number of joint initiatives. Already in 1982, the executive *Groupe Interforce Antiterroriste* (GIA) was set up in response to a series of politically inspired violent events and the explosion in front of a Brussels synagogue. Rather uniquely, this service unites members of the different police and security forces. GIA compiles all information collected by the different police and security services on terrorism and subversion, functions as an advisory centre for the National Magistrate (see below), the local magistrates and the investigators, and co-operates internationally with comparable units (De Cock 1992: 32). In 1994, a General Police Support Service (*Algemene Politiesteundienst*) was created to improve the co-ordination between the police services and to centralize the co-ordination of international police activities. As a consequence, it accommodates liaison officers, SIRENE, SIS, Interpol NCB and the Belgian satellite of the Europol Drugs Unit. A central service for the fight against Economic and Financial Crime was also created in 1994 and provides support to the police services in the area of money laundering, carousels, insider trading, swindling and fraud against the EU.

Within the judiciary, a National Magistrate (Deputy Attorney General) was established to improve the efficiency of national policing activities and international co-operation. The main tasks include the co-ordination of investigations into terrorism, drug-trafficking and organized crime, and the supervision of the National Squad and the GIA. The installation of the National Magistrate has accelerated decision-making processes in the operational sphere (e.g. in the case of cross-border surveillance) (De Cock 1992: 33). The 'Dutroux Affair', in which a formerly convicted paedophile was released from prison and kidnapped and murdered a few young girls, has given a strong impulse to the reform of the Belgian policing system. Following the work of a parliamentary inquiry committee ('Commissie Verwilghen') it has been proposed to create a federal police force in which the national investigation teams of the Gendarmerie and Judicial Police are fused, and to introduce 'interpolice zones' in which all three police forces are integrated at the local level.[5]

England and Wales

The organizational model of policing in England and Wales is based on a decentralized, county-oriented system: there are 43 different police forces. The Association of Chief Police Officers (ACPO) expects major amalgamations between these forces.

Reasons for this are that the statutory procedures for police amalgamations have been simplified and that the Home Secretary can determine the police force boundaries by his own orders (Loveday 1995: 147).

The moderately decentralized county-model of policing (Walker 1991: 8) reveals contrastive centralization tendencies even stronger than those in other EU Member States. The main impulse for the creation of law enforcement units at the national level has been given by the need for more efficiency in the fight against organized crime. Yet, as Benyon (1986: 20) notes, centralization has been a tendency that goes back to the 1964 Police Act. This Act resulted in the reduction of the number of police forces, an increase in the role of the Home Office and the Inspectors of Constabulary, and the increasingly prevalent central arrangements for a diversity of functions.

In more recent times, the creation of the seven Regional Crime Squads has been the output of a strategy to enlarge the scale of law enforcement activities in a move to improve police efficiency. These units support the local police in the investigation of serious crime in the region; they also have a role at the national and international level. The Regional Crime Squads are directed and co-ordinated by a National Co-ordinator, and they employ undercover policing methods in the investigation of serious and organized crime. At the regional level, there are also Regional Criminal Intelligence Services and Special Drug Units. Regional Crime Squads have a specific task in co-operating with HM Customs and Excise, and with the National Criminal Intelligence Service (NCIS), which was created in 1992. NCIS was restructured in October 1994. Apart from an administrative division, it now includes an HQ Division (Operations Support Unit, International Co-ordination, Policy and Research Unit and Strategic and Specialist Intelligence Branch),[6] a UK Division (co-ordination of the five regional NCIS-bureaux in London, Birmingham, Bristol, Manchester and Wakefield; Scottish/Irish Liaison Unit) and an International Division (National Central Bureau Interpol and network of European drugs liaison officers). Many specialist services have been accommodated within these divisions. Examples are the Organized Crime Unit, the Economic Crimes Unit, and the Drugs Unit; there is currently an experiment with a Vehicle Intelligence Unit.

The integration of the Scottish and Northern Irish police forces within NCIS has not yet been achieved, which is due to budgetary and organizational difficulties. These forces have liaisons at NCIS and have access to the Integrated National Criminal Intelligence System (INCIS). NCIS is not the only illustration of an attempt to establish a vertically structured organized-crime strategy. The creation of the Serious Fraud Squad for instance is a central desk for serious fraud and resulted from the 1987 Criminal Justice Act. Responsibilities for the investigation and prosecution of serious fraud cases remain seated within the police organization, despite the creation of the Crown Prosecution Service (CPS) in 1985. The CPS meant a restriction of the discretionary autonomy of the police organization with regard to the prosecution of criminal acts. The CPS does not, however, unlike the prosecutor's services in most other Member States, have a co-ordinating or supervisory role in the criminal investigation itself, which means it has no control in the choice of police investigation methods. Centralization tendencies in the policing system in England and Wales are not applicable to the whole range of policing activities. The basic concept of community policing prevails even today, and recent reforms allegedly reinforce the role of local police authorities. The government has claimed that the Police and Magistrate's Court Act 1994 will significantly reduce central government controls over police, but these will be partly counterbalanced by measures such as national key objectives – the main purpose of which is to refocus policing priorities according to the policies set by the Government – and the introduction of NHS-like performance tables and performance indicators of the Audit Commission. Moreover, the central determination of policing priorities may be reinforced by a growing role for Her Majesty's Inspectorate of Constabulary, as it is an essential source of professional advice on policing matters (Loveday 1995: 146).

Despite noticeable centralization tendencies mentioned above there is a parallel strategy to strengthen the local control of Chief Constables. The creation of national or central structures and initiatives does not flow from a desire to enlarge the scale of all policing activities, but just of those activities that target supra-local crime, such as drug-trafficking, money laundering, serious fraud, football hooliganism and illegal immigration. This demonstrates the workings of the subsidiary principle: everything that can sensibly be done at the local or regional level, remains at that level.

Germany

The federal constitution of Germany is responsible for a high level of autonomy of the police forces at the level of the *Land*. Each *Land* has its own Police Act and its own *Landeskriminalamt*. There is, however, a measure of uniformity which is guaranteed by the need to comply with federal standards for the protection of human or basic rights. A non-binding model to which the *Länder* police could voluntarily align their police laws was largely implemented after it was adopted by the Interior Ministers of the Federation and the *Länder* (Cullen 1992: 34, 35).

Due to Germany's federalized policing system, the organizational units for the fight against organized crime do not only exist at the national level (*Bundeskriminalamt* or BKA), but also at the level of the *Länder* (*Landeskriminalämter* or LKAs) and the larger cities. The responsibilities of these entities are ordered hierarchically: the BKA is responsible for international cases and cases within its own remit, the LKAs are responsible for cases between the Länder and in the Länder themselves, and the large cities concentrate on cases in the region (Busch and Funk 1995). The number of organizational units that specifically engage themselves with organized crime have increased considerably. They are centres of expertise for CID information, intelligence and covert policing methods. Activities within these units are usually kept separate from traditional repressive policing activities which are performed during official criminal investigations. Although the police are an independent organization within the criminal justice system, the *Staatsanwaltschaft* (Prosecution Service) is responsible for directing the criminal investigation activities of the police. The police is as such accountable to the *Staatsanwaltschaft* and requires approval in advance for the use of covert policing methods. A problem for the prosecution is that police competencies have been widened and that the police have become far more professional in the employment of investigation methods. The professionalization and specialization of the executive police forces make control of the prosecution service over the kind of methods that are employed much harder (Lillie 1994: 631). The police are one step ahead of the prosecution as far as information is concerned. Contacts with informers and sting-operators are solely conducted by the police, often without with the knowledge of the prosecution. *Post hoc* validity and plausibility control by the prosecution can be obstructed because police do not always report used undercover methods (Lillie 1994: 630). Some wonder whether the extension of police powers should not have been accompanied by a more profound structural revision of the German code of criminal procedure (Lillie 1994: 626).

Despite these less optimistic noises, the creation of central organizational units is in a certain way echoed within the *Staatsanwaltschaft*. The *Staatsanwaltschaften* now has unit supervisors or prosecutors that closely collaborate with the *Kriminalpolizei* in analysing organized crime developments. The Federal Prosecution Service (I) now has a central co-ordinator who oversees the activities of the co-ordinators in the I; he is also responsible for furthering the exchange of information and experience at supra-local level between the police and the prosecution. All measures essentially flow from the Common Guidelines of the Ministers and Secretaries of Justice (federal and land level), which were issued at the end of 1990. The main objective of these guidelines has been to improve the co-operation between police and prosecution, and to guarantee that all parties have an equal insight in criminal investigations with supra-regional ramifications. This insight and knowledge pertains to crime fighting strategies, criminal procedures, the use of undercover policing methods and witness protection, confiscation, international mutual legal assistance and so on. Meetings and discussions about these take place on an annual basis.

It has been argued that decision making structures within the German police were rationalized with the development of streamlined command by means of consolidating central instances of decision making (Cullen 1992: 51).

The Netherlands

A major reorganization within the Dutch police was completed in 1994, when the municipal police (I) and the state police (I) were merged into one police service and divided into 26 forces. The 26th police force, the KLPD, incorporated previously existing structures and provides national services to the other 25 forces. The new system is based on a moderately decentralized model of policing, and the line of command has a dual system of central and decentral control. The Ministers of Justice and the Interior each maintain their central control over law enforcement and policy, and the OM or Prosecution Service has been given a larger margin of supervision and control over criminal investigation activities. At the regional level, the local government of the largest municipality in the region, the chief public prosecutor and the chief constable of the regional police force, negotiate about the budget and policing priorities. One of the most important reasons for creating one single police force out of the municipal and the state police was the existence of overlapping competencies between forces. The purpose of the reorganization was to improve overall efficiency and co-ordination. A secondary, but not unimportant objective, was the improvement of international police co-operation. Within the semi-decentralized Dutch police system, inter-regional units fulfil an important co-ordinating function between the regional and the national and/or international level. The soon to be reorganized five Regional branches of the CRI channel information from the central to the decentral level and vice versa. They are also responsible for the intelligence to and from Regional Criminal Intelligence Departments (RCIDs), which are not always centrally organized (Paulissen 1994). The *Binnenlandse Veiligheidsdienst*, the Dutch Secret Service, also has a decentralized set-up with the *Regionale Inlichtingendiensten* (RIDs).

During and after the reorganization of the Dutch police service, a void emerged at the national, operational level (e.g. Bruinsma *et al.* 1994). The demise of one of the five Inter-regional Crime Squads (IRTs – which specifically engage in the fight against criminal groups active at the supra-regional level), the resignation of the Minister of Justice and the Minister of the Interior during the spring of 1994, and the subsequent parliamentary enquiry[7] on undercover policing methods gave rise to profound debates about the organizational and accountability links between different segments of the criminal justice system. The recent creation of a National Crime Squad (*Landelijk Rechercheteam*, LRT) within the KLPD signals closer ties between police and prosecution and demonstrates a desire to push the supervision of supra-regional criminal investigations in the central direction of the minister or procurator general. A national undercover team was recently created to meet international demands,[8] and a Central Control Committee (*Centrale Toetsingscommissie*) was installed to evaluate weighty national and international requests for undercover action.

Also the reorganizations within the prosecution service have been and will be rigorous. Most of the measures to be implemented flow from recommendations listed by a special Committee (Commissie Openbaar Ministerie 1994), which concluded that the prosecution service should take its central co-ordinating role in the criminal justice system more seriously, and that it should exercise tougher supervision over the police service. The three most significant measures include the creation of the National Crime Squad (LRT, see above); a national Prosecution Office which incorporates the two National Prosecutors, and which will engage itself with the national and international fight against serious organized crime, terrorism, financial investigations and mutual legal assistance requests which can not be handled by the regional prosecution offices (*Landelijk Bureau Openbaar Ministerie*); and the creation of a National Prosecution Board (*Landelijk OM College*), consisting of three to five procurators general, which will direct the nineteen courts, five district courts and the General Prosecution Counsel.

These reorganizations are meant to create more uniformity among the prosecutorial districts and to relieve the prosecutorial services at subordinate levels from time-consuming administrative tasks in order to reserve more room for the traditional judicial tasks.[9] The reorganizations are also unambiguously related to an increasing concern about crime with national and international ramifications, and to a need for co-ordination of the criminal investigations that focus on drug-trafficking and/or international, organized crime.

Centralization tendencies are prominent, but certain fundamental regional characteristics are left unscathed. Similarly to Germany, the UK and Belgium, the creation of central initiatives has been related to concern over international crime, and with the belief that it can be combated more effectively and efficiently at the national level. Also the prevention of redundancy and duplication of efforts, and the international requirement of a transparent contact and accountability structure lie at the root of these reorganizations.

A Collapse of Extremes: Fading Differences between Police Systems

The response to the internationalization of crime has been an enlargement of scale in the police organizations of Belgium, England and Wales, Germany and The Netherlands. Specialist executive and supportive tasks have to a large extent been centralized, while public order maintenance and the repression of (mostly petty) crime have remained at the local level (i.e. Treur 1995). Gradually, the organizational workings of the subsidiary principle make themselves clear both nationally and internationally: central agencies should only be geared into action in the case of supra-regional, national or international investigations (Van der Landen 1994: 928; Den Boer 1996). The creation of central units both within the police and the prosecution service has been a noticeable development without regard to whether or not the police system has a hierarchical, centralized structure. Perhaps enlargement of scale and the creation of central units has been easier to implement in countries with a uniform, hierarchically structured police organization. But in any case policing systems in northern West Europe slowly arrive at a mixed police organization, in which centralized and decentralized styles are no longer diametrically opposed but combined in one model. This development suggests there has not been a choice between alternative organizational styles, but rather a superimposition of central units in moderately decentralized police organizations and an introduction of regional units in hierarchically structured police organizations, in other words: a multiplication of police activity (Levi 1995). The political climate has been very favourable to this expansionism (Hermans 1994) and the enlargement of scale has stimulated the political significance of police and criminal justice (Boek 1995: 313). This has had a two sided effect, namely that although the professional elite still exercises a strong autonomous voice in the direction of politics, renewed political attention has also reinforced the control of government over policing (Hermans 1994).

International pressures to adapt national criminal justice programmes (in particular in the sphere of drugs and organized crime) to internationally agreed standards exposes the success and failure of law enforcement in individual countries to much more external scrutiny than before. As anti-crime strategies have become a major focus of many international platforms (United Nations, G7, EU, etc.), effective and efficient policing at the national level has become one of the dominant fields of evaluation in international diplomatic circles. Senior Dutch and Belgian officials would not deny that some centralization initiatives have been modelled on the American FBI, and even seem to suggest that pressure exercised by American diplomats encouraged the creation of national undercover teams and support services.

The watchful eye of international diplomacy, the emergence of international criminal justice performance tables and the promotion of organized crime to prime target for international law enforcement have all contributed to an intensified competition between police organizations. Co-operation against organized crime has paradoxically been paralleled by a competition between police organizations, both between states and within nation states (Van Reenen 1989). Community policing and crime prevention programmes acclaim less visible reward, certainly internationally, than eliminating large international criminal groups. Police organizations have therefore begun to aspire to law enforcement strategies and to the use of innovative and high-tech policing methods. They have generally adopted a more commercial attitude and attempt to profile themselves as a modern organization in a competitive environment (Walker 1993: 41). The speed of innovations within the police organizations has increased: the life cycle of police knowledge, policing products and services is becoming shorter as changes in the environment of the police organization demand a fast and flexible adaptation (Horn and Cozijnsen 1995: 29).

Furthermore, by taking on board new security threats, such as international organized crime and illegal immigration, West European police organizations are undergoing a shift from what Brodeur (1983) has called 'low policing' to 'high policing', and from what Marenin (1982) has called policing of the 'general' to the 'specific' order of the state. Both authors have in mind a shift from policing which is concerned with the maintenance of order and the suppression of crime (low policing, general order) to the protection of the state and dominant political actors (high policing, specific order). The old dividing lines between police and intelligence service are beginning to erode (Anderson et al. 1995: chapter. 5; Pouw 1995: 4). Indeed, the fight against organized crime has been inspired by the belief that it has destabilizing effects on the democratic order of nation states, and that as such 'the state' – and not so much 'the community' – has to be protected against this form of crime. As the security threat has been redefined to include forms of crime that undermine the stability of the state, forms of political and/or undercover policing have entered the realm of ordinary policing, which is generally accompanied by the gradual introduction of undercover methods such as infiltration, buy-and-bust techniques, controlled delivery and covert surveillance (Anderson et al. 1995, chapter 5).[10] This is not to say that the shift to proactive, undercover policing pervades all segments of the police organization, but that certain parts of it have been mobilized and specialized to combat supra-regional, high profile crime.

Three developments flow from this. First, the enlargement of scale and the covertness of policing techniques makes policing both more and less controllable. More controllable, when we consider that the centralization of anti-organized crime initiatives is paralleled by a strengthening of accountability structures, particularly with regard to prosecutorial and ministerial control. Less controllable, when we take into account that centralized structures are bureaucratic, further removed from the citizen and not subject to local and regional forms of social control (Boek 1995: 390, Buruma 1990: 45). Less controllable also when we consider that undercover police action is usually staged against individuals who have not been officially charged with a criminal offence, and that the information obtained by the police is not collected on the basis of public consent.

Second, in targeting international organized crime, the ordinary police organization has propelled itself into a competition with state intelligence services and intelligence departments of multinational companies. Intelligence services, who were more or less forced to redefine their remit after the collapse of the iron curtain, possess a vast experience in the sphere of undercover policing and rely on a solid international infrastructure of contacts and co-operation, something that is jealously guarded by the police service. In some countries this situation caused inter-agency friction and competition. The Special Branch of the London Metropolitan Police was less than enthusiastic about the move from terrorist related intelligence to MI5 for instance. The battle for information – still the single and most important asset for all criminal investigations – also rages between the police and the private, commercial domain. Many car companies, banks, insurance and credit card companies which operate internationally have created their own intelligence departments, where crucial information is collected but not necessarily shared with the police. The advantage these company intelligence departments have is that they can operate within a very specific, narrowly defined domain of interest, and that they own the resources to mount international intelligence gathering – all this outside the 'burden' of public accountability. The latter circumstance may be one of the reasons why in some cases police resort to private security agencies. Some believe that because private security agencies can operate outside rigid accountability structures, police approach them to perform activities which are at best semi-legal.

Third, police organizations face a competition from non-state policing initiatives. These include the intelligence departments and security agencies in the private domain (Hoogenboom 1986, Johnston 1992, Walker 1996), but also the emergence of a policing capacity within the European Union (UCLAF, Europol). The competition at the national level (intelligence services, private security agencies) and at the international level (international 'performance tables', non-state policing structures) places police organizations in nation states in a new position, one in which they have to emphasize their own capacities. The competition factor affects all police organizations in West Europe in an equal manner.

Figure 4.1 represents a global inventory of the convergence and divergence between police organizations in Belgium, England and Wales, Germany and The Netherlands. The number of similarities reveals a strong convergence between the police systems, particularly in the domain of organizational structure, crime analysis, law enforcement priorities, police methods, contextual factors and the relationship with the profession and politics.

Figure 4.1   Inventory of shifts towards convergence and divergence in Belgium, England and Wales, Germany and the Netherlands

Convergence	Divergence
Centralization and enlargement of scale due to internationalization of policing and demand for better national accountability structures.	Control of Prosecution Service differs greatly between continental and Anglo-Saxon countries: in continental countries the prosecution authorizes and often supervises methods of investigation. Despite this formal control of the prosecution, police show a strong urge for autonomy.
Analysis of crime patterns: steady increase of crime in most countries.	
Law enforcement priorities: organized crime, drugs and money laundering have become chief targets.	
Shift from repressive/reactive policing to preventive/proactive policing. Traditional political or high policing methods have entered the domain of ordinary policing.	
Police face competition from intelligence services and from non-state policing initiatives (private security and supranational frameworks).	
Position of professional elite is strong *vis-à-vis* politics, and policing has attracted renewed political attention: nation states seek to reinforce their position in the face of erosion of sovereignty and demise of prior common security threat.	

Law Enforcement Co-operation Across Borders: Comparing Models

International police co-operation is an important lever for the growth of police knowledge about managerial strategies, police tactics and organizational styles. As such it contributes significantly to a convergence between organizational models and styles of policing. Although this is not a new feature – the British model of decentralized, local policing had a considerable influence in other European countries just over a century ago (Horn & Cozijnsen 1995: 3) – the police nowadays certainly have far more opportunity to travel abroad and have access to information about police organizations in other countries. International co-operative structures, such as the International Police Working Group on Undercover Policing, provide ideal platforms for the exchange of knowledge and expertise, mostly also because the swapping of information tends to be case orientated and concrete.

Police officers are generally more enthusiastic about informal and pragmatic international co-operation ('horizontal co-operation'), than about formal and pro-grammed international co-operation ('vertical co-operation') (Den Boer 1996). The reason for this is simple: formal co-operation is usually centrally directed and much more a matter of high politics. This means that practical and operational input of police officers tends to be marginalized at the central level (e.g. the European Union). Practitioners feel effectively shut out from these vertical co-operation structures. Their political influence halts at the national border, which marks the existence of a close relationship between policing and the nation-state (Walker 1994a). The revenge of the practitioners is anything but sweet: their frustration about the lack of direct polit-ical influence is translated in the expression of distrust toward supranational policing initiatives such as the Europol Drugs Unit (Pouw 1995: 112). Police officers in various EU Member States have great difficulty in sending their sensitive data to Europol (already a problem at the national level) and hence make it perform like a lame duck (see Fijnaut & Verbruggen 1997). The trust of the policing community in supra-national law enforcement initiatives is meagre, but then again the centralization at national and international level requires time to mature and settle.

The absence of trust can also be explained by the fact that vertical co-operation structures lack an identifiable central authority and common accountability mechan-ism. Moreover, the European Union, to which the Europol Drugs Unit is attached, is an abstract entity of which the boundaries are still shifting. 'Vertical' police co-operation is also tiresome and time-consuming, because agreement has to be reached between all 15 parties and agreed criminal justice priorities need to be down-loaded into the national police organizations. In a fast moving and competitive environment, police officers tend to favour their self-regulated 'horizontal' co-operation structures (e.g. the International Working Group on Undercover Policing) with the danger that they are starving the 'vertical' co-operation structures from their practical input.

Although vertical and horizontal police co-operation both contribute to the elim-ination of differences between police systems – and thus to a gradual harmonization – horizontal co-operation tends to have a more profound effect on convergence. As horizontal, informal co-operation is usually unhindered by politics, it tends to be highly dynamic; as it is generally propelled by pragmatic and case oriented needs, it tends to be tailored for its purpose and circumvents redundancy of effort; and as it is driven by professional rather than political interest, it offers more (individual!) stimulus and reward to law enforcement officials.

The purpose of this argument has not been to oppose horizontal and vertical co-operation structures, but to make some observations about their relative influence on convergence without saying too much about the obstacles that stand in the way of approximation. Three obstacles may countervail the aforementioned convergence tendencies: structural differences between criminal justice systems (such as the relationship between police and prosecution), systemic differences between rules of criminal procedure (such as the use of anonymous evidence in court), and cultural differences related to policy preferences and law enforcement priorities (such as varying criteria for the prosecution of drug-related offences). It goes beyond the purpose of this chapter to analyse the balance between stimulus factors and obstacles in the furthering of international co-operation. Another question that cannot yet be answered within this context is whether a convergence of police systems has its own dynamic, derived from forms of horizontal and spontaneous co-operation, or whether convergence should be interpreted as a variable of centrally co-ordinated action.

Notes

1. A part of this chapter was presented at the Europol Drugs Unit, The Hague, 31 May 1995. ('A Comparison of Accountability Systems for the Use of Undercover Policing Methods in Some EU Member States', mimeo).
2. When this chapter was revised (April 1998), 13 of the 15 Member States of the European Union had signed up to the Schengen Agreement, which provides for the abolition of border controls and lists series of compensatory measures that warrant a better security (e.g. agreements about external border controls, police co-operation, judicial co-operation, direct and automated information exchange). The United Kingdom and Ireland were the only EU Member States that had not become members, partly because they wanted to maintain their passport union and partly also because they did not want to jeopardize their security situation. However, the Treaty of Amsterdam, which was signed on 2 October 1997, has made it possible, via a special protocol, for these two Member States to 'opt into' various provisions of the Schengen Agreement, such as cross-border police competencies. Norway and Iceland have become Associate Members of the Schengen group which allows the Nordic countries to maintain the Nordic Passport Union.
3. SIRENE stands for Supplementary Information Request at the National Entry.
4. E.g. *Rapport Onderzoek naar het functioneren van de RCID Kennemerland*, Rijksrecherche Fort Team, SDU Uitgevers, Den Haag, 1996.
5. Enquête Parliamentaire sur la manière dont l'enquête, dans ses volets policiers et judiciares a été menée dans l'affaire Dutroux-Nihil et consorts, Chambre des Représentants de Belgique, Session Ordinaire 1997–1998, 16 Février 1998, 713/8–96/97.
6. NCIS HQ now also includes a European Police office (Europol) desk; two NCIS representatives are based at the Europol Drugs Unit at The Hague.
7. *Inzake Opsporing. Enquêtecommissie Opsporingsmethoden.* SDU Uitgevers, s-Gravenhage, 1996.
8. NRC, 7 July 1995.
9. Minister van Justitie, *Plan van aanpak. Reorganisatie van het Openbaar Ministerie*, May 1995.
10. Pouw (1995: 65) implies that after Europol will have gained responsibility over terrorism (two years after ratification of the Europol Agreement), the Intelligence Services will have a lot more input in international police co-operation fora. This may have an impact that goes further than erosion of differences between the police and the intelligence services at the national level, namely a cross-border harmonizing effect on the dividing lines between police organizations and intelligence services.

Bibliography

Anderson, M., M. den Boer, P. Cullen, W. Gilmore, C. Raab, N. Walker 1995. *Policing the European Union*. Oxford: Clarendon Press.

Benyon, J. 1986. Policing in the limelight: citizens, constables and controversy. In *The Police. Powers, Procedures and Proprieties*, J. Benyon & C. Bourn (eds). Oxford: Pergamon Press.

Boek, J.L.M. 1995. *Organisatie, functie en bevoegdheden van politie in Nederland*. Arnhem/ Antwerpen: Gouda Quint/Kluwer.

Boer, M. den 1996. Justice and home affairs cooperation: attachment without integration. In *Policy making in the European Union*, 3rd edn. H. Wallace & W. Wallace (eds). Oxford: Oxford University Press.

Brodeur, J.P. 1983. High Policing and low policing: remarks about the policing of political activities. *Social Problems* **3**, 507–20.

Bruinsma, G.J.N., M.R. Daniel, G.J. Veldhuis 1994. Enkele verwaarloosde organisatorische vraagstukken van de Interregionale Rechercheteams (IRTs). *Delikt en Delinkwent* **24** (10), 1056–1069.

Buruma, Y. 1990. Het naderende einde van het souvereine strafrecht: een tendens in het zicht van 1992. *Grensoverschrijdend strafrecht*. Arnhem: Gouda Quint bv, 23–46.

Busch, H. & A. Funk 1995. Undercover tactics as an element of preventive crime fighting in the Federal Republic of Germany. In *Undercover. Police Surveillance in Comparative Perspective*, C. Fijnaut & C.T. Marx (eds). Deventer: Kluwer International.

Cock, P. de 1992. The Belgian police and European police cooperation. Working Paper VII, Working Paper Series *A System of European Police Cooperation*. Edinburgh: University of Edinburgh.

Cullen, P. 1992. The German police and European police cooperation, Working Paper II, Working Paper Series *A System of European Police Cooperation*. Edinburgh: University of Edinburgh.

Commissie Openbaar Ministerie 1994. *Het functioneren van het Openbaar Ministerie binnen de Rechtshandhaving*. 's-Gravenhage.

Fijnaut, C. & G.T. Marx (eds) 1995. *Police Surveillance in Comparative Perspective*. The Hague, London, Boston. Kluwer Law International.

Fijnaut, C. & F. Verbruggen 1997. The eagle has not landed yet. The federalisation of criminal investigation: precedents and comparisons. In *Undercover policing and accountability from an international perspective*, M. den Boer (ed.). Maastricht: EIPA, 129–41.

Hermans, L.M.L.H.A. 1994. Politie en Politiek. Meer dan ooit tevoren hebben politie en politiek met elkaar te maken. In *Handboek Politiemanagement*. Alphen a/d Rijn, Samsom H.D. Tjeenk Willink: B1140–1–B1140–12.

Hert, P. de. 1997. The Belgian National Magistrate: A Function to Become Europeanized? In *Schengen, Judicial Cooperation and Policy Coordination*, M. den Boer (ed.). Maastricht, EIPA, 135–62.

Hoogenboom, A.B. 1994. *Het politiecomplex. Over de samenwerking tussen politie, bijzondere opsporingsdiensten en particuliere recherche*. Arnhem: Gouda Quint.

Hoogenboom, A.B. 1986. *De Privatisering van de politiefunctie*. Den Haag.

Horn, J. & A. Cozijnsen 1995. Probleemgerichte aanpak van onveiligheid. Inhoudelijke en organisatorische voorwaarden voor innovatie bij de Nederlandse politie. In *Handboek Politiemanagement*. Alphen a/d Bijn, Samsom H.D. Tjeenk Willink: A1120–1–A1120–31.

Johnston, L. 1992. *The rebirth of private policing*. London/New York, Routledge.

Landen, D. van der 1994. Naar een GeUNIEficeerd strafrecht? *Delikt en Delinkwent* **24**, afl. 9: 921–39.

Levi, M. 1995. Covert policing and the investigation of 'organized fraud': The English experience in international context. In *Undercover. Police surveillance in comparative perspective*, C. Fijnaut & G.T. Marx (eds). Deventer: Kluwer International.

Lillie, H. 1994. Das Verhältnis von Polizei und Staatsanwaltschaft im Ermittlungsverfahren. In *Zeitschrift für gesamte Strafrechtswissenschaft* **6** (3), 625–43.

Loveday, B. 1995. Reforming the police: from local service to state police? *The Political Quarterly* 141–56.

Marenin, O. 1982. Parking tickets and class repression: the concept of policing in critical theories of criminal justice. *Contemporary Crises* **6**, 241–66.

Mawby, R. 1990. *Comparative policing issues. The British and American experience in international perspective*. London: Unwin Hyman.

Nadelmann, O. 1993. *Cops across borders: the internationalization of US criminal law enforcement*. University Park, PA: Penn State Press.

Paulissen, W. 1994. CID centraal of decentraal? *Tijdschrift voor de Politie* (April) **4**, 21–3.

Pouw, J.F.M. 1995. *Naar een 'Europees binnenlands veiligheidsbeleid? Europese samenwerking en de 'autonomie' van nationale veiligheidsdiensten*, The Hague: Netherlands Institute for International Relations.

Rambach, P.H. 1993. Belgien. *Besondere Ermittlungsmaßnahmen zur Bekämpfung der Organisierten Kriminalität*. W. Gropp (ed.). Freiburg i. Breisgau, Max Planck Institut für ausländisches und internationales Strafrecht, 13–54.

Reenen, P. van 1989. Policing Europe after 1992: cooperation and competition, *European Affairs* **2**, 45–53.

Team Consult 1987. *De politiediensten in België* (April).

Treur, J.H.F. 1995. Centralisatie en decentralisatie bij de Nederlandse politie: een hoopvol perspectief? *Handboek Politiemanagement*. Alphen a/d Rijn, Samsom H.D. Tjeenk Willink: C1210–C1220.

Walker, N. 1991. The United Kingdom police and European police cooperation. Working Paper III, Working Paper Series *A System of European Police Cooperation*. Edinburgh: University of Edinburgh.

Walker, N. 1993. The accountability of European police institutions. *European Journal on Criminal Policy and Research* **4** Vol. 1 (Police cooperation and private security).

Walker, N. 1994a. European integration and European policing: a complex relationship. In *Policing across national boundaries*, M. Anderson & M. den Boer (eds). 22–45. London: Pinter.

Walker, N. 1994b. Reshaping the British police: the international angle. *Strategic Government* **1** Vol. 2, 25–34.

Walker, N. 1996. Policing the European Union: the politics of transition. In *Policing change: changing police. International perspectives*, O. Marenin (ed.). 251–77. Current Issues in Criminal Justice. New York: Garland Press.

Walker, N. 1997. Deficient Weaponry, Reluctant Marksmen and Obscure Targets: Flaws in the Accountability of Undercover Policing in the EU. In *Undercover policing and accountability from an international perspective*, M. den Boer (ed.). Maastricht: EIPA, 205–16.

Wyngaert, Christine Van den. 1997. Organized Crime, Proactive Policing and International Cooperation in Criminal Matters: Who Controls the Police in a Transnational Context? In *Undercover policing and accountability from an international perspective*, M. den Boer (ed.). Maastricht: EIPA, 163–77.

CHAPTER 5

Post-Socialist Policing: Limitations on Institutional Change

LOUISE I. SHELLEY

Introduction

The Soviet Union created a model of policing. This model of policing was exported and imposed on diverse countries. As the former socialist countries confront the communist legacy, they are trying to develop police forces and legal systems more suited to their emergent political systems.

Most studies in the past have focused on change in the police force(s) of a particular country. These diverse analyses reveal that police forces change, often dramatically, as a result of major economic, social or political changes within a particular country. Change also occurs as a result of pressures within the society for police reform often as a consequence of an incident of devastating police brutality. A transition away from an authoritarian government also provides the impetus for transformation of the police.

The transformation of the police since the fall of the Berlin Wall and collapse of the Soviet Union is different from most of the analyses in this book. First, Soviet policing was a standardized system of policing which existed in a vast territory that extended from East Germany to the Pacific Ocean. It was developed in Moscow and exported throughout the socialist societies. Second, the changes occurring in post-socialist policing were not planned but are a result of the unexpected collapse of the USSR. Consequently many countries are not equipped to deal with the changes in policing now required.

Under the Soviet system, little allowance was made for the vast cultural differences among the many socialist states and their different legal traditions. The Ministry of Interior Academy in Moscow trained personnel from all over the former Soviet Union, Eastern Europe, Africa, Cuba, the Middle East and other parts of Asia.[1] With the collapse of the Soviet Union, the many countries emerging from this shattered empire are seeking to develop their own identities. The former Soviet Union is now divided into 15 countries, Czechoslovakia has split and East Germany has been reunited with West Germany. Countries such as Kazakhstan, Tadzikistan and Kyrgyzstan which never sought independence are forced to develop their own policing without direction from Moscow. Germany seeks to obliterate any legacy of communist policing by imposing Western German forms of policing on its citizens in the East. Many countries in Eastern Europe and the Baltics seek, in an environment of severe fiscal limitations, to create more democratic policing.

With such a diversity of post-Soviet experiences, it is not possible in one chapter to examine all aspects of the movement away from the model of socialist policing. As diverse countries try to establish a distinct national identity, the transformation of their police forces remains a primary objective of many of the successor states. All the former socialist states are left with a common legacy: demoralized and corrupted police forces with little or no respect for citizens' rights. Whereas some post-socialist states such as Germany, Hungary and Estonia have devoted considerable resources to the creation of more democratic police forces, in some successor states such as Uzbekistan and Tadzikistan the police are much more authoritarian than in the final years of the Soviet period. The situation in Russia has deteriorated since the Soviet Union's collapse.[2]

Presently, it is impossible to analyse policing in the post-Soviet states without addressing the Soviet legacy. Because forces of nationalism are strongly affecting decisions concerning future directions of policing, in a couple of decades there will be very distinct differences in the styles and structures of policing observable in the former socialist states. Yet such a profound change has not occurred because no country, apart from Germany (Ewald 1995), has been able to commit the resources to completely transform its system of policing. Instead, the former socialist states at present have more or less democratic versions of Soviet policing.

The problems of crime, corruption and organized criminality are now so severe in most former socialist states that it undermines possibilities for positive change. While many foreign countries, particularly the United States and western Europe, are committing significant resources to aiding the transformation process in policing, it is premature to suggest that the training and advice leads to sustained change in these police departments.

The Soviet Legacy

During 74 years of Soviet rule, the militia was transformed from a militarized body suppressing political opposition to a law enforcement body responsible primarily for social and economic order. This transformation was similar to that which has been observed in the police forces of other industrialized societies: over time, a distance was gradually established between the police and the nation's political structure. Yet, because the Soviet militia functioned as a tool of the Communist Party, the relationship between the militia and the political structure in the USSR and other socialist states remained much closer than in democratic societies, allowing the Party to close that distance at the end of the Soviet era and direct the militia once again to suppress political opposition.

Despite its final effort to democratize during the *perestroika* years, the Soviet militia remained an authoritarian police force which retained elements of continental, colonial and communist police traditions. These elements remain present in the transitional police forces of the newly independent states today, even in the absence of Marxist ideology, the Communist Party and the Soviet state. In Eastern Europe, the Baltics and Central Asia, the consequences of long term colonization are a major impediment to the creation of independent, democratic police forces.

During *perestroika*, Communist Party General Secretary Mikhail Gorbachev attempted to reverse the relationship between the Soviet state and citizen. This allowed an opportunity for change both within the USSR and in the states of Eastern Europe. Instead of tolerating the arbitrary exercise of police power, he hoped to establish a socialist, law-based state in which institutions and individuals would be subordinate to the law. The state, however, faced the dilemma of how to liberalize while maintaining order and centralized control. Not only did the militia lose credibility among those it policed, it lost credibility among those charged with executing its orders. The departure of numerous personnel in many socialist states at the end of the 1980s evidenced a serious morale problem and left the police without the qualified, experienced personnel needed to fulfil the body's ever more difficult duties (a problem which has only intensified since the collapse of the USSR and the socialist bloc). In the late *perestroika* period, moreover, when central political authority no longer prevailed, non-Slavic militia officers actively sided with republican interests against the Soviet state in many of the republics.

As the USSR began to splinter, militiamen became executors of the policies of a weak state, one which could not even guarantee their security. Record numbers of militiamen were attacked and killed by fellow citizens in the late 1980s as they sought to control nationalist movements, ethnic violence and increasingly vicious criminals. By the time the regime collapsed, Soviet citizens could no longer count on the most fundamental law enforcement services needed to protect them from rising crime and the operations of ever-expanding organized criminal groups.

Deteriorating police performance increasingly prompted many people to take policing into their own hands by creating private police forces and citizen militias independent of the Communist Party. These new forms of law enforcement, together with the efforts of the Soviet republics to exert more control over their ministries of internal affairs, were part of a general trend away from centralized control toward greater republican and regional sovereignty in the country.

Police forces in Eastern Europe benefited from the diminution of Moscow's control by trying to shape their police to their more market oriented economies and to the growth of civil societies. In Hungary, thousands of personnel were dismissed who could not adhere to the new constitutional demands in the society (Pinter 1995). Police had to tolerate market activity and increasing participation of citizens in political and social life of the society. They were increasingly trained to respect the rule of law and rights of citizens. Control by Moscow declined, however, without the consciousness or framework of legal norms that sustain democratic societies and democratic police forces.[3] The attainment of more democratic police forces is a long term goal that will be achievable by only a small proportion of the countries to emerge from the socialist system.

Post-Soviet Policing

After the communist regimes of Eastern Europe collapsed, an acute examination of past policing techniques occurred in Hungary, Germany, Poland and Czechoslovakia. The attention given to policing in these countries was based on the conviction that close scrutiny of existing police practices was vital to democratization (Vigh & Katona 1993). Not surprisingly, many police methods were deemed incompatible with a democratic society in these nations, among them covert policing techniques, forced citizen collaboration with law enforcement bodies and the practice of planning the administration of justice. The former socialist states of the region have tried different reform approaches in order to limit police intrusion into private life. Poland has replaced many of its regular policemen, preferring inexperienced beginners to corrupt professionals insensitive to legal norms. West Germany has forced former East German policemen to adopt West German police techniques (in Berlin, police from the former German Democratic and Federal republics are paired in patrols). Hungary has abolished the network of informants that served as the foundation for undercover police work in that country, and Czechoslovakia, in destroying its secret police apparatus, has set a precedent for the ordinary police in the contemporary Czech and Slovak republics.[4]

The destruction of the communist system in the former Soviet Union has not been so thorough. The contemporary Russian state, together with many other successor states to the USSR, failed to exploit the impetus for change that followed the unsuccessful coup attempt and subsequent break-up of the Soviet Union in 1991.[5] Reformers have been more successful in removing symbols of state coercion such as the statue of Feliks Dzherzhinsky (the founder of the Soviet security police) before the KGB headquarters in Moscow than in restructuring law enforcement bodies. The superstructure of the Soviet state has collapsed, but the institutions of the Soviet period remain very much intact; the commitment to democratization and political change on the part of certain internal affairs personnel has yet to be matched by the kind of institutional changes that would promote a more open and accountable police.

Citizens in Russia feel very dissatisfied with the law enforcers with almost half of those surveyed reporting themselves to be completely dissatisfied with the police. The main reasons for their dissatisfaction are their bureaucratism, lack of responsiveness and respect of the citizenry. Citizens also cited problems of physical force, illegal conduct and demand for bribes as further reasons for their disregard for the police (Kuzminskii *et al.* 1994). This response to law enforcement is not confined to Russia but is a legacy of the police–citizen relations of the Soviet period. The lack of systemic change contributes to a perpetration of the same attitudes and policies. There is more rhetoric concerning respect for human rights than actual change.[6]

The continued executive practice of issuing classified normative acts, some of which directly affect citizens' rights and freedoms, offers concrete evidence of the unchanged institutional environment.[7]

The police forces of post-Soviet states remain true to the continental police model in their structure, functions and operations. Unlike several post-communist nations in Eastern Europe, the range of functions performed by the police in the newly independent states of the former USSR has not contracted. Several of these states have adopted new statutes on the regular police that grant the police the same duties it possessed in the Soviet period. Despite general acknowledgement of the fact that the passport and registration system violates basic human rights, most of these states have also preserved this significant militia control over the populace. The registration system is often used in a discriminatory fashion to harass ethnic minorities and to keep asylum seekers from exercising their rights.[8] Even more disconcerting, police forces in some of these states have used their new-found independence to secure or enhance their power at the expense of citizens' rights. In Russia, for example, the former Supreme Soviet Committee on Defence and Security was dominated by security, interior ministry and military industrial personnel (only a few of whom were inclined to reform) and the March 1992 Law on Security identified internal affairs organs as part of the security apparatus.[9]

The 1994 report of Russian Ombudsman Sergei Kovalëv documented two major violations committed by law enforcement personnel in 1993. First, following the attack on the parliament in October 1993, many individuals – including former deputies and staff members – who left the Russian 'White House' were beaten by members of the militia in the courtyards of neighbouring homes and on the streets. Brutal beatings also occurred at several police stations and at militia headquarters at Petrovka 38. Many of the detained later claimed that militiamen had shouted anti-Semitic and anti-Caucasian insults at them. Second, during the state of emergency which followed, approximately 10,000 individuals were expelled from Moscow by the militia, most of them non-Russian. The ombudsman's office has suggested that these expulsions resembled an ethnic cleansing.[10]

A recent report conducted by Helsinki Human Rights Watch reports that in the period from 1992–5, there has been a campaign of harassment and physical violence against ethnic minorities, and foreigners from the third world. The abuses include restrictions on 'freedom of movement, including arbitrary detention, arbitrary house searches and invasion of privacy, extortion, and physical assault.'[11] Those victimized include not only the Caucasians cited in the ombudsman's reports but individuals from the Middle East, Central Asia, the Asian subcontinent and Africa. Informants and undercover techniques are still used widely to detect criminals and penetrate society in most of the successor states to the USSR. Having failed to incorporate the concept of civil liberties into law enforcement, police operations in these states – in bona fide continental tradition – continue to emphasize the supremacy of the state over the individual. In Kazakhstan, the powers of law enforcement agencies have been enhanced and the militia is now authorized to perform 24 different types of operations, including secret entry of apartments, houses and offices of private enterprises. All investigative functions formerly divided among the police, procuracy and security police have now been combined into one large investigatory agency. The new Russian law on police operations, separate from that on state security, gives law enforcement personnel great latitude in the use of investigative methods and institutes only weak legal safeguards against police abuses, including the misuse of deadly force.[12]

Russian society, moreover, has yet to create a real division of political powers or to develop any kind of popular legal consciousness. Militiamen retain the right to engage in surveillance activity, monitor mail, eavesdrop on telephone conversations and other forms of communication and to use technical devices that are not life-threatening in order to monitor citizen behaviour. It is small comfort that the Russian militia can employ such methods only with the permission of the courts or the procuracy.[13] The need to use such methods to effectively address organized crime has raised serious questions about the introduction of a powerful organized crime law without proper legal safeguards.[14]

The political functions associated with the continental police model also remain intact in many of the newly independent states; militiamen continue to suppress ethnic disorder, police political protests and monitor members of political opposition groups. In certain Central Asian countries, Interpol (acting under the authority of the Ministry of Internal Affairs) has been used to locate Uzbek dissidents who have taken refuge in Kazakhstan. Such dissidents have then been detained and returned to Uzbekistan, where they were subjected to political repression.[15] And although the Communist Party is no longer the life force of these states, several of these countries have yet to recognize an individual's right to political expression without state intervention. Although a unified Ministry of Internal Affairs no longer controls policing in the entire territory of the former USSR, republican ministries of internal affairs remain. Most of these bodies remain unchanged from their Soviet incarnations and continue to manage law enforcement in the newly independent states with the same personnel, the same mandate and many of the same laws of Soviet times. Co-ordination of law enforcement among these states, moreover, is now being justified by the threat of organized crime, which has rapidly moved to exploit the porous borders between them. Although vital, such co-operation threatens in the short-run to re-establish ties that existed at the national ministerial level during the Soviet period.

It is an altogether disturbing fact that the law enforcement bureaucracies of the successor states to the USSR have the power to perpetuate Soviet police traditions in the absence of the Communist Party of the Soviet Union and its system of social controls. The state's penetration of private life through the security police and the militia remains a fact of life in most post-Soviet states. The *Tajik* legislature, for example, passed a new law on the militia in 1992 that requires state bodies, labour collectives and official and public associations to assist the regular police in its activities – continuing communist practice in the absence of communist ideology.[16] Co-operation between law enforcement agencies and the military also endures in many of these nations. In Russia, armed forces personnel were first directed to perform police work in January 1991.[17] By continuing to combine these different parts of the state control apparatus, the Russian state remains wholly within the continental tradition.

The communist element of policing should eventually disappear in post-Soviet states with the delegitimation of basic communist ideology. Property relations of the communist regime, however, remain extant in most of these countries, particularly with respect to land ownership, with state- and publicly-owned property in these nations only gradually being privatized. Thus it is highly likely that state paternalism will endure even in the absence of regimes structured to deliver all essential social services to the population. Finally, the post-Soviet police forces of the successor states have also inherited the law enforcement problems of the Soviet period. Independence has not eliminated the causes of endemic corruption, the lack of legal consciousness or the severely limited technical capabilities of the police. (While the number of Russian militia officers may have recently increased, the quality of their professional training has declined.)[18] In fact, many of these problems have been exacerbated by the collapse of the imperial centre.

Growing state corruption and organized crime in the successor states also have had major repercussions on law enforcement in the former Soviet republics. In 1993, for example, Russian police officials suggested that 13,000 internal affairs employees were directly collaborating with organized criminal groups and many more were accepting bribes from so-called 'mafias'. Russian law enforcement personnel suggest that there is pervasive corruption from organized crime. In Krasnodar and Dagestan, militia personnel have even beaten up judges.[19] In only two months in late 1994, 324 violations committed by Ukrainian MVD personnel were publicly disclosed and 43 criminal cases were initiated against MVD employees.[20] The poor salaries of militiamen, flourishing corruption at top leadership levels of the successor states and the difficulties of surviving hyperinflation have made police corruption as severe a problem, if not more so, than it was at the close of the Soviet regime.

In Russia, law enforcement personnel in several major cities have set up an independent police union to address the problems of institutionalized corruption and lack of respect for the law by senior officials. Members of the independent law enforcement unit who were sent without authorization to fight in the *Chechen* war protested through this union (Panasenko 1995a). Unions have also protested the failure to augment pensions of retired personnel or pay salaries of law enforcement personnel as mandated by the law. They are also investigating corruption by higher law enforcement officials in the distribution of housing to police personnel (Panasenko 1995b). Membership in these unions is small because members and their leaders have been harassed. But in 1996 with new leadership at the top of the Russian Ministry of Interior there has been some responsiveness to the issues raised by the independent unions.[21]

Demoralized by the low pay and insecurity of their work in state law enforcement bodies, numerous militia personnel in Russia and other successor states are leaving for the private sector.[22] The new private enforcement bodies, often staffed and run by former MVD and KGB personnel, work directly or are managed by organized crime groups. Firms are forced to contract for their services or face extortion by organized crime groups. A serious problem of professional ethics has accompanied the process of privatization and these independent agencies are seen as key nodes in organized crime accountable to no one. The Head of the Russian State Duma

Committee on Security, Viktor Iliukhin, estimates that there are now approximately 800,000 individuals working in private security forces, many of them controlled by organized crime. Rather than represent a new form of policing, privatization merely continued the worst of Soviet policing practices while freeing private police forces from legislative and institutional controls.[23] The process of privatization is facilitating crime not only in the law enforcement sector. Privatization in the successor states has also been criminalized since its inception. Many investors who have participated in privatization came from the former shadow economy. That is, in the past they acted as speculators, racketeers and extortionists. According to estimates of the Russian Ministry of Interior in mid-1993, 40,000 enterprises were controlled or established by organized criminal groups, with law enforcement personnel complicit in much of this illegal activity (Glinkina 1994). Privatization, moreover, is occurring against a background of severe economic and political crisis – almost one-half of the former Soviet republics are now party to serious inter-ethnic conflict or civil war. Under such conditions, observance of legal norms is continually subordinated to the survival of the state and its citizens.

Given the newly independent states' financial straits, shortages of militia cars, typewriters, telecommunications equipment and even gasoline are more serious problems today than they were for the Soviet militia during the waning days of the USSR. In most Eastern European countries, limited funds are available for new equipment and training programmes to modernize their police forces. In all the former socialist societies, under-equipped police forces are a poor match for increasingly sophisticated, well-equipped professional criminal organizations. During the socialist period, brutal enforcement techniques combined with forced citizen compliance meant that clearance rates for reported crimes and conviction rates for criminal offences were quite high. These statistical indicators have declined significantly, a consequence of more accurate data reporting and of the increased capabilities of the criminals to exploit gaps in law enforcement. Many former members of the police and security apparatus of many socialist countries are key participants in criminal organizations, being particularly capable of exploiting the weaknesses of the current governmental police forces. In all these countries, the state is now competing with criminal organizations for experienced law enforcement personnel. In some countries, individuals enter police schools to receive training and then leave shortly after completion of their studies to join the private security forces run by criminal groups able to offer more attractive salaries. The police forces of most of the successor states remain severely understaffed and it is difficult to locate replacements for departing personnel, a situation that threatens to endure for some time to come.

The Colonial Legacy

In addition to their continental and communist heritage, the structure and composition of post-Soviet police institutions represents one of the most concrete legacies of Soviet colonialism. Slavs enjoyed a visible presence in the militia forces of all former republics of the USSR, a staffing pattern required to reinforce the authority of the central Russian state. While some of the newly independent states of the region have forced Slavic (or Russified) personnel off their police forces, many others lack qualified replacements for law enforcement bodies (Beckelhimer 1993). In countries, such as the Baltics, where militia personnel were viewed as part of the oppressive force, it is very hard to recruit local cadres for law enforcement work. Moreover, the low wages paid for police work in all the former socialist states makes it particularly difficult to attract personnel. Nowhere do citizens view police work as a key element of state building of a more democratic society. The ideological commitment to the building of socialist society meant that ethnic differences were subordinated to larger societal objectives. As new territories fell under Soviet influence, the entire population was subjugated and no attention was paid to minority populations and their rights. Many Eastern European countries and successor states, have inherited the long standing problem of suppressed ethnic groups who in this more democratic environment seek expression of their rights. The law enforcement apparatuses are not sensitive to this problem. Slavic personnel continue to operate in the security police of most Central Asian nations; the same situation largely holds for the militias of these countries.

As in other parts of the world, colonial relationships continue between the former imperial centre and the periphery of the Soviet empire, largely because many former Soviet republics did not acquire autonomy – economic or otherwise – with independence. Unlike the Baltic states and Ukraine, not all of these new countries fought, or even sought, to become sovereign nations, a status they achieved as a result of the collapse of the empire. Russia's assertion that it has a legitimate right to intervene in these countries on behalf of the 25 million Russians living outside Russia's borders adds additional weight to the colonial character of the relations between the former imperial centre and the 'near abroad'. Although the political ties among the socialist bloc have collapsed, the ties among the criminal populations of the Soviet successor states and the Eastern European countries endure. Therefore, while the ties among the law enforcers are weak, the ties among the criminals are not. They exploit the weaknesses in law enforcement for their own advantage.

Western Assistance Programmes

Many European countries and more recently the United States have provided assistance to the police forces of the former socialist states. This assistance has been provided by individual donor nations and there has been limited co-ordination among countries providing law enforcement training. In the first years following the collapse of the Berlin War, most assistance was provided by individual countries in Western Europe. The limited capacities of Europol and the bureaucratic problems inherent in the European Union have inhibited a co-ordinated European response.

For the past three years, Europe 2000 has been holding seminars on organized crime for legal professionals in different countries in Eastern Europe. These efforts complement those of individual institutions in Western Europe that are trying to maintain contact with their counterparts in law enforcement institutions in many countries in Eastern Europe, the Baltics and some of the successor states. Much of the assistance from European countries comes from those with immediate geopolitical and economic interests. For example, the Scandinavian countries have been particularly involved in the Baltic states while Austria and Germany have been most visible in Eastern Europe. The German police training academy has been working with Belarus. But the assistance has been by no means limited to these countries. For example, Italian police have trained colleagues in Hungary. The consequence of this unfocused assistance is that many police personnel in recipient countries feel themselves confused by the contradictory advice which has been offered them.

American law enforcement assistance has arrived much later than that offered by most Western European states. But once American assistance was provided, it came with an intensity unmatched by European counterparts. Americans have also tried to co-ordinate western law enforcement assistance through a training academy in Budapest[24] an initiative that has met with only limited support from other donor countries. The US Congress, alarmed by the collapse of order in the former socialist countries and the rise of organized crime, allocated $30 million to assist the Central European and NIS states fight organized crime and corruption. The initiative, co-ordinated by the Bureau of International Narcotics and Law Enforcement Affairs, draws on United States government law enforcement personnel to provide training in investigations, management skills and forensic skills. Seminars are held by the Federal Bureau of Investigation, US Customs Service, Drug Enforcement Assistance Administration, Department of State's Bureau of Diplomatic Security, Bureau of Alcohol, Tobacco and Firearms, US Secret Service and Financial Crimes Enforcement Network (FinCen) of the US Department of the Treasury.[25] The philosophy behind this programme is that international organized crime is exploiting the weaknesses in law enforcement in the former socialist states and is using these countries as safe havens for operation. Therefore, American aid is to develop partnerships for investigating transnational organized crime and is to prevent the further expansion of organized crime from Eastern Europe and the former USSR into the United States. There are three foci of the American effort. They include combating international organized crime, financial crime and a counter-narcotics programme. Courses are offered on such subjects as detecting and preventing counterfeiting, investigating crimes in the banking sector including money laundering, and control over narcotics production and distribution.

The most significant component of this effort was the establishment of an international law enforcement academy for personnel from the former Soviet Union and Central Europe. Training programmes began in 1995 although the official opening of the institution was only in Spring 1996. American law enforcement personnel are providing most of the instruction although the Americans seek the financial and professional involvement of their Canadian and Western European counterparts. The centre will provide longer professional development courses for mid-level personnel and short term courses on combating organized crime, narcotics trafficking and financial crime. A particular concern in the initiation of these programmes is that training is not being provided to corrupt law enforcement personnel, who will be better equipped for illicit conduct after these courses. The US governmental effort to ensure that allocated funds have been expended has not always allowed for the targeted assistance that is necessary to prevent the misuse of these programmes.[26]

The Post-Soviet Future

To date, most of the newly independent states have been unable to reconceptualize policing. While it may be premature to expect major restructuring of law enforcement agencies and practices in these nations, their failure to address one of the more important authoritarian legacies of the Soviet period inhibits their ability to democratize. The future development of police forces in the successor states will depend on the type of societies that emerge in these countries. Twenty years from now, it is unlikely that these 15 countries will have similar police forces. The more western parts of the former Soviet Union may well strive to implement European models of policing, while many of the Islamic countries of Central Asia may eschew western legal models and follow law enforcement models closer to Turkish and/or Iranian experience. Whatever course they follow, the communist legacy of the Soviet regime and, in many cases, the colonial legacy of Russian rule, will continue to weigh heavily on law enforcement in these nations for years to come.

Sadly, many of the newly independent states seem to have traded one form of violence for another. Whereas once state repression was accentuated and civilian violence relatively insignificant, today nearly one-half of the former Soviet republics cannot control crime or ethnic and nationalist violence within their borders. If these countries continue to live in a state of war for a protracted period, it is possible they may choose the *Hobbesian* alternative and create authoritarian governments (with authoritarian police forces) in order to put an end to constant conflict. Should such a scenario prevail, the continental police tradition will be further perpetuated in these nations.

If, however, the new states of the region succeed in creating individual property and distributing it with some equity within their societies, they will create a bulwark against unlimited state authority. These nations would then have the opportunity to develop civil societies and civil liberties and gradually require that their police forces operate according to the rule of law. Movement away from communist property relations should force these states to accept the idea that certain areas of human conduct are outside the purview of government and state regulation and thereby reduce the degree of interventionist policing known in the former Soviet Union. While it is too early to be assured of either of these two scenarios, law enforcement in most of the former Soviet republics is clearly in a precarious state.[27] The morale of law enforcement agencies is at an all-time low – they can neither control escalating crime, nor handle the increasingly sophisticated activities of organized criminal groups which threaten not only their own societies, but those of many other nations in the world. With the declining authority of the security police and the army in these nations, only the militia remains, affecting the ability of the successor states to both stabilize and control organized crime. Far from being of interest only to specialists of the region or an impediment to democratization, the current condition of militia operations in the Soviet successor states is thus an issue of global concern.

Notes

1. Interview with personnel of the MVD Academy in Moscow in May 1995.
2. The Helsinki human rights group in Russia met in May 1996 and proclaimed the situation in law enforcement in Russia a serious threat to human rights.
3. Several noted specialists have examined the legal framework that underlies democratic societies and police forces, among them see Bittner (1980), Emsley (1983), Liang (1992), Reiner (1985) and Reiss (1971).
4. Presentations at the conference on Social Changes, Crime and Police, 1–4 June 1992, Budapest, Hungary sponsored by the Department of Criminology at Eotvos Lorand University. See also Vigh & Katona (1993).
5. It may be that part of the reason Russia has been unable to reform its law enforcement agencies is that certain elements of the militia, as well as the Alpha Division of the KGB, sided with Yeltsin against the coup perpetrators in August 1991. MVD troops again supported the Russian president in October 1993, when they helped to storm the Russian parliament building; their support subsequently earned the MVD both material benefits and political protection in the Yeltsin regime. Ironically, the pro-democracy stance of these groups in the MVD and security police may have shielded more conservative co-workers from harsh reprisals.
6. See for example 'Prava cheloveka i status pravokhranitel'nkh organov', *Gosudarstvo i Pravo* **11**, 1994, 81–126, a discussion from the Ministry of Interior Institute in St Petersburg on the need for human rights and democratization.
7. See 'Human Rights Committee Chairman Describes Abuses', Foreign Broadcast Information Service, *Daily Report: Eurasia* (hereafter FBIS, *Daily Report*), 1 September 1994: 7.
8. Human Rights Watch/Helsinki **7** (12) 'Russia: Crime or Simply Punishment/Racist Attacks by Moscow Law Enforcement' September 1995: 3.
9. For the composition of the Supreme Soviet committee, see Waller (1993a). For more information on the 1992 Law on Security, see Waller (1993b).
10. 'O sobliudenii prav cheloveka i grazhdanina v rossiskoi Federatsii za 1993 god' (report of the Office of the Russian Ombudsman presented at a meeting of the Human Rights Commission under the President of the Russian Federation, Moscow, 14 June 1994).
11. Human Rights Watch, 1995: 1.
12. On police powers in Kazakhstan, see 'New Law Boosts Powers of Police', FBIS, *Daily Report* 26 October 1994, 41. For the text of the new Russian law, see 'Ob operativno-rozysknoi deiatel'nosti v Rossiiskoi Federatsii', Russian Federation Law 892, *Vedomosti s'ezda narodnykh deputatov Rossiiskoi Federatsii i Verkhovnogo Soveta Rossiiskoi Federatsii* **17** (23 April 1992): 1222–3. Information on the weak safeguards this law contains against police abuses was provided by Russian Ombudsman Sergei Kovalëv in a September 1994 interview in Washington, DC.
13. 'Ob operativno-rozysknoi deiatel'nosti'.
14. This theme was a central part of the discussion at the first round table of the organized crime study centre of Moscow State University on 2 November 1995.
15. September and October 1994 interviews with Central Asian human rights figures in Washington DC.
16. See 'Law on Militia', Foreign Broadcast Information Service, *Daily Report: Central Eurasia/Laws*, 1 September 1992, 113.
17. 'On Co-operation between the Police and Units of the USSR Armed Forces in Ensuring Law and Order in Combating Crime', decree of the President of the Union of Soviet

Socialist Republics, translated in 'Are Police-Army Patrols Constitutional?' *Current Digest of the Soviet Press* (hereafter *CDSP*) **18** (5) (1991): 7.

18. 'MVD Personnel Chief Astapkin Discusses Militia Crime', FBIS, *Daily Report*, 13 October 1994, 47–8.

19. On Russian militia co-operation with organized criminal organizations, see 'Alarm, jetzt kommen die Russen', *Der Spiegel* **25** (1993): 105. On Krasnodar and Dagestan, see 'Revamped Justice System Suffers Birth Pangs', *CDSP* **36** (34) (1994): 10.

20. 'Radchenko on Crime Problem, MVD', FBIS, *Daily Report*, 14 November 1994, 67.

21. Meetings and conversations with Valery Inozemtsev, head of the independent policemen's union in Ekaterinburg in 1995 and 1996.

22. 'MVD Personnel Chief Astapkin Discusses Militia Crime', 47–8.

23. July 1994 interview with Viktor Iliukhin, Moscow.

24. 'Interview with the Honourable Richard A. Clarke', *Trends in Organised Crime* **1** (3), 1996: 7.

25. Announcement of Anti-Crime Training and Technical Assistance Program, US Department of State, Office of International Criminal Justice, 1996.

26. The author who has critiqued these government programmes during their initiation phase raised many concerns about the lack of targeted assistance in intra-governmental memos.

27. In Russia, politicians of the left and right agree that the socio-economic situation, rather than the MVD, is most to blame for the current crime situation. See 'Softer version of Law Against Organised Crime Adopted', FBIS, *Daily Report*, 28 November 1994: 31.

Bibliography

Beckelhimer, M.J. 1993. Estonia's men in blue. *The Baltic Observer*, **59.15**, 6.

Bittner, E. 1980. *The functions of police in modern society*. Cambridge, Mass.: Oelgeshlager, Gunn & Hain.

Emsley, C. 1983. *Policing and its context, 1750–1870*. London: Macmillan.

Ewald, U. 1995. The effect of social changes upon crime. In *Social changes, crime and the police*, L. Shelley & J. Vigh (eds). Chur, Switzerland: Harwood Academic Publishers.

Glinkina, S.P. 1994. How organized crime is hijacking privitization, *Demokratizatsiya* **2.3**, 388.

Kuzminskii, E.F., I.N. Mazaev, I.B. Mikhailovskaia 1994. Militsiia: naselenie analiz vzasmootnoshenii. In *Prestupnost: chto my znaem o nei; militsiia: chto my dumaen o nei*, I.B. Mikailovskaia (ed.). Moscow: Human Rights Group.

Liang, H-H. 1992. *The rise of modern police and the European state system from Metternich to the Second World War*. Cambridge: Cambridge University Press.

Panasenko, S. 1995a. Omon: Blizhe k Groznomu, *Vechernii Ekaterinburg*, 17 January, 2.

Panasenko, S. 1995b. Kvartiry dlia mairov, *Vechernii Ekaterinburg*, 19 April, 3.

Pinter, S. 1995. The effect of social changes on the police. In Shelley & Vigh (eds) op cit.

Reiner, R. 1985. *The politics of the police*. Brighton: Wheatsheaf.

Reiss, A.J. 1971. *The police and the public*. New Haven: Yale University Press.

Vigh, J. & G. Katona 1993. *Social changes, crime and police*. Budapest: Eötvös Loránd University Press.

Waller, J.M. 1993a. Russia's security and intelligence services today, *ABA National Security Law Report* **15.6**, 5.

Waller, J.M. 1993b. Russia's legal foundations for civil repression, *Demoksatizatsiya* **1.3**, 111.

CHAPTER 6

Post-Colonial Systems

BANKOLE A. COLE

Introduction

The study of colonial policing was, until very recently, a relatively under-researched area (Cain 1979, Mawby 1990). Today, an excellent body of historical material exists on British colonial policing (Anderson & Killingray 1991, ibid. 1992). In contrast, however, very little has been written on policing in the colonies of other European countries such as Germany, France or Belgium. The study of colonial policing provides an important insight into the development of policing in post-colonial countries which account for more than half of the total world population. In addition, it provides a useful foundation for an effective comparative study of policing in the world. As Anderson & Killingray (1991) argued, the colonial dimension provides a very interesting addition to the existing western writings on the social history of crime and the role of the state in seeking to prevent crime and maintain social order. This chapter is concerned with colonial policing and its impact on post-colonial police systems. The focus of the chapter is the development of police systems resulting from western European colonization of the developing world, with particular reference to African, Asian as well as some Central and Latin American countries. The main aims are:

(1) to identify and discuss the distinctive features of colonial policing in terms of their structures and functions.
(2) to discuss the specific impact of colonial policing on policing in post-colonial countries
(3) to examine the current debate on the 'imperial linkage' with reference to the impact of the colonial experience on post-colonial policing in the 'mother-countries'.

Colonial Policing

It is not possible to generalize on the form of colonial policing,[1] but there are certainly identifiable and distinctive features and similarities in terms of the structure and functions of colonial police forces. The historical development of policing in the colonies took place mainly as a by-product of the global expansion of capitalism in the nineteenth century; but their origins could be traced as far back as the fifteenth century, to the Portuguese and Spanish occupation of Central and South America, followed by British and French settlements in North America, New Zealand and Australia. A clear distinction eventually emerged between the development of policing in colonies that were annexed for the purpose of settlement and the development of policing in the 'pacified' colonies annexed mainly for the purpose of trade. Generally, civilian policing structures were predominant in 'settlement' colonies of North America, Canada and Australia whilst para-military policing was common in 'pacified' colonies located mainly in Africa, Asia, Central and South America. In the latter, two-tier policing systems were operated whereby urban areas where European settlers, administrators and traders lived (usually designated 'colonies') were policed differently compared with the rural areas where the bulk of the 'natives' lived (usually designated 'protectorates') (Killingray 1986).

Historical evidence reveals that civilian police forces were established in the German European townships of Windhoek and Swakopmund in Southwest Africa (Bley 1971); the French 'communes' and European settlements in Algeria, Cochin-China (South Vietnam), Senegal, French Equatorial Africa, New Caledonia and the New Hebrides (Roberts 1963, Suret-Canale 1971, US Naval Intelligence Division 1943, Thompson & Adloff 1960); the Spanish colonial township of Santiago in Chile (Galdemes 1964); the Portuguese colonial settlement of Rio de Janeiro in Brazil (Prado 1967); and also in the various British colonial settlements in East and West Africa (Newbury 1965, ibid. 1971, Anderson 1991). Policing the 'protectorates' was more varied and complex. Generally, policing in these areas developed in an ad hoc fashion, in reaction to particular needs but more importantly in reaction to the nature of the local acceptance or resistance to colonial rule. Pacifying the 'natives', protecting colonial economic interests, upholding the legitimacy of colonial political authorities and maintaining basic essentials of law and order in order to open up trading routes, were some of the factors that prompted the establishment of police forces in the protectorates. The complexity of protectorate policing, however, lies mainly in the lack of a clear distinction between policing and military action. Most of the colonial senior police officers in Africa and Latin America were recruited directly from the imperial armies, and the majority of the police forces in these protectorates were para-military units. They operated alongside the imperial armies in the joint efforts of opening up the 'hinterlands' for trade, maintaining internal security and protecting the European settlements from possible invasions from hostile 'natives' (McCracken 1992, Gutteridge 1970, Levene 1963). In fact, in many of the pacified territories, police and military duties were interchangeable. Most colonial military operations in the empires were concerned with internal security and could, therefore, be classified as policing. In the Belgian Congo, for example, the main tasks of the *Force Publique*, the Belgian colonial army were defined in the decree of 1885 as:

> To assure the occupation and defence of the colony, to maintain peace and public order, to prevent insurrection and to overlook and assure . . . the execution of laws, decrees and rules, especially those which are relative to the police and general security (Gutteridge 1970: 297).[2]

In the French colonies generally, the distinction between *l'armee, la gendarmerie* and *la police* was often blurred in the protectorates where all military and law enforcement institutions were often under military commanders, usually the *Commandant de cercle* (Bidwell 1973, Coquery-Vidrovitch 1969). In French West Africa, the *cercle* police forces performed military functions in place of the army in most parts of the protectorates, under the command of the *Commandant de cercle*. Similarly, the French mounted mobile police force (the *meharistes*) was a para-military police force that was used in the 'pacification' of the Sahara region in North Africa and Northeastern Chad in the nineteenth century (Suret-Canale 1971). In British colonial Africa and the Caribbean, para-military police forces were established initially as back-ups for the British imperial armies and gunboats, but they were destined to replace the soldiers in later years, as climatic conditions and economic factors made the recruitment of soldiers from Britain difficult (Newbury 1965, ibid. 1971, Johnson 1991). The Armed Hausa Police in West Africa was, in this regard, a typical example (Tamuno 1970). Similarly, in Fascist Libya, the local Arabic word for police – *shurtah* – connotes the idea of a para-military security force (Stanford Research Institute 1969). In contrast, German colonial police forces were organized strictly along military lines, with ranks similar to those of the German army. In German Southwest Africa, for example, the colonial police officers had to undergo military training and were under the control and supervision of the German colonial army (Rafalski 1930). In practice, therefore, colonial police officers in the protectorates performed multiple roles which included mainly enforcing the law, maintaining internal security, and fighting wars.

Examples of police-military collaboration in the protectorates were many, especially in regions where warring 'tribes' and local protests against colonial authorities created acute public order problems. In Africa, police-military collaboration was common during the period of the 'scramble' when European claims to the monopoly of trade in various areas of influence within the continent had to be backed by evidence of 'effective occupation' (see Fieldhouse 1973). With new rules imposed by the Berlin Conference of 1884–1885, all the European powers in the continent could no longer tolerate acts of defiance from the 'natives' that implied ineffective occupation and had, in many cases, to impose their political authority over rebellious 'tribes' by force (Uzoigwe 1985, Robinson & Gallagher 1975, Bley 1971). Some of the existing para-military police forces took up active military roles while others became para-military units within existing imperial armies. The evidence that police and military duties were similar and interchangeable during the colonial era could not be better expressed than in 1898 when, at the height of the 'scramble', Lord Chamberlain merged all the police forces and colonial armies in British West Africa to form the West African Frontier Force – a military organization that eventually placed the whole of modern Nigeria, Sierra Leone, Ghana and the Gambia firmly under British rule (Ukpabi 1966, Newbury 1971).

Nevertheless, protectorate policing was not all in all para-military policing. Various forms of civilian policing were set up, in many places alongside the para-military forces. Generally, civilian policing appeared to prevail during the latter years of colonization. Most of the colonizers concentrated on establishing civil police forces after the pacification process was completed and the colonial states were well established. The most conspicuous features of civil policing during the colonial era, however, were the various forms of local police systems that were set up at territorial, village or district level. Many of these forces were set up as parts of established local government structures, often referred to as 'native' or 'tribal' administration.

'Native' administration policing took several forms but there were two main types outstanding. On the one hand, in communities where established traditional political authorities administered justice and enforced the law, a system was practised whereby these traditional authorities (for example, the Mandarins in French Indo-China and the Hausa-Fulani Emirs in British Northern Nigeria) were left to continue in this tradition but under the watchful eyes and supervision of colonial administrators (Roberts 1963, Osborne 1969, Adeleye 1977, Robb 1991). On the other hand, and in the majority of cases, local dignitaries or other persons loyal to the colonial governments were put in charge of 'native' administration and, as part of their duties, they were empowered to appoint police officers for their local areas.[3] Examples of the latter system could be found in most parts of the British Empire, German East Africa, Fascist Ethiopia and some parts of Spanish Latin America (Afigbo 1972, Austen 1968, Sbacchi 1985, Killingray 1986, Fagg 1963, Davis 1968, Crowder 1968).[4] Generally, 'native administration' policing provided cheap ways of policing vast areas of colonial territories. French West Africa, for instance, covered an area of over three million square kilometres – an area nine times the size of France itself. The same could be said for Portugal, Germany and Britain. Although colonial civil police forces (both 'native' and imperial) were generally small in size and police-citizen ratios were generally very large,[5] the close link between the police forces and colonial political authorities, and the back-up easily provided by the colonial armies, were enough to coerce respect for their authority, even in the most remote parts of the empires.

A major misconception about colonial policing is the assertion that it was mainly public order policing – a viewpoint which over-emphasizes the confrontations with 'natives' and creates an impression of colonization as dealing mainly with anarchy and 'barbarism'. But the colonial society was not, in itself, crime free. Crime in the colonial society could be linked, although not entirely, to new socio-economic problems created by the colonial political economy. Hence, some of the colonial police forces were established specifically to control crime. For example, the first police organization in the Spanish colony of Chile (known as the Queen's Dragoons) was created in 1758, to supplement the efforts of the *serenos* (night-watchmen) in the fight against a rising wave of crime and insecurity in the Spanish city of Santiago and its environs, caused by armed bandits and robbers (Galdemes 1964). Likewise, in colonial Brazil, unemployment and poverty created severe crime problems. The first civil police institution in the city of Rio de Janeiro, for example, was set up specially to deal with crime and muggings carried out, as in Chile, by armed bandits and highway men (the *capoeiras*). In the rural areas of Brazil, rich landowners' private militia (the *condottieri*) worked together with the *Corpus de Ordenanca* (the territorial militia or Home Guard) in the war against banditry, inter-familial violence and crime in the 'backlands' (Alden 1968, Prado 1967, Vianna 1949, de Souza 1972, Russell-Wood, 1975). Similarly, the *gendarmes* in French Equatorial Africa, like the *Ordenancas* in Brazil, were concerned with controlling crime in the rural areas, most of which occurred mainly in the form of illegal immigration and contraband trade across the frontiers, fraud in the mining enterprises and black marketeering (Thompson & Adloff 1960). Various accounts of the use of the police to control crime also existed in many parts of the British empires (Anderson & Killingray 1992, Tamuno 1970, Willis 1991, Throup 1992). It is important to note, however, that in the empires, crime control was generally secondary to the maintenance of internal security and public order. The link between colonial policing and colonial political economy cannot, however, be over-emphasized, for the fundamental basis of all colonialist ventures is economic imperialism. Colonial empires were essentially markets and trading centres that operated for the benefit of western European economies. In practice, the majority of European colonial possessions, particularly those in Africa, were basically factories run on principles of efficiency and productivity secured, if need be, by force (Roberts 1963, Newitt 1981). In Indo-China, South America and Africa, the benefits of the colonies were seen mainly in terms of their ability to support profitable trade in local commodities as well as provide markets for Europe's redundant capital. Accordingly, economic considerations significantly guided the process of the development of policing in almost all western European colonies. This was evidenced, firstly, in the role played by concessionaire and chartered companies in the policing of colonies and secondly, in the roles that colonial police forces generally played in the protection of imperial economic interests in the colonies.

Concessionaire and chartered companies were, in the first place, representatives of industrialists and capitalists in Europe. Most of them were created in the nineteenth century, particularly during the period of the scramble, primarily to fill an administrative vacuum in the colonies and maintain European colonial authority at a minimal expense to the 'mother-countries'. Most importantly, they were established to protect colonial economic interests in specific areas of influence. Their duties were to administer and defend the colonial territory in return for the fiscal advantages of running lucrative trade monopolies. Examples included the Royal Niger Company (British: Nigeria); the East India Company (British: India); the *Neu Guinea Kompagnie* (German: Papua New Guinea); the *Deutsche Kolonialesellschaft fur Sud-west Afrika* (German: Southwest Africa); the *Woermann, Jantzen and Thormalen* (German: Togo and Cameroon); the *Deutsche Handels und Plantagen-Gesellschaft* (German: Western Samoa); the *Deutsche Ostrafikanische Gesellschaft* (German: East Africa); the British South Africa Company (British: South Africa), the East Africa Company (British: East Africa), the Mozambique Company (Portuguese: Mozambique); the Niassa Company (Portuguese: Angola and Mozambique) and the Zambezi Company (Portuguese: Angola). These chartered companies held sovereign rights over vast areas of land and millions of people. French concessionaire companies operating in Equatorial Africa in the late nineteenth century, for example, were given:

> ... exclusive rights over all agricultural, forest and industrial exploitation for thirty years, and after that period outright ownership of whatever land they had developed and any forests in which they had regularly collected rubber. In exchange, they were to pay the state a sum that varied with the size of their concessions, plus fifteen per cent of their annual profits. They were also to build roads and maintain order (Thompson & Adloff 1960: 13).

In order to defend the colonial territories and maintain law and order, the chartered and concessionaire companies had the power to establish armed guards, private militia or para-military police forces. The functions of these police forces or private militia, however, depended on the specific needs of the colonial power concerned. In British Africa, the concerns were mainly to secure recognition for Britain's claims to the monopoly of trade in her areas of influence in the African hinterland, prevent foreign encroachment on British areas of trading activities by rival French and German traders, expand Britain's areas of influence in the continent and ensure that Britain's claim to effective occupation was not threatened by the natives themselves. Consequently, the chartered company police forces that were set up took an active part in the signing of treaties of protection with African chiefs and also in wars against defiant 'native' traders and businessmen (Dike 1956, Anene 1966). The British Royal Niger Company's Constabulary was a typical example of a company para-military police force that took active part in the wars of pacification and the signing of treaties of protection with local chiefs – an activity that brought the vast hinterland of the middle belt of modern Nigeria under British protection in the late nineteenth century (Flint 1969). Similarly, Adolf Luderitz's *Deutsche Kolonialesellschaft fur Sud-west Afrika* (DKGfSWA) and Carl Peters' *Gesellschaft fur Deutsche Kolonisation* (GfdK) signed treaties with African chiefs and brought vast areas of Southwest Africa and East Africa under German rule (Smith 1978, Firth 1972).

In contrast, Portuguese chartered company police forces in Angola and Mozambique were not involved in pacification wars against the 'natives' nor in the signing of treaties of protection. Instead, they were used to coerce the local populations into compliance with colonial tax and labour laws designed to ensure a regular supply of cheap labour on company-owned plantations and *prazos* (Newitt 1981). Under Portuguese colonial labour laws, all 'natives' had a moral and legal obligation to work either for a company or the colonial government. If the 'natives' failed to contract themselves to an employer for work, they could be forcibly contracted by the colonial administration (Newitt 1981). This legal provision empowered the Portuguese chartered company police forces in Angola and Mozambique to round up workers in seasons when demands were high and to force them to work on the plantations. Thus, the Portuguese company police forces helped to support a system of 'corporate feudalism' (Newitt 1981) upon which depended the survival of Portuguese colonial ventures in Africa.

For the 'natives' in the pacified protectorates, colonial policing, in several ways, signified the invasion of an alien force representing an unquestionable political authority. The use of the police generally to manage and control the local population, particularly the labouring classes, was a common feature of policing in the protectorates. Classic examples could be found in the protectorates of South Africa and the Caribbean (see Johnson 1991, Grundlingh 1991, Nasson 1991). Fear, intimidation, oppression and control were, for many pacified communities, the trademarks of colonial policing both in times of peace and war. Numerous incidents of illegal raids, pillage and extortion, corruption and mindless brutality by colonial policemen exist in written and oral histories of colonial policing (Banda 1971). In French Equatorial Africa, for example, accounts of police brutality by both company and imperial police forces were reported on several occasions when the local population refused to comply with unreasonable labour and taxation demands (Deschamps 1962, Thompson & Adloff 1969). In a police raid against a village in the French Congo, Gide (1927) recounts that:

> There were thirty-two victims: twelve men were shot, fifteen women slaughtered with the machete and five children burnt in a hut . . . [In addition] police and irregular troops used in these operations were required to confirm their military exploits by bringing to the commandant the ears and genitalia of their victims (Suret-Canale 1971: 85).

Similar accounts of police brutality and abuse of power in the course of enforcing colonial laws and economic policies were also reported in the British, German and Portuguese colonies (Iliffe 1969, Newitt 1981, Cole, 1988). Sir Frederick Lugard, in his progress report on Northern Nigeria (1902) noted the fact that the mere mention of the word 'police' was enough to command unquestioned obedience and respect. This enabled the colonial policemen to commit numerous acts of lawlessness 'all of which they did saying that they were "consul's men" and could not be touched'.[6] Sir (later Lord) Lugard observed that impersonating a police officer was a common method adopted by criminals in Northern Nigeria to blackmail, terrorize, rape and collect illegal tolls from innocent but ignorant local peoples.[7] He argued that the success of this crime was due to the 'uncomplaining acquiescence of the people and their extraordinary credulity' but also accepted the fact that, 'throughout Africa – East and West – much injustice and oppression has been unwittingly done by our forces, acting on crude information and accusations of slave-raiding brought by enemies of the accused to procure their destruction'.[8]

Abuse of power and police brutality were not confined to imperial police officers alone, but were even more pronounced among 'native' police officers. In British Africa where the majority of colonial 'native' police forces were created, the image of the policeman was generally that of a law unto himself. In colonial Northern Nigeria, the activities of the Native Administration police forces earned them the distrust and outright hostility of the indigenous peoples, leading to their social isolation. Oral historical accounts of 'native' policing in the Tiv region of central Nigeria reveal that the Native Administration policeman was a powerful figure in the community, placed in the same respectable position as the staff-chiefs and 'native' council members. They were corrupt and they frequently abused their powers (East 1939). To the 'natives', the 'chiefs' and their policemen were simply agents of a new authoritarian political order that was generally unaccountable to the local peoples. This position was legitimized by the unreserved backing that was frequently given by colonial governments to the 'chiefs' and their policemen whenever they abused their powers (Afigbo 1972, Killingray 1986). As the latter maintained:

> Policing throughout the colonial period was imposed on the people and never enjoyed their consent . . . colonial policing had little to do with serving the community and everything to do with upholding the authority of the colonial state (Killingray 1991: 123).

The most obvious feature of colonial policing, therefore, is the close link that it had with colonial politics. Colonial police forces were the most visible symbols of imperial political power, both during the era of pacification and also when the colonial states were fully consolidated. In almost all the European colonies, colonial police forces maintained a position very close to colonial political authorities. In many cases, they operated as a crucial part of the colonial governments. The 'native' police forces, for example, were part and parcel of the colonial political system of divide and rule.

The political role of colonial police forces was particularly visible during the years of decolonization (mainly between the 1940s and 1950s) when challenges to the authority of the colonial state, manifested in waves of nationalist movements and anti-colonial uprisings, led to a more active political role for the majority of the colonial police forces. In the British colonial possessions in Africa, South-east Asia and the Middle-East, these political events were unprecedented. The result was that the colonial police forces in these regions were drawn into areas of policing to which they were ill-equipped to respond. These included the gathering of political intelligence and counter insurgency operations (Anderson & Killingray 1992). Under the pressure of the new political environment, the colonial police forces had to reform 'and to reform fast' (Rathbone 1992). Many of the police forces in the British colonies, in the 1940s and 1950s eventually acquired sophisticated riot-control and surveillance equipment, whilst many established riot squads (for example, Police Mobile Forces) and set up local police intelligence units, with links with the British Special Branch, in order to monitor the activities of trade unionists, 'terrorists' and 'militants', 'communists' and students. The flow of personnel between the colonies was very pronounced during these periods as 'experts' from regions with experience in riot-control and political policing (for example, Palestine, Kenya, Malaya and Cyprus) were drafted into areas with little experience of counterinsurgency operations (Anderson & Killingray 1992).

Similar changes were reported in French and Portuguese colonies during the years of decolonization. In Portuguese Africa, the Portuguese colonial police forces were involved in the efforts of the Portuguese colonial governments to suppress the anti-colonial political activities of the *mesticos* in the 1920s and 1930s (Newitt 1981). Likewise, the use of the colonial police forces to subdue nationalist and religious uprisings and labour unrest were common throughout the French colonies of North and West Africa during the same period (Crowder 1968, Suret-Canale 1971,

Galdemes 1964, Deschamps 1962, Thompson & Adloff 1969). Generally, twentieth century colonial police history, specifically during the period of decolonization and especially after 1945, was dominated by quasi-military like police operations against those who challenged the legitimacy of colonial rule. Colonial policing continued as an effective arm for defending the legitimacy of the colonial states and political economy. Police–army co-operation was revived whilst the colonial police forces drifted backwards into para-military policing. In relation to the British Empire, the main consequence of this development was that the colonial police forces 'suffered from becoming too prepared to cope with internal subversions and armed revolts, while normal police work and crime prevention and investigation were neglected' (Throup 1992: 147). The police were expected to combat crime, quell disorder, police political dissidents and then facilitate the smooth running of the colonial economy by enforcing labour and tax regulations. The result was the emergence of a modernized but over-burdened and over-politicized colonial police institution (Arnold 1992).

Policing the Post-Colonial State

The true form of the post-colonial state is still a subject of controversial political debate. Existing literature maintains that the basis of the post-colonial state, particularly in Africa, is, in fact, the colonial state (Joffe 1978, Stark 1986, Leys 1976). Although many post-colonial countries have, since independence, experimented with different types of governments, most of them have preserved in their new political structures several features of the colonial state, some practically in their original forms. This is particularly true of policing. Many retained the para-military component of their inherited police forces, but mainly as special units in predominantly colonial-like civilian police structures. The former French, Portuguese and Spanish colonies, for example, adopted police structures similar to those of their 'mother-countries', with the French system adopted in almost carbon copies in West and North Africa.[9] The independent Federal Republic of Brazil, representing a former Portuguese colony, has a decentralized police structure consisting of two semi-autonomous police forces: The Federal Police, administered centrally by the *Departmento de Policia Federal* (DPF)[10] and the State (civil) Police Forces under the direct supervision of state governors (Weis *et al.* 1975a). Likewise, Mexico has a police structure that is complex and decentralized in a manner similar to the police system in semi-federalist Spain. In addition to a Federal Police Force under the command of the *Direccion General de Policia y Transito*, there are state police forces, municipal police forces and even private police forces – all operating independently of each other (Weis *et al.* 1975b).

By contrast, the development of policing in the former British territories in Africa and India was shaped, significantly, by political events during the period of decolonization. In Africa, the complexity of the political situation, brought about mostly by the interference in 'nationalist' politics of ethnic and religious sentiments, led the British government to express a preference for centralized police forces in her pacified colonial possessions, in spite of her keenness on local government policing.[11] Central government control and administration of the police appeared to be a rational choice in the sense that it was the most likely option to ensure the impartiality of the colonial police forces after independence (Anderson & Killingray 1992). Post-colonial politics in Africa and India did turn out to be generally turbulent during the early years of independence. Under a rather chaotic political environment, the idea of national police forces began to gain grounds as an indispensable means for ensuring the political unification and survival of the new states. In response to these crises, India, for example, shelved the idea of any radical overhaul of its inherited colonial police organization. The Indian prime minister, Jawarharlal Nehru was quoted, in 1947, as saying that 'first things must come first and the first thing is the security and stability of India' (Arnold 1992: 58).

Today, police forces in the former British colonies in Africa and India, unlike those in the 'mother-country', are national institutions under central government control. Many of those former British colonies that retained their pre-existing 'native' authority police forces after independence and placed them under regional political control (for example, Nigeria) were forced to dissolve them or absorb them into national police forces either following the misuse of local police forces for political ends[12] or generally on the onset of authoritarian and military governments. Where police forces still exist locally, in provinces or regions, they are mainly contingents of the national police forces, under centralized command structures.[13] Central government control of police administration and operations is now enforced in several African constitutional provisions on the police. Many of these provisions, however, are based on former colonial arrangements. An example is the constitutional provision that grants to heads of governments (presidents) powers similar to those of their colonial counterparts (the consuls and governor-generals), to appoint national, regional or local police chiefs,[14] and for these police chiefs to be under the general orders and command of the heads of government.[15] There are provisions, too, that confer on heads of government the power to give directives to their police chiefs on law and order issues and not be questionable in any court of law on what and if any directives have been so given.[16]

The assertion that features of colonial policing did not disappear after independence is also applicable to those post-colonial countries, where the upsurge of revolutionary ('anti-colonial') ideas have shaped political developments since independence (for example, Libya, Burkina Faso, Angola, Mozambique, Chile, Cuba, Vietnam and Cambodia). These countries continued in the colonial tradition with regard to the structure and functions of their police forces, including police–state relations and para-military policing (Whitaker et al. 1973). The Chilean national police force (the Carabineros de Chile), for example, is a para-military police force created under President Ibanez as a means for dealing with anti-government protests in the 1920s. During the 1920s and 1930s, the Carabineros de Chile and the Chilean army operated, in the colonial fashion, as effective arms of successive Chilean military juntas with which they suppressed political oppositions resulting, for example, from labour and trade union militancy spearheaded by the Chilean Workers Confederation (the CTCH) and the upsurge of communism (Loveman 1979). Thus, the colonial tradition of political policing was continued in Chile after independence (Galdemes 1964). In fact, since the 1973 military coup d'état, the *Carabineros de Chile* has been part and parcel of Chilean military governments with its top Generals holding political offices in Chilean military governments (Nunn 1976).

Similarly, in independent Cuba, the adoption of a Marxist–Leninist government since the Castro revolution has meant a greater political role for the Cuban national revolutionary police force. Political policing in post-colonial Cuba actually began before the revolution of 1959 when, ironically, it involved the use of the police to suppress the rise of communist ideas during the Cuban crisis of the 1930s (Perez 1993). From what appeared to be their first experience of political policing since independence, the Cuban national revolutionary police gradually became entrenched in Cuban revolutionary politics, operating under a persistent atmosphere of political 'crises' and 'revolutions'. The Cuban police force is now part of a network of state security systems including the Cuban secret police – the *Departmentot de Seguridad del Estado* (DSE), the *Comites de Defensade de la Revolucion* (CDR) and the *Direction General de Inteligencia* (DGI). Since the 1959 revolution the functions of the police have been mainly to fight against 'social and political dissidents' and eradicate 'counter-revolutionaries' (Black *et al.* 1976).

In many respects, political policing appears to be the most obvious colonial legacy for most post-colonial countries in the developing world. Policing in the post-colonial state is largely a central government affair. The legitimacy of the police institution in the post-colonial state, as in the colonial state, is linked to the political authority of central governments. In many cases, the control of the police has simply changed hands from one authoritarian government to another. In Africa, the inherited colonial police institutions have, since independence, continued to play a significant role in the political processes of power entrenchment and regime legitimization by different factions of the post-colonial political classes (Sklar 1979, Cole 1995). Although most African laws and constitutions uphold the common law doctrine of constabulary independence,[17] recent events in some African countries reveal that, in practice, the operational autonomy of African police chiefs is not fully guaranteed in the existing constitutional arrangements on police governance. Many African political leaders have been able to continue in the colonial tradition of using the police and their chiefs for political ends. These have included the use of the police to oppress and intimidate political opponents and dissidents, trade unionists, university lecturers and students; and to control the working classes generally (see Cole 1988). This position is most visible under military governments when African police chiefs, like their counterparts in Latin America, are usually members of government ruling councils or cabinets.

In addition, the colonial encounter could be argued to account for many of the problems now faced by several post-colonial police forces, particularly those in Africa. Police corruption, brutality, inefficiency and isolation are problems of policing in many post-colonial African countries today that could be traced to the colonial experience (Wasikhongo 1976, Cole 1988, Igbinovia 1985, Carter & Marenin 1977, Odekunle 1979). The colonial public image of the police as agents of unquestionable government authority persists in Africa and this has enabled police officers with an inclination towards abuse of power to do so with impunity (Cole 1990a, ibid. 1990b). This situation is fuelled by the fact that most African countries, particularly those that were former British (and French) territories, have retained colonial legal and political arrangements that do not allow for any democratic control or administration of their police forces. There is practically no democratic input into policing issues at the local level. There is virtually no political platform in these countries upon which policing issues are debated or even challenged. Needless to mention is the fact that there are no effective review mechanisms to enable the public to call their police forces to account for how they choose to enforce the law and deal with members of the public. For example, there are no democratic institutions that oversee the operation of the police complaints systems. In addition, there are no provisions in many of these countries for an independent review of police decisions, for example those that are made in the police station (Cole 1990a, ibid. 1990b). All these go to support an argument that many police forces in Africa are yet to be fully democratically accountable to the various peoples and social groupings that they police. Furthermore, the colonial experience did have negative effects on the development of police roles and functions. Post-colonial policing is still generally concerned with law enforcement and the maintenance of internal security. Other similarly important areas of police work like police welfare roles and community policing are yet to emerge as significant features of policing in many post-colonial countries in the developing world, particularly those in Africa. Whilst it could be argued that there is no sound foundation in the colonial experience upon which to build such developments, a lot could be said for the lack of resources that would enable these countries to expand their policing functions beyond the colonial tradition. More importantly, there appears to be a general lack of political will, particularly in most post-colonial African countries today, to bring about radical changes. That radical changes are needed is a fact that cannot be ignored.

The Impact of the Colonial Experience on the Policing of the 'Mother-Countries'

Discussions on colonial policing are now emerging in support of the notion that the empires were systems in which ideas flowed not only outwards from the metropole but also backwards (Anderson & Killingray 1991). Accordingly, British police historians and criminologists like Michael Brodgen maintain that the development of policing in modern England should not be seen in isolation from the development of policing in the British colonies. Much literature now exists on the 'lessons' from Northern Ireland, the Middle-East and other parts of the British Empire and their possible impact on the development of policing in England and Wales (see for example, Brodgen 1987a; ibid. 1987b, Davis 1985, Hillyard 1987). A major support for this argument is often presented in the fact that many of the officers who returned from service in the colonies took up senior appointments in the Metropolitan Police and the English county police forces. This, it is believed, might have had some influence on recent developments, especially in relation to the growth of para-military policing in Britain. These arguments should be viewed with caution. There is no historical evidence to support any assertion that the colonies were testing grounds for policing ideas destined for mainland England. Moreover, whereas it could be argued that the British police today are close to becoming carbon copies of their colonial counterparts, there is nothing to sustain the claim that these developments are informed directly by the colonial experience. However, a link could possibly be found in the fact that the issues that led to the development of imperial policing in the colonies are similar to those that have shaped the development of policing in Britain since the 1970s, under the political leadership of the British Conservative Party. These include the need to manage the unpredictable crises of capitalism, including the need to control the 'dangerous classes' or the 'enemies within', in order to protect the socio-economic and political interests of the ruling classes. The consequence for modern Britain has been a notable drift towards colonial-like policing methods designed to achieve the same results (see Fine & Millar 1985). After all, specific socio-political and economic environments produce specific policing styles. Authoritarian governments thrive upon authoritarian policing. A common denominator, it appears, is the Tories' habit of authoritarianism. As Brodgen noted:

> Perhaps what were previously considered to be aberrations from the norm of police work – such as the use of aggressive Police Support Units and of 'alien' white police officers in the black ghettos in the British mainland of the 1980s, may in fact be central to British practice (Brodgen 1987b: 181).

What is being witnessed in Britain, therefore, is not a crude transfer of colonial policing styles or an unmistakable replay of colonial policing but a consolidation of conservative policing.

In relation to the other European colonial powers, there is no indication of any direct influence on their policing brought about by the colonial experience. The French Police, for example, have always been centralized, government controlled and essentially concerned with political control (Mawby 1992). In addition, there is a strong para-military element in French policing which is traditional and, therefore, could not be linked to the colonial experience. Political policing, central government control of the police and para-military policing are, in fact, established features of 'continental' policing (see Mawby 1990). If there was any influence of colonial policing on continental Europe, the institutions most likely to have been affected are the military organizations (for example, the French Foreign Legion), not the police forces. It is safe, therefore, to argue that the flow of policing ideas between France, Germany, Italy, Spain and Portugal and their colonies have not been mutual.

Summary and Conclusion

The study of colonial policing is now becoming an interesting area of inquiry in the debates on the policing of the world. It has been shown that colonial policing has distinctive features irrespective of the European colonizer involved; be it French, British, German, Spanish or Portuguese. The baseline is that policing the empires developed largely in response to several imperial demands, the most important of which was the global expansion of capitalism, particularly in the nineteenth century, and the need to control international markets in raw materials as well as outlets for Europe's industrial goods. As Anderson and Killingray (1991) argued, the police forces that eventually emerged in the colonies were essentially 'hybrids', with many having characteristics that did not mirror police models in the 'mother-country' but were shaped by colonial events and needs. A dual system of policing was adopted with civil policing featuring mostly in settlement colonies and a mixture of civilian and militaristic policing in the protectorates.

The impact of colonial policing on the colonized are many and varied. The link between policing and military action in the pacified territories, and the use of the colonial police forces generally to maintain unfavourable colonial tax and labour policies earned them the reputation of being nothing but instruments of state coercion, representing an unquestionable political authority and existing only to serve the political and economic interests of the colonialists. Incidents of police brutality, corruption, violence, murder and abuse of power punctuated almost every decade of colonial police history. The political image of the colonial police was most visible during the period of decolonization when development in colonial policing shifted rapidly towards political policing against the 'enemies' of the colonial states. However, the colonial policing legacy did not disappear in the developing world after independence, even in those post-colonial states that adopted anti-colonial revolutionary governments. Many post-colonial states continued in the colonial tradition of political policing, using the police as the most visible symbol of political power and control, to legitimize and entrench largely authoritarian governments. Thus, in many respects, the post-colonial police forces, like their colonial predecessors, are still misused and abused. The question of their autonomy is yet to be resolved in constitutional arrangements that emphasize government control. Various accounts of the police in Africa continuing in the colonial tradition as agents of the state against trade unionists, students and political opponents, persist. Similar use of the police for political ends are visible in the former Spanish, Portuguese and French colonies in Africa, Central and Latin America. In a nutshell, the strategic position that the police occupied in the colonization process together with their operation as an arm of authoritarian governments ever since have enabled them to consolidate their position as an instrument of the central state which functions to perpetuate existing power relations in the interest of the different factions of the post-colonial political classes.

Evidence of 'imperial linkage' in policing are clear in terms of the export of policing ideas from Europe to the colonies, particularly after their independence. On the one hand, French, Portuguese and Spanish models of policing were adopted in many of their former colonies. Former British colonies in Africa and India, on the other hand, adopted centralized policing systems, quite different from the police system in Britain. Whilst central government control of the police appears to be appropriate for most post-colonial societies, especially those with a history of interference in politics of ethnic and religious sentiments, it simply reinforces the colonial image of the police as a government force.

The notion that colonial policing might have influenced the development of policing in the 'mother countries', however, needs further proof. With regards to France, Germany, Spain and Portugal, there is no direct indication of a transfer of policing ideas from the colonies to the mother countries. Similarly, there is no evidence to back up the argument of some British historians that the colonial experience significantly influenced current developments in contemporary British policing. What is defensible is the similarity in the issues underpinning policing in the colonies and in England today. Political policing, racist policing, the use of the police to suppress workers, centralization of police operations and their link directly with central government are features of 'Tory policing' both in the colonies and now in modern Britain. Hence, it is argued that the link appears to be the Tories' habit of authoritarianism. As Brodgen (1987b) argued, these so-called new developments in Britain could, perhaps, be common features of British policing, wherever it is practised. Nevertheless, the colonial tradition did have far-reaching consequences for the development of policing in the world. For example, it led to the global transfer of western policing ideologies and technology to the developing world. It has also meant, however, the imposition of a global impression of policing as a government force and not a public service. Lack of police autonomy and democratic accountability, and the restriction of police roles mainly to law enforcement are colonial traditions that are still upheld in most post-colonial countries today. As Anderson & Killingray (1991) argued, although African police forces have developed technologically as a result of the colonial experience, this development is yet to be matched by an equally progressive move towards policing by consent. However, whilst the form that the democratic accountability of the police should take in multi-ethnic states, such as those in the developing world, is an issue that requires serious thoughts, the need to democratize the administration, management and control of the police cannot be ignored in any discussion of the future of policing in these countries. The outlaw of the local voice in policing in many African constitutions marginalizes the local populations from any democratic control of their police. Integrating effective local participation in police administration into the existing constitutional arrangements is a positive change that should be considered. Similarly, the need to diversify police roles to include more welfare duties and elements of crime prevention and community policing strategies, cannot be overemphasized in any debate on the future of policing in these countries.

However, there appears to be a general lack of political will, particularly in Africa, to make radical changes for the future. For many post-colonial African countries, the inherited colonial tradition is simple, manageable and perhaps cheap. For these countries, therefore, the crucial issues and priorities are those of the needed resources that would make the police more effective in their jobs and, perhaps, effect a total overhaul of the police image, to make them more acceptable to the peoples they should serve. Whilst structural changes are achievable, more so as western support and financial assistance have been substantial in recent years (for example, from the ODA in England), unfortunately, there is very little indication that the required political and legal changes are feasible in the near future.

Notes

1. The focus of the chapter is 'modern colonialism' beginning with Portuguese and Spanish colonization of South America in the fifteenth century and extending up to the early twentieth century. Other forms of colonization before the fifteenth century are not considered.
2. It was only after the first world war that the *Force Publique* was re-organized into two sections, consisting of a military wing and a para-military police force or *gendarmerie* (Cornevin 1967).
3. Examples of these local government administrators included the 'warrant chiefs' in British Eastern Nigeria, the *akidas* in German Tanzania, the Eritrean and Somalian *askaris* in Fascist Ethiopia and the Indian *alcalde embarrados* (the staff-bearing magistrates) in Spanish Latin America.
4. See also PRO CO 1037/28: 'Native Authority police forces – Northern Rhodesia; PRO CO 1037/32: Reorganisation of Somali Police Force 1955–6'.
5. For example, in the mid-1950s, there was in French West Africa, one gendarme per 6,000 inhabitants and 15,000 square kilometres (Thompson & Adloff 1969: 232).
6. PRO FO 84/2111: MacDonald to Sir Percy Anderson. Private letter, 8 August 1891.
7. Northern Nigeria: Report for the Period from 1st January to 31st March 1901, *British Parliamentary Papers*, 1902 cd. 788–16, p.10.
8. Northern Nigeria: Report for the period from 1st January to 31st March, *British Parliamentary Papers*, 1902 cd. 788–16, p.11.
9. Since Germany lost all her colonies in 1914, the European countries that took over her colonies (mainly France) super-imposed their own systems of policing on the former German colonies.
10. The DPF deals with planning, national co-ordination, technical services, maritime, air, drug trafficking, national security, public order, censorship and the collection and dissemination of police intelligence (Weis, *et al.* 1975: 376).
11. See for example PRO CO 1015/224: Minutes by Sir Charles Jeffries on 'functions of the Federal Police Service, Central African Federation 1952–1953', 18 December 1952; PRO CO 1037/48: 'Nigerian Police Force: establishment and strength, 1956'.
12. During the Nigerian First Republic, the regionally controlled local government and 'native' administration police forces were used as instruments of oppression in the hands of ethnically-controlled regional governments in a bitter political struggle against political opponents (see Post K.W.J. 1963, Mackintosh 1966, Sklar 1963).
13. See for example, The Police Act (The Gambia) 1966, s.3; The Police Force Ordinance (Tanzanian) Cap 322, s.3; The Constitution of the Republic of Ghana, 1979, s.172(1) (2); The Police Ordinance (Sierra Leone), 1950 s.3; The Constitution of the Federal Republic of Nigeria, 1989, (suspended), s.212(1); The Constitution of Uganda, 1963, s.80(1); The Police Ordinance (Malawi) Cap 64 s.3; The Laws of Botswana (Cap 63 part II s.2), Swaziland, (Cap. 93 s.2) and Lesotho (Proclamation No 27, 1957, s.2).
14. See for example, The Constitution of the Republic of Ghana 1979, s.172 & 174; The Constitution of the Federal Republic of Nigeria, 1989 (suspended), s.213(1); The Police Ordinance (the Sudan) 1954, s.5 & 8; The Constitution of Malawi, s.92; The Laws of Botswana (Cap 63, part II s.3), Swaziland (Cap 93, s.3) and Lesotho (Proclamation No 27, 1957, s.3). In some countries, these powers are often exercised with the assistance of national political bodies like 'police councils'.

15. See for example, The Police Ordinance (Zambia) 1953, Cap 44, s.39(1); The Police Ordinance, 1950 (Sierra Leone), s.6; The Police Ordinance (Malawi) Cap 64, s.7; The Police Ordinance (Kenya) Cap 84, s.4(1) (2); The Police Act (Swaziland) 1957, s.5(1); The Police Ordinance (The Sudan) 1954, s.5; The Constitution of Uganda 1963, s.80(3).

16. See for example, The Constitution of Uganda, 1963, s.8. Similar provisions exist in the constitutions of Kenya, Tanzania, Nigeria and Ghana.

17. See for example, The Police Act (The Gambia) 1966 s.6; The Constitution of Uganda, s.8; The Police Ordinance (The Zambia), Cap 44 1953, s.7(1); The Police Force Ordinance (Tanzania) Cap 322, s.8(1) (2); The laws of Botswana, Cap 63, Part II s.4; Swaziland, Cap 93 s.4 and the Laws of Lesotho Proclamation No 27 of 1957 s.5(1). See also the Nigerian case of *State v Commissioner of Police Anambra State* [1982] 2 N.C.R. 252.

Bibliography

Adeleye, R.A. 1977. *Power and diplomacy in Northern Nigeria 1804–1906*. London: Longman.

Afigbo, A.E. 1972. *The Warrant Chiefs: indirect rule in south-eastern Nigeria 1891–1929*. London, Longman.

Alden, D. 1968. *Royal government in colonial Brazil with special reference to the administration of the Marquis of Lavraido, viceroy 1769–1779*. Berkeley and Los Angeles: University of California Press.

Anderson, D.M. 1991. Policing, prosecution and the law in colonial Kenya. In *Policing the empire: government, authority and control 1830–1940*, D.M. Anderson & D. Killingray (eds), 183–200. Manchester and New York: Manchester University Press.

Anderson, D.M. & D. Killingray (eds) 1991. *Policing the empire: government, authority and control 1830–1940*. Manchester and New York: Manchester University Press.

Anderson, D.M. & D. Killingray (eds) 1992. *Policing and decolonisation: politics, nationalism and the police 1917–1965*. Manchester and New York: Manchester University Press.

Anene, J.C. 1966. *Southern Nigeria in transition 1885–1906: theory and practice in a colonial protectorate*. Cambridge: Cambridge University Press.

Arnold, D. 1992. Police power and the demise of British rule in India, 1939–47. In *Policing and decolonisation: politics, nationalism and the police 1917–1965*, D.M. Anderson & D. Killingray (eds), 42–61. Manchester and New York: Manchester University Press.

Austen, R.A. 1968. *North-western Tanzania under German and British rule: colonial policy and tribal politics*. Connecticut: New Haven.

Banda, H.K. 1971. Introduction. In *A history of the Malawi police force*. Marlow: C. Zomba.

Bidwell, R. 1973. *Morocco under colonial rule: French administration of tribal areas 1912–1956*. London: Frank Cass.

Black, J.K., H.I. Blutstein, J.D. Edwards, K.T. Johnston, D.S. McMorris 1976. *Area handbook for Cuba*. Washington DC: US Government Printing Office.

Bley, H. 1971. *South-West Africa under German rule 1894–1914*. English edn. London: Heinemann.

Brodgen, M. 1987a. The emergence of the police: the colonial dimension. *The British Journal of Criminology* **27** (1), 4–14.

Brodgen, M. 1987b. An act to colonise the internal lands of the island: empire and the origins of the professional police. *International Journal of the Sociology of Law* **15**, 179–208.

Cain, M. 1979. Trends in the sociology of police work. *International Journal of the Sociology of Law* **7**, 143–67.

Calvert, P. 1973. *Mexico*. London: Ernest Benn Ltd.

Carter, M. & O. Marenin 1977. Police in the community: perceptions of a government agency in Nigeria. *African Law Studies* **9**, 28.

Cole, B.A. 1988. *Police power and accountability in the Nigerian criminal process*. PhD thesis, Centre for Criminology, Department of Law, University of Keele, England.

Cole, B.A. 1990a. An experience in a Nigerian police station. *Police Journal* **63** (4), 312–20.

Cole, B.A. 1990b. Rough justice: criminal proceedings in Nigerian magistrates courts. *International Journal of the Sociology of Law* **18** (3), 299–316.

Cole, B.A. 1995. Democratisation and law enforcement. Paper presented at the conference on 'Transitions in West Africa – Towards 2000 and Beyond', University of Central Lancashire, Preston.

Coquery-Vidrovitch, C. 1969. French colonization in Africa to 1920: administration and economic development. In *Colonialism in Africa 1870–1960: the history and politics of colonialism 1870–1914*, Vol. 1, L.H. Gann & P. Dignan (eds) 165–98 Cambridge: Cambridge University Press.

Cornevin, R. 1967. De la force publique a l'armee nationale congolaise. *Le Mois en Afrique* **14** (Feb), 74–112.

Crowder M. 1968. *West Africa under colonial rule*. London: Hutchinson.

Davis, H.E. 1968. *History of Latin America*. New York: The Ronald Press Company.

Davis, J. 1985. Review of Emsley, policing and its context. *International Journal of the Sociology of Law* **13**, 293–5.

Deschamps, H. 1962. *Traditions orales et archives au Gabon*. Berger-Levrault: Paris.

Dike, K.O. 1956. *Trade and politics in the Niger Delta 1830–1885*. Oxford: Clarendon Press.

East, R. 1939. *Akiga's story*. Oxford: Oxford University Press.

Fagg, J.E. 1963. *Latin America: a general history*. New York: The Macmillan Company:

Fieldhouse, D.K. 1973. *Economics and empire 1830–1914*. London: Cox & Whyman.

Fine, B. & R. Millar (eds) 1985. *Policing the miners' strike*. London: Lawrence & Wishart.

Firth, S.G. 1972. The New Guinea Company 1885–1899: a case of unprofitable imperialism *Historical Studies* **15** (3), 61–77.

Flint, J.E. 1969. Nigeria: the colonial experience from 1880 to 1914. In *Colonialism in Africa 1870–1960: the history and politics of colonialism 1870–1914*, Vol. 1, L.H. Gann & P. Dignan (eds) 220–60 Cambridge: Cambridge University Press.

Galdemes, L. 1964. *A history of Chile* translated and edited by I.J. Cox. New York: Russell & Russell.

Gide, A. 1927. *Voyages au Congo*. Paris: Gallimard.

Grundlingh, A. 1991. 'Protectors and friends of the people'?: the South African Constabulary in the Transvaal and the Orange River colony, 1900–1908. In *Policing the empire: government, authority and control 1830–1940*, D.M. Anderson & D. Killingray (eds), 168–82. Manchester and New York: Manchester University Press.

Gutteridge, W.F. 1970. Military and police forces in colonial Africa. In *Colonialism in Africa 1870–1960: the history and politics of colonialism 1914–1960*, Vol. 2, L.H. Gann & P. Dignan (eds) 286–319. Cambridge: Cambridge University Press.

Hillyard, P. 1987. The normalisation of special powers: from Northern Ireland to Britain. In *Law, order and the authoritarian state: readings in critical criminology*, P. Scraton (ed.) 279–312. Milton Keynes: Open University Press.

Igbinovia, P.E. 1985. Police misconduct in Nigeria. *Police Studies* **8**, 111–22.

Iliffe, J. 1969. *Tanganyika under German rule 1905–1912*. Cambridge: Cambridge University Press.

Jeffries, C. Sir. 1952. *The colonial police*. London: Max Parish.

Joffe, H. 1978. The state in post-colonial societies: an overview of the works of Alavi, Saul, Shivji, Mamdani and Leys. *African Perspectives* **7**, 27–37.

Johnson, H. 1991. Patterns of policing in the post-emancipation British Caribbean, 1835–95. In *Policing the empire: government, authority and control 1830–1940*, D.M. Anderson & D. Killingray (eds), 71–91. Manchester and New York: Manchester University Press.

Killingray, D. 1986. The maintenance of law and order in British colonial Africa. *African Affairs* **85** (340), 411–37.

Killingray, D. 1991. Guarding the extending frontier: policing the Gold Coast 1865–1913. In *Policing the empire: government, authority and control 1830–1940*, D.M. Anderson & D. Killingray (eds), 106–25. Manchester and New York: Manchester University Press.

Levene, R. 1963. *A history of Argentina*. New York: Russell and Russell Inc.

Leys, C. 1976. The over-developed post-colonial state: a re-evaluation. *Review of African Political Economy* **5**, 39–48.

Loveman, B. 1979. *Chile: the legacy of Hispanic capitalism*. New York: Oxford University Press.

Mackintosh, J.P. 1966. *Nigerian government and politics*. London: George Allen & Unwin Ltd.

Mawby, R.I. 1990. *Comparative policing issues*. London: Unwin Hyman.

Mawby, R.I. 1992. Comparative police systems: searching for a continental model. In *Criminal justice: theory and practice*, K. Bottomley, T. Fowles, R. Reinder (eds), 108–32. London: BSc/ISTD.

McCracken, J. 1992. Authority and legitimacy in Malawi: policing and politics in a colonial state. In *Policing and decolonisation: politics, nationalism and the police 1917–1965*, D.M. Anderson & D. Killingray (eds) 158–86. Manchester and New York: Manchester University Press.

Nasson, B. 1991. Bobbies and Boers: police, people and social control in Cape Town. In *Policing the empire: government, authority and control 1830–1940*, D.M. Anderson & D. Killingray (eds), 236–54. Manchester and New York: Manchester University Press.

Newbury, C.W. 1965. *British policy towards West Africa: select documents 1786–1894*. Oxford. Clarendon Press.

Newbury, C.W. 1971. *British policy towards West Africa: select documents 1875–1914*. Oxford: Clarendon Press.

Newitt, M. 1981. *Portugal in Africa: the last hundred years*. London: C. Hurst and Co.

Nunn, F.M. 1976. *The military in Chilean history. Essays on civil-military relations 1810–1973*. Albuquerque: University of Mexico Press.

Odekunle, F. 1979. The Nigeria police force: a preliminary assessment of functional performance. *International Journal of the Sociology of Law* **7**, 61–85.

Osborne, M.E. 1969. *The French presence in Cochin-china and Cambodia: rule and response 1859–1905*. Ithaca: Cornell University Press.

Perez, L.A. Jr. 1993. Cuba c. 1930–1959. In *Cuba: a short history*, L. Bethell (ed.) 57–93. Cambridge: Cambridge University Press.

Post, K.W.J. 1963. *The Nigerian federal elections of 1959*. London: Nigerian Institute of Social & Economic Research.

Prado, C. Jr. 1967. *The colonial background of modern Brazil*. Berkeley and Los Angeles: University of California Press.

Rafalski, H. 1930. *Vom niemandsland zum ordnungsstaat geschichte der landespolizei*. Berlin.

Rathbone, R. 1992. Political intelligence and policing in Ghana in the late 1940s and 1950s. In *Policing and decolonisation: politics, nationalism and the police 1917–1965*, D.M. Anderson & D. Killingray (eds) 84–104. Manchester and New York: Manchester University Press.

Robb, P. 1991. The ordering of rural India: the policing of nineteenth-century Bengal and Bihar. In *Policing the empire: government, authority and control 1830–1940*, D.M. Anderson & D. Killingray (eds), 126–50. Manchester and New York: Manchester University Press.

Roberts, S.H. 1963. *The history of French colonial policy 1870–1925*. London: Frank Cass and Company Ltd.

Robinson, R. & J. Gallagher 1975. *Africa and the Victorians*, 2nd edn. London. Macmillan.

Russell-Wood, A.J.R. (ed.) 1975. *From colony to nation: essays on the independence of Brazil*. Baltimore: The John Hopkins University Press.

Sbacchi, A. 1985. *Ethiopia under Mussolini: fascism and the colonial experience*. London: Zed Books Ltd.

Sklar, R.L. 1963. *Nigerian political parties*. Princeton, New Jersey: Princeton University Press.

Sklar, R.L. 1979. The nature of class domination in Africa. *Journal of Modern African Studies* **17** (4), 531–52.

Smith, W.D. 1978. *The German colonial empire*. Chapel Hill: University of North Carolina Press.

de Souza, A. 1972. The cangaco and the politic of violence in northeast Brazil *In Protest and resistance in Angola and Brazil*, R.H. Cihilcote (eds), 109–31 Berkeley. Los Angeles: University of California Press.

Stanford Research Institute 1969. *Area handbook for Libya*. Washington DC: US Government Printing Office.

Stark, F.M. 1986. Theories of contemporary state formation in Africa: a re-assessment. *Journal of Modern African Studies* **24** (2), 335–47.

Suret-Canale, J. 1971. *French colonialism in tropical Africa 1900–1945*. Translated from the French version by Till Gotheiner. London: C. Hurst and Company.

Tamuno, T. 1970. *The Police in modern Nigeria 1881–1965*. Ibadan: University of Ibadan Press.

Thompson, V. & R. Adloff 1960. *The emerging states of French equatorial Africa*. Stanford, California: Stanford University Press.

Thompson, V. & R. Adloff 1969. *French West Africa*. New York: Greenwood Press Publishers.

Throup, D. 1992. Crime, politics and the police in Kenya, 1939–63. In *Policing and decolonisation: politics, nationalism and the police 1917–1965*, D.M. Anderson & D. Killingray (eds) 127–57. Manchester and New York: Manchester University Press.

US Naval Intelligence Division, 1943. *Indo China*. Geographical Handbook Series. BR 510 (Restricted).

Ukpabi, S.C. 1966. The origins of the West African Frontier Force. *Journal of the Historical Society of Nigeria* **3** (3), 485–501.

Uzoigwe, G.N. 1985. European partition and conquest of Africa: an overview. In *Africa under colonial domination 1880–1935*, A. Adu Boahen (ed.) 19–44. General History of Africa Vol. 7. UNESCO.

Vianna, O. 1949. *Instituicoes politicas Brasileiras*. Rio de Janeiro: Livraria Jose Olympio Editora.

Wasikhongo, J.M.N. 1976. The role and character of police in Africa and western countries: a comparative approach to police isolation. *International Journal of the Sociology of Law* **4**, 383–96.

Weis, T.E., J.K. Black, H.I. Blusten, K.T. Johnston, D.S. McMorris, 1975a. *Area handbook for Brazil*. Washington DC: US Government Printing Office.

Weis, T.E., J.K. Black, H.I. Blusten, K.T. Johnston, D.S. McMorris 1975b. *Area handbook for Mexico*. Washington DC: US Government Printing Office.

Whitaker, D.P., J.M. Heimann, J.E. MacDonald, K.W. Martindale, R.S. Shinn, C. Townsend 1973. *Area handbook for the Khmer Republic (Cambodia)*. Washington DC: US Government Printing Office.

Willis, J. 1991. Thieves, drunkards and vagrants: defining crime in colonial Mombasa, 1902–32. In *Policing the empire: government, authority and control 1830–1940*, D.M. Anderson & D. Killingray (eds), 219–35. Manchester and New York: Manchester University Press.

CHAPTER 7

Policing in Japan:
East Asian Archetype?

F. LEISHMAN

Introduction

The difficulties facing any writer attempting to compare policing systems between
and within geographical regions are many and daunting, as other contributors to
this volume have already testified. Even in an ever more closely integrating Europe,
Western scholars and practitioners of policing, with few rare exceptions, still have
a tendency not to look much farther than their own national borders and when they
do so, they must generally confront and attempt to overcome the impediments of
meaningful access, cultural literacy, ethnocentric bias and, importantly, language.
Too often, comparative policing studies imply predominantly English-speaking country comparisons and far too frequently the Anglo-American experience and the
liberal-democratic traditions which spawned it are the principal referents and/or
taken-for-granted exemplars.

The same 'gang of four' methodological problems already mentioned, apply *a
fortiori* to considerations of policing in the East which (after Rozman 1991) is taken
here to mean the East Asian region, encompassing Japan, China, North and South
Korea, and the 'three little Chinas' of Taiwan, Hong Kong and Singapore. Access
to academics, particularly to those scholars native or otherwise who are likely to
make uncomfortably critical observations on human rights and equal opportunities
issues, has tended to be relatively restricted in most of the constituent countries of
the region. Though reunification with capitalist South Korea in the next century may
eventually prise open windows of opportunity for would-be comparative researchers,
North Korea remains for the time being secretive and largely impenetrable to outside observers. Meanwhile, the sheer vastness, populousness and diversity of China,
coupled with the formidable linguistic, cultural and political barriers which that
country presents, render it an extremely difficult choice of comparator. For example,

109

statistical information on crime in China has only recently become more readily obtainable and, while apparently exhibiting one of the lowest recorded crime rates in international comparisons, there is a broad measure of agreement that the publicly available data grossly under-represent the true extent of crime in China (Dutton & Lee 1993, Yang 1994). Qualitative data on Chinese policing, such as representations in officially sanctioned police procedural magazine stories (Kinkley 1993) and content analysis of official police newspapers (Fu 1994), may appear to indicate a tilt toward the goals of greater police autonomy and professionalism, but with a post-Mao 'structural legacy' of an extremely low police-to-population ratio of about 1: 1,400 (Dutton & Lee 1993), tight party control over policing seems likely to be in place for some time. One of the absorbing issues for the future will be the effect on policing in Hong Kong following the island's return to China in 1997, and of its consequent impact on other areas of Chinese settlement such as Taiwan and Singapore.

Notwithstanding the economic crises affecting the region in late 1997 and throughout 1998, it is generally agreed that the twenty-first century is still set to see an ascendant East Asia with Japan, along with a revitalized China, occupying pivotal positions in the affairs and attentions of the post-millennial world. It is therefore a timely point at which to reflect upon policing arrangements in Japan, which, in many ways, cast the capitalist developmental template which some in the region have already followed and which others are now emulating. The following section considers the historical background to the modern Japanese police system, then focuses on contemporary and emergent issues. The final part of the chapter returns to the broader question of whether policing in Japan is best understood as conforming to an identifiable 'oriental' model.

Continuity and Change in Japanese Policing

In one of his more recent contributions to the literature, Professor David Bayley noted that '[n]ational police forces have personalities just as the people they serve do' (1995: 87), noting later in the same piece that 'police institutions are not blank slates. Traditions count' (ibid.: 89). Drawing on a majestic historical sweep, Bayley argues persuasively that from the eighteenth century onwards, the development of police institutions has been characterized by borrowing and adapting models from elsewhere. In the world, as well as a regional context, policing in Japan offers an instructive case study in eclecticism, adaptation and tradition. It should be noted from the outset that, in contemplating policing in Japan, it is of paramount importance to be alive to the distinction between dyads such as *tatemae* (public behaviour) and *honne* (real feelings), and *omote* (front) and *ura* (back), which pervade Japanese society and inform our understanding both of its institutions and interpersonal relations. In Japan (as elsewhere in East Asia) choosing the appropriate 'face' for a particular occasion is a vital social survival skill and control mechanism, while losing face is an affront to be avoided at all costs (Hendry 1995).

Historical background

During the Edo era (1600–1867), Japan entered a period of self-imposed national isolation under the centralized administration of the Tokugawa shogunate. Confucian principles, imported from China in the seventh century, were consciously drawn upon to bolster an already minutely regulated feudal society based upon strict hierarchical principles (Hendry 1995). Tokugawa Japan possessed a fairly sophisticated policing apparatus, administered by personnel of the ruling *samurai* class, though neighbourhood groups of five households (*gonin-gumi*) were held collectively responsible for order maintenance in their areas. Precedent and individual decrees formed the basis of Japanese criminal justice until 1742, when the shogun Yoshimune promulgated the *kujikata osadamegaki*, a secret, two-volume compilation of acts and precedents which remained in force until the end of the Tokugawa period (Oda 1992). This outlined the functions of various officials and also permissible forms of torture used in extracting confessions, which the Japanese, like the Chinese, have long considered to be a prerequisite for criminal conviction. In spite of the harshness of many of the procedures and punishments laid down in the *osadamegaki*, officials evidently discharged their duties with discretion, restraint and leniency, sometimes colluding with suspects to 'bend' confessions in the direction of less serious or less shameful offences (Hiramatsu 1989: 123).

In the mid-nineteenth century, Japan was forced to face up to the fact that its future as an independent sovereign nation depended on its ability to 'catch up' economically, militarily and politically. The shogunate finally collapsed, the authority of the Emperor (Meiji) was restored, and Japan embarked upon a rapid modernization programme, borrowing and adapting what was seen as the 'best from the West' in agriculture, education, science and technology. The same approach was applied to policing and criminal justice, which became heavily influenced by models borrowed from continental Europe, notably France and Prussia, whose codified penal law, powerful procuracy and highly centralized police administration seemed natural choices to follow in the quest to meet both internal and external pressures for reform (Westney 1982, Mitchell 1992).

The Tokyo Metropolitan Police was formed in 1874, headed by Toshiyoshi Kawaji, a former samurai from Kagoshima who had earlier been despatched to Europe to examine policing arrangements there. Regarded as the Japanese police's 'founding father', Kawaji's view was that 'government should be seen as the parent, the people as the children and the policemen as the nurses of the children' (van Wolferen 1989: 183). Like its contemporary European counterparts, Japan's new police were charged with a wide range of administrative functions and a special brief for political surveillance. Control was consolidated in a powerful Home Ministry (*Naimusho*) and, on the recommendation of advisers from Berlin, a network of police-boxes was established in rural and urban areas in all prefectures of Japan, providing the highly centralized system with a prominent local presence. By the end of the Meiji period in 1912, there were over 15,000 rural residential police posts (*chuzaisho*) and urban neighbourhood offices (*koban*) in Japan (Ames 1981: 23), a combined total virtually equivalent to that of the present day.

Meiji Japan's first Criminal Code (1880) was based upon the French Code with a smattering of Belgian and Italian law, while the less liberal Prussia provided the pattern for its subsequent revision in 1907 (Oda 1992). The 1908 Prison Law (*kangoku ho*), established two sites for pre-trial detention; facilities run by the prison system under Ministry of Justice control, and 'substitute prisons' (*daiyo kangoku*), cells adjacent to police stations in which lengthy interrogations were and still are conducted (Bennett 1990, Mitchell 1992). A brief flowering of democracy in the 1920s withered all too quickly as Japan embarked upon the expansionist policies which were to culminate in involvement and defeat in World War II. As the decade wore on, the military-bureaucratic nexus assumed total control of government and judiciary and the police acquired additional responsibilities connected with censorship, regulation of public morals and mobilization for the war effort. A 'thought police' (*tokko*) combined with a reactivated *gonin-gumi* system became key elements in suppressing political heterodoxy until Japan's surrender in 1945 (Aldous 1997, chapter 2). Among other excesses and abuses, the period was characterized by 'fascism by the procuracy' (*kensatsu fassho*), which at its worst involved prosecutors and judges fabricating cases against dissidents from whom confessions had been forcibly extracted (Johnson 1972: 161).

The US Occupation of Japan (1945–52) set in train a number of reforms aimed at demilitarizing and democratizing the country. Key reform documents were the 1947 Constitution of Japan and the 1948 Code of Criminal Procedure, both heavily influenced by US law and both of which remain in force today. The pre-war Home Ministry was disbanded and a number of senior bureaucrats and police officers were 'purged'. The 1948 Police Act aimed to reconstruct Japanese policing along American lines through a radical decentralization programme, with municipal forces for towns with populations above 5,000 and a National Rural Police Force to cover the smaller towns and villages. Democratic control and political neutrality were to be maintained by the establishment of national and prefectural public safety commissions (*koan iinkai*). However, on the grounds of geography, cost-effectiveness, efficiency and – back to Bayley's opening quote – tradition, the measures were not a complete success.

Recentralization, though to a much lesser degree than had existed pre-War, was effected under the 1954 Police Act, which gave each prefecture and major metropolitan area (*todofuken*) its own force, while a National Police Agency (NPA) was established to facilitate central government oversight. Ames has described the resultant hybrid system as 'an imperfectly blended amalgam of the authoritarian, powerful and highly centralised . . . and the democratic and decentralized' (Ames 1981: 215), suggesting that the *honne* is closer to the former.

Contemporary structure and accountability

Long regarded as a country with exceptionally low crime rates (Adler, 1983), Japan, with over 124 million people densely packed in the habitable areas of its four main islands (Government of Japan, 1994), has one of the highest population to police officer ratios in the developed world at 561:1 (NPA 1995a: 108). Prefectural police personnel are, in the main, *local* government employees, while officers of the rank of senior superintendent and above are *national* public servants employed by the Tokyo-based NPA. The top positions in all 47 prefectural forces are held by NPA personnel.

The NPA is headed by Japan's highest ranking police officer, the Commissioner-General, and has responsibility for setting national standards of policing and drafting associated legislation. Other duties include the co-ordination of prefectural police activities, such as major criminal investigations and response to large-scale emergencies. The NPA is supervised by a National Public Safety Commission – an administrative committee chaired by a cabinet minister and comprising five other members who must not have been in police or prosecution-related public service in the previous five years. Commissioners serve for a five-year term and, although appointees of the Prime Minister, there is a stipulation that no more than three members may belong to the same political party. The Commission endorses basic policy, which the NPA in turn passes down to the prefectural forces, each of which is supervised by a public safety commission of three or five members depending on its size. Like their national counterpart, the local committees give formal approval to a broad policy agenda but may not specify operational details, though they do have a remit in disciplinary and licensing matters. Thus, as Ames notes, at both national and local level, public safety commissions 'ostensibly function as buffers between police and politicians to prevent bias and untoward influence, yet they do not insure public control over the police organisation' (1981: 218). The police (like bureaucrats in other Japanese public services) are very much considered to be the 'experts' who generally exert considerable influence over local as well as national policy-making (Neary 1992), though as Bayley notes, senior police officers are sometimes summoned before prefectural assemblies to answer questions about police performance and local crime issues (1991: 63).

At each prefectural police headquarters, activity is organized in core departments which are replicated throughout Japan; administration, community safety, criminal investigation, traffic, and security. The fundamental bases for day-to-day local policing, however, remain the urban *koban* and the rural *chuzaisho* to which about 40 per cent of the nation's officers are assigned and from which the 'service-to-the-citizen' face (Hoffman 1982) of the Japanese police is projected. According to Archambeault and Fenwick, this orientation is a manifestation of a management style which:

> creates an atmosphere which encourages teamwork and collective responsibility; the police officer is taught to see [his] efforts as contributing to the best interests of the police team, which is merely an extension of society itself (1985: 3).

That contrasts markedly with police in both South Korea and the United States which, they suggest, exhibit management approaches less participable than Japan's. While Bayley underlines the positive outcomes which may be generated by the 'chemistry of membership' of such an organization (1991: 65), initial inaction and unfortunate delays in responding to major crimes and incidents may be the negative obverse of the Japanese police's deliberative decision-making culture (McCarthy 1993).

Koban *activity*

The *koban* system has been the principal focus of academic field studies of Japanese police-work (Ames 1981, Bayley 1976, ibid. 1991, Murayama 1990, Parker 1984) and has attracted the attention of numerous Western police practitioners (e.g. Alderson 1984). The *koban*, with its reassuringly familiar red lamp (*akai monto*), is generally favourably portrayed as an ideal of 'communitarian' policing, nostalgically associated in the West with some long-lost golden age. Interestingly, there may also be similar wistfulness in fin de siècle Japan itself, as an editorial in the *Japan Times* newspaper seemed to suggest:

> The changes Japanese society is undergoing pose difficult new challenges for the nation's police that can best be met by all of us co-operating, Japanese and foreigner alike. A return to the days of the friendly neighbourhood police box – with an international flavour – would be a good place to start (*Japan Times*, 9 August 1992).

In the rural context, the *chuzai-san*, who lives with his family in a house behind the police office and whose wife shares to a significant extent in his work, is expected to integrate into the life of the community and cultivate the trust of local people. The *chuzai-san* and his wife are traditionally accorded considerable prestige and are often consulted about a range of family and personal matters, in addition to dealing with accidents and complaints. Incidentally the male pronoun is used here, because that reflects the actuality of the situation. Accounting for a mere 2.6 per cent of prefectural police officers in 1994 (NPA 1995b), women are still very much under-represented in Japanese policing: ethnic minorities are not represented at all. However, since the implementation of the Equal Employment Opportunity Law in 1986, the situation with regard to women is gradually improving. In 1990, out of 47 prefectures, only 31 were recruiting policewomen, two years later the number had risen to 43 (NPA 1992, ibid. 1994). Indeed there is some evidence to suggest that as the number of suitably qualified male applicants declines, more efforts are being made to recruit capable Japanese women graduates (see Brown *et al.* in this volume).

Chuzaisho still outnumber *koban*, but over recent years, their numbers have declined, reflecting both continued urbanization and rural depopulation, and the Japanese police's responsiveness to such population movements. Of approximately 3,200 cities, towns and villages in Japan, about a third are officially designated as depopulated areas (*kaso-chiiki*) (Kawai 1994). In 1990, there were 8,901 *chuzaisho* compared with 8,698 three years later, while in the same period, *koban* numbers rose from 6,392 to 6,495 (NPA 1991, ibid. 1995(b)). *Koban* vary in size and construction, blending in where they can. In slum and entertainment districts, for example, there exist *manmosukoban* ('mammoth' koban!) from which as many as 30 officers may patrol. These, however, are rare and the norm is a smaller two-storey station, with resting facilities upstairs and an office below, staffed on a 24 hour basis by a dozen or so officers working a three-shift rota. The scope of friendly service activity provided by *koban* officers is legendary: advising on addresses in Japan's largely unnamed streets; lending out unclaimed found umbrellas to commuters caught in showers; ensuring drunken *sararimen* get the last train home; and counselling on 'citizen's troubles' (*komarigoto sodan*). By the year 2020, over a quarter of Japan's 128 million people will be aged 65 or over (Arai 1994: 9), an estimated half of whom will be 75 or more years old: so *koban* officers may be expected to extend further their service involvement with the country's expanding 'silver generation'. Almost all *koban* produce mimeographed neighbourhood newspapers and, in many localities, officers run classes in the martial arts and other sports for children, a tried and tested means of reinforcing traditional Japanese values such as discipline, endurance and respect for authority. In addition to patrolling their areas on foot and on regulation pedal cycles, the *omawari-san* (literally 'honourable Mr/s go-around') visit households, shops and companies on their patch (*junkai renraku*). While the *tatemae* was that all premises were visited twice a year, the *honne* has for some time been, as Murayama's (1990) study suggested, rather different. Changing family and work patterns, not to mention increased social mobility and anonymity have made it difficult for officers to retain the continuity of contact that was possible in earlier decades. This raises the issue of how the *koban* system is adapting to the Japan of the twenty-first century.

The linkage of Japan's apparently low crime rates with the cosy neighbourhood orientation of the *koban* has become something of a commonplace (and often uncritically accepted) assertion. However, a series of distressing child murders in the late 1980s and early 1990s, followed by a postwar peak in 1993 of 1.8 million recorded penal code offences, concentrated many minds on the criminogenic consequences of Japan's 'thinning' social relations (NPA 1993). As the deputy director of the NPA's Community Policing Affairs Division stated in 1995:

> the demise of the sort of society based on shared territorial bonds has undermined the effectiveness of the koban system. Also, given the concern for protecting the privacy of individuals, it is now difficult to maintain the same kind of close relationship that used to exist . . . (quoted in Kondo 1995).

A package of reform measures has been put in place. Firstly, the NPA has set about promoting *koban* as 'community safety centres', embarking on a renovation programme which will provide most police-boxes with a meeting room geared towards residents' participation in crime prevention and other community meetings. Under police leadership, a raft of partnership projects and campaigns has been launched in an apparent attempt to regenerate community involvement in policing, including the establishment of *koban* and *chuzaisho* Liaison Councils. According to the NPA, the number of such councils had risen ten-fold from 6,125 in 1992, to 67,243 by the end of 1993 (NPA 1994 ibid. 1995(a)). Secondly, serious efforts appear to have been made to raise the profile of *koban* activity within the police organization. Patrol work has been elevated from sub-departmental status to become the core business of the renamed Community Safety Department, which received extended coverage in Chapter 1 of the 1994 *White Paper on Police* (*keisatsu hakusho*), a symbolically significant shift to a position more usually reserved for 'sexier' topics such as *boryokudan* (gangsters), crimes committed by foreigners, drugs and terrorism. A programme of police rank redistribution carried out over the last five years (Leishman 1994) has also sought to create double the number of assistant inspectors (*keibuho*), a substantial proportion of whom now work as co-ordinators of groups of adjacent *koban* in an apparent bid to maximize efficiency and reconcile competing public demands for both regular patrolling and a reassuring presence at individual police-boxes. The replacement of patrol officer and sergeants' posts with more senior ranks should boost morale and may add to the attractiveness of a police career at a time when there is a seeming reluctance among younger Japanese men to enter occupations which smack of any of the 'three k's' – *kitsui* (hard), *kitanai* (dirty) and *kiken* (dangerous). Thirdly, the NPA is apparently striving to augment *koban* resources by installing picture-phone 'robo-cop' systems and enhanced fax facilities, while at the same time re-employing retired officers as civilian '*koban* counsellors' to deal with routine matters and cover for patrol officers when they are out and about.

Systematic, scholarly evaluations of the progress and impact of these initiatives in the closing years of this century may offer instructive lessons for Japan and other societies in the next.

Crime, conformity and control

In spite of the recent upward trend in recorded crime, Japan's 30-year-old reputation as a 'country with safe streets' remains robust, with findings from the International Crime Survey (ICS) suggesting a victimization rate about 10 per cent lower than the European average (Mayhew 1994). However, a recent study drawing on criminal and other homicide statistics has questioned the extent to which the low crime image accurately reflects overall risks to public safety in Japan, and urges that future research should pay more attention to underlying political-economic rather than cultural factors (Fujimoto & Park 1994). That sentiment echoes Mouer and Sugimoto (1986) who argued that, typically, when seeking to explain Japan's low crime rate, insufficient weight has been ascribed to structural factors such as the significant private and voluntary sector involvement in law enforcement, a longstanding phenomenon in Japan (Mawby 1990, Miyazawa 1991). There has, rather, been a tendency among Western observers to focus on what Thornton and Endo (1992) dub the *haji* (shame) factor, on which Braithwaite (1989) elaborated for his important theory of symbolic 'reintegrative shaming'. This posits that shaming in Japan occurs in an optimal way: potent enough to prevent repeat offending, but not sufficient to stigmatize and push offenders into subcultural behaviour. Kersten (1993), however, suggests that subcultural groupings in Japan, such as *bosozoku* ('hotrodder') and *yakuza* (organized crime syndicate) gangs are, in fact, 'numerically significant and culturally visible', while journalist Karl Taro Greenfeld's highly readable *Speed Tribes* (1995) reveals an ugly *ura* to the *omote* of Japan as a highly conformist society, a phenomenon which was brought chillingly to the world's attention in Spring 1995 by the existence and activities of the apocalyptic *Aum Shinri Kyo* cult (see also Downer 1995).

While Japan's significant rate of suspension of prosecution (Castberg 1990), for example, may lend some support to Braithwaite's thesis, it is difficult to disagree with Professor Miyazawa (1993) that 'ethnographic studies comparing Japanese reality to that in other countries may affect and perhaps undermine the persuasiveness of [it]'. The author of the only academic observational study of criminal investigation work in Japan, Miyazawa (1992) believes that Japanese police investigators are probably less interested in reintegration than in extending the already considerable legal resources available to them to achieve crime control objectives. Prosecutors and detectives operate within a system which aims implicitly for 'resolution of all cases' (*zenken kaiketsu*) and, that an indicted suspect in Japan has 'literally but one chance in a thousand of avoiding conviction' (Bennett 1990: 67), is surely telling testimony of some measure of success. Under the *daiyo kangoku* system mentioned earlier, pre-trial detention of up to 23 days is possible, during which time suspects may be interrogated relentlessly and without access to lawyers. The system has been roundly criticized by legal academics and practitioners in Japan and elsewhere (Watson 1995). Given Japan's prominence in the manufacture and marketing of state-of-the-art audio-visual equipment, it is a strange irony that confessions, still very much seen as the 'king of evidence' (*shoko no o*), are not video-taped or tape-recorded, nor even recorded verbatim. Rather, investigators write up the results of their labours in statement form, which the weary suspect is expected to sign. It all seems somehow reminiscent of the *ginmi tsumari no kosho* (formal written confession) described in the eighteenth century *osadamegaki* and it is therefore unsurprising that Professor Hiramatsu asked:

> Has the modernization of the system . . . really completely reformed the *actual substance* of the criminal trials represented by Tokugawa criminal policies and the *fundamental nature* of the criminal policies that have been passed down from the Edo era? (1989: 128; emphasis in the original).

It is a question which is likely to be the subject of continued debate into the twenty-first century, as the fledgling duty attorney scheme (*toban bengoshi seido*), presently operated on a voluntary basis by Japanese Bar Associations, becomes more fully established, and as internal and external pressure for reform gathers momentum (Watson 1995). Having said that, however, there were indications in the wake of the Tokyo and Yokohama nerve gas attacks and attempted assassination of the NPA Commissioner-General in 1995 of a mood more inclined toward enhancement rather than curtailment of the investigative powers available to police, with the Japanese Justice Minister hinting that telephone tapping and undercover operations may be authorized by government in the future (Lloyd Parry 1995).

While it is not inappropriate to conclude of contemporary Japan that 'the protection of human rights has reached a highly advanced and sophisticated level' (George 1990: 107), it remains the case that the Japanese police, and in particular the detective branch, operate in a highly 'enabling' legal and cultural environment (Miyazawa 1992: 2–9), in which 'the concept of individual freedom is of secondary importance to the perceived necessity for public safety and social control' (Cleary

1989: 147). The tension between these conflicting claims will surely only be resolved once the 'dark cloud' to which Watson (1995) alludes has been dispersed. Finally, whereas studies of Japanese patrol activity have tended to portray a police service with strikingly different core philosophy and values, it would appear from Miyazawa's research that Japanese detectives have much in common with their Western counterparts with regard to their sense of justice and perceptions of, for example, 'good arrests' and appropriately condign sentencing. Furthermore, the tension between Packer's (1968) 'due process' and 'crime control' models of justice appears to apply to the handling of criminal cases in Japan also, as evidenced by the two ideal types of investigator identified by Miyazawa; the 'policemen's police' and the 'citizen's police':

> The 'policemen's police' refers to an investigative officer who acts with procedural restraint out of fear that the reputation of the police will be damaged. The 'citizen's police' refers to an investigative officer who plunges forward with bold investigations in response to citizens who demand the arrest of criminals and the reparation of injuries (Miyazawa 1992: 177).

Omote and *ura* at work yet again?

East Asian Reflections

In seeking to explain the economic success and public orderliness of Japan and other East Asian societies, politicians, economists and social commentators have increasingly turned to the shared cultural heritage of the region for clues. In the contemporary East Asian context, the legacy of Confucianism can be seen to have contributed significantly both to continuity and control, as well as to the dynamism of change, whether toward socialism or capitalism, as has happened variously within the region, a contrast nowhere more starkly illustrated than by the two Koreas (Rozman 1991).

The Confucian heritage

> The Master said, 'Guide them by edicts, keep them in line with punishments, and the common people will stay out of trouble but will have no sense of shame. Guide them by virtue, keep them in line with the rites, and they will, besides having a sense of shame, reform themselves' (*Analects*, II.3).

The teachings of Confucius and of his disciple Mencius are at the very heart of the Chinese intellectual tradition, and evoke many of the core values evident among the peoples of the East Asian region today. What is not being proposed here is some crude cultural reductionism which suggests that the sayings in the *Analects* account for the characteristics of modern East Asian societies, any more than the bible does for the West. However, as Rozman argues, in spite of its imprecision, the concept of 'Confucian values' can usefully be employed to embrace 'a complex of attitudes and guides to behaviour that spread from China' (1991: 7), and which can in turn be utilized to define the contours of social control in constituent countries of the region. Many minds were concentrated on this idea by the case of Michael Fay, an 18-year-old American youth who, in 1994, was sentenced to corporal punishment in Singapore for vandalism (Wiechman 1994). At the time, the Fay case stimulated much debate about Eastern versus Western approaches towards social control, epitomizing for many the relative social, moral and, by extension, economic decline of the Western way. Indeed, in an interview unrelated to the Fay case, Singapore's long-time leader Lee Kuan Yew opined that:

> Westerners have abandoned an ethical basis for society, believing all problems are solvable by a good government, which we in the East never believed possible . . . The fundamental difference between Western concepts of society and government and East Asian concepts . . . is that Eastern societies believe that the individual exists in the context of the family' (Zakaria 1994: 112–3).

It was a viewpoint which doubtless struck a chord with many in the West disenchanted with domestic perceptions of high crime, low productivity and fragmenting social cohesiveness. In comparing Western and East Asian control tendencies, Rozman (1991: 16ff) notes the emphasis in the latter on personalized 'moral suasion', while the former sets greater store on the rule of law and on institutional checks and balances. Broadly speaking then, whereas the East takes as its starting point the Confucian assumption of the fundamental goodness of human nature and the positive effects of benevolent actions and leadership, in the West more reliance is placed on legal institutions and *their* perfectibility. In terms of social relations, the East Asian worldview is orientated towards familism, paternalism and interdependence, with a strong work ethic and regard for seniority and hierarchy, with teachers being accorded pronounced respect, a key factor underlying the impressive educational attainments of pupils in Japan, South Korea and elsewhere in the region. By contrast, in the West, individualism, legality, independence and freedom are the prized attributes. Thus, while praising Confucian values for the discipline and determination of families, workers and schoolchildren in East Asia, Western commentators will allude to constraints upon and violations against the rights of individuals. Whereas the East Asian may tolerate extensive policing and social control provided they guarantee order, the Westerner, naturally more suspicious of state surveillance, may be prepared to accept higher crime levels as the trade-off for less intrusive policing and unwanted interference.

These embedded views can be traced back to differences between the more moralistic tenets of the Chinese tradition which emphasized ethical loyalty to one's family or group, in contrast to the stronger *legalistic* concepts which prevailed in medieval Europe and from which derived the notions of individual freedom and equality which flourished in eighteenth and nineteenth century Western Europe and North America. As noted in Mawby (1990), from as far back as third century BC China, Confucian teachings stressed the importance of the ethical (*li*) over the more formal (*fa*) dimensions of social control, and it is a view which resonates around the modern states of the region, where resort to law and litigation may still be interpreted as a shameful failure to maintain proper, harmonious social relations.

An oriental model of policing?

The dichotomy between legalism and moralism is fundamental to the typology of approaches to policing and social control offered by Bayley (1982); authoritarian, Anglo-Saxon and oriental. It is a taxonomy worthy of re-examination, not least because it constituted a rare, if not unique, attempt to construct a specifically 'Eastern' model of policing contrapuntal to an Anglo-American ideal.

According to Bayley, authoritarian systems are characterized by formal, often repressive social control by a state police which possesses a broad mandate to regulate the minutiae of social life, including even precursory criminality. Historical examples were located in continental Europe and the former Soviet Union, while contemporary manifestations exist in certain African and South American states. In the Anglo-Saxon model, said to be found in Britain, North America, India and Australasia, the police are less penetrative of society than their authoritarian counterparts and, while it is accepted that they do perform an array of 'servicing' tasks, police organizations are more generally geared toward emergency response and law enforcement than routine intervention in neighbourhood life. In oriental systems, argues Bayley, police are used as an important element in social control, but in contrast with the other two models, tend to maintain order through harnessing the forces of informal social control. Rather than swish the cloak of legal authority, they lead by example and persuasion, cultivating community involvement in crime control through extensive, service-style interactions with the citizenry. This conforms closely to the ideal of the *koban* and also with the mass policing movements in the People's Republic of China, which range from 'help and education' groups composed of teachers and other community figures to 'aged persons' associations geared towards the prevention of crime and maintenance of public order. However, as Sun and Ching (1993) note, some of the latter exist in name only and, as such, may tell us more about the failings of official policing in China rather than its success.

While he never made claims of completeness, the adequacy of Bayley's troika as a comprehensive typology of world policing styles is clearly open to question. Where, for instance, do contemporary Western and Northern European models of policing fit in? Its validity was further criticized by Brewer *et al.* (1988: 227–30) on the grounds that its implicit assumption of homogeneity of policing style between geographically and culturally contiguous states, though seductive, is misleading and fails adequately to explore either the relationship between police and state or, importantly, the mix of social control styles which might be encountered within the same jurisdiction. If forced to choose between the three alternatives, it is a moot point as to whether Singapore, for example, more appropriately qualifies for the 'authoritarian' category (see, for example, Tremewan 1994) or the 'oriental' label, on account of its community policing set-up (see Bayley 1989). And how are we supposed to deal with the English common-law tradition which underpins Singaporean law (see Wiechman 1994), as well as that of the US: Anglo-Saxon? In a similar vein, Brewer and his colleagues (1988: 220) note that liberal-democratic states like Britain at various times redefine certain activities as threats to public order, and pass measures which may impinge on civil liberties in such a way as to qualify for the 'authoritarian' epithet. The Criminal Justice and Public Order Act 1994 which created new offences specifically targeted at those pursuing alternative lifestyles is an example of the kind of control which Brewer *et al.* probably had in mind. The Brewer *et al.* alternative typology which embraced three state control strategies (criminalization, accommodation and suppression) succeeds to some extent. However, by focusing too narrowly on public order policing, they neglected to deal with 'policing' in its widest sense, including the capacity of a society to police itself, an important element which Bayley did reflect upon. While Brewer *et al.* rightly suggested that cultural traditions and values are 'not passive agents' in the policing process, their discussion about the extent to which history and heritage may predispose a state toward particular styles of policing and social control mixes is underdeveloped.

Toward an alternative framework

The construction of *ideal-types* is a Weberian device for ordering concepts in such a way as to render comparisons possible, the underlying presumption being that in the real world *ideal-types* will be encountered not in pure form, but rather in clusters. Thus typologies enable us to make sense of combinations, facilitating identification of the dominant elements or style at a given point in time (Black 1976: 5). With inspiration from Black, Packer (1968), Rozman (1991) and Bayley's more recent work (1995), the Bayley (1982) and Brewer *et al.* (1988) typologies have been synthesized and realigned to produce a new typology (Table 7.1) which seeks to accommodate many of the dimensions incorporated in the earlier attempts. For example, the 'communitarian' tendency which in many respects comes closest to Bayley's oriental ideal, removes the concept from a specific geographical location, to identify instead an orientation which is evident in Western innovations such as community policing programmes, neighbourhood watch and diversion schemes, as well as in Japan's *koban* system. Moreover, in an age increasingly characterized by globalization (Zalewski & Enloe 1995), it seems somehow more appropriate and less ethnocentrically biased to suggest a 'democratic' orientation rather than an Anglo-Saxon one (Bayley 1995).

Following Bayley (1995), the typology is premised on the notion that a jurisdiction's policing institutions have a 'personality', in the way that individuals within each society do. Such personalities are not homogeneous, but rather multi-faceted and complex clusters, at times and in certain circumstances more inclined toward one tendency than others. Table 7.1 further takes as a starting point the idea that using policing as an access point may tell us more about a culture or society, than a culture or society can ever tell us about its policing.

Table 7.1   Three policing and society tendency types

	Democratic	Authoritarian	Communitarian
Authority type	rational-legal	central-bureaucratic	moral-paternalistic
Cultural orientation	individualism	statism	groupism
Mode of conflict resolution	forensic	repressive	conciliatory
Dimensions of public police	reactive detached suspected specialist	deterrent intrusive feared omnipotent	preventive pervasive respected generalist

Japan: archetypal or atypical?

The alternative typology is presented at this stage as little more than a crude pro-totype for possible future use by comparative policing researchers in the iden-tification and assessment of policing 'tendency clusters'. Each tendency is an ideal type, unlikely to exist in its pure form, but most likely to be found in clusters of two or more. It would seem that, in contemporary East Asia, the clusters tend to be hybrids of the authoritarian and communitarian types, while the Japanese cluster, like Western European, North American and Scandinavian combinations, contains all three tendencies, exhibiting as it does more of a democratic hue than other East Asian clusters. Comparing Japanese and South Korean policing, Lee noted:

> The Japanese force displays a 'softer' authoritarianism and functions within a more highly sophisticated 'new democracy', more supportive of it, and more law-abiding and conformist. The Korean 'democracy' has so far survived on much shakier ground than the Japanese (1990: 106–7).

While acknowledging that Taiwan and South Korea are becoming more tolerant of opposition, Rozman (1991) notes that East Asia's one-party political rule reflects a general lack of democratic institutions, including, one may surmise, democratic policing institutions:

> [o]nly Japan has found a way, within this context, for national leaders to resign after short terms in office and for rival parties to function as legitimate opposi-tion with an unquestioned opportunity to oppose and defeat the governing party.

As Bayley (1995: 89) comments, '[t]he character of government is more important for the reform of policing than the reform of policing is for the character of govern-ment' and, while it is by no means clear in what direction the awakened giant of China will turn, there is, according to South Korea's Kim Dae Jung, reason to be optimistic about the prospects for twenty-first century East Asia:

By the end of its first quarter, Asia will witness an era not only of economic prosperity, but also of flourishing democracy . . . The world economy's changes have already meant a greater and easier flow of information, which has helped Asia's democratization process (1994: 192–93).

As this chapter has attempted to illustrate, Japan possesses – albeit to varying degrees – all three of the characteristics of policing which, Bayley (1995: 89) argues, can contribute most to democratic nation-building; responsiveness to disaggregate public needs, adherence to principles of human rights, and open, participative and self-critical management. As such, its policing system is a worthy object of further comparative research and evaluation. While other Asian countries (Singapore, Thailand and Malaysia) and some American cities (Philadelphia, Detroit and also San Juan, Puerta Rica) have experimented with *koban* transplants, there has sadly been little in the way of meaningful cross-national comparative assessment. Generally speaking, compared to other police institutions which possess Bayley's core democratizing features, Japan's police has not been as open to external academic scrutiny and independent evaluation (Araki 1988, Miyazawa 1990). Notwithstanding the excellent efforts of bodies such as the National Research Institute for Police Science and of individual Japanese scholars, academic researchers within and outside Japan are still largely dependent on studies conducted in the 1970s and early 1980s for much of their source information on Japanese policing which, like so many of that country's other institutions, has become to a significant extent shrouded in an aura of 'cultural uniqueness'. As we have seen, many of the contemporary changes and debates surrounding policing in Japan are by no means unique and offer compelling reasons for the adoption of a more open policy towards independent empirical and comparative research by Japanese and foreign academics. It is sincerely to be hoped that late-twentieth century collaborative ventures in the basic and applied sciences between Japan and other countries will be mirrored by similar successful developments in the spheres of criminology and police science in the next.

Acknowledgements

The author would like to acknowledge the generous support of Japan Foundation Endowment Committee Grant No 802, and also thank Dr Chris Aldous, for helpful comments on an earlier draft.

Bibliography

Adler, F. 1983. *Nations not obsessed with crime*. Littleton, Colorado: Fred B. Rothman.
Alderson, J. 1984. *Law and disorder*. London: Hamish Hamilton.
Aldous, C. 1997. *The Police in Occupation Japan*. London: Routledge.
Ames, W. 1981. *Police and community in Japan*. Berkeley: UCLA Press.
Arai, E. 1994. Aging society through graphs. *Pacific Friend* (June), **9**.

Araki, N. 1988. The role of police in Japanese society. *Law and Society Review* **22**, 1033–6.

Archambeault, W.G. & C.R. Fenwick 1985. Differential effects of police organizational management in a cultural context: comparative analysis of South Korean, Japanese and American law enforcement. *Police Studies* **8**, 1–12.

Bayley, D.H. 1976. *Forces of order*. Berkeley: UCLA Press.

Bayley, D.H. 1982. A world perspective on the role of police in social control. In *The maintenance of order in society*, R. Donelan (ed.). Ottawa: Ministry of Supply and Services.

Bayley, D.H. 1989. *A model of community policing: the Singapore story*. Washington: National Institute of Justice.

Bayley, D.H. 1991. *Forces of order*, 2nd edn. Berkeley: UCLA Press.

Bayley, D.H. 1995. A foreign policy for democratic policing. *Policing and Society* **5**, 79–103.

Bennett, F. 1990. Pretrial detention in Japan: overview and introductory note. *Law in Japan* **23**, 67–71.

Black, D. 1976. *The behavior of law*. New York: Academic Press.

Braithwaite, J. 1989. *Crime, shame and reintegration*. Cambridge: Cambridge University Press.

Brewer, J. *et al.* 1988. *The police, public order and the state*. London: Macmillan.

Castberg, A.D. 1990. *Japanese criminal justice*. New York: Praeger.

Cleary, W. 1989. Criminal investigation in Japan. *Californian Western Law Review* **26**, 123–48.

Confucius 1979. *The Analects*. Harmondsworth: Penguin.

Downer, L. 1995. Coming of age in Japan. *Prospect*, November, 50–5.

Dutton, M. & T. Lee 1993. Missing the target? Policing strategies in the period of economic reform. *Crime and Delinquency* **39**, 316–36.

Fu, H.L. 1994. A bird in the cage: police and political leadership in post-Mao China. *Policing and Society* **4**, 277–91.

Fujimoto, T. & W-K. Park 1994. Is Japan exceptional? Reconsidering Japanese crime rates. *Social Justice* **21**, 110–35.

George, B.J., Jr 1990. Rights of the criminally accused in Japan. *Law and Contemporary Problems* **53**, 71–107.

Government of Japan 1994. *Japan Statistical Yearbook 1995*. Tokyo: Management and Coordination Agency.

Greenfeld, K.T. 1995. *Speed tribes*. London: Boxtree.

Hendry, J. 1995. *Understanding Japanese society*, 2nd edn. London: Routledge.

Hiramatsu, Y. 1989. Summary of Tokugawa criminal justice. *Law in Japan* **22**, 105–28.

Hoffman, V.J. 1982. The development of modern police agencies in the Republic of Korea and Japan: a paradox. *Police Studies* **5**, 3–16.

Johnson, C. 1972. *Conspiracy at Matsukawa*. Berkeley: UCLA Press.

Kawai, S. 1994. Turning things around: a depopulated town fights for its survival. *Pacific Friend* (April), 10–16.

Kersten, J. 1993. Street youths, bosozoku, and yakuza: subculture formation and societal reactions in Japan. *Crime and Delinquency* **39**, 277–95.

Kim, D-J. 1994. Is culture destiny? The myth of Asia's anti-democratic values. *Foreign Affairs* **73**, 189–94.

Kinkley, J.C. 1993. Chinese crime fiction. *Society* **30**, 51–62.

Kondo, H. 1995. Koban: now an English word. *Pacific Friend* (February), 17–19.

Lee, S-Y. 1990. Morning calm, rising sun: national character and policing in South Korea and Japan. *Police Studies* **13**, 91–110.

Leishman, F. 1994. Under Western eyes: perspectives on policing and society in Japan. *Policing and Society* **4**, 35–51.

Lloyd Parry, R. 1995. Baffled Japan may try phone taps. *The Independent* (21 April).

McCarthy, T. 1993. Police accused of bungling in kidnap tragedy. *The Independent* (23 August).

Mawby, R.I. 1990. *Comparative policing issues*. London: Unwin Hyman.

Mayhew, P. 1994. Findings from the International Crime Survey. Home Office Research & Statistics Department Research Paper No. 8. London: Home Office.

Mitchell, R.H. 1992. *Janus-faced justice*. Honolulu: University of Hawaii Press.

Miyazawa, S. 1990. Learning lessons from Japanese experience in policing and crime: challenge for Japanese criminologists. *Kobe University Law Review* **24**, 28–61.

Miyazawa, S. 1991. The private sector and law enforcement in Japan. In *Privatization and its alternative*, W.T. Gormley (ed.), 241–57. Madison: University of Wisconsin Press.

Miyazawa, S. 1992. *Policing in Japan*. Albany: State University of New York Press.

Miyazawa, S. 1993. The enigma of Japan as a testing ground for cross-cultural criminological studies. Revised version of paper presented at the 11th International Congress on Criminology, Budapest, Hungary.

Mouer, R. & Y. Sugimoto 1986. *Images of Japanese society*. London: KPI.

Murayama, M. 1990. *Keira keisatsu no kenkyu*. Tokyo: Seibundo.

Neary, I. 1992. Japan. In *Power and policy in liberal democracies*, M. Harrop (ed.), 49–70. Cambridge: Cambridge University Press.

NPA, 1991. *The police of Japan 1991*. Tokyo: National Police Agency.

NPA, 1992. *White Paper on the police 1991*. Tokyo: National Police Agency.

NPA, 1993. *White Paper on the police 1992*. Tokyo: National Police Agency.

NPA, 1994. *White Paper on the police, 1993*. Tokyo: National Police Agency.

NPA, 1995a. *White paper on the police, 1994*. Tokyo: National Police Agency.

NPA, 1995b. *The police of Japan 1995*. Tokyo: National Police Agency.

Oda, H. 1992. *Japanese law*. London: Butterworths.

Packer, H. 1968. *The limits of the criminal sanction*. Oxford: Oxford University Press.

Parker, L.C. 1984. *The Japanese police system today*. Tokyo: Kodansha International.

Rozman, G. 1991. The East Asian region in comparative perspective. In *The East Asian tradition: Confucian heritage and its modern adaptation*, G. Rozman (ed.), 3–42, Princeton: Princeton University Press.

Sun, G-C. & M-K. Ching 1993. Alternative policing and crime control in China. In *Alternative policing styles: cross-cultural perspectives*, M. Findlay & U. Zvekic (eds), 71–90. Deventer: Kluwer Law and Taxation Publications.

Thornton, R.Y. with K. Endo 1992. *Preventing crime in America and Japan: a comparative study*. New York: M.E. Sharpe.

Tremewan, C. 1994. *The political economy of social control in Singapore*. London: Macmillan.

Watson, A. 1995. The dark cloud over Japanese criminal justice: abuse of suspects and forced confessions. *Justice of the Peace and Local Government Law* (5 & 12 August) 516–37.

Westney, D.E. 1982. The emulation of western organizations in Meiji Japan: the case of the Paris prefecture of police and the keishicho. *Journal of Japanese Studies* **18**, 307–42.

Wiechman, D. 1994. Caning and corporal punishment: viewpoint. *CJ International* **10**, 13–19.

van Wolferen, K. 1989. *The enigma of Japanese power*. London: Macmillan.

Yang, C. 1994. Public security offences and their impact on crime rates in China. *British Journal of Criminology* **34**, 54–68.

Zakaria, F. 1994. Culture is destiny: a conversation with Lee Kuan Yew. *Foreign Affairs* **73**, 109–26.

Zalewski, M. & C. Enloe 1995. Questions of identity in international relations. In *International relations theory today*, K. Booth & S. Smith (eds). Cambridge: Polity Press.

PART 3

Policing Issues in International Perspective

Introduction

It is scarcely surprising to find that when we review policing issues of current topicality in England and Wales we find consistent references to the situation in North America. For example both Adler (1990) and Heidensohn (1992) look to the US for examples of how the place and role of women in policing might be improved. Similarly recent debates over the desirability of arming the English police were conducted against a backcloth of studies from the US where about 70 police are currently killed on duty each year (Maguire & Pastore 1994: 357), where the crime rate is markedly higher, and where an armed police raises equally controversial issues concerning civilian deaths (Binder & Scharf 1982, Fyfe 1981, ibid. 1988, Geller 1982; McKenzie & Gallagher 1989).

In some cases experiences from other countries receive equal attention. We have already noted the wealth of Japanese research on community policing, and debates on policewomen frequently refer to the Dutch experience where a previously poor record on the deployment of female officers has been transformed through a recent series of proactive policies (Cadman 1991). Nevertheless, lessons from further afield than the Anglo-American 'alliance' are not plentiful, partly because research has not been done, or perhaps not presented in English, partly because of a reluctance to look for ideas in more 'alien' police systems. As already discussed, such concerns are valid and we should take care before transplanting practices from one country to another. Nevertheless it may be advantageous to see how current issues are being handled in as wide a variety of societies as is possible.

Clearly a whole range of current policing issues are just as relevant in an international context as they are locally. If we wish to understand the dramatic increase in private policing (Shearing & Stenning 1987, Johnston 1992), it is important to realize that it is a trend common to most Western capitalist societies, and incidentally in Eastern Europe too. If we are concerned at the role of the police in public order situations it is important to see how far differences elsewhere in training, deployment etc. (Brewer *et al*. 1988, Roach & Thomaneck 1985) produce different results. When we consider the importance of occupational subculture(s) within the police (Reiner 1992), it may be useful to ask how far the structure and content of such subcultures is reproduced in other societies. And where the British police are prevented from striking, we may wish to evaluate this policy in the light of experiences from abroad where the police have struck (Ayres 1977, Clark 1975, Pfuhl 1983, Takala *et al*. 1979). This raises a difficulty in international research that has already been alluded to, namely the problem of definition. For example, where other nations allow their police to form unions, is this really much different from Britain, or is it more a matter of different ways of defining 'union'? And if we wish to assess police services for crime victims, do we mean by 'victim services' police services that are oriented towards welfare, help or support for victims or services that victims themselves consider appropriate? While we may assume the former, we should not then necessarily expect victims to evaluate the police more positively as a result of such changes!

The chapters in this section thus consider a range of issues from an international perspective. Inevitably there is a concentration on British and North American experiences, and evidence from developing societies is less readily available than that from other industrial societies, especially the capitalist West. Nevertheless, contributors raise a number of issues that can be further developed as more information becomes available. In Chapter 8 Barry Loveday, a prolific critic of shifts in the local accountability of the English police, considers the accountability issue in an international context. Almost immediately here the question of definition is raised, and Loveday's approach is distinct from that of earlier commentators. Regan (1984), in an earlier comparison of Britain, France and West Germany, defined accountability in terms of the extent of centralization, the scope of the police role and the degree of political control. In contrast Bayley (1983) identifies two dimensions on which accountability might be measured: internal/external and specialized/non-specialized. This provides a fourfold classification of accountability mechanisms, and Bayley then concentrates on one of these, external specialist mechanisms.

On one level, Loveday's approach is more akin to that of Regan. He focuses on accountability in terms of the extent to which the police are accountable politically at local level or are subject to centralizing influences, and takes England, the USA and France as examples where, according to previous critics, police accountability is distinctly different. However a closer review of the English, US and French police leads him to conclude that earlier models were of questionable validity in the past and may be even less appropriate today. One of the problems underpinning the topicality of police accountability is that of violence in police/public encounters, most notably where fatalities occur. While much concern in Britain in the 1980s arose where violent encounters have led to the injury or death of members of the public, a parallel theme has been the danger faced by the police in carrying out their duty while armed only with a truncheon, and recent debates over the routine arming of the police and moves towards provision of side batons and CS gas sprays reflect both a political acceptance that policing has become more dangerous and the need to ensure accountability to the law, through regulation of the appropriate use of additional weaponry. These issues, especially concerning the regulation of use of firearms (McKenzie & Gallagher 1989) are particularly familiar to an American audience (see above) and it is thus not surprising that Tank Waddington introduces Chapter 9 with a comparison of the British and US situations. However, Waddington then focuses on the English experience compared with that in Ireland and other colonies, and argues that the decision on whether or not to arm the police is symbolic of police/public relations and the context within which policing takes place. In this sense Waddington sees the arming of the colonial police and continental police systems as unproblematic. Rather it is the arming of civilian police forces, like the Japanese, Swedish and US, that is problematic, and while failing to fully explain this he argues that the enhanced armed capability of the police in the USA and Britain may reflect a shift in policy-makers' perceptions of the status of the policed. Essentially then, for Waddington the key issue in arming the police is not the relationship it has with crime (or violence) but what it implies about 'police', 'policed' and police/public encounters, reiterating many of the issues raised by Cole in Chapter 6. For many, community policing is the opposite of paramilitary policing. For others it is the panacea as old, crime-focused and detection-led policing strategies become recognized as failures (Bayley 1994). However, like the concept of paramilitarism community policing comes in various guises, broadly encompassing decentralization of policing, police involvement in community problem-solving, community participation in the policing process and a greater degree of community involvement in police decision-making (Mawby 1990). In Chapter 10 Mike Brogden, in a review of community policing initiatives worldwide argues that the concept is essentially American and that the failure to establish community policing in continental European (or ex-colonial?) systems reflects the very different histories and cultures of policing there. Moreover he argues that if community policing is as American as cherry pie, the cherries are somewhat bitter; where 'community policing involves engagement in a world of inequity' it commonly results in the shoring up of that inequity rather than adopting the more radical approach of community advocacy and a positive discriminatory deployment of resources.

One theme that is often implicit in discussions of community policing is the notion of the police as a service, with victims of crime as consumers of that service. However it is a common assumption of researchers that police services to victims have traditionally been inadequate. In Chapter 11 Rob Mawby reviews policies aimed at improving the 'victim-proneness' of the police and takes examples from recent cross-national research to demonstrate national differences in public perceptions of the ways in which the police handle crime victims. Intertwined with the conception of police as force or service is the place of women in policing. As Jennifer Browning, Anita Hazenberg and Carol Ormiston note, the notion of policing as concerned with violence and control has been one bar to the acceptance of women; policework is synonymous with 'man's work'. In a meticulous critique of the emergence of women in a wide range of police systems, Brown et al. provide a review that is both depressing and familiar. Lack of male applicants and the advent of police problems that could be identified as women's work resulted in the introduction of policewomen in different societies but at the same time ensured that women's role in policework was a peripheral one. While research, legislation and litigation have, along with other pressures, led to an improvement in the situation, the authors conclude that policing has impacted on policewomen, but policewomen have as yet had little effect on policing itself; at best they may have improved policing through their own particular approaches to their work. Not until women attain at least 25 per cent of staff – a level nowhere near achieved in any society – might women make a significant impact on the organization.

While there has to date been no research on women within the private police, it seems unlikely that their role in the private sector is any different. It is though important here to remind ourselves that the public sphere holds no monopoly over policework. Indeed as Les Johnston observes in Chapter 13, private policing has increased in recent years and in North America at least the private police outnumber their public counterparts. Even in Central and Eastern Europe it is possible to chart the dramatic rise of the private sector, with perhaps even more worrying implications given the apparent involvement of 'retired' and disgraced state police (often the former secret police) as the new entrepreneurs (Borger 1994; Janinski 1995). While, given the dearth of material, Johnston's discussion largely centres on Britain and North America, he argues that 'current expansion is linked to structural changes whose impact is global'. The paradox here, however, is that this structural uniformity leads to social diversity as policing is dispersed among a variety of providers. Johnston's chapter is a useful reminder of many of the lessons to be learnt from Part 3. Contributors have identified a number of issues that, far from being culturally specific, are common to police systems across the world. Yet the way these issues are defined and interpreted, the pulls and pushes that determine change, raise further questions for both policy-makers and academics. None of the contributors here offer too many solutions to the issues facing the police in different societies. What they do, instead, is to invite comparison, and, as Bayley suggested in Chapter 1, such comparison is the first step towards a clearer understanding of the issues involved.

Bibliography

Adler, Z. 1990. Hill Street clues; the US record on promoting women, *Personnel Management*, August, 28–33.

Ayres, R.M. 1977. Case studies of police stations in two cities, *Journal of Police Science and Administration* **5**, 19–31.

Bayley, D.H. 1983. Accountability and control of police: lessons for Britain. In *The future of policing*, T. Bennett (ed.). Cambridge: Cropwood Papers, Institute of Criminology.

Bayley, D.H. 1994. *Police for the future*. New York: Oxford University Press.

Binder, A. & P. Scharf 1982. Deadly force in law enforcement, *Crime and Delinquency* **28**, 1–23.

Borger, J. 1994. Poland's old security men strike again, *Guardian*, 15 November.

Brewer, J.D., A. Guelke, I. Hume, E. Moxon-Browne, R. Wilford 1988. *Police, public order and the state*. London: Macmillan.

Cadman, G. 1991. Going Dutch on equality. *Police*, June, 16–17.

Clark, G. 1975. What happens when the police strike? In *Criminal law in action*, W. Chambliss (ed.). Santa Barbara: Hamilton.

Fyfe, J.J. 1981. Observations on police deadly force. *Crime and Delinquency* **27**, 376–89.

Fyfe, J.J. 1988. Police shootings: environment and licence. In *Controversial issues in crime and justice*, J.E. Scott & T. Hirsch (eds). Beverley Hills, Calif.: Sage.

Geller, W.A. 1982. Deadly force: what we know. *Journal of Police Science and Administration* **10**.

Heidensohn, F. 1992. *Women in control? the role of women in law enforcement*. Oxford: Clarendon Press.

Janinski, J. 1995. Crime control in Poland: an overview. In *Crime control in Poland*, J. Janinski & A. Siemaszko (eds). Warsaw: Oficyna Naukowa.

Johnston, L. 1992. *The rebirth of private policing*. London: Routledge.

Mawby, R.I. 1990. *Comparative policing issues: the British and American experience in international perspective*. London: Routledge.

Maguire, K. & A.L. Pastore (eds) 1994. *Sourcebook of criminal justice statistics – 1994*. Washington, DCUS Department of Justice, Bureau of Justice Statistics.

McKenzie, I.K. & G.P. Gallagher 1989. *Behind the uniform: policing in Britain and America*. Hemel Hempstead: Harvester Wheatsheaf.

Pfuhl, E. 1983. Police strikes and conventional crime. *Criminology* **21**.

Regan, D. 1984. Police status and accountability: a comparison of the British, French and West German models. Paper presented at the European Consortium for Political Research, Salzburg.

Reiner, R. 1992. *The politics of the police*. Brighton: Wheatsheaf.

Roach, J. & J. Thomaneck (eds) 1985. *Police and public in Europe*. London: Croom-Helm.

Shearing, C. & P. Stenning 1987. *Private policing*. Beverley Hills, Calif.: Sage.

Takala, H., T. Makinenn, R. Siren 1979. The police strike in Finland. In *Police and the social order*, J. Knutsson, E. Kuhlhorn & A. Reiss (eds). Stockholm: National Swedish Council for Crime Prevention.

CHAPTER 8

Government and Accountability of the Police

B. LOVEDAY

Introduction

This chapter will look at current debates surrounding the accountability of the police service in England and Wales, and issues related to the government of the police in the United States and France. It will also consider the application of typologies of police systems first developed by John Stead in his influential study of the French police in the 1950s. These typologies have a continuing application in terms of developing models of police systems. Traditionally examples of the typologies developed by Stead have been relatively easy to identify and may, in part, have reflected the divide between European and Anglo-American police and legal systems. Stead was to develop three typologies of police systems which he classified as fragmented, combined and national centralized systems. Traditionally the police systems of the USA and Britain would be classified as respectively fragmented and combined where a large number of police forces operated in relative isolation or where local and central government were jointly responsible for the government of the police. Similarly, France has traditionally been identified as being a clear example of a national centralized police system. This relatively easy allocation of existing police systems to particular typologies made in the past may now need to be reviewed.

A central feature of government of the police remains the degree to which the police force can be made accountable for what it does. The debate on accountability has a long history and in terms of the typologies identified each demonstrates a different form of accountability. National police systems are, theoretically at least, made accountable at national political level, usually by way of clear ministerial responsibility to a national parliament or Assembly. In France, the Minister of the Interior has traditionally been identified as the senior minister responsible for what the national police do. In fragmented police systems, the accountability mechanism is much more local and diffuse. Here, as in America, many police forces will be viewed as being immediately accountable to the local electorate, if only because the sheriff may often be an elected official or may hold an office which is the gift of an elected mayor. In between the national centralized and fragmented models, lies the combined system where an element of balance between central and local government is designed to maximize the accountability and responsiveness of the police to the public interest. Yet it is apparent that each model and police system may not provide a degree of accountability which the public sees as appropriate. National police systems may be the responsibility of ministers who, as in France, have demonstrated until recently an ability to protect police interests (and perhaps their own), from effective parliamentary scrutiny (Hayward 1983). A local fragmented police system, as in the United States, may be prey to partisan interests, influence and advantage. In combined systems, the very division of responsibility may enable the central government to exercise power without responsibility as in Britain. The problem is, of course, compounded by the differing perceptions of what constitutes effective accountability in relation to the police service. As Geoffrey Marshall (1978) argued, the debate over police accountability revolved around the competing claims of direct and indirect accountability. In England, anyway, Marshall was to conclude that indirect explanatory accountability was probably preferable to direct or mandatory accountability, which might degenerate into over-partisan direction exercised by local political elites. Elsewhere concern over the independence of the police has not proved to be so salient. In national, centralized systems, the activities of the police will necessarily be ultimately a political responsibility. In fragmented systems the mechanism of accountability is likely to be direct and mandatory rather than indirect and explanatory. For a variety of reasons, which are explained in this chapter, the assumptions surrounding the status and accountability of police systems in the three countries reviewed may need to be challenged. Nevertheless the forms of accountability (either direct or indirect) remain of general application and provide a useful device in the development of a comparative analysis of a number of police systems.

The application of direct and indirect forms of accountability may also be linked to the extent to which central or local government is able to exercise some degree of influence over what the police do and to whom they are answerable. Thus in England and Wales, where traditionally the police are viewed (at least by themselves) as being highly accountable, if not the "most accountable police service in the world", the central-local government relationship has proved to be highly significant (Mark 1978). This has been particularly important during a period when there has been a dramatic change in the relationship and balance between central and local government and in which centralization of public services has proved to be the most lasting legacy of the conservative government from 1979 to 1997 (Jenkins 1995). Developments in Britain provide a contrast to France, where, over the same period, successive governments under the Presidency of Mitterand, were to encourage decentralization in a country which traditionally exhibited highly centralized control of public services. Both appear to contrast with the patchwork pattern of police responsibility identified in the United States, where a local fragmented system pertains. To what extent do these systems fit the typologies to which they have been traditionally assigned?

Accountability Issues in England and Wales

The problem of the accountability of the police has been a continuing issue of debate in Britain. Debate over the extent to which the police service could be held accountable either locally or centrally in England and Wales was to reach a high watermark during the 1980s as a consequence of local authority interest and also because of central government policies which remained, in the industrial relations field, heavily dependent on the police enforcing the 'rule of law'. Thus in the 1981 local elections to the Metropolitan counties, Labour groups were to identify the police service (probably for the first time) as a priority interest. Over a period of five years, until their abolition following the Local Government Act of 1985, the police authorities for these areas were responsible for opening up debate about policing and the police service to a degree never before experienced. In this they were undoubtedly helped by the serious disturbances which occurred in many Metropolitan areas in 1981. Beginning in Brixton, London in 1981 the disturbances quickly involved communities in Manchester, Birmingham and Merseyside. The later Scarman Inquiry was to discover that, at least in part, the riots had been a result of intimidatory police activity; and a collapse in police community relations particularly with the ethnic minorities. Equally disturbingly, the police service appeared to be caught completely off guard by the disturbances even though, as in Liverpool, the local authority departments were aware that social unrest could be expected (Merseyside Police Committee 1985).

The local authority interest in policing and the often conflictual relationships which were experienced by chairs of local police authorities and their chief officers provided an interesting backcloth to the debate over whether the police were made sufficiently accountable for their actions. While the British police claimed that theirs was essentially a local service which contrasted with the centralized police systems elsewhere in Europe, the reality did not seem to sustain this carefully nurtured image. If policing was local it was so because each police area was the immediate responsibility of a local 'chief constable'. Thereafter the ability of the local community or local authority to effectively influence policing strategy became somewhat tenuous, where much could depend on the personality and style of the chief police officer.

The ability of the chief officer to decide how (or whether) to respond to local requests concerning policing activity was (and remains) based on the convention of constabulary independence, which chief officers claimed was enshrined in both case law and the 1964 Police Act. As Geoffrey Marshall was to demonstrate in a series of highly influential (and insightful) monographs, the claims to the convention of constabulary independence, particularly in relation to case law, was itself extremely tenuous (Marshall 1965, ibid. 1978, ibid. 1985). In analysing both the Fisher Oldham case of 1930 along with the 1968 Blackburn case, Marshall (1984) was to conclude that neither provided a sufficiently strong argument to sustain the legal basis of constabulary independence while the oft-quoted Denning dictum which claimed that no one could instruct a chief constable as to his duty, could, he concluded be best described as 'obiter'.

The continuing argument over the accountability of the police was to be further fuelled by what appeared to be a systematic use by central government of the police service to achieve highly political outcomes during the course of the Miners' dispute of 1984/5 and the Wapping dispute of 1986. Although at the time the government (and police service) were to strenuously deny any overt political interference in policing the Miners' strike, the determination of a Thatcher government to beat the NUM pickets meant that encouragement from the centre was always likely. Later, some chief officers were to question the way in which the government had in fact actively intervened and encouraged the police during the strike (personal communication). Although the police (and government) were to claim that the police alone via the National Reporting Centre based at Scotland Yard were immediately responsible for co-ordinating policing activity during the strike, it became clear that the police had not been able to exercise entire autonomy during the period the NRC was activated. Later, officers involved at the NRC were to describe daily (morning) visits made by Home Office officials who clearly identified and articulated ministerial expectations for the day and who provided a ready conduit between the police and government (personal communication). Later, some chief officers were to refer to direct and regular calls made from Downing Street to individual force headquarters, where chief officers were encouraged to pursue the government strategy against the NUM (personal communication).

If a conflict between chief officers and their police authorities raised doubts about the local nature of police accountability, the Miners' strike was to raise fundamental questions about the national dimension of policing in Britain, particularly the extent to which central directives could over-ride local priorities and interests. More than anything else, the Miners' strike demonstrated that when push came to shove, the local police authority played at best second fiddle to central government and at worst was an irrelevance. Local police authorities were required to finance local police forces but could exercise no influence on how the money was spent and what the police did. The 1980s were therefore a watershed in policing. If before then the fiction of local accountability was sustained largely because of indifference to the exact relationship between the force and the police authority, this rather abruptly ended when increasingly local (usually) Labour councillors expressed greater interest in what the local police force did and what it cost.

It is certainly the case that for many chief officers the new interest in what they did and particularly what this cost came as something of a surprise. From offering platitudes about Britain's 'policing advantage' and local community links, chief officers were increasingly confronted by vocal minorities and local politicians who were no longer prepared to accept either the platitudes or the complacency upon which they appeared to be based. From a position best described as an arrogant expectation of unquestioning acceptance of police decision making, chief officers were rather quickly made the object of intense, immediate political interest which increasingly questioned the comfortable assumptions which surrounded the work of the post-war police service.

1964 and All That

Those politicians and academics who researched the issue of police accountability rather quickly learned that along with the convention of constabulary independence, which appeared to defy all attempts of establishing some influence over policing locally, the 1964 legislation on police also provided considerable protection to the police against what was usually described as unwarranted attacks on their independence from politically motivated critics. The 1964 Police Act gave very considerable powers to the Home Secretary and indeed preceding the Act, the 1962 Royal Commission Report was to argue consistently for a bigger and far more influential role for central government in the government of the police. This overt argument for greater centralization was justified by reference to the 'needs of modern society' and similar ephemeral claims which in retrospect had little rational basis. The huge amalgamation programme beginning in 1966 is usually identified as the consequence of the 1964 Police Act. Certainly that amalgamation was, it could be argued, to greatly weaken the claim to local policing in Britain. But other features of the legislation were to be perhaps of greater significance. Thus under the 1964 Act, the Home Secretary was to be made jointly responsible for the efficiency of police forces. He became the ultimate disciplinary appeal body and also made the final decision on the retention or dismissal of chief officers. The explicit nature of the centralization of the police promulgated by the 1964 Act did appear to be at variance with the tradition of local policing which successive governments claimed the Act was designed to protect.

It is probably the case that 'local policing' was a concept which in the official mind at this time was something which could only be sustained if this was determined by the chief police officer. Certainly no police authority sought an active role in determining policing policy. In the main, it must be said, most local police authorities (LPAs) were happy to leave policing to the chief officer. This may perhaps have reflected a perception that any intervention on their part would have been viewed as unwelcome or unacceptable by the chief constable. Whatever the explanation, successive local authority association surveys picked up evidence which suggested that both administration and policy was left to the chief constable by the LPA. This political indifference may well have encouraged the police in the view that any question of their role was a threat to their 'independence'. Many other problems which characterized the internal structure of the police may have been generated (or at least sustained) by the absence of any real external challenge to what the police did and didn't do in the decades preceding the 1964 Act and those which followed it. Cumbrous, hugely expensive and inefficient administrative hierarchies were allowed to develop which increasingly sucked in mainly uniformed personnel at a real cost to operational policing patrol activity. A steady increase in the number of officers at higher ranks pushed up the 'oncost' of the police hierarchy, usually at the expense of visible patrol activity. Specialization, the growth in the size of police forces and the attendant bureaucracy together continued to erode the availability of uniform officers for patrol activities. This was, of course, unfortunate if only because it was the patrol function alone which was of immediate interest and concern to the general public who ultimately paid for the service. All the evidence produced as a result of public surveys clearly indicated that uniform presence on the street remained (and remains) the critical test of police effectiveness among the public. For a variety of reasons, not least the professionalization of the service, which encouraged greater specialization, it was in just this area that the police found it increasingly difficult to provide this basic service (Loveday 1990).

By the mid-1980s the position of the police was seen as being unsustainable. The police force did not appear to be locally accountable if only because at crucial times the chief constable could appeal to the Home Secretary to curb perceived local 'political interference'. Alternatively he refused to respond to requests made locally by reference to operational independence. But if local accountability was limited, by reference to the convention of constabulary independence, this did not appear to preclude central intervention. As has been demonstrated regularly by way of Home Office Circulars which are viewed rather more as commands than advice, the Home Secretary can 'recommend' on occasion radical change which is automatically accepted by chief officers. A classic example of this would probably be the Home Office Circular recommending police authorities and forces to establish local police consultative groups in 1983. Only one police force decided against the introduction while the rest conformed to central 'advice' even though doubts were expressed as to the utility of such a comprehensive exercise (Savage & Wilson 1987).

Home Office influence has increased in a variety of other ways. The increasing significance of HMIC has been an important factor in encouraging greater conformity among police forces. Moreover, the status of HMIC in relation to the local police authority was to be very forcibly demonstrated in an important appeal court case in 1988. In Regina vs Secretary of State for the Home Department, ex parte Northumbria Police Authority, it was discovered that the Home Secretary enjoyed a prerogative power which enabled him, on the advice of HMIC, to provide such equipment as a chief constable felt necessary to keep the Queen's peace in his area. Behind this deceptively reassuring judgment lay a major political issue which Northumbria Police Authority had sought to confront. This was the ability of the police force to purchase plastic bullets and CS gas (or any other anti-riot equipment) when the police authority specifically rejected their use (or their retention) by its police force. The position adopted by Northumbria may have been influenced in part by a view that this equipment had no part to play in a policing system based on consent. Additionally past experience (as in Merseyside), had demonstrated that mistakes could be made when the use of the wrong CS cartridges had occasioned serious injury to members of the public during the 1981 disturbances. The Northumbria case therefore represents a significant marker for LPA influence and also suggests that where an exclusive bilateral dialogue has been allowed to develop between Home Office and chief officers, this has inevitably been at the expense of the police authority which has continued to lose influence in the development of policing strategies. Subsequent research into the Association of Chief Police Officers demonstrated the significance of the national dimension in policing while also highlighting the influence now exercised by this association across a range of police responsibilities (Cope *et al.* 1998).

A Policing Revolution?

Although the Labour Party was, via the Straw Police Bill of 1979, prepared to identify the kind of reforms needed to improve local accountability of the police, it has been the Conservatives who have ultimately determined what shape police reform would actually take. While Labour was in control of most Metropolitan police authorities through the 1980s and into the 1990s under Joint Board arrangements, Conservative control of central government enabled them to dictate change. As with other public services, the police have been subject to reform pressure to bring it into line with other services subject to 'social market' solutions. Following more than a decade of Government support to (and use of) the police, it became apparent that it was increasingly exasperated by the apparent inability of the police to control crime and by the apparent lack of effective management of the service observable to its critics. It became clear that before her reluctant departure from Downing Street, even Mrs Thatcher was prepared to consider radical change to improve the quality of the service. In 1989, for example, the introduction of a 'second' officer tier into the police service was under serious consideration.

Following Mrs Thatcher's departure, it became apparent that a residual antipathy towards the police for its failure to deal with the crime problem existed within the Major Government. Kenneth Baker, when Home Secretary, was to discover how his colleagues viewed the police service. While in public they supported the police, privately they castigated them for their evident failure on the 'crime issue', despite the injection of massive resources in policing over the previous decade (Baker 1992). More police officers and much better police pay and pensions did not appear to have had any significant effect on the ability of the service to fight crime. More police officers in service appeared to be only matched by more recorded crime, which had, by 1991, doubled from the figure inherited by the Conservative Government from Labour in 1979, undermining the government's image as the party of 'law and order'.

If the 'crime problem' and police failure to deal with it provided one explanation for police reform, another was the view within Government, following its fourth election success of 1992, that it no longer needed the police to impose market-led programmes on recalcitrant public services. The massive decline in the number of strikes along with the absence of any organized opposition to the Government within organized labour, meant that its earlier commitment to the police service could be safely diluted. It was, therefore, of no real surprise to discover that shortly after his arrival at the Home Office, Kenneth Clarke was to demonstrate an eagerness to reform the police service which he had shown earlier in both the Health and Education Departments. Claiming that the police service was administered rather than managed, he established an inquiry into police pay and responsibilities, led by Sir Patrick Sheehy. More significantly, Mr Clarke was to directly recruit Eric Caines, formerly Chief Personnel Officer in the Health Department, to the Sheehy Inquiry. Eric Caines had been influential in introducing the internal market arrangements into the Health Service and was clearly committed to similar market solutions for the police.

It is quite clear that both the Sheehy Inquiry and evident ministerial indifference to declining police morale came as a surprise to the police service. For a variety of reasons, many within the police service believed that they would always be protected from the reforms meted out to other public services. The Sheehy Report of 1993 demonstrated just how far the Major Government was removing itself from the earlier commitment to the police demonstrated during the Thatcher period. A series of recommendations, which clearly shocked the police service, was to include, *inter alia*, fixed five-year contracts for all police officers, which could be renewed; structural severance to get rid of officers surplus to requirements; the use of a matrix of police duties to reward officers by way of bonus payments; and the introduction of local wage arrangements. The market solution proposed by Sheehy was based on a view within the Inquiry team that the police service was mismanaged, highly wasteful and bureaucratic and that of all public services was the most in need of major reform. As a unique mass rally of police officers held at Wembley in 1993 was to demonstrate, the police were prepared to openly demonstrate their opposition to a set of proposals which were based very largely on a blueprint prepared for the NHS.

Police Reform

The Thatcher period saw the extensive use of the police service in a number of high profile industrial strikes. The combination of the Edmund Davies pay award and government commitment to an expansion of the police service through the 1980s, meant that by the end of the decade the police had become a high-cost service which did not appear to be able, by way of internal reform or reorganization, to improve its own performance. A combination of extended hierarchies, organizational culture and the lack of effective management had resulted in the police service taking on all the finer characteristics of a beached whale. Although ACPO was, much later, to engender internal change particularly by way of its important Statement of Common Purpose, it became increasingly clear that for the Major Government the police service needed the kind of management and market disciplines which had been introduced into other public services. As noted earlier one of the consequences of this was to be the creation of the Sheehy Inquiry. A much more significant development however proved to be the decision to initiate reform of the tri-partite structure of police chiefs, police authorities and the Home Secretary. Beginning with a statement to the House of Commons, the then Home Secretary Kenneth Clarke outlined his plans for reform in a subsequent White Paper on Police Reform. The immediate justification for reform related to the apparent failure of the police to deal with the crime problem, which was judged to be a reflection of the relatively little amount of time devoted by the police to 'crime fighting'. Police forces in future would be required to target crime fighting and this would be encouraged by the introduction of management structures which would reward successful policing activity and penalize poor performance. A commitment to managerial accountability by way of the use of a wide range of comparative performance data would also, it was believed, require the police to prioritize activities and make more effective use of manpower. To encourage all of these activities a review of police Core and Ancillary duties was established by the Home Office to identify 'core functions'. In a proposal closely linked to the Sheehy Inquiry all officers would be placed on fixed contracts renewable after five years and offered performance pay. As a central element to contractual accountability proposed by the Home Secretary, the streamlined police authorities would be required to become fully involved in monitoring police activity and setting objectives for the police force. Reducing the number of local police authority members from an average of 35 to 17 was designed to create a decision making body rather than sustain a situation in which the committee was merely a public arena for the chief officer.

To encourage their deliberations a slimmed down police authority would be led by a Chairman selected by the Home Secretary who would also (it was expected), nominate the seven other independent members to the newly constituted police authority. The proposal to give the Home Secretary such an enormous patronage base in the police service was bound to engender opposition. This was to be fully experienced during the passage of the Police and Magistrates Courts Bill when, in the House of Lords, four former Home Secretaries were to attack the proposal which threatened to centralize the police service to a degree never before contemplated by a central government department.

Police and Magistrates Courts Act (1994)

Following the emasculation in the House of Lords of a number of clauses within the Bill, the government was to finally get its police legislation through by accepting a number of amendments. The most important changes resulted in allowing the police authority to choose its own chairperson, to increase the number of elected members, to provide them with a simple majority in the police authority and also to introduce a system of independent nominees which made the Home Secretary's involvement in their selection slightly less intrusive. One consequence of these amendments has been to create a rather arcane selection procedure which provides a significant Home Office veto power on independent members. In the selection procedures of 1994/5 for independent members, questions were to be raised about the apparent bias in terms of Home Office choice of nominees which appeared to penalize both women and members of the ethnic minorities. It also became apparent that Conservative Party 'business managers' had been involved in vetting the shortlists of nominations returned to the local police authority (Loveday 1995).

It is, as yet, uncertain how well the new police authorities will discharge their responsibilities. It is, however, increasingly the case that local police authorities are subject to national demands. In future the Home Secretary will determine national objectives for all police forces. Police training, once the shared responsibility of the local and central government, has been effectively nationalized under a new national director of training, based at the Police Staff College, Bramshill. Police funding is now subject to strict central government control, while the work of both police and police authorities will be reviewed by a central government inspectorate (CoLPA 1995).

Other pressures may also tend to undermine the local structure of policing in Britain. Successive police Commissioners for the Metropolitan Police service have argued for either a national police or for a national police agency to be superimposed on existing local police forces. This British 'FBI', as it is sometimes termed, could become the operational arm of the National Criminal Intelligence Service (NCIS) which began to operate across England and Wales in 1992. Further pressure to nationalize policing arrangements could emanate from the European Union, particularly since the Maastricht Treaty, and a European commitment to a Euro-police force and further European co-operation (Walker 1994). Planned regional government in Britain by New Labour may also generate pressures for further amalgamation to create police forces with boundaries coterminous with those of regional government.

The Remainder of the British Isles

Consideration of policing arrangements has been largely directed to England and Wales. It is, however, noticeable that within the United Kingdom, a variety of other police systems operate independently of it. (See Chapter 3 in this volume.) In Scotland, for example, police investigations are supervised by the Procurator Fiscal, the equivalent of a French examining magistrate. The Procurator Fiscal is responsible for taking witness statements, directing an investigation and formulating criminal charges. There is no office similar to this in England and Wales. Elsewhere, as in Northern Ireland, the police force (RUC) was, until the reforms of the mid-1970s the responsibility of the Stormont Government. It was, in effect, a national police force responsible to an elected minister. Following a review in Northern Ireland, the police were to become the joint responsibility of the police authority in Northern Ireland (PANI) and the Secretary of State for Northern Ireland. These reforms followed the independent Hunt Report which recommended major changes to the RUC and its relationship with Government. In the Channel Islands, police arrangements are further removed from the mainland. In both Jersey and Guernsey, locally elected constables (*centenaires*), continue to work alongside professionally paid police forces. Thus in Jersey, the States of Jersey police are required to work alongside elected and local constables. The police are accountable to the State's government and ultimately via the island's Governor to the Home Secretary, whose department continues to have a residual responsibility for the islands. These differing police systems are of great and particular interest. However, it does remain the case that for the majority of the UK population, the policing arrangements in England and Wales will be those most commonly experienced.

Application of Typologies to Police Systems

Using the typologies developed by John Stead in his evaluation of comparative police systems, some attempt can now be made at classifying the police system of England and Wales (Stead 1965, ibid. 1957). Stead was to identify three police models which he classified as fragmented, combined and national centralized systems. For Stead the appropriate classification of the police system of England and Wales appeared to fit easily into the combined police system, in which the national and local government co-operated and shared responsibility for establishing and running a police service. While it is important not to exaggerate the case, it is clear that at least since 1964 and particularly since 1979, it has been difficult to sustain the claim that policing in England and Wales was in any real sense a local responsibility. The effective operation of the police since 1964 has been towards centralization by way of what became an exclusively bilateral dialogue between chief officers and the Home Office. In effect, while chief officers laid claim to constabulary independence *vis-à-vis* local government they surrendered it in relation to the Home Department. This tendency to fight local intervention while acting as the willing servants of a central government department was of course encouraged by a Conservative Administration which under both Thatcher and Major was responsible for undermining local authority responsibilities and centralizing power to an extent not experienced since 1945. For a variety of reasons therefore, the police system in England and Wales has for some time exhibited, albeit on a de facto basis, many of the characteristics of the national centralized system which traditionally the British establishment has abhorred. The experience of the 1980s, particularly the Miners' dispute of 1984/5, only served to reinforce the de facto nature of the national police force which operates in England and Wales. But far worse than this, the police system and Police Acts have given the Home Secretary power without responsibility which has enabled him to influence all that the police do without being made directly accountable to either Parliament or the people for what he asked of the service. Ultimately within a quasi-national police system the issue of greatest concern has not been the lack of accountability of the police but the absence of any mechanism to bring the Home Secretary to account for what he has encouraged the police service to do (Reiner 1992).

America: a Fragmented Police System?

If the English system of a combined and local police service is really a national centralized police service in disguise, what then of the American system, which, according to Stead's typology is fragmented and heavily localized in terms of accountability and administration? The fragmentation which is seen to characterize the American police system is inevitably a reflection of the federal structure of that country and the very strong commitment to state and local government which provide the checks and balances to executive power (see Chapter 3 in this volume) which has been sustained by recent Supreme Court rulings. In effect, the political pluralism which it is claimed characterizes the USA is reflected in a range and variety of police agencies which operate within it. Federal, state and the local (municipal) police agencies along with sheriff departments and highway patrols all provide policing services. Most recently the total number of police agencies has been computed to stand at just under 20,000. This is roughly half the number estimated in

1967 by the President's Commission on Law Enforcement which demonstrates the lack of reliable data on the American Police (Walker 1992). Overwhelmingly the largest number of police agencies are local municipal forces and employ only a small number of people.

The plethora of agencies at a local level, it might be thought, would reinforce the fragmented nature of the American policing system. Some townships have privatized their local police service entirely. On the other hand, a long term policy goal of many leading professionals has been towards consolidation of smaller police jurisdictions to provide fewer more effective units of policing, but the value of larger police forces has been challenged by reference to the level of patrol activity actually achieved by large and medium sized police forces in America (Walker 1992). The traditional emphasis has been on diversity and the evident difficulty of persuading communities to relinquish their own local police service in the interest of a future gain in efficiency.

Yet the emphasis placed on the number and variety of police agencies in America may not always have resulted in greater local accountability, which presumably continues to be a primary defence of local policing in that country. This may have reflected the policy of the Federal Bureau of Investigation (FBI) and its former director Edgar Hoover, who ran the bureau from 1924 through to 1972. From a position of unchallenged power in the US Department of Justice building, Hoover was able, it has been argued, to personally manipulate American law enforcement by the utilization of a variety of techniques and ploys which effectively meant the FBI almost became the national police agency for the country (Murphy & Plate 1977: 87). Hoover was to develop a strategy to control the selection of local police chiefs which, it has been argued, was institutionalized with the creation, in 1935, of the national police academy at Quantico, Virginia. Although proclaimed as a major contribution to improving American police work, the underlying rationale of the academy was much less positive or altruistic. As was to be argued subsequently by Patrick Murphy (Murphy & Plate 1977: 88), the national academy quickly became, in the police world, a 'certification pit-stop' before advancement up the American police career ladder. No-one who wished to get anywhere in policing was likely to be successful without an FBI 'academy ticket' (Murphy and Plate 1977: 7). For those many police chiefs who gained entry to the academy, the catch became that certification by the academy was the same thing as certification by the director, as Hoover was not only the academy's Dean but also its Director of Admissions. Each year 200 police officers after suitable screening would be invited to Washington. The critical test was whether these future local police chiefs could be counted on to render obedient service to the FBI director and pledge complete support to the local branch of the FBI whenever needed. Special FBI agents, it is argued, on a regional basis became highly influential in providing information to the director as to which police officers could be of use to the FBI (Murphy & Plate 1977: 89). Special agents also had responsibility to 'plug into' the local power structure and convey useful information to the director. Additionally, and on an informal basis, local mayors who selected the police chief would want to stay friendly with the FBI (Murphy & Plate 1977: 87). In terms of chief officer selection, a special agent of the FBI 'would only have to make a suggestion one way or the other and would find his suggestion taken very seriously indeed' (Murphy & Plate 1977: 89). Ultimately, it was to be argued that Hoover's domination of local police departments 'helped immensely' in whatever actual success in enforcing the law the FBI achieved. Moreover, the national dimension of influence exercised by the FBI may have been reinforced by Hoover's domination of the International Association of Chief Police Officers (IACP). Control of the IACP was one means of eliminating any challenges to Hoover at a local level (Murphy & Plate 1977: 89). This along with unfettered access by FBI agents to all local police files meant that local accountability may have existed in name only. Moreover the systematic abuse of constitutional safeguards and indi-vidual rights by the FBI was, long term, to seriously damage the image and prestige of the American police forces generally (Murphy & Plate 1977: 85). So too was the director's politically expedient use of racism to cement alliances with powerful com-mittee chairmen on Capitol Hill, which may have reinforced a perception amongst the black community that the police nationally were unjust in enforcing the law and discriminated against them (Murphy & Plate 1977: 94). Ironically, the centralizing nature of the FBI under Hoover was to be consistently defended by reference to the 'loathsome spectre of a national police force' which Hoover argued would be the alternative and which would clearly threaten local interests and local police jurisdic-tions (Murphy & Plate 1977: 95). The influence of Hoover on policy-making was manisfested in an interesting monograph on the Department of Justice published in 1967. While the Director, it is argued, emphasized it was an investigatory not a policy-making body, the author went on to note that:

> There can be no doubt that in exercising its investigatory function, the FBI gathers data that influences policy decisions of the executive branch and often legislation by Congress (Huston 1967: 235).

Nevertheless, as the same writer noted:

> As more than 40 years as head of the FBI have embedded in Hoover's thinking definite ideas about methods of law enforcement, law-makers and administra-tors recognize that his experience qualifies him to advise on certain matters of policy. However reluctant he may be, the fact remains that he does give advice in public and in private on what he thinks should be done (Huston 1967: 236).

Since the departure of Edgar Hoover and the decision of successive FBI directors to improve the status and direction of that organization, particularly in relation to fighting organized crime and drugs, there has been increased FBI intervention in local policing (Poveda 1990).

Federal intervention in the policing of the individual states has been an increased phenomenon in the USA. It may be the case that the very number of small police agencies makes this inevitable. It might be possible to argue that using the typologies developed by Stead the American police system might be best characterized as a combined system rather than a fragmented one. Thus for a long period of its history and during the formative years of many police departments, the police under Edgar Hoover's FBI began to assume, it has been argued, the characteristics of a national police system (Murphy & Plate 1977). The arguments presented by former police commissioner Murphy may, however, be viewed as extreme. Against that interpretation it could be argued that the influence of local politics continues to sustain a local and highly fragmented police system. Indeed the influence of the FBI in opposing consolidation of small agencies by reference to the 'menace of a national police force' only reinforced such fragmentation.

On a wider level, the potential influence of federal government in the policing of the United States has followed on from successive Supreme Court rulings, which enabled federal intervention in inter-state trade. Wherever an offence crosses state boundaries, there is likely to be federal involvement. The development of highways, along with greater mobility of offenders, has offered many more opportunities for federal involvement in the policing of the United States. Nor is 'policing' merely a responsibility confined to the FBI. Over time, a plethora of federal agencies have been established to deal with specific types of offence. Indeed it has recently been argued that no fewer than 63 federal agencies have police, investigation and enforcement or arrest powers (Torres 1995: 287). The best example of this would of course be the Drugs Enforcement Agency (DEA). Here the widespread use and sale of drugs has provided considerable opportunity for federal involvement in policing. At a local level, some police chiefs may welcome federal involvement which could arguably 'nationalize' America's policing response to serious crime (Ahern 1972). Along with the FBI and DEA, other federal agencies include the US Treasury Department's Alcohol, Tobacco and Firearms Division, which among its many duties has a responsibility for federal gun law enforcement, a responsibility which was to be displayed quite spectacularly at Waco in 1993.

Both the Justice and Treasury departments also claim extensive law enforcement responsibilities. The Treasury Department has immediate responsibility for Alcohol, Tobacco and Firearms and in some respects competes with the Drugs Enforcement Agency. Additionally, the Federal Internal Review Service employs officers for a variety of duties and the overlapping jurisdictions of federal bureaux may lead to rivalry and some inefficiency. This has been perhaps best evidenced in the competition between the FBI and DEA in recent years (Bailey 1995: 243). Competing investigations conducted by the US Customs Service, Internal Revenue Service and US Secret Service, each of which employ large numbers of federal investigators, provide a further example of this within the Department of the Treasury (Torres 1995: 287).

As numerous examples of failed attempts at consolidation of local police forces has demonstrated, the very number and size of police departments in the United States may have encouraged further federal involvement. Local police departments, which continue to demonstrate varying standards in terms of professionalism, and low levels of resources, have tended to trigger greater federal intervention as the crime rate has risen. As has been noted elsewhere, the large number of small police forces has meant that they have only a limited service capacity, low professionalism and an inability to respond to 'area-wide' crime. Consolidation has, however, proved difficult to achieve as local electorates have been unprepared to lose control of 'their' police departments by way of proposed amalgamations. If consolidation remains politically unfeasible, then further intervention, federal or otherwise, can be expected. For many police professionals, the solution to the chaos of local and weak police departments is to encourage much greater federal involvement in policing arrangements at state and local level. This may, however, only sustain the traditional relationship between FBI and state and local police agencies which it is argued has been historically one of 'menace and mutual distrust' (Murphy & Plate 1977: 82).

The National Police of France

An alternative to the Anglo-American police systems is the highly centralized European police systems of which France might be thought of as the best example of a state-led and national centralized police force. Certainly the French policing experience has been traditionally cited as the most extreme form of centralized police activity in Europe in which the "rights of man" (and the individual) have had to compete with the collective interests of the state. Observers have frequently concluded that in this apparently unequal contest individual rights have been sacrificed to state interests. The police system has been more concerned with protecting the interests of the state than with the rights of the individual (Coatman 1959). Indeed the same commentator in the late 1950s was to argue in relation to the French police that:

> it is not too sweeping a judgement to say that the French police system could be fitted more easily than that of any other Western countries into the pattern of totalitarian government . . . The political activities and the building up of dossiers of persons unconnected with crime which form so large a part of the work of the police of totalitarian countries has been among the activities of the French police since the days of the first Napoleon (Coatman 1959: 77–8).

Along with the dirigiste nature of policing in France, has gone unofficial acceptance of very wide discretion given to the police in carrying out their duties. As was argued elsewhere:

> The French police are allowed a latitude – license would not be too strong a word – in their dealings, not only with suspected and arrested persons, which is probably unique in Western democratic countries (Coatman 1959: 75).

This assessment probably exaggerates both the extent of police activity and state direction while minimizing similar characteristics elsewhere. This picture of the police of France has moreover been overtaken by recent developments which have had a significant impact on policing in France. First, it was never easy to describe the police system as national, at least until after 1966 when the police of Paris lost its individual identity and was amalgamated into the National Police administered by the Sureté Nationale (Journés 1993). Second, while it was possible to describe the policing as a national function, it was never a unified national police system. Thus the Police Nationale are the responsibility of the Ministry of the Interior while the higher status Gendarmerie remain the responsibility of the Ministry of Defence.

One interesting feature of the division of responsibilities between the two police forces is the continuing conflicts which have developed over time between them (Gleizal *et al.* 1993: 202). This interesting tension between the two services was to reach a high point in the Jobic affair in 1987 when officers of the Gendarmerie arrested a very senior officer of the National Police in Paris (Guyomarch 1991). The very division of responsibilities between the two police forces provides some interesting checks and balances to the ubiquitous style of policing which has been condemned in the past by many commentators on French policing. As has been argued, there is a continuing lack of co-operation between these two forces and to date no significant move towards unification of police structures has been attempted (Guyomarch 1991). Indeed such tensions as exist can be, and have been, exploited by politicians to encourage greater police responsiveness. In 1987 for example, the Minister of Defence was to allow the Gendarmerie to operate in plain clothes. In the early 1980s the National Police was to be humiliated publicly by the decision of the then President Mitterand to transfer responsibility for his personal protection to the Gendarmerie (Guyomarch 1991: 325). This 'institutionalized tension' between the two forces has been important in retarding any development of a unified professional police strategy and may have actually encouraged greater political accountability of the services. This fragmentation, officially sustained by central government departments, is further encouraged by the complete absence of any coherent professional police organization. This is in part the effect of unionization of police officers. The unionization of the National Police has generated conflicts between unions exhibiting differing political tendencies who recruit from the same organization. The FASP (autonomous federation of police unions) for example, which represents pro-socialist views, has often been in conflict with the USCP which gives its support to centre right parties. The rise and fall in influence of these two unions has faithfully reflected the changes in power at the centre as the Gaullest PRP has been replaced by the socialist party and vice versa. Strong law and order policies pursued by the right received the support of the USCP. Significantly the socialist reforms of the early 1980s received the support of FASP then and thereafter. This was most notable with Interior Minister Deferre who offered FASP a sympathetic ministerial ear while other unions closer to the PRP Party were kept at arms length (Guyomarch 1991: 325). The fragmentation between police forces has therefore also been matched by fragmentation within the National police itself which has received Ministerial blessing as one way of exercising influence by the application of the well established principle of 'divide and rule'.

The fragmented nature of French policing would not be complete without reference to a real power which can be exercised at local level and which was to substantially increase during the 1980s. As has been argued by one commentator, the extent of centralization in France (in relation to the police) can be exaggerated and is limited through a series of checks and balances which exist in relation to local government. Under the Law of 1884, which is now seen as the basis of municipal freedom in France, the Mayor was given responsibility for public order in his commune (Journés 1993: 283). The Mayor was also given responsibility to appoint all municipal employees, including police constables and inspectors. While this responsibility is balanced by the authority of the Prefect who has a greater role in the recruitment of police in towns with populations of over 40,000 inhabitants it is interesting to note, as Journés has argued, that it was not until 1941 in a Law passed by the Vichy government of that year, that the National Police were given responsibility for towns with populations of over 10,000 inhabitants.

The centralist tendencies of the Vichy government and those experienced during the immediate post-war period have, in the 1980s and the 1990s, been challenged by a growing interest in the decentralization of policing. There are, as has been argued recently not two but three police systems in France (Journés 1993: 283, Gleizal *et al*. 1993: 266). The third police system is the steady increase in the French Municipal police which have been seen as a local response to the perceived failure of the National police to deal effectively with crime and delinquency in the cities and towns of France (Gleizal *et al*. 1993: 206). Although it is argued that the growth of Municipal police has been the responsibility of right-wing mayors and that the Municipal police enjoy no clear legal status (Guyomarch 1991: 331), it is noticeable that the growth of Municipal police (often in competition with the National Police) has been the most interesting policing development in contemporary France. In 1986 Guyomarch (1991: 331) estimated that 530 Municipal police forces were in existence and of these 107 directly competed with the National police in terms of duties, responsibilities and structures.

Additionally while the Municipal police have been characterized as a creation of the Right, it is clear that the impact of the Bonne-Maison report, which concluded that crime prevention rather than crime control techniques would be effective in the fight against crime, has encouraged their wider application. By 1992 some 700 crime prevention committees had been established in France (Journés 1993). Given the real deprivation experienced in many of the suburbs of France's larger cities it has been argued that:

the primary aim has been to approach the problems of public safety and public security in partnership terms between state and local government (Journés 1993: 286).

This partnership has allowed French Mayors to establish Municipal police forces to provide more general police patrols in their towns. There are now some 10,000 Municipal police officers who work in some 2,860 localities (Journés 1993: 286). At least a third of those officers employed at Municipal level carry firearms and the expectation must be that they will be allowed to develop a wider competence which could go beyond specific crime prevention functions and bring them into direct competition with the National Police. These interesting features are a continuing phenomenon within the French policing system and mean that it may be difficult to place the French police system in terms of control and accountability within the national centralized police model traditionally associated with France (Stead 1965). Indeed the fragmented and conflictual nature of the police system which demonstrates pluralistic rather than unified characteristics may be better placed in one or other of the alternative typologies developed by Stead. The French system could arguably be classified as a combined police system and this looks likely to become more appropriate as decentralized Municipal police forces continue to grow. The high degree of fragmentation exhibited by the division and competition between and within individual police forces is also of interest here. These divisions provide important opportunities to influence and direct the police while also making each more potentially accountable. The divisiveness which characterizes the police system of France is also sustained by the direct entry system and officer class which operates in both National Police and Gendarmerie. It is thus difficult if not impossible to sustain a collective view of policing strategy when such different and competing interests coexist.

Conclusion

This brief evaluation of current developments in policing, police organizations and accountability provides a descriptive rather than definitive statement. Nevertheless, the application of typologies used most frequently to demonstrate the differences between local 'Anglo-American' police systems and National centralized (French European) police systems may be a little misleading. It is perhaps a matter of interest that Anglo-American commentators on policing systems have been all to ready to congratulate themselves that their 'policing system' provided all the characteristics usually associated with local pluralistic liberal democracies. Unfortunately, the erosion of local competence and powers, most pronounced in Britain, may require the application of a more detached and objective judgement. If Anglo-American police forces have been subject to both formal and informal centralizing tendencies, in France the movement in recent years has been in an altogether different direction. In France formal structures built around a local government system which appears to enjoy a greater protection than anything on offer, for example, in Britain have catered for the rapid expansion of local Municipal police forces. While it would be wrong to exaggerate the importance of this development in relation to the role of the National Police and Gendarmerie, it would seem that for the future, France may provide us with an example of local accountability of police. In contrast to this, local accountability in Britain has been steadily eroded by the encroachment of the central department and the centralizing policies of the previous Conservative government. To what extent either policy will be sustained or reversed by New Labour – in contemporary England – must remain at this time a matter of conjecture.

Bibliography

Ahern, J.F. 1972. *Police in trouble*. Hawthorn Books Inc.
Bailey, W.G. 1995. *The Encyclopaedia of Police Science*. New York: Garland Publishing Inc.
Baker, K. 1992. *Turbulent years, my life in politics*. London: Faber.
Coatman, J. 1959. *Police*. Oxford: Oxford University Press.
Cope, S., S.P. Savage, S. Charman 1998. *New Public Management and the New Police Governance: The Association of Chief Police Officers and Police Accountability*. Paper presented at the Annual Conference, Political Studies Association 1998, Keele University.

Gleizal, J., J. Gatti-Domenach, C. Journés 1993. *La police, le cas des démocraties occidentales*, Themis Droit Public. Press Universitaires de France.

CoLPA: Committee of Local Police Authorities 1995. ACC: London.

Guyomarch, A. 1991. Problems of law and order in France in the 1980's: politics and professionalism. *Policing and Society* **1**.

Hayward, J.E.S. 1983. *Governing France: the one and indivisible republic*. London: Weidenfeld.

HMSO, 1962. Royal Commission on the Police.

HMSO, 1989. Audit Commission. Police Paper No. 9.

HMSO, Audit Commission. Police Paper No. 12.

HMSO, 1993. Audit Commission. Helping with Enquiries. Police Paper No. 13.

HMSO, Inquiry into Police Responsibilities and Rewards, Report Vol. 1.

Huston, Luther A. 1967. The Department of Justice, Praeger Library of US Government Departments and Agencies, New York, 1967.

Jenkins, S. 1995. *Accountable to none: the Tory nationalisation of Britain*. Harmondsworth: Penguin.

Journés, C. 1993. The structure of the French police system: is the French police a national force? *International Journal of the Sociology of Law* **2**.

Loveday, B. 1990. The road to regionalisation. *Policing* **6**, Winter.

Loveday, B. 1995. Who are the new independent members? *ACC County News*, April.

Mark, R. 1978. *In the office of constable*. London: Collins.

Marshall, G. 1965. *Police and government*. London: Methuen.

Marshall, G. 1978. Police accountability revisited. In *Policy and Politics*, Butler Halsey (eds). Basingstoke: Macmillan.

Marshall, G. 1984. *Constitutional conventions: the rules of forms of political accountability*, Chapter 8. Oxford: Clarendon Press.

Marshall, G. 1985. The police. In *The Changing Constitution*, Jowell & Oliver (eds). Oxford: Clarendon Press.

Merseyside Police Committee 1985. Role of the Police Committee. Merseyside County Council.

Murphy, P.V. & T. Plate 1977. *Commissioner: a view from the top of American law enforcement*. Simon & Schuster.

Poveda, Tony G. 1990. *The FBI in transition*. Brooks Publishing Co.

Reiner, R. 1992. *Chief constables*. Oxford: Oxford University Press.

Reiner, R. & S. Spencer 1993. *Accountable policing: effectiveness, empowerment and equity*. London: Institute of Public Policy Research.

Savage, S. & C. Wilson 1987. Ask a policeman: community consultation in practice. *Social Policy and Administration*.

Stead, P.J. 1957. *The police of Paris*. London.

Stead, J. 1965. The police of France. *Medico-Legal Journal* **33**.

Torres, D.A. 1995. Federal police and investigative agencies. In *The Encyclopaedia of Police Science*, Second Edition, W.G. Bailey (ed.). New York & London: Garland Publishing Inc.

Walker, N. 1994. Reshaping the British police: the international angle. In *Policing Papers Strategic Government* **2**. No. 1. ACC Spring.

Walker, S. 1992. *The police in America, an introduction*. New York: McGraw-Hill.

CHAPTER 9

Armed and Unarmed Policing

P.A.J. WADDINGTON

Introduction

Americans and the British have a mutual fascination for each other's police, at the heart of which is their contrasting relationship with the gun. Americans are incredulous that the British 'bobby' is able to fulfil his or her duties without carrying a gun. Reciprocally, the British are addicted to the media portrayal of the gun-toting American cop shooting it out with sundry 'bad guys'. When the issue of armed policing arises in Britain, the question that is habitually asked is whether Britain is adopting the American model. However, this comparison is misleading. Most police forces throughout the world are routinely armed, but share few of the other characteristics of American society. If we are to appraise armed and unarmed policing rationally, then we must do so from a wider comparative perspective.

Britain and Ireland: Twin Experiments in Policing

Perhaps the most instructive comparison is to be found within the British Isles that plays host to two very different models of policing, that of Great Britain and other residents in the island of Ireland. Both policing systems sprang from much the same origins. Sir Robert Peel and his coterie of reformers were instrumental in the creation of both the force that evolved into the Royal Irish (later Ulster) Constabulary (RIC and RUC) and the London Metropolitan Police (the Met.) that became the model for policing throughout the mainland. The two systems embodied the same vision of policing and were opposed on essentially the same grounds, that they were an expensive threat to liberty. Yet, from such similar origins the two policing systems followed starkly divergent paths. In Ireland the Peace Preservation Force rapidly became an armed paramilitary gendarmerie, housed in more or less fortified barracks from which they patrolled the surrounding area often as quasi-infantry

151

columns. They were subjected to armed attack and made frequent recourse to their weapons (Palmer 1988). As the terrorist campaign grew in strength so policing became increasingly violent and oppressive, a development that was epitomized by the paramilitary irregulars deployed as a last desperate attempt to impose British rule on Ireland, the 'black and tans'. As the IRA campaign increased in ferocity and the partition of Ireland approached, the RIC virtually failed to operate as a police force at all (Bowden 1978) and the Cabinet was advised in 1920 that it 'would soon be little better than a mob' (Townshend 1992).

In London and thence progressively throughout the rest of England and Wales, the development of policing was very different. The London Metropolitan Police remained lightly armed, carrying only a truncheon and a rattle (with which to summon assistance), and even these accoutrements were carefully hidden from view. The police of London had ready access to weapons kept at police stations and seem to have been prepared to employ them (Emsley 1991), but the overt appearance given to the people of London was of an unarmed and vulnerable body of men. Indeed, it was the murder of Constable Culley at the riot of Coldbath Field in 1833 that is credited by some historians as creating a wave of sympathy for this erstwhile unpopular force which was then translated into general public acceptability (Critchley 1970, 1978). At various points during the nineteenth century there would have been little opposition to transforming the Met into an overtly armed force, but these opportunities were deliberately avoided. Thus, the Met refused to capitalize upon public expressions of outrage at the periodic gruesome murder of police officers. In 1883, when police policy-makers succumbed to anxieties arising from a wave of armed burglaries, officers on outer divisions were authorized to carry a pistol on night duty, but this change in policy was never publicly announced and officers were required to carry their weapon covertly. When the problem abated the policy was just as quietly reversed (Gould & Waldren 1986).

What general lessons about armed policing can be gleaned from these divergent histories? The main lesson is that the nature of policing, including the role that weapons play, cannot be divorced from the context in which policing takes place. Particularly influential are whether the civil population are considered 'citizens', the relationship of the police to the military, and the scale of resistance to state authority.

Citizenship

The principal distinction between Londoners and the peasantry of rural Ireland, was that the former enjoyed the status of citizens and the latter were denied it. Who was being policed had an enormous influence upon the shape that policing took, and particularly the weaponry that could be employed against them. Irish peasants and native peoples throughout the empire were considered a subject and potentially rebellious population on whom it was the police task to impose colonial rule. Whilst Peel encountered resistance to his Peace Preservation Force on the grounds that it would threaten liberty, it was not the liberty of Catholic peasants that was at issue, but the freedoms of the Protestant Ascendancy (Palmer 1988). The point emerges even more clearly in the South African context where the policing task was aimed as much at subduing Boer resistance as it was designed to subjugate native Africans (Brogden 1989, Grundlingh 1991, Brewer 1994).

However, it would be a mistake to crudely characterize the relationship between colonial populations and their respective police as inevitably typified by coercive threat. First, in many colonies police jurisdiction was divided either territorially or functionally, so that European colonists were served by civil police whilst the native population was often subjected to more oppressive paramilitary treatment (Anderson 1991, Throup 1992, see also Cole in this volume). Secondly, the police provided the colonists with order and security. Perhaps the most successful colonial police was the Northwest Mounted Police, the Canadian 'Mounties', who, despite being a paramilitary force modelled explicitly on the RIC (Morrison 1975, 1991), became a symbol of Canadian nationhood. The 'Mounties' could acquire a favourable public image despite their paramilitarism, because 'the public' they served comprised settlers who welcomed the order that they represented. Colonial policing, therefore, starkly illustrates the influence that citizenship has upon policing: settlers received civil policing whilst native peoples were subjected to paramilitary suppression.

Just as colonial policing reflected the socio-political conditions within which it operated so the policing of Continental Europe reflected, and still reflects, its wider context. Policing throughout Europe was a creature of the strong state of absolute monarchies, autocratic empires and, latterly, dictatorships (Emsley 1983, Roach & Thomaneck 1985). In pre-revolutionary France, for example, there developed an intricate spy network as well as an armed gendarmerie because the general population (including courtiers) were perceived to present a continuing threat to the state (Stead 1983).

In mainland Britain, by contrast, the principal objection to the 'police idea' was of the threat to liberty of 'free born Englishmen' (Palmer 1988) even though the franchise was still denied to most. When the yeomanry attacked the illegal gathering at St Peter's Field in 1819 they caused the comparative low number of 11 fatalities, yet this incident created a political furore. Even disenfranchised, predominantly working class, members of an illegal assembly were not an 'enemy' to be hacked down by the sabres of the military. More restrained methods would need to be devised and this was one of the principal arguments for the creation of a professional police. But this restraint was not limited to the police alone. Britain avoided much of the turmoil that afflicted continental Europe and elsewhere because its political institutions successfully incorporated the emerging industrialized working class into social, economic and political institutions. This was not achieved without disorder and occasional violence by the police and military, but the scale of repression was minor compared to that elsewhere.

Police–Military Relations

The most obvious expression of citizenship lies in the relationship of the military to the civil population. What characterizes both the military and the police is the use of force (Manning 1980). What distinguishes them is how that force is used. The military aim is to eliminate the enemy. This can be seen in military tactics, weapons and munitions that are designed to create a 'field of fire' in which the likelihood of survival is minimized. Soldiers are required to obey superior orders, especially when ordered to 'fire' or 'cease fire'. Civil police, however heavily armed they may be, do not aim to eliminate their adversaries who are still citizens, even if they are also armed criminals. Typically, if engaged by an armed adversary, fire is returned. Once resistance is overcome, further use of force is not only redundant but also usually illegal (Waddington 1990). Civil police are characteristically individually liable for their actions in using force and cannot claim that they were acting under superior orders (Brownlee 1989).

An abiding paradox of the history of policing is that as the military acquired the capacity more effectively to suppress the civil population by force, so they became increasingly uneasy about involvement in civil conflict (Vogler 1991). The distinction between domestic citizens and foreign enemies was drawn progressively more clearly throughout the nineteenth and early twentieth centuries. This distinction continues to create difficulties for military forces that provide 'aid to the civil power', where their task is more that of a police force than an army (Everlegh 1979, Rowe 1985). It is particularly problematic in counter-terrorist operations where both sides may consider themselves at war, but the state is loathe to accord the status of 'combatant' to those who oppose it (Urban 1992).

Blurred though it sometimes is, the division of labour between the police and the military has been crucial to the development of policing in all societies. In some societies the police are progressively differentiated from the military and continue to adopt the style and manner of militarism. Elsewhere, the police arise in opposition to the military eschewing military traditions. In Ireland, for long a troubled province, the military had played a prominent role in the suppression of rebellion (Kee 1972). The Peace Preservation Force rapidly became a substitute means of repressing dissent and equally rapidly acquired the means of doing so, military weapons and modes of deployment. In doing so, the force replicated a much wider pattern: it became effectively a gendarmarie.

The gendarmaries of Continental Europe are explicitly para-military. For example, French Gendarmes are accountable not to the Ministry of the Interior, but to the Minister of Defence. In times of war they have an explicitly military role and are equipped as a light infantry division for the purpose. In peacetime, their task is to maintain order in the rural hinterland of France, and especially to guard the principal highways. The firearms that Gendarmes routinely carry are not necessitated by their exposure to crime and violence, for they are spared responsibility for policing the main centres of population where crime flourishes. Firearms are, like the uniform they wear, an echo of their military origins and traditions (See Emsley 1983, Stead 1983, Roach 1985). If the police of Ireland inherited many of the features of the gendarmaries of Europe, they also acted as midwife to a distinct, but similar, tradition of colonial policing. Ireland was the first colony to be 'policed' and it continued to influence the conduct of colonial policing throughout the era of the British Empire.

Although the 'Irish model' was adapted to the varying conditions of colonialism (Hawkins 1991), it remains true that the officer cadres of colonial police forces were trained in Dublin and many were recruited from the RIC, and later the RUC, often to supply a more robust approach to policing. It was also a distinctly militarized form of policing in which heavily armed columns of police ventured into the hinterland to 'show the flag' and subjugate by force a rebellious native population (Finnane 1987, Ahire 1991, Anderson & Killingray 1991). Such paramilitarization could, until recently, be clearly seen in the South African Police (SAP) and reflected in the weaponry they regularly deployed in the townships. Thus, SAP officers routinely patrolled in detachments of a dozen in military-style personnel carriers on which were mounted belt-fed general purpose machine-guns. Each officer was equipped with an assault rifle, sub-machine-gun or pump-action shotgun and would deploy from the carrier in a defensive military formation. Officers were routinely trained in the use of such military weapons as light and heavy mortars. During the State of Emergency that accompanied the final days of apartheid, police officers were indemnified against using force 'in good faith'. In all these respects, they unwittingly, but eloquently, demonstrated that they were indeed an 'army of occupation', rather than a police force (Nathan 1989, Brewer 1994). Indeed, so blurred was the distinction between the military and the police in the apartheid state that the SAP fought as a light infantry regiment in the border wars that characterized the final phase of apartheid's nemesis (Cawthra 1993).

The British police are distinctive not simply because they were created as an unarmed force, but because their lack of armaments was a conscious repudiation of the military model. When the Met. took to the streets of London in 1829 they did not inherit a tradition of unarmed policing, far from it: what policing there was, was invariably armed. The Bow Street Runners, mounted patrols and river police all carried sabres and pistols; even the decrepit watchmen known as 'Charlies' were equipped with various weapons albeit that they may have had difficulty using them. Peel's 'New Police' was designed to be the antithesis of the continental gendarmaries that the English feared as a threat to their liberty. As pre-existing police forces in London were gradually assimilated into the Met. so they were disarmed (Gould & Waldren 1986). An unarmed civil police could not win the compliance of the civil population by fear and coercion, as could their militarized counterparts. Their authority would rest upon respect rather than fear – what is sometimes misleadingly described as 'policing by consent'.

Of course, myth played a significant role in the process of legitimating police authority. The unarmed constabulary was not nearly as vulnerable as it appeared. The military continued to provide a lethal long-stop for the remainder of the century and beyond. In 1911 the Scots Guards were deployed to engage a suspected gang of foreign anarchists, which they did to devastating effect in the Siege of Sidney Street. The military continued to be used to suppress violent public disorder some-times by the use or threat of lethal force (Geary 1985, Weinberger 1991). At the more prosaic level, clearly policing was a pretty rough and tough business in which police officers needed to be competent street fighters (Cohen 1979, Brogden 1991).

Yet, even when the patina of sentiment is stripped from the history of policing in Britain, it remains the case that the police have remained lightly and covertly armed and used force much more sparingly than elsewhere for more than 150 years. This has been the genuine triumph of Peel's legacy of creating an unarmed civil police.

The conscious political decision to create an unarmed constabulary was not unique to Britain – two other police forces in Eire and New Zealand were disarmed for essentially the same purpose of symbolizing a particular relationship between the state and civil population. Whilst the *Garda Siochana* inherited many features of the despised RIC that preceded it, the one notable exception was that Gardia did not carry weapons (Townshend 1992). More remarkable, perhaps, was the experience of the New Zealand Police (Hill 1986, 1991) which was originally a paramilitary colonial force that forcibly subjugated the Maoris and then transformed itself into an unarmed police on the lines of the London Metropolitan. In Britain, Eire and New Zealand, policing became unarmed not because of a rational calculation of how best to enforce the law or protect police officers, but in order to fulfil a symbolic purpose.

Resistance to State Authority

There is no simple relationship between crime levels and armed policing. The London of the mid-nineteenth century was a tumultuous place yet its police were unarmed. Today Switzerland and Japan enjoy enviable reputations for low levels of crime, but the police in both these countries routinely carry sidearms. Hawkins & Ward (1970) found that those Australian states that routinely carried weapons not only shot suspects more often than their counterparts who did not carry weapons so freely, but were themselves more likely to be victims of armed attack. Indeed, the most vulnerable police in the world have been the most heavily armed: South Africa, Northern Ireland (during 'the troubles') and, to a lesser extent, the United States. On the other hand, the police of Britain, Eire and New Zealand have enjoyed historically low casualty rates.

Far more influential than crime rates is the extent to which state authority is challenged. Where that occurs policing is almost invariably coercive. In the frontier conditions of early colonialism, policing could involve punitive raids on dissident tribes, burning villages and executing tribal leaders as an example to others (Ahire 1991). As settlements grew, and with it greater stability was acquired, so policing in those areas became more civil (Johnson D.H. 1991, Johnson H. 1991, Killingray 1991). Later, as independence movements grew and with them resistance to colonialism, so the police became increasingly paramilitary, despite attempts to adopt a more civil style of policing (Smith 1992). Only, it seems, in Malaya did a police facing an insurrectionary movement succeed in developing a civil approach designed to win the 'hearts and minds' of the population (Stockwell 1992); elsewhere resistance was met with armed oppression.

The American Anomaly

So far no mention has been made of what often appears to be the archetype of armed policing – the American cop. This has been deliberate, first to avoid the often facile comparison between Britain and America. Commentators on armed policing often suggest that if the British police were to be armed then the streets of London would become like those of New York. Why, one wonders, would London not become like Oslo or Zurich? Secondly, and more importantly, America is an anomaly: like the British, Americans did not subscribe to the vision of the strong state that underlay both the Continental European gendarmaries and colonial styles of policing. Yet, unlike the British, policing in the United States was armed almost from the outset, despite attempts to adopt the London model of an unarmed constabulary (Miller 1977). America represents an anomalous situation in which the frontier was policed by civil means.

Civil armed policing

As in Britain, policing in America grew in opposition to the military. Policing was always an intensely civil matter in the United States, even more so than in Britain. The revolutionary antecedents of the United States and its history as a magnate for oppressed peoples seeking a new life has bequeathed a political culture that values individual liberty and fears state power. The police, as custodians of the state's monopoly of legitimate force have always been regarded with scepticism: more a potential threat to liberty than a protection against lawlessness and disorder. Policing was destined to become local and democratic. The paradox is that the most overt symbol of police power, the gun, became inextricably part of the American style of policing.

Policing in America began in the cities, which emulated Peel's 'New Police', but it was fashioned by the frontier. In stark contrast to the colonial model represented by its near neighbour, the Canadian 'Mounties' (Morrison 1991), settlers were left to enforce their own law and order. It was here that the vigilante tradition grew and prospered, since there was no state authority to speak of (Kopel 1992). The legacy of this vigilante tradition continues to be felt in the plethora of local police forces too numerous to itemize, each of whom continues to guard its independence jealously. The Federal Bureau of Investigation seeks to spread standards of best practice through its training programmes, but until recently policy varied enormously between forces, not least in connection with the use of firearms (Milton et al. 1977). In many forces individual officers are obliged or allowed to purchase their own weapons. Some may opt for revolvers, whilst others prefer self-loading or 'semi-automatic' pistols and there may even be a variety of calibres in use. Insofar as uniformity has begun to be imposed it has been through the influence of the courts, both in constitutional and civil liability cases. Increasingly, police forces are enunciating common policies and training officers better in order to demonstrate to the courts that they are fulfilling their responsibilities in the event that officers do open fire on others. It remains instructive, that it is through the courts' reaction to incidents that uniformity of policy is being imposed upon the American police, not by proactive federal government initiative.

Citizenship and minorities

Although American political culture is firmly rooted in the rights of individual citizens, respect for individuals has not been uniformly enjoyed by all sections of the civil population. This has had a profound influence upon policing generally, and the police use of weapons in particular. In the colonial and post-colonial era Native Americans and slaves were formally denied citizenship and, as a result, not only received little protection from law enforcement officers, but were often the target of oppression. The emancipation of slaves after the Civil War only marginally reduced the oppression of black Americans. They continued to be exposed to informal methods of 'policing' such as periodic lynchings (Tolnay & Beck 1992). Equally, a persistent feature of policing in America has been the exposure of black Americans to police violence (Hawkins H. & Thomas 1991), most notably the frequency with which they are shot and killed by police officers (Takagi 1974, Goldkamp 1976, Meyer 1980, Milton et al. 1982). This may suggest naked racism of the most violent kind, but Fyfe has shown that the race effect in individual cases is attributable to the greater likelihood that black offenders are armed and involved in serious offences (Fyfe 1982b). However, others have shown that the percentage of non-whites resident in an area is a better predictor of police killings of blacks than other variables related to the crime rate (Liska & Yu 1992). These data suggest that in cities with high ethnic minority populations, the police feel themselves to be under greater threat and more likely to respond forcefully to situations. What is undoubtedly true is that black Americans have still to acquire full de facto citizenship in American society and that this is reflected in the greater propensity for police to use force against them.

This denial of de facto citizenship has not been restricted only to black Americans, but in an earlier era to working class and immigrant labour. Here again, the distinctive American pattern is revealed, for much of this violence was perpetrated not by the official police, but by the private police forces of corporate employers (Weiss 1986, 1987), albeit that they were often supplemented by troops. As Taft & Ross have documented, labour disputes in the period stretching from the end of the nineteenth century to the mid-1930s were often bloody affairs, with very significant body counts (Taft & Ross 1979). For example, as recently as 1913 during a miners' strike in West Virginia an armoured train was used by the mine company's police to attack a tented colony of strikers, firing over 200 rounds in the process.

Resisting state authority

The real anomaly of the American experience is that armed policing did not follow resistance to the state, as it did in other frontier territories. Settlers were not a subject and rebellious population to be suppressed like native peoples throughout the British Empire. The turmoil of the frontier and cities of the eastern seaboard as immigrants flocked to the new continent was expressed as criminality. However, a more recent contribution of America to armed policing arguably does owe something to popular resistance to the state. In 1968, at the height of campus unrest prompted by opposition to the Vietnam War and a succession of 'long hot summers' of ghetto riots, the Los Angeles Police introduced the idea of Special Weapons and Tactics (SWAT) (Beck 1972). These are more or less dedicated teams of highly trained officers who are used for the more difficult and sensitive armed operations. They are equipped with military weapons and other equipment, such as assault rifles and distraction grenades (Clapp 1987). SWAT teams spread rapidly throughout the major law enforcement agencies, local, state and federal, suggesting that they represented more than a limited operational response to specific policing problems. The weaponry, tactics and even the acronym 'SWAT', seems indicative of a quasi-military reaction to widespread disaffection amongst the civil population, especially black Americans who, in the 1960s, still were denied full citizenship.

Closing the Police–Military Gap

The Americans were not alone in developing SWAT units, albeit that similar squads throughout the world acquired less dramatic designations. In London the Metropolitan Police had created D11 in 1966. Combat-ready, these forces appear virtually identical: a dark blue or black hooded coverall; respirators; body armour with ceramic plates; radios with ear-pieces and throat microphones; carrying Heckler and Koch MP5 sub-machine guns supplemented with 9mm self-loading sidearms; and also equipped with tear-smoke, distraction grenades, and various devices for removing doors and windows. Members of these squads are skilled in techniques of rapid entry, including abseiling down the outside of buildings, and practice engaging armed adversaries. In other words, they bear a striking similarity in appearance, weapons and tactics to military special forces such as the renowned British Special Air Service (SAS). Does this, therefore, suggest that the distinction between military and police is becoming blurred? Are police forces throughout the industrialized world moving towards the military end of the spectrum?

The appearance, weapons and tactics of these units are largely dictated by operational necessity. Officers need a hooded coverall to save them from contamination in the event that CS irritant is used in an assault, an operational possibility that also dictates the need for respirators. The dark colour and absence of insignia on the coverall are designed to deny adversaries a clear target at which to fire. The Heckler and Koch MP5 has earned an enviable reputation for reliability in circumstances where unreliability could easily prove fatal. Tactics such as abseiling are necessitated by the need to gain entry to premises for the purposes of hostage-rescue.

Beneath these surface considerations, lies a deeper and more problematic issue: the tactic of engaging an armed adversary. The police preference in Britain and elsewhere is to contain, if possible, an armed adversary (Waddington 1991a). Hence, a typical hostage situation will involve police laying siege to the 'stronghold' (usually a building or room within a building, but which might be a train, plane, boat or other vehicle) until the hostage-taker surrenders him- or (much more rarely) herself. Hostage rescue, by contrast, involves rapidly entering a 'stronghold' engaging the hostage-taker and rescuing the hostage. The almost inevitable corollary of such an operation is that the hostage-taker(s) will be killed. As officers burst into the premises, they will have only a brief moment in which to identify an armed adversary and overpower him. This will be accomplished with necessary speed and aggression, and will take place to the accompaniment of distraction grenades, CS and much shouting, screaming and general commotion. The idea that officers would not eliminate any armed adversary they encountered in these circumstances is frankly absurd. The irony is that police, at least in Britain, are placed in this quasi-military role because of the distinction that is drawn between the military, whose task is to deal with an enemy, and the police, whose task it is to tackle criminals. Thus, the expertise of the SAS cannot be used against those criminals who adopt the same tactics as terrorists.

The gap between the police and the military is most perilously jeopardized by terrorism. In those countries where terrorism flourishes policing tends to be paramilitary. In this respect Northern Ireland has merely conformed to the general rule for the past quarter of a century. The question is whether that process of paramilitarization leads to police and the military acting as 'aid to the civil power' to view suspected terrorists not as citizens committing criminal acts, but as an enemy. Certainly, the status of terrorists seems genuinely ambiguous: they claim to be waging a 'war' against the state whom they oppose, a claim that implicitly denies their citizenship of that state. On the other hand, the British government allocates responsibility for armed operations against terrorists to the military. Does this mean, that like a foreign enemy in wartime, terrorists can be eliminated by military means? Urban (1992) has persuasively argued that at various times throughout the Northern Ireland 'troubles' military units, principally the SAS, have 'ambushed' suspected 'Active Service Units' (ASUs) of the Provisional IRA (PIRA), rather than seeking to arrest them. Certainly, it is difficult to reconcile the operation at Loughgall in 1987 with a police action. Urban estimates 1,200 rounds were fired at the terrorists, some from belt-fed general purpose machine-guns, riddling some of the vehicles being used and killing those inside who were out of view of the soldiers (Urban 1992). As Urban concludes, the manner of this and other attacks is entirely consistent with a military ambush where the tactic is to eliminate the enemy by creating a field of fire in the 'killing zone' so intense that survival is minimized. That soldiers revert to their basic training and ideology is hardly surprising, but there have been allegations that specialist police units in Northern Ireland have adopted this military style of engagement. It was this that led to the 'shoot to kill' allegations (Asmal 1985, 'United Kingdom: Northern Ireland' 1988) and the inquiry headed by John Stalker, Assistant Chief Constable of the Greater Manchester Police in 1984 and taken over by Colin Sampson in controversial circumstances in 1986 (Taylor 1987, Stalker 1988). Certainly, there is plentiful comparative evidence that when the state is perceived to be under threat, recourse is made to illegal methods of suppressing that threat, such as the 'death squads' of some South American states (Bowden 1978).

Restraining the Use of Force

The prospect that police might be tempted or driven to use an increasing measure of force raises the issue of how this might be restrained. This poses, in its starkest terms, the ultimate paradox of policing, 'who guards the guardians?' This is so not least because opening fire upon an armed adversary is quintessentially a matter of individual discretion. In most jurisdictions individual police officers are held personally liable for inflicting injury or death. The decision whether or not to open fire is one that must be taken in an instant. It will depend, inevitably, upon the subjective assessment by the officer of the scale and immediacy of the threat posed by an adversary and the opportunities for dealing with the situation by alternative means. Controlling such discretion seems to pose formidable problems. Would an officer, faced with a potentially life-threatening situation, be influenced by force policy or even the law?

Strange as it may seem, changing departmental policy has had a significant impact on the frequency with which police use their weapons in the United States (Fyfe 1978, 1982a, Chapman 1982, Sherman 1983, Wilson 1980). However, this may tell us more about the laxity with which many American police departments approached policy in this connection (a notable illustration of which was a departmental policy that prescribed only 'Never take me [the gun] out in anger, never put me back in disgrace'!). This is one conclusion to be drawn from Sherman's analysis of three departments that effected such change, since there was a marked reduction in shots fired in dubious circumstances following the implementation of the policy. However, shots fired in more obviously serious circumstances remained at their previous levels (Sherman 1983). Nevertheless, the apparent influence of changes in departmental policy upon individual behaviour in highly charged situations does weigh against the fatalistic view that little or nothing can be done to alter how 'street cops' exercise their discretion.

The question, therefore, arises whether police in other jurisdictions should be given less latitude in the use of lethal force. From this perspective, the vagueness of British law has attracted considerable criticism. Section 3 of the Criminal Law Act 1967 states that 'Any person may use such force as is reasonable' for a lawful purpose (identical provisions apply in Northern Ireland). In addition, the common law on self-defence and breach of the peace may have some bearing on the judgement of a court (Harlow 1974, Ashworth 1975). Critics (Asmal 1985, 'United Kingdom: Northern Ireland' 1988, Kitchin 1989), have argued that the law is far too permissive and that it should be more narrowly defined, stipulating the conditions under which legal force may be used. This, critics hope, would reduce the opportunity for police and military personnel to shoot unarmed suspects and escape punishment. But would it? There are several reasons to doubt that it would.

The first is raised by Harding (1970) in his classic examination of police killings in Australia. That is the 'stranglehold' that police everywhere have over the investigation of alleged misconduct by fellow officers. This ranges from failing to test thoroughly the justification offered by officers for opening fire to the fabrication of evidence by the means of 'throw-down weapons' planted on the bodies of those shot by police to 'justify' recourse to lethal force. Clearly, this is a formidable obstacle. What is, perhaps, more puzzling is that this 'stranglehold' is not used to greater effect. Why do SAS units, who are accused of callously gunning down terrorists in pre-planned ambushes, fail to take the precaution of supplying their victims with 'throw-down weapons' after the smoke has cleared? On the other hand, the experience of John Stalker suggests that not only the police, but other agencies of the security forces, will obstruct investigations that threaten to expose wrongdoing by their personnel (Stalker 1988).

A second reason for doubt is whether juries would convict officers who killed suspects in contravention of narrowly defined laws. Although it is difficult to disentangle this from the possibility that police have a 'stranglehold' over the investigation, experience does not suggest that juries are eager to convict police officers or soldiers who mistakenly shoot even wholly innocent people. The British police officers who shot Stephen Waldorf, John Shorthouse and Cherry Groce were all tried for very serious offences and all were acquitted (see Waddington 1991a for details). In each case the jury accepted that the defendants were placed in a difficult situation not out of volition but because it was their duty, and that they made a tragic mistake. Even when convicted of murder, those who find themselves in this position are likely to arouse public sympathy rather than opprobrium, as the case of Pte Lee Clegg has recently illustrated. Clegg was a soldier manning a roadblock in Northern Ireland when a car attempted to speed through the checkpoint without stopping. A number of shots were fired at the car and Clegg appears to have fired a shot once the car had halted. This fateful shot killed the passenger, a 14-year-old schoolgirl. Clegg served four years of a life sentence for the murder of the girl before being released on licence following a campaign for his release in which Members of Parliament participated vocally.

The third reason for doubt is that the very vagueness of British law might actually prove a greater restraint than the drawing of firm legal boundaries. What critics need to explain is why shooting by the police is so exceptional in the United Kingdom. What is fascinating about Northern Ireland is not that the security forces might have been tempted to 'ambush' suspected terrorists, but that in the context of an insurrectionary war they have done so with such infrequency. The law may be much less important than general cultural expectations that regard the use of firearms by the British police to be exceptional. This is reinforced by the fact that police are not routinely armed, armed operations increasingly being the responsibility of specialist units, and training that emphasizes the need for caution (Waddington 1991a).

Arming an Unarmed Police

Can the British police continue to maintain their unarmed status? The issue has been hotly debated during the 1990s, culminating in a ballot of Police Federation members in 1995 that overwhelmingly rejected routine arming. However, the Commissioner of the Metropolitan Police, Sir Paul Condon, has remarked that policy on arming police will be 'incident driven'. The prospect is that each future murder of a police officer will incrementally shift policing towards greater use of firearms until every British 'bobby' will carry a gun on his or her hip. Certainly, the recent history of police weapons policy has been 'incident driven'. The deployment of armed response vehicles (ARVs) was a clear illustration of this. A Home Office Working Party rejected such a deployment in 1985 (Home Office 1986). However, following the massacre of 16 people by a deranged gunman in the small country town of Hungerford in 1986, an inquiry by Charles McLaughlin advocated the adoption of ARVs despite his conclusion that the presence of ARVs at Hungerford would most likely have led to increased casualties since the ARV crews would have been outgunned by Michael Ryan (Waddington 1991). Imagining that routinely carrying a gun would offer better protection to police officers seems profoundly mistaken. The general experience worldwide is that whilst all but a handful of police forces are armed, rates of crime, armed crime and attacks on police vary enormously. It seems that carrying a gun on one's hip is largely irrelevant to police vulnerability. This is because it seems that many attacks are entirely unpredictable (Bristow 1963, Cardarelli 1968). The annual supplement to the FBI's Uniform Crime Report detailing the circumstances in which officers have been killed on duty pays eloquent testimony to this. What does seem to have reduced fatalities amongst American law enforcers has been the widespread adoption of body armour.

The likelihood that the British police will carry firearms may have less to do with the incidence of armed crime than with the status of the civil population as 'citizens'. The emergence of a social structure divided at least as much by race as it has been by class, and the concentration of ethnic minorities in deprived areas could encourage the development of 'internal colonialism' (Brewer 1994). The consistent pattern in policing has been that where the civil population or section of it is excluded from the status of 'citizen' it is subjected to more oppressive forms of policing. That is the most frightening prospect that currently faces the future of unarmed civil policing in Britain.

Bibliography

Ahire, P.T. 1991. *Imperial policing: the emergence and role of the police in colonial Nigeria 1860–1960*. Milton Keynes: Open University Press.

Anderson, D.M. 1991. Policing, prosecution and the law in colonial Kenya, c. 1905–39. In *Policing the empire: government, authority and control, 1830–1940*, D.M. Anderson, D. Killingray (eds), 183–200. Manchester: Manchester University Press.

Anderson, D.M. & D. Killingray (eds). 1991. *Policing the empire: government, authority and control, 1830–1940*. Manchester: Manchester University Press.

Ashworth, A.J. 1975. Self-defence and the right to life. *Cambridge Law Journal* **12**, 338–45.

Asmal, K. 1985. *Shoot to kill? International lawyers' inquiry into the lethal use of firearms by the security forces in Northern Ireland*. Dublin: Mercier Press.

Beck, G.N. 1972. SWAT – the Los Angeles Police Special Weapons and Tactics teams. *FBI Law Enforcement Bulletin* 8–30.

Bowden, T. 1978. *Beyond the limits of the law*. Harmondsworth: Penguin.

Brewer, J.D. 1994. *Black and blue: policing in South Africa*. Oxford: Clarendon.

Bristow, A.P. 1963. Police officer shootings – a tactical evaluation. *Journal of Criminal Law, Criminology and Police Science* **54**, 93–5.

Brogden, M. 1991. *On the Mersey beat.* Oxford: Oxford University Press.

Brogden, M.E. 1989. The origins of the South African Police – Institutional versus structural approaches. In *Acta juridica*, W. Scharf (ed.), 1–19. Cape Town: Faculty of Law, University of Cape Town.

Brownlee, I.D. 1989. Superior orders: time for a new realism? *Criminal law review* 396–411.

Cardarelli, A.P. 1968. An analysis of police killed by criminal action: 1961–1963. *Journal of Criminal Law, Criminology and Police Science* **59**, 447–53.

Cawthra, G. 1993. *Policing South Africa.* London: Zed Books.

Chapman, S.G. 1982. Police policy on the use of firearms. In *Readings on the police use of deadly force*, J.J. Fyfe (ed.), 224–57. Washington, DC: Police Foundation.

Clapp, W.M. 1987. *Modern law enforcement weapons and tactics.* Northbrook, Ill.: DBI Books.

Cohen, P. 1979. Policing the working class city. In *Capitalism and the rule of law*, B. Fine, R. Kinsey, J. Lea, S. Picciotto, J. Young (eds), 118–36. London: Hutchinson.

Critchley, T. 1970. *The conquest of violence.* London: Constable.

Critchley, T.A. 1978. *A history of police in England and Wales.* London: Constable.

Emsley, C. 1983. *Policing and its context.* London: Macmillan.

Emsley, C. 1991. *The English Police: a political and social history.* Hemel Hempstead: Harvester Wheatsheaf.

Everlegh, R. 1979. *Peacekeeping in a democratic society.* London: Hurst.

Finnane, M. 1987. *Policing in Australia: historical perspectives.* Kensington, NSW: New South Wales University Press.

Fyfe, J.J. 1978. Administrative interventions on police shooting discretion. *Journal of Criminal Justice* **7**, 309–23.

Fyfe, J.J. 1982a. Administrative intervention on police shooting discretion: an empirical examination. In *Readings on police use of deadly force*, J.J. Fyfe (ed.), 258–81. Washington, DC: Police Foundation.

Fyfe, J.J 1982b. Race and extreme police-citizen violence. In *Readings on police use of deadly force*, J.J. Fyfe, (ed.), 173–94. Washington: Police Foundation.

Geary, R. 1985. *Policing industrial disputes: 1893 to 1985.* Cambridge: Cambridge University Press.

Goldkamp, J.S. 1976. Minorities as victims of police shootings: interpretations of racial disproportionality and police use of deadly force. *Justice System Journal* **2**, 169–83.

Gould, R.W. & M.J. Waldren 1986. *London's armed police.* London: Arms and Armour.

Grundlingh, A. 1991. 'Protectors and friends of the people'? The South African Constabulary in the Transvaal and the Orange River Colony, 1900–08. In *Policing the empire: government, authority and control, 1830–1940*, D.M. Anderson & D. Killingray (eds), 168–82. Manchester: Manchester University Press.

Harding, R.W. 1970. *Police killings in Australia.* Sydney: Penguin.

Harlow, C. 1974. Self-defence: public right or private privilege? *Criminal Law Review* 528–38.

Hawkins, G. & P. Ward 1970. Armed and disarmed police: police firearms policy and levels of violence. *Journal of Research in Crime and Delinquency* **7**, 188–97.

Hawkins, H. & R. Thomas 1991. White policing of black populations: a history of race and social control in America. In *Out of order?*, E. Cashmore & E. McLaughlin (eds), 65–86. London: Routledge.

Hawkins, R. 1991. The 'Irish model' and the empire: a case for reassessment. In *Policing the empire: government, authority and control, 1830–1940*, D.M. Anderson & D. Killingray (eds), 18–32. Manchester: Manchester University Press.

Hill, R. 1986. *History of the New Zealand police – the theory and practice of coercive social and racial control in New Zealand, 1767–1867*. Wellington, New Zealand: Historical Publications Branch, Department of Internal Affairs.

Hill, R.S. 1991. The policing of colonial New Zealand: from informal to formal control, 1840–1907. In *Policing the empire: government, authority and control, 1830–1940*, D.M. Anderson & D. Killingray (eds), 52–70. Manchester: Manchester University Press.

Home Office 1986. *Report by the Home Office Working Group on the police use of firearms*. London: Home Office.

Johnson, D.H. 1991. From military to tribal police: policing the Upper Nile Province of the Sudan. In *Policing the empire: government, authority and control, 1830–1940*, D.M. Anderson & D. Killingray (eds), 151–67. Manchester: Manchester University Press.

Johnson, H. 1991. Patterns of policing in the post-emancipation British Caribbean, 1835–95. In *Policing the empire: government, authority and control, 1830–1940*, D.M. Anderson & D. Killingray (eds), 71–91. Manchester: Manchester University Press.

Kee, R. 1972. *The green flag: a history of Irish nationalism*. London: Weidenfeld and Nicholson.

Killingray, D. 1991. Guarding the extending frontier: policing the Gold Coast, 1865–1913. In *Policing the empire: government, authority and control, 1830–1940*, D.M. Anderson, & D. Killingray (eds), 106–25. Manchester: Manchester University Press.

Kitchin, H. 1989. *The Gibraltar report: an independent observer's report of the inquest into the deaths of Mairead Farrell, Daniel McCann and Sean Savage, Gibraltar September 1988*. London: National Council for Civil Liberties.

Kopel, D.B. 1992. *The Samurai, the Mountie, and the Cowboy*. New York: Prometheus.

Liska, A.E. & J. Yu 1992. Specifying and testing the threat hypothesis: police use of deadly force. In *Social threat and social control*, A.J. Liska (ed.), 53–68. Albany: State University of New York.

Manning, P.K. 1980. Violence and the police role. *Annals of the American Academy of Political and Social Sciences* **452**, 135–44.

Meyer, M.W. 1980. Police shootings at minorities: the case of Los Angeles. *Annals of the American Academy of Political and Social Science* **452**, 98–110.

Miller, W.R. 1977. *Cops and bobbies: police authority in New York and London, 1830–1870*. Chicago: University of Chicago Press.

Milton, C.H., J.W. Halleck, J. Lardner, G.L. Abrecht 1977. *Police use of deadly force*. Washington, DC: Police Foundation.

Milton, C., J.W. Halleck, J. Lardner, G.L. Abrecht 1982. Analysis of shooting incidents. In *Readings on police use of deadly force*, J.J. Fyfe (ed.), 42–64. Washington, DC: Police Foundation.

Morrison, W.R. 1975. The North-West Mounted Police and the Klondike gold rush. In *Police forces in history*, G.L. Mosse (ed.), 263–75. Beverly Hills: Sage.

Morrison, W.R. 1991. Imposing the British way: the Canadian Mounted Police and the Klondike gold rush. In *Policing the empire: government, authority and control, 1830–1940*, D.M. Anderson & D. Killingray (eds), 92–104. Manchester: Manchester University Press.

Nathan, L. 1989. Troops in the townships 1984–1987. In *War and society*, J. Cock & L. Nathan (eds), 67–78. Cape Town: David Philip.

165

Palmer, S.H. 1988. *Police and protest in England and Ireland, 1780–1850*. Cambridge: Cambridge University Press.

Roach, J. 1985. The French police. In *Police and public order in Europe*, J. Roach & J. Thomaneck (eds), 107–42. London: Croom Helm.

Roach, J. & J. Thomaneck (eds) 1985. *Police and public order in Europe*. London: Croom Helm.

Rowe, P.J. 1985. Keeping the peace: lethal weapons, the soldier and the law. In *Military intervention in democratic societies*, R. Rowe & C.J. Whelan (eds), 197–215. London: Croom Helm.

Sherman, L.W. 1983. Reducing police gun use: critical events, administrative policy, and organisational change. In *Control in the police organisation*, M. Punch (ed.), 98–125. Cambridge, Mass.: MIT Press.

Smith, C. 1992. Communal conflict and insurrection in Palestine, 1936–48. In *Policing and decolonisation: politics, nationalism and the police*, 1917–65, D.M. Anderson & D. Killingray (eds), 62–83. Manchester: Manchester University Press.

Stalker, J. 1988. *Stalker*. London: Penguin.

Stead, P.J. 1983. *The police of France*. New York: Macmillan.

Stockwell, A.J. 1992. Policing during the Malayan Emergency, 1948–60: communism, communalism and decolonisation. In *Policing and decolonisation: politics, nationalism and the police, 1917–65*, D.M. Anderson & D. Killingray (eds), 105–26. Manchester: Manchester University Press.

Taft, P. & P. Ross 1979. American labour violence: its causes, character, and outcome. In *Violence in America*, H.D. Graham & T.R. Gurr (eds), 187–241. Beverly Hills: Sage.

Takagi, P. 1974. A garrison state in a 'democratic' society. *Crime & Social Justice 5*, 27–33.

Taylor, P. 1987. *Stalker: the search for the truth*. London: Faber & Faber.

Throup, D. 1992. Crime, politics and the police in colonial Kenya, 1939–63. In *Policing and decolonisation: politics, nationalism and the police, 1917–65*, D.M. Anderson & D. Killingray (eds), 127–57. Manchester: Manchester University Press.

Tolnay, S.E. & E.M. Beck 1992. Toward a threat model of southern black lynchings. In *Social threat and social control*, A.J. Liska (ed.), 33–52. Albany: State University of New York.

Townshend, C. 1992. Policing insurgency in Ireland, 1914–23. In *Policing and decolonisation: politics, nationalism and the police, 1917–65*, D.M. Anderson & D. Killingray (eds), 22–41. Manchester: Manchester University Press.

United Kingdom: Northern Ireland 1988. *Killings by security forces and 'supergrass' trials*. London: Amnesty International.

Urban, M. 1992. *Big boys' rules*. London: Faber & Faber.

Vogler, R. 1991. *Reading the riot act: the magistracy, the police and the army in civil disorder*. Milton Keynes: Open University.

Waddington, P.A.J. 1990. 'Overkill' or 'Minimum Force'? *Criminal Law Review*, 695–707.

Waddington, P.A.J. 1991a. *The strong arm of the law*. Oxford: Clarendon.

Weinberger, B. 1991. *Keeping the peace? policing strikes in Britain, 1906–1926*. Oxford: Berg.

Weiss, R.P. 1986. Private Detective Agencies and Labour Discipline in the United States, 1855–1946. *Historical Journal* **29**, 87–107.

Weiss, R.P. 1987. From 'slugging detective' to 'labour relations': policing labour at Ford, 1930–1947. In *Private policing*, C.D. Shearing & P.C. Stenning (eds), 110–30. Newbury Park, California: Sage.

Wilson, J.Q. 1980. Police use of deadly force. *FBI Law Enforcement Bulletin*. August, 16–21.

CHAPTER 10

Community Policing as Cherry Pie

M. BROGDEN

Community Policing as Contextual

Policing is bedevilled by definitional problems. Given the different origins of police forces internationally – legally, culturally and organizationally – the prospects of reaching an agreed definition of 'the police' results in little more than the functionalist aphorism 'Policing is what people in blue (or whatever colour), police officers do'. Varying codes of law govern police duties. Restrictive in the Code Napoleon, permissive in common law, they contribute one source of the miasma. Culture, from the generalities of national tradition to the specifics of the canteen culture of the police, has inspired different police styles and conventions. Historical patterns of organization, from the centralized High Police of Marshall Fouche to the local structures of the Vigilantes of the American Frontier, determined future practices and legitimation. The development of community policing in different national and local contexts reflects the tensions between the legal, cultural, and organizational structures of policing. The complexity of that contextual mesh – law, culture, and organization – prevents easy transplants – whether it be from small town America to the urban ghettoes or from Newport Mews to downtown Antwerp. As several commentators have noted (Bayley 1984), the origins of the *Koban* system in Japan (and Singapore) cannot be understood without contextualization within Japanese culture and society. Conversely, the absence of community policing models, for example, in Austria and in Belgium, needs to be understood from within the specifics of historically-derived law, culture, and organization. Community policing, as popularized from its North American roots, is as American as cherry pie. It is not a model that can be culturally transplanted to domains with different structures and traditions. The 'failure' of community policing in much of Western Europe, as in the cities of North America, is partly one of implementation. But the larger impediment is its alien legal, cultural, and organizational history.

Community Policing as Ahistorical – History and Legitimation

History has warped Anglo-Saxon notions of community policing. An ahistoricity has produced a myopia over the source of failure of most community policing pro- grammes. The substitution of pragmatism for historical understanding has blinkered the advocates. The same historical material can both legitimate and disavow com- munity police origins (Monkkonen 1981). A police commander, seeking justification for a new community policing scheme preaches 'Inside everyone of our policemen and women, there is tithingman waiting to get out' (quoted in Brogden 1982). Such mythology locates the original constable as an equal amongst equals, policing the community of *his* fellows.

Alternatively, that functionary of early modern England can be portrayed as an official imposed on the community by the Norman overlord, to hold the community to ransom for any actions which infringed the latter's sovereignty. The tithingman, the mythical source of community policing, can be pictured more critically. Even within one country, history tells different stories and offers different legitimation for community policing. Differences are noted if they lie across the Pacific but not if they exist across the Straits of Dover. Models developed without historical contextualization are doomed. For example, Moir (1990) notes that community policing developments in Australia failed to recognize the traditional unpopularity historically of the police. This long-term community distrust cannot be ignored. Constructing community policing without regard to historical perceptions of the police is shortsighted. This ahistoricity (and sometimes ethnocentric history) derives from the hegemony of North American scholarship in police studies. Research has recently suggested that *rural* policing practices contain many lessons for the recon- struction of *urban* policing on community lines (Weishett *et al.* 1994). The rural and small town policing of the United States may have been the taken-for-granted model for the urban developments.

New developments in Western European countries tend to be conflated in the com- munity policing literature as a reaction to the crime-fighting model. Commentators on the 'collapse' of traditional policing have generally failed to recognize that they are referring to a specific 'crime-fighting' prototype. 'Traditional' has been used as a synonym for crime-fighting. In fact, at least three models of state policing are evid- ent in Western society. There is the centralized, gendarmerie model (see, for example, Liang 1991) of most of Western Europe, a version that draws originally upon the Pax Napoleon era in centralized or federalized organization and state-defined duties. In its crudest form, that model is concerned with order-maintenance on behalf of the central state (and, to a lesser extent, the social order of the streets in terms immortalized by Fouche). It features a para-military, hierarchical structure with a minimum of legal and organizational discretion for the rank-and-file officer. When writers refer to the collapse of traditional policing, this model is largely ignored, its practices not subject to evaluative scrutiny.

In the xenophobia of the Anglo-American literature, traditional policing is epitom- ized as 'bandit-catching' or crime-fighting policing (Brogden & Shearing 1993). Here, the major *raison-d'être* of the force is to 'catch criminals' rather than to enforce social order. Organizationally, it contains a range of specialisms with priority being given to criminal investigation. Discretion is common but formally bounded by the limits of the criminal law. It is this model to which commentators refer when they talk of the crisis in traditional policing. Finally, we have the hugger-mugger of community policing, in its many guises and variations. Organizationally, community policing is decentralized, with a 'flattened' pyramid structure. The police organization functions to solve problems, often independently of whether those problems are located within the remit of the criminal law. Professional discretion is paramount in the search for resolutions, not all of which may involve a legal, or indeed, a criminal sanction.

Certain contemporary police organizations often reflect different components of these models. Thus the Garda of the Irish Republic and the Royal Ulster Constabulary both represent paramilitary forms of organization while simultaneously practising discretion from within the permissive parameters of common law. Similarly, the former South African Police acted as an internal army of occupation while operating traditional common law powers of arrest and prosecution. Lack of appreciation of different historical orthodoxies results in an assumption of evolutionary progression from crime-fighting towards community policing.

Community Policing as Atheoretical – the Equity Example

Community policing, whether as a philosophy or as a programme for implementation, features not only an ahistorical rendering but also a theoretical nihilism, a vacuum which betrays the inertia of police scholarship. The orthodox references derive almost entirely from the unilinear work of Herbert Goldstein (1963, 1990) who contributes a quasi-functionalist approach to the concept, primarily via his emphasis on discretion and problem-solving. In the late 1960s, the American research literature focused on police application of the law (Goldstein 1963, LaFave 1965) and especially on how discretion could be guided in the dichotomy between law enforcement and social order (Skolnick 1966). Law and order were often incompatible goals and led to police deviance in the attempt to resolve that dilemma. Central concerns in this literature were to develop administrative devices for controlling the police discretion, to determine their own resolution to that conflict between law and order (Goldstein 1967, Krantz *et al.* 1979). Hence, Goldstein's construction (1979) of the concept of *problem-oriented* policing as a way of developing administrative policies that would guide the exercise of discretion. Such discretion could only be controlled and equitably directed, Goldstein argued, by developing an analysis of the problem which discretion was being used to resolve. The criminal law was *only one* device which the police could use to address problems equitably.

The concern with equity directs attention to a theoretical contribution which may loosen that functionalist stranglehold. Equity in policing is increasingly perceived as a problem. No longer (as in the earlier evaluative studies) are communities regarded as homogeneous units consisting of citizens with legal and social rights. Social inequality is recognized. The implementation studies reveal that wealthier city areas with less crime tend to be the locus where community policing is most in demand, and where the few successful schemes operate. Lower class, more hetero-geneous communities (Skogan 1990) characterized by high property and violence rates, represent unfertile ground for community policing. Community police officers develop affinity with the more powerful pressure groups that conservatively support policing and consequently succumb to providing them with a larger share of policing resources (Bayley 1988), a practice that is reinforced by the orthodox rank-and-file culture.

Community policing involves engagement in a world of inequity. Police may act in discriminatory fashion in conducting a futile attempt to solve problems deriv-ing from social inequity. Broadening of the mandate through community policing may result in the partisan exercise of authority (Manning 1988). For example, the Portland, Oregon, police trained landlords in 'tenant management' in order to keep 'undesirables' out of public property, a practice that raised major civil liberties questions. In Mission, Texas, the Police Department provided full-time Education Resource Officers for school classes (in the context of an anti-drugs campaign), thereby threatening the professional rights of schoolteachers (Eck 1993). Where the police become dependent upon community wishes, discrimination may result from inequitable community power. The dilemma in a heterogeneous society or com-munity is one of the police deciding whose interests and values should be upheld, often resulting in political decision-making. In Short's (1983) example of the Devon and Cornwall decision over the policing of a nuclear site, the police commander was able to make political determinations about the organization and lifestyles of local communities. Bayley (1988) argues that intensive community policing may mean an increased risk that the law will be enforced in discriminatory, unequal ways, that reflect the distribution of neighbourhood political power. Equity in community policing is no longer simply defined as adherence to the rule of law or to numerical parity. The Goldstein model cannot solve the equity problem in the American ghetto or in other national contexts.

Community policing is consistently faced with making decisions regarding equity. Traditional community relations to the police institution implied a passive role ('do we get our fair share of police services?'). But for many active community groups, equity is more about participatory management and power sharing. This perspect-ive raises the question of equity to a new level: towards citizen involvement in decision-making, in community defence, in problem-solving, and in various commun-ity empowerment schemes. Public officials and police may withdraw support from neighbourhoods that cannot be organized and where there is little affinity to policing. As the police cannot withdraw completely from a neighbourhood, these areas will receive reactive incident-based policing which may accentuate class divisions (Eck & Rosenbaum 1994). Problems therefore arise of *equity* in community policing – how should police resources be distributed? To those that are articulate and powerful but have insignificant crime and quality of life problems or to the more inarticulate crime-ridden localities? Nothing in the work of Goldstein or in Bayley, gives guid-ance to the resolution of that question – how to resolve the quandary of delivering equal services in an unequal society? Pragmatic community policing fails to offer guidance on the critical issue of discriminatory practice. Eck & Rosenbaum (1994) have been the only scholars to attempt to deal with the problem of equity. However, they can only suggest changes in the procedural rules to deal with the equity dilemma.

A more erudite origin (and one that is implicit in much of the Left Realism approach to criminology in North America and in the UK), lies in the contributions of the Bolshevik jurist, Pashukanis (1978), who first raised to critical legal scrutiny the conflict between *social* equality and *legal* equality. Legal equals, citizens (Balbus 1973), are often social unequals – as determined by factors of race, of gender, and of socio-economic class. Where power, resources, and social problems are unequally distributed, Community policing – if it is to deal with causes rather than symptoms – has to discriminate in favour of those who suffer most. Equal treatment of all citizenry (a goal made more difficult by the greater political power of the wealthy groups) ignores the relative problems of those in the downtown districts. Calls for help, for service, are on any subjective scale more critical when they come from the most disadvantaged. Dealing with the problems of the disadvantaged (the unstated perplexity at the core of community policing's concerns with quality of life issues) lies not in guaranteeing *parity* of community policing services independently of variations in community power.

Pashukanis' work, elucidated from the complexity of legal theory to the problematics of community policing, infuses the training package constructed for community policing within the new South African Police Service. If law and the work of law enforcement personnel are to service quality of life concerns, they must act in a positively discriminatory fashion. Community policing has to deal unequally with people who are nominally legal equals. Dealing with the 'clients' for police services according to their social needs not according to their political 'pull', becomes a central motif. A bicycle stolen from Soweto is to be treated more seriously than a BMW stolen from a prosperous white suburb like Randburg. Community police officers are mandated to act in unequal fashion, to treat people in terms of the social category of need, not as individual citizens, with different qualitative requirements of the new community police.

In South Africa, state policing always served an unequal social order. The new community police training system was structured not to eliminate discrimination, but rather to reverse its flow. Community policing if it is to take the problem of equity seriously, the quality of life issues at the core of the philosophy, has to act with inequality on behalf of the poor and oppressed. Where the officer is politically empowered by the community, he/she may be transformed from being a community resource to a community advocate – acting on behalf of the community against the legitimate authorities (Carter 1995). The implementation findings on the failure of community policing in America's inner cities highlight not just the problems of practice, but the barrenness at the central theoretical core of the quasi-functionalism of its academic proponents. Such accounts offer little guidance to policing practice in those downtown districts or to the policing problems of other societies.

The failure of the quasi-functionalism of Goldstein to deal with the key problems of equity has not prevented the model being exported by the international police salesforce to Western European countries, where the blend of law, of culture, and of organization contains different presumptions regarding the police role. Community policing, especially with regard to the question of equity, *needs* to be understood primarily in terms of local exigencies – whether the legal powers of the police officer allows the development of the kind of extra-legal practices required by community policing, whether the political culture of the particular society provides for an acceptance of state police officers conducting activities outside more general public order and crime related functions (and within that broader culture, the specific local police culture), and whether the inherited organizational structure of the particular police institution allows for the degree of decentralization of command and discretion central to the community policing practices.

Community Policing as an Evolutionary Response to an American Policing Dilemma

Proponents of community policing claim that traditional policing (i.e. crime-fighting policing) has simply failed to 'deliver the goods' and that community policing is the evolutionary response. Traditional policework ignores the factors that most communities regard as a priority. In Wilson & Kelling's (1982) 'Broken Windows' argument, a police department that focuses solely or even primarily on serious crime will not be of much use to a community struggling to 'keep its head above water'. Quality of life matters are a communal priority, not the serious crime perceived by the police culture, by forms of police organization, and by police command. In effect, traditional policework '. . . for most police departments (is) patrol, emergency responses, and investigation' (Sparrow *et al.* 1990). The vast majority of calls to the police are to do with other things than serious crimes whereas police departments traditionally tend to see the former as garbage work (Moore & Trojanowicz 1988), rather than dealing with quality of life issues that dominate, for example, Police Liaison Committees (Moore 1992, Morgan & Maggs 1985). Further, the kind of crime that terrifies citizens the most – mugging, robbery, rape, homicide – is rarely encountered by police on patrol. Police officers spend most of their time passively patrolling and providing emergency services.[1]

Any attempt to improve police performance along traditional 'crime-fighting' lines has little value. There is no productivity gain from doing more of the same (Bayley & Skolnick 1986). The central police tactic in dealing with crime and fears of crime, that of randomized patrol, is largely a waste of resources (Kelling *et al.* 1974). Such patrols do not reassure citizens enough to affect their fear of crime nor engender greater trust in the police (Bayley & Skolnick 1986).[2] Increasing the number of police and police budgets rarely reduces crime rates or raises the proportion of crimes solved (Bayley & Skolnick 1986, Audit Commission 1991, Bayley 1994). Saturation policing works temporarily but may displace crime, and may be dysfunctional for long-term police community relations. Improving response time to emergency calls has no perceptible effect on the likelihood of arresting criminals (Scott 1981, Spelman & Brown 1984). What most victims want is predictable, rather than rapid response. Traditional policing is most fallible in dealing with so-called 'victimless' crimes – such as drug abuse and prostitution (Moore 1983). Crimes are not solved – in the sense of offenders being arrested and prosecuted – through criminal investigations conducted by detectives and police departments (Greenwood *et al.* 1977, Mawby 1979) but because offenders are immediately apprehended or someone identifies them. The success of police in criminal investigations has no appreciable effect on public security. Enhanced clearance rates are not related to changes in the level of crime.

> If criminals noticed the increased efficiency of the police, they certainly didn't seem to care (Bayley 1994: 5).

These studies have all emphasized that community policing arose as a response to North American policing problems – for example, in Edmonton, the police department developed community policing in order to achieve a reduction in the perceived excessive number of calls for police service (Koller 1990). These studies also spurred interest in developing universal alternatives to the traditional random patrol, rapid response, and follow-up investigation. Other writers have noted more structural factors in attempts to transform the crime-fighting model – such as fiscal constraints and demographic factors (zero population growth, an ageing population, and rural–urban migration) (Murphy & Muir 1985); emergency planning which needs greater citizen involvement (Scanlon 1991); and variations in political power (Heywood 1979). In practice, the police devote most resources to traditional, bureaucratically safe approaches that no longer work, if they ever did, and have been overtaken by structural changes (Bayley 1994).

Policy alternatives indicated included police involvement in organizing neighbourhoods and in building police community relations as a means of controlling fear of victimization (Wilson & Kelling 1982). Hence, traditional (crime-fighting) policing has been faced with several inter-linked crises – of operations (policing practices are highly ineffective at dealing with crime); of efficiency in crime prevention, especially in the failure to enlist the potential of citizens and communities in this process of crime prevention (Bayley 1994), and in dealing with the symptoms rather than the causes of crime; of professionalism (the lack of relations between higher police pay, codes of conduct, and effectiveness); and of accountability (Moore 1992). The response to these crises has led to a greater concern for community interaction and sensitivities, and recognition that quality of life factors are more important to the communities than are crime control, emergency response, and justice functions (Moore 1992). Crime absorbs minimal police time and therefore logically, the majority of duties should not be organized around a lesser practice. Fear of crime is perhaps a more important organizing core (Moore 1992). This recognition of the fear of crime creates two difficulties for the police. The police do not claim expertise on factors that contribute to that fear or on effective methods of reducing it. The fear of crime is often associated with the presence of a racially or ethnically dissimilar group. Consequently, the police can find it difficult to respond to divergent community interests and to provide an equitable service to all groups within the community.

The central message of these studies was that they forced police departments to focus attention on different purposes and different values. They encouraged the police to think beyond traditional law enforcement and to include objectives of crime prevention, fear reduction, and improved responses to general emergencies (Moore 1992). They required the police to be more imaginative in developing alternative responses to that of the criminal law (Bayley 1994). Finally, the varied research led to an organizational transformation – from a centralized command-and-control bureaucracy to a decentralized professional organization (Moore 1992).

Community policing in North America developed haphazardly through a combination of recognition of the failings of traditional policing together with a variety of local ad hoc innovations and improvisations (Eck 1993). Hence, community policing from this perspective has generally followed an evolutionary trajectory, drawing deeply on Anglo-American roots, concerns, and police models. Organizational and structural problems could be resolved by a new policing philosophy which recognized the fundamental importance of community problems, priorities, and relationships. The problems of the Anglo-Saxon crime fighting models were to be resolved by an historical resurrection of the solution in the community. The tithingman was re-born.

The Constituents of Community Policing as a Reaction to Crime-Fighting Failures

Community policing developed in response to these crises in the Anglo-Saxon model in two ways – pragmatically and as a philosophy (Trojanowicz & Bucqueroux 1994). Incremental, ad hoc, 'bolting-on' of schemes have been the dominant form of development. Common themes that characterize that pragmatism include four items – community crime prevention schemes; an increase in the number of foot patrols; development of localized command structures; and creation of systems of local accountability (Bennett 1994, Skolnick & Bayley 1987, Mawby 1990, Moir 1990).

An alternative approach to the location of conventional practice is to document the key themes that appear in the academic literature, distinguishing between the theory/philosophy of community policing and its actual practice (Skolnick & Bayley 1987). It is not the programme in itself that constitutes community policing but rather the philosophy behind the programme.[3] Hence the common themes within the philosophy are problem-solving of non-crime issues; partnerships between police and public; new forms of accountability; and power-sharing between community and police over police decision-making. Similarly, community policing operates at an ideological level to emphasize notions of service, flexibility, consumer responsiveness, conciliation, and negotiation. Community policing is about emphasizing and encouraging the development of preventive policing and non-conflictual aspects of policing, giving those aspects more status than is currently the case. Those practices may occur independently of a commitment to the philosophy of community policing (Mastrofski 1988). Bayley (1994) notes variations on several dimensions:[4] in personnel arrangements (it may be practised by all officers of force, irrespective of continual assignment, or delegated to CPOs and to beat officers); in organizational responsibility (it may be given to existing commands, such as patrol or criminal investigation, or to a specially created command); in deployment patterns (community police officers (CPOs) may be dispersed on to beats, formed into special squads to operate over wider areas, or based at headquarters); in technology (officers may work on foot, on bicycles, from mobile police stations, or from cars and vans); in function (in Edmonton, CPOs respond to emergency calls whereas Detroit's mini-station squads do not; problem solving is emphasized in some forces but not in others); in forms of consultation (some CPOs are responsible for liaising with community bodies, others have no such function but interact informally with the public on the beat); in co-ordination procedures (formal mechanisms established for that purpose or on a case-by-case basis); and in public participation (police departments may encourage citizens to join them in their work or keep them at arm's length).

Noteworthy from Bayley's listing is that (apart from a reference to the Japanese Koban) all the examples are drawn from police forces with an Anglo-American inheritance. Given Bayley's scholarship and erudition, it is remarkable that he does not espouse a central critique. Community policing is merchandise constructed incrementally within a particular police tradition, one whose success (or more commonly failure) needs to be linked critically to that tradition. Exporting community policing models is subject to all the caveats of other forms of colonialism, as the limited evidence of community policing schemes in Western Europe demonstrates.

Community Policing in Europe

Community policing processes in Western Europe vary dramatically. In countries such as Holland and Sweden, community policing has become the dominant philosophy (National Institute of Justice 1989). As in Canada, community policing has assumed orthodoxy rather than representing a radical challenge. In countries with quite different gendarmerie traditions of policing, such as France and Austria, little occurs under the community policing rubric. In the former Soviet bloc countries, cultural, organizational, and legal factors (together with political and economic exigencies) prevent any notable developments.

The critical decisive factors appear to be the combination of traditional forms of police organization, the cultural perception of the state police function, and the extent to which the criminal law is permissive or limiting in relations to police powers and duties. The development of community policing, in the tradition espoused by Goldstein, relates to a combination of decentralized organizational structures, a perception of the state police as being non-threatening (public consent), and a legal mandate which does not specify the limitations of the police function. In other words, Goldstein's work is situated within the specifics of a particular policing tradition.

Not that a combination of these factors is all-determining. Community policing can also develop in a country in which police functions have been legally limited. But the other elements of a decentralized organizational tradition, and a positive perception of the state police must be present. Community policing may grow indigenously, as in the Japanese tradition of the Koban, or it can be adapted given a particular combination of a 'push' factor – the diffusion[5] of new ideas on policing, and the receptivity of local conditions through that mix of organization, police status and legal mandate.

In the Scandinavian nation-states, independently of legal tradition, the other factors of organization and status lend themselves to such community policing developments. In Denmark, Neighbourhood Police Stations are common and some quarter of police officers function as community police (Boyle 1990). Danish police engage in various preventive policing measures within a broad rubric of community policing – a limited number of officers are assigned as 'education' police, with the main task of developing a positive relationship between the police and youngsters.[6] The City of Copenhagen also employs 15 specialized units within police stations to bring together schools, social workers, and the police, and Neighbourhood Police Houses provide a trouble-shooting base for a variety of police–community functions (National Institute of Justice 1989). The central mission of Swedish schemes started from a crime reduction exercise, with major crime prevention strategies and built-in assessment measures (Kuhlhorn & Svensson 1982). For example:

> Scandinavian ministations are especially attractive, warmly furnished, inviting places, where neighbourhood residents talk to the police about a variety of 'problems' – a husband's excessive drinking, child's failure to meet school obligations – that do not bear directly on crime (National Institute of Justice 1989: 10).

However, there are certain tensions in Swedish practice because of the centralized nature of the Swedish police system. Norway produces similar evidence with several detailed but essentially experimental locations for community policing posts. As with Sweden, there exists considerable friction between rhetoric and practice in Norway's case because of the problems of a conservative police culture (National Institute of Justice 1989). The Dutch police have been pioneers in community policing despite the older gendarmerie tradition and appear to have developed community policing as an indigenous alternative to the Anglo-Saxon model. The picture is complicated however by the multiplicity of forces and jurisdictions (Kruissink 1993). Considerable autonomy is exercised by local police forces as compared with the national institutions. Peculiarly, the police have a more ubiquitous role than in most other societies, being involved in issues of public health, in economic matters, and in matters of the quality of life in general (Fitzsimmons & Lavery 1976, Shane 1980). There is considerable experimentation prompted by evaluative studies on police service output and on a recognition of the original omnibus role for policing. The community policing picture appears to owe more to indigenous Dutch factors than to the import of Anglo-American notions (Van der Meeberg 1991).

Conversely, where the combination of traditional organization, legal mandate and the cultural location of the state police operate at the extreme, community policing schemes have been given little sustenance. For example, the French conception of the police role and organization prevents any major innovations. Juvenile squads work closely with other agencies but the French police are committed primarily to a state-defined public order role (Friedman 1991). The most proximate French approach to a community policing strategy is the 'Bonnes Maison' strategy for crime reduction. Critical in this context, is the importance of the joint agency Crime Prevention panel (Cornish 1991). Similarly, in Belgium, community policing remains fragmentized. Few of the 1980s innovations (such as neighbourhood constables, NWS, specialized 'social' patrol (Antwerp), team policing, and project surveillance) have survived. The operation of CPOs focuses mainly on information gathering, responding to citizen requests and on preventive actions. But generally, there is little commitment to community policing (Hendrieck *et al.* 1990). Elinerts *et al.* (1993) provide the only (critical) substantive documentation of Belgian community policing, arguing that the drive towards community policing was prompted by political and state policing scandals. In 1990, it was proposed to use the local municipal police as the cornerstone of community policing with the two national forces as complementary agents. The police function in the localities was to shift from reactive to proactive practices with more emphasis on crime prevention. Two years later a notion of 'Safety Contracts' between the local municipality and the central Ministry emerged with the model Contract suggesting eight different initiatives, one of which emphasized 'community policing philosophy'. In practice, Belgium has seen few relevant developments. The major impediment to the development of community policing in Belgium has been its rule-bound nature:

> Work is primarily committed to the development and control of rules and procedures; no time is left for real management, crime analysis or policy plans (Elinerts *et al.* 1993: 170).

Legal rules in particular are restrictive and the management and structures of Belgian policing are perceived to be incompatible with a community policing philosophy.

Austria (Proske 1994) provides another example of a Western Europe nation where the community policing approach is the antithesis of policing tradition. There are no documented community policing schemes. They are absent because of the centralized nature of Austrian policing, the belief that such policing would be seen as 'snooping' – there is, for example, much opposition to any development of NWS – and a dominant conservative view of police function as traditionally conceived. Crime reduction and prevention is conducted through a privatization of lower level police functions in the service of the argument that criminality is better resolved by releasing professional police from extraneous duties. In Germany, which again has a policing system developed from the gendarmerie tradition, there has been a general reluctance to move towards community policing (Feltes & Rebscher 1990) despite a major critique of both ordering and crime-fighting police functions (Feltes 1993). There are only isolated manifestations of the practices that occur under community policing rubric elsewhere; for example, foot patrols primarily to deal with the fear of crime (Koetsche 1990) and police consultancy bureaux for specific campaigns (Steinhilper 1979). But officers involved feel that they have low status (Feltes 1993).

Community policing in the Republic of Ireland represents the outcome of developments where gendarmerie history has been weaned through culture and common law to the potential development of appropriate schemes. But those schemes have generally derived from ad hoc initiatives, owing more to a search for instant solutions, independently of larger departmental considerations. According to Aylward (1993), the combination of terrorist threat and the homogeneity of the population has kept Community policing concerns in the background until recently. Present changes, he argues, are due to the urbanization process and the relatively high proportion of young people in the population as compared with the rest of Europe. O'Reilly (1993) notes several factors contributing to the fragmentary development of Community Policing – such as the lack of correlation between police resources and the recorded crime rate (enhanced technology simply meant vastly increased costs with no obvious benefit in terms of crime control); the legal redefinition of rights;[7] increased crime due to the breakdown of informal social controls; and a recognition that the historical development of a centralized structure and national organized police service prevented any local accountability. Until recently, ventures have concentrated on inter-agency relationships, such as developing schemes for marginal young males in Outward Bound Schemes, and similar activities (Tansey 1993). O'Reilly (1993) dates development from the first NWS in 1984, followed by a 'Community Alert' scheme for old people in rural areas with the Neighbourhood Garda programme following in 1986. Police officers are given responsibility for a homogeneous, physically distinct area. The central function is to make the neighbourhood a better place in which to live. The primary difference from earlier forms of patrol was that officers (within certain defined limits) could negotiate their working hours to take account of local events (Boyle 1990). However, Boyle notes a negative evaluation on those limited schemes in terms of an over-ambitious and ill-conceived development of NWS practices. Participating officers showed little enthusiasm for the specific practice although most officers enjoyed a higher degree of general job satisfaction.

Community policing as conceived in the Anglo-American contexts, has no evident manifestation in the former Soviet bloc countries. Gaberle (1993) in Poland, notes a general tendency in recent years to develop local police forces (such as under the Town Guard schemes) to deal with most everyday affairs instead of a centralized police. Szikinger (1993) in Hungary, suggests one key reason for the absence of community policing development – the historical investment of power in the police by the previous state has engendered distrust of police incursions into the community. Centralized organization, cultural perception of the role and practices of the state police, and legal limitations of the police mandate – apart from a range of factors in relation to resources and tradition – militate against community police development.

Community Policing Elsewhere

This brief overview of community policing is necessarily limited. Such a review ignores the developments in Australasia. Signally, it also leaves out of discussion the debate regarding the Japanese 'Koban' system (see Leishman in this volume). The latter is the primary example of an indigenization of community policing developing, which appears to have no obvious source within Western tradition. The importance however of Japanese community policing is not that it provides an alternative model to Anglo-Saxon notions. Rather it signifies the importance of context to community policing – where culture, law, and organization furnish appropriate prerequisites. One of the problems in considering the Japanese system is that many of the Western commentators have taken an uncritical view of the Koban system. Indeed, the Koban system has been regarded with much of the same myopia as were the early community policing schemes in the West (Bayley 1984, ibid. 1988, Jon & Quah 1987). The criticisms have mushroomed (Kusada-Smick 1990). Japan represents a relatively homogeneous structured society with particular *cultural* features that have resulted in a specific perception in Japanese society of the relationship between the police and the society. Many of the earlier commentators appear to fail to recognize the reality of Koban practice, providing an unjustified rosy-hewed picture.

Bayley (1989) has also extolled the Singapore system of community policing which is portrayed as deriving directly from the Koban and was instituted as deliberate policy to replace the inheritance of the previous colonial policing structure. Other authors have been more cynical about the Singapore model – for example, the failure to take into account the larger structural features of the country (Friedman 1991). There is no evidence that the Koban actually results in decreased burglary rates. In reality, there is no mobilization of local people or communities in the Anglo-American community policing sense. The police are unwilling to reveal much about themselves to community. There is also indicative evidence that the Koban police act arbitrarily against minorities. The Koban is often staffed largely with elderly officers, those who have failed in other sections, and young probationers. In sum, the Japanese model may suffer, in the Western commentaries, from a confusion between rhetoric and practice. As with the Anglo-American model, structural factors make it unsuitable for transplanting in other societies.[8]

The Failure of Community Policing – Law, Organization and Culture

A policing philosophy, informed by a particular view of policing the Anglo-Saxon inheritance as modified by local exigencies, has been exported through a process of diffusion to Western countries. New missionaries have spread a particular policing creed. A unilinear perception of police development has been assumed, a process occurring largely independently of local police mandates, cultures, and patterns of organization. What appeared to offer promise in small-town America, and in the prosperous white suburbs, is being exported by a new brand of academic and police salespeople to all and sundry.

My own experience, in contributing to the transformation of the South African police, bears some witness to that police evangelism. The new courses provided for the South African Police Service at Technikon SA, in Roodepoort, embody the belief that problem-solving community policing can be transplanted uncritically to the black townships. They ignore major salient features of the townships – from particular factors such as features of self-policing by the Peoples Courts under apartheid, to the factors of local tradition and custom, to the violent crime-ridden legacy of apartheid to those urban slums (see Brogden & Shearing 1993). The empirical studies which have evaluated community policing practices are now legion (Brogden & Nijhar 1995). But the central problem – one rarely raised by the critics – is its contextual and ethnocentric character. Police organizations with no traditions of decentralized decision-making encounter major problems. The decentralization required by community policing, and the resultant increased autonomy of the rank-and-file, may have three effects on the urban police institution. It may mean a loss in effective management control as a consequence of decentralization. Similarly, it may result in a loss of wider accountability and control. Finally, loss of external and internal supervision may lead to a breakdown of professional standards of behaviour by police officers.

Over time, traditional centralized authority may re-assert itself (Schwartz & Clarren 1977, NIJ 1989, Eck 1993). Organizations may pay lip-service to decentralization in terms of developing specialist units (Murphy 1990) and of cultivating de-centralized inter-agency links (Sadd & Grinc 1993). Organizational decentralization and consequent local development of inter-agency links may be actually counter-productive (Liddle & Bottoms 1991) and result in an inter-agency power struggle (Sampson et al. 1988, Moore & Brown 1981, Carter 1995). Decentralization outside tradition suggests that much community policework may become routinized. Ritual takes over with statistical devices constructed to justify practices. 'Doing-nothing' becomes the dominant way of spending time (Bennett & Lupton 1990, Brown & Iles 1985, Knutsson 1991, NIJ 1989). Buerger (1994) notes that there is a 'mystical belief' that simply taking the police officer out of the patrol car and placing him/her on foot, will somehow guarantee community consultation. Specialization without decentral-ized tradition will lead to organizational schisms and confusion (Moore 1992, Pate & Shtull 1994). The empirical evidence of decentralized organization, implanted where there is no tradition, suggests that community policing is the antithesis of acceptable policing in countries with strongly centralized police organizations.

Secondly, independently of organization impediments, cultural factors both within the police organization and in the relationship between the police and the com-munity impede effective community policing (Grinc 1994). The specifics of canteen culture constitute one hurdle (Eck & Spelman 1987, Irving et al. 1989, Lurigio & Skogan 1994, Chatterton 1991, NIJ 1989, McNeece & Shader 1995). Lower ranking officers using a variety of techniques resist change from their crime-fighting self image (Sadd & Grinc 1993). In a social context which emphasized the police public order function, development of close relations ran contrary to traditional cultural practice. The schemes fell foul of police culture which preferred isolation to close engagement with the community (Moore 1994). Where a police organization has distinct managerial and rank-and-file cultures (Ianni & Ianni 1983), community policing becomes more improbable (Buerger 1994, Carter 1995, Rosenbaum et al. 1994). This problem could be overcome by new forms of participatory management (Wycoff & Skogan 1994). But, critically, the location of the police institution within national and cultural matrices provides the major determining factor. Small-town America may be favourably disposed towards the Burger-bar police officer. However, the French gendarme inherits a different tradition.

Finally, as in the Belgian case, the existence of a strict rule-defined mandate (whether it be the legal rules governing police mandate or the procedural rules of police practice) affects the climate for community policing. The lack of a specified legal mandate for the police may expand the police mandate into community policing. Mastrofski (1988) argues that four systems of rule-bound accountability may be diminished by community policing – the system of criminal, civil, and administrative law; the police department's formal internal system of command; peer groups both within and outside the police who provide, formally and informally, work standards for the police; and informal rules and guidance from the community in the form of the expectations of those who are policed – including press, interest groups, and civic leaders. The development of community policing strategies has major legal implications. Broadening the police function from crime-fighting into the diverse world of community crime prevention means that police officers will depart from the relatively clear restraints of the criminal law to areas governed by vaguer maxims (Bayley 1988). Hence community policing is only possible when the constitutional rights of citizens are vague rather than distinct, and especially where the police mandate is permissive rather than restrictive.

Notes

1. While foot patrol does not reduce crime, it can however increase public satisfaction with the police service and can also reduce the fear of crime.
2. There is of course a more detailed critique, including evidence that two-person cars are not more effective in reducing crimes or in catching criminals than are one-person police cars. The latter generate fewer complaints from the public. Mobile car patrols inhibit police officers from developing community contacts (see Brogden & Nijhar 1995).
3. For example, foot patrols that are constituted for purely budgetary reasons would not qualify as Community Policing (Skolnick & Bayley 1988).
4. Dealing with Community Policing by relying on secondary material, tells us little about the specificity of local schemes. At the national level, there may be little evidence of Community Policing developments. But at the local level, there may be spontaneous ad hoc developments, where decentralized organization is an established feature. For examples of the extreme variations within one country – Canada see Brogden & Nijhar (1995).
5. See Monkkonnen 1981 for a Weberian approach to the diffusions of policing ideas in the nineteenth century.
6. For example, by teaching courses in safety, crime prevention and drug prevention to school children.
7. That legal change prevented the Garda operating in traditional ways giving – arguably – more rights to suspects; changed perceptions by the public of what was acceptable in the way of force.
8. For an account of an attempt at reverse police colonization – experimental attempts to adapt the Koban system within United States cities (see Milton 1995).

Bibliography

Audit Commission 1991. *Reviewing the organisation of provincial police forces*. London HMSO.

Aylward, S. 1993. Community policing in Ireland: political and historical aspects. In *Community policing: comparative aspects of community oriented police work*, D. Dolling & T. Feltes (eds).

Balbus, I. 1973. *The dialetics of legal regression*. New York: Russell Sage.

Bayley, D.H. 1983. Accountability and control of police: lessons for Britain. In *The future of policing*, T. Bennett (ed.). Cambridge: Cropwood Papers.

Bayley, D.H. 1984. Community policing in Japan and Singapore. In *Community policing*, J. Morgan (ed.). Australian Institute of Criminology.

Bayley, D.H. 1988. Community policing: a report from the devil's advocate. In *Community policing: rhetoric or reality?* J.R. Greene & S.H.D. Mastrofski (eds). New York: Praeger.

Bayley, D.H. 1989. Community policing in Australia. In *Australian policing*, D. Chappell & P. Wilson (eds). Sydney: Butterworths.

Bayley, D.H. 1994. International differences in community policing. In *The challenge of community policing – testing the promises*, Part IV, D.P. Rosenbaum (ed.), 278–85. Los Angeles: Sage.

Bayley, D.H. & J.H. Skolnick 1986. *New blue line: police innovations in six American cities*. New York: Free Press.

Bennett, T.H. 1994. Recent developments in community policing. In *Police force, police service: care and control in Britain*, M. Stephens & S. Becker (eds). London: Macmillan.

Bennett, T.H. & R. Lupton 1990. *National review of community-oriented patrols: report to the Home Office Research and Planning Unit*. Cambridge: Institute of Criminology.

Boyle, M. 1990. *The Experience of Neighbourhood Policing in Dublin*. MA Thesis, University of Exeter.

Brogden, M.E. 1982. *The police: autonomy and consent*. London: Academic Press.

Brogden, M.E. 1985. An agenda for post-Troubles policing in Northern Ireland. In *The Liverpool Law Review* **17** (1), 3–27.

Brogden, M.E. & C.D. Sheering 1993. *Policing for a New South Africa*. London: Routledge.

Brogden, M.E. & S.K. Nijhar 1995. *A bibliography of community policing overseas*. Belfast: Northern Ireland Office.

Brown, D. & S. Iles 1985. *Community constables: a study of policing initiatives*. Research and Planning Unit Paper 30. London: Home Office.

Buerger, M.E. 1994. A tale of target-limitations of community anticrime actions. *Crime and Delinquency* **40**, 3, 411–36.

Carter, D. 1995. *Community policing and political posturing: playing the game*. Annual Conference of the Academy of Criminal Justice Sciences, Boston.

Chatterton, M. 1991. Organisational constraints in the use of information and information technology in problem-focused area policing. Paper presented at the British Criminology Conference, University of York.

Cornish, P. 1991. Overseas models of community policing. In *The police and the community in the 1990s* **5**, 187–99. S. McKilloop & J. Vernon (eds). Australian Institute of Criminology: Canberra, ACT.

Eck, J.E. 1993. Alternative futures for policing. In *Police innovation and control of the police*. D. Weisburd & C. Uchida (eds), 59–79. New York: Springer.

Eck, J.E. & D.P. Rosenbaum 1994. Community policing in theory: The new police order:

effectiveness, equity and efficiency in community policing. In *The challenge of community policing – testing the promises.* D.P. Rosenbaum (ed.). Los Angeles: Sage.

Eck, J.E. & W.W. Spelman 1987. *Problem-oriented policing in Newport Mews.* Washington, DC: Police Executive Forum.

Elinerts, C., E. Enhus, T. Van den Broek 1993. Community policing in Belgium. In *Community policing: comparative aspects of community-oriented police work.* D. Dolling & T. Feltes (eds), 159–75.

Feltes, T. 1993. Foreword: police research in Germany. In *Community policing: comparative aspects of community-oriented police work,* D. Dolling and T. Feltes (eds).

Feltes, T. and E. Rebscher (eds). 1990. *Police and the Community: Contributions Concerning the Relationships between Police and Community and Concerning Community Policing.* Holzkirchen: Felix-Verlag.

Fitzsimmons, S.J. & W.G. Lavery 1976. Social economic accounts system: towards a comprehensive community-level assessment procedure. *Social Indicators Research* **2**, 389–452.

Friedmann, R.R. 1991. *Community policing: comparative aspects of community-oriented police work.* New York: Harvester.

Gaberle, A. 1993. Civic militia and police in the Republic of Poland. In *Community policing: comparative aspects of community oriented police work,* D. Dolling & T. Feltes (eds).

Goldstein, H. 1963. Police discretion: The ideal versus the real. *Public Administration Review* **23**, 140–48.

Goldstein, H. 1967. Towards a redefinition of the police function. In *Administration of Criminal Justice,* Report No 7. Chapel Hill: University of North Carolina.

Goldstein, H. 1979. Improving policing: a problem-oriented approach. *Crime and Delinquency* **25**, 236–58.

Goldstein, H. 1987. Towards community-oriented policing: potential base requirements and threshold questions. *Crime and Delinquency* **33**, 6–30.

Goldstein, H. 1990. *Problem-oriented policing.* New York: McGraw-Hill.

Greenwood, P.W., J.M. Chaiken, J. Petersilia 1977. *The criminal investigation process.* Lexington, Mass: Lexington.

Grinc, R.M. 1994. Angels in Marble: Problems in stimulating community involvement in community policing. *Crime and Delinquency* **40**, 3, 437–68.

Hendrieck, C., E. Enhus, C. Elinerts 1990. Neighbourhood policing: report on a Belgian experiment. In *Police and the community: contributions concerning the relationships between police and the community and concerning community policing,* T. Feltes & E. Rebscher (eds). Holzkirchen: Felix-Verlag.

Heywood, R.N. 1979. Perspectives of crime prevention. *Canadian Police Chief* **68**, 3, 25–9.

Ianni, E.R. & F.A.J. Ianni 1983. Street cops and management cops: The two cultures of policing. In *Control in the police organisation,* M. Punch (ed.), 251–74. Cambridge: MIT Press.

Irving, B., C. Bird, M. Hibberd, J. Willmore 1989. *Neighbourhood policing: the natural history of a policing experiment.* London: Police Foundation.

Jon, S.T. & S.R. Quah 1987. *Friends in Blue: The Police and the Public in Singapore.* Singapore: Cambridge University Press.

Kelling, G.L., T. Pate, D. Dieckman, C.E. Brown 1974. *The Kansas City preventative patrol experiment: a summary report.* Washington DC: The Police Foundation.

Knutsson, J. 1991. Community-oriented policing. Paper presented at Garda Siochana Conference, Dublin.

Koenig, D.J., J.H. Bhana, R.L. Petrick 1979. *Team policing in St Paul, Minnesota: an evaluation of two years of implementation.* St Paul, Minn: Team Police Evaluation Unit, Police Department.

Koetsche 1990. Model police programmes in Hamburg. In *Police and the community: contributions concerning the relationships between police and community and concerning community policing*, T. Feltes & E. Rebscher (eds). Holzkirchen: Felix-Verlag.

Koller, K. 1990. *Working the beat: the Edmonton neighbourhood foot patrol*. Edmonton, Alberta: Edmonton Police Service.

Krantz, S., B. Gilman, C. Benda, C. Hallstrom, E. Naddworny 1979. *Police policymaking*. Lexington, MA: D.C. Heath.

Kruissink, M. 1993. Measuring police performance: evaluation of the Dutch police. In *Community policing: comparative aspects of community oriented police work*, D. Dolling & T. Feltes (eds), 99–109.

Kuhlhorn, E. & B. Svensson (eds). 1982. *Crime prevention* **9**. Research and Development Divisions, National Swedish Council for Crime Prevention, Stockholm.

Kusada-Smick, V. 1990. *Crime prevention and control in the United States and Japan*. Transnational Juris Publications.

LaFave, W.R. 1965. *Arrest: the decision to take a suspect into custody*. Boston: Little Brown.

Liang, H-H. 1991. *The rise of modern police and the European state system from metternich to the Second World War*. Cambridge: Cambridge University Press.

Liddle, M. & A.K. Bottoms 1991. *The five towns crime prevention initiative*. London: Home Office.

Lurigio, A.J. & W.G. Skogan 1994. Winning the hearts and minds of police officers: an assessment of staff perceptions of community policing in Chicago. *Crime and Delinquency* **40**, 3, 315–30.

McNeece, C.A. & M.A. Shader 1995. *Community policing: three models in three cities*. Presented at the Annual Meeting of the Academy of Criminal Justice Sciences, Boston.

Manning, P.K. 1988. Community policing as a drama of control. In *Community policing: rhetoric or reality?* J.R. Greene & S.D. Mastrofski (eds).

Mastrofski, S. 1988. Community policing as reform: a cautionary tale. In *Community policing: rhetoric or reality?* J.R. Greene & S.D. Mastrofski (eds). New York: Praeger.

Mawby, R. 1979. *Policing the city*. Farnborough: Saxon House.

Mawby, R.I. 1990. *Comparative policing issues*. London: Unwin Hyman.

Milton, S. 1995. *Community policing and youth development: American variations on Japanese themes*. Eisenhower Foundation.

Moir, P. 1990. Community policing – questioning some basic assumptions. In *The police and the community in the 1990s* **5**, S. McKillop & J. Vernon (eds). Australian Institute of Criminology, Canberra, ACT.

Monkkonen, E.H. 1981. *Police in urban America*. Cambridge, Mass.: Cambridge University Press.

Moore, C. & J. Brown 1981. *Community versus crime*. London: Bedford Square Press.

Moore, M.H. 1983. Invisible offences: a challenge to minimally intrusive law enforcement. In *Abscam ethics: moral issues and deception in law enforcement*, G.M. Caplan (ed.). Washington DC: Police Foundation.

Moore, M.H. 1992. Problem-solving and community policing. In *Modern policing: crime and justice* **15**, M. Tonry & N. Morris (eds). Chicago: University of Chicago Press.

Moore, M.H. 1994. Research synthesis and policy implications. In *The challenge of community policing – testing the promises*. Part VII, 2855–300, D.P. Rosenbaum, (ed.). Sage Publications.

Moore, M.H. & R.C. Trojanowicz 1988. Corporate strategies for policing. *Perspectives on policing* **6**. Washington, DC: National Institute of Justice & Harvard University.

Morgan, R. & C. Maggs 1985. *Setting the PACE: police community consultation relationships in England and Wales.* Bath: Bath University Press.

Murphy, C.J. 1990. Community policing in Canada: pretence and reality. In *Police and the community: contributions concerning the relationships between police and community and concerning community policing,* T. Feltes & E. Rebscher (eds). Holzkirchen: Felix-Verlag.

Murphy, C. & G. Muir 1985. *Community-based policing: a review of the critical issues.* Ottawa: Solicitor General of Canada.

National Institute of Justice 1989. *Community policing: issue and practices around the world.* Washington: National Institute of Justice.

O'Reilly, T.J. 1993. The development of community policing initiatives in Ireland. In *Community policing: comparative aspects of community oriented police work,* D. Dolling & T. Feltes (eds). op cit.

Pashukanis, E. 1978. *Law and marxism: a general theory.* London: Ink Links.

Pate, A.M. & P. Shtull 1994. Community policing grows in Brooklyn – an inside view of New York city police departments model precinct. *Crime & Delinquency* **40**, 3, 384–410.

Proske, M. 1994. Community policing in Austria. In *Community policing: comparative aspects of community oriented police work,* D. Dolling & T. Feltes (eds). op cit.

Rosenbaum, D.P., D.L. Wilkinson, S. Yeh 1994. The impact of community policing on police personnel: a quasi-experimental test in two cities. *Crime and Delinquency* **40**, 3, 331–53.

Sadd, S. & R. Grinc 1993. *Issues in community policing: an evaluation of eight innovative neighbourhood oriented policing projects.* New York: Vera Institute of Justice.

Sampson, A., P. Stubbs, D. Smith, G. Pearson, H. Blagg 1988. Crime localities and the multi-agency approach. *British Journal of Criminology* **28**, 478–93.

Scanlon, J. 1991. Reaching out: getting the community involved in preparedness. *Canadian Police College Journal* **15**, 1–25.

Schwartz, A.I. & S.N. Clarren 1977. *The Cincinnati team policing experiment: a summary report.* Washington, DC: The Urban Institute and Police Foundation.

Scott, E.J. 1981. *Calls for service: citizen demand and initial police response.* Washington DC: US Department of Justice, National Institute of Justice.

Shane, P.G. 1980. *Police and public: a comparison of five countries.* St Louis: Mosby.

Short, C. 1983. Community Policing – beyond slogans. In *The Future of Policing,* T. Bennett (ed.). Cambridge: Institute of Criminology.

Skogan, W.G. 1990. *Disorder and community decline: crime and the spiral decay in American neighbourhoods.* New York: Free Press.

Skolnick, J.H. 1966. *Justice without trial: law enforcement in a democratic society.* New York: John Wiley.

Skolnick, J.H. & D.H. Bayley 1987. Theme and variation in community policing. In *Crime and Justice* **10**, 1–37. N. Morris & M. Tonry (eds). Washington DC: National Institute of Justice.

Sparrow, M.K., M.H. Moore, D.M. Kennedy 1990. *Beyond 911: a new era for policing.* New York: Basic.

Spelman, W. & D.K. Brown 1984. *Calling the police: citizen reporting of serious crime.* Washington, DC: US Department of Justice, National Institute of Justice.

Steinhilper, G. 1979. Crime prevention in Federal Germany. *International Crime Police Review* **34**, 325, 34–7.

Szikinger, I. 1993. Community policing in Hungary: perspectives and realities. In *Community policing: comparative aspects of community oriented police work,* op cit. D. Dolling & T. Feltes (eds).

Tansey, M.N. 1993. Community policing in Ireland: policing neighbourhoods. In *Community policing: comparative aspects of community oriented police work*, D. Dolling & T. Feltes (eds).

Trojanowicz, R.C. & B. Bucqueroux 1994. *Community policing: how to get started*. Cincinnati: Anderson Publishing.

Van der Meeberg 1991. Community policing in the Netherlands. *Community-oriented policing seminar*. Trevi Group: Dublin.

Weisheit, R.A., L.E. Wells, D.N. Falco 1994. Community policing in small town and rural America. *Crime and Delinquency* **40**, 4, 549–67.

Wilson, J.Q. & G.L. Kelling 1982. Broken windows: the police and neighbourhood safety. *Atlantic Monthly* **249**, 3, 29–38.

Wycoff, M.A. & W.G. Skogan 1994. The effect of a community policing management style on officers attitudes. *Crime and Delinquency* **40**, 3, 371–83.

CHAPTER 11

Police Services for Crime Victims

R.I. MAWBY

Introduction

The emphasis of the police on action, excitement and 'thief catching' stands at the opposite end of the spectrum to community policing. It also contrasts vividly with the perception of the police as providing a *service* for crime victims, a notion that has become more acceptable in England and Wales in recent years where victims have been identified as consumers of police services. Indeed, as performance indicators have become a more central feature of evaluations of policework in a number of countries (Bayley 1994: 94–101, Terlouw *et al.* 1994), so 'soft' measures of performance, such as victims' satisfaction with police action, have been incorporated alongside 'hard' measures such as crime and clearance rates.

In fact, victims' evaluation of police action are important for at least three reasons. First, the police are highly dependent upon the public, and especially victims, for bringing crime to their attention and providing leads on the offender (Greenwood & Chaiken 1977, Mawby 1979, Reiss 1971). Conversely if victims feel that the police do not provide a useful service they may fail to report crimes or even take unsanctioned vigilante action (see Johnston in this volume). Second, despite the emergence of victim assistance programmes in many countries (Mawby & Walklate 1994) the police is still the main agency with which victims have contact. As a result, police response to victims may be the most significant post-crime experience. As Joutsen (1987: 212) notes:

They are generally the first representatives of the State to come into contact with the complainant. Furthermore their intervention will come at a time when the complainant is most likely to be suffering from the immediate shock of the offence. Their attitude will considerably influence not only what the complainant decides to do but also what impression he received of the administration of justice, and of how the community as a whole regards the offence.

Third, and underpinning this, partly because the police have prioritized an action-orientation, partly because, unlike victims, they tend to become immune to the impact of crime, the police traditionally have provided a very poor service for victims and in many cases their response may have exacerbated the effects of the crime – that is, resulted in secondary victimization. Moreover this response seems common across a range of police systems:

> There is ample evidence from in-depth interviews that victims are particularly sensitive to the way they are personally approached by police officers. According to several researchers, many victims experience an acute need to be 'reassured' by the police. Others state that victims expect the police to recognize their status as someone who has been wronged by a fellow citizen. Many victims express dissatisfaction with police officers who are distrustful, callous or cynical. Such observations are often viewed as evidence of secondary victimization . . . Police officers must be taught that their deskside manners are as important to victims as bedside manners of doctors are to patients (van Dijk 1985: 154, 162).

There is, encouragingly, some evidence that police 'deskside' (or 'crime-side'?) manners have improved since Van Dijk was writing, and much of the evidence is reviewed in the following sections. Before that however it is important to clarify two definitional issues: what do we mean by 'services for victims', and about what sorts of crime are we talking?

At first sight the notion that the police should improve the service they provide for victims appears straightforward. However, while authors such as Van Dijk use the concept to imply a more needs, help, or welfare oriented approach towards victims, this is only one way of looking at it, and one that may be at odds with consumer evaluations. Thus while we may consider 'victim-proneness' as a service where victims are treated as people rather than numbers, given practical advice and emotional support, and referred on – where necessary – to other specialist agencies, and we may evaluate the police in these terms, we should not assume that *victims* will necessarily evaluate the police in the same way or prioritize these features of police action. At the extreme, for example, victims *may* rate police more favourably where the police adopt a crime-fighting stance and show scant regard for victims' feelings! We should not therefore unintentionally equate '*victim-proneness*' with *victim-approval*.

The second distinction that it is important to make at this juncture is according to the offences under consideration. Traditionally the police have been heavily criticized for their treatment of victims of rape or domestic violence. Less emphasis was placed, however, until recently, on police response to victims of other crimes, for example property crimes. For this reason alone it seems important to distinguish between these two broadly defined groups of victims. In the following section, therefore, the focus is on the policing of rape and domestic violence. Then the emphasis shifts to police response to victims of conventional crimes, especially but not exclusively burglary.

Police Response to Rape and Domestic Violence

Some of the earliest, and most significant, critiques of the way the police handled crime victims concerned violent offences against women, notably rape and domestic violence. Spawned by the women's movement in the 1970s, a range of critics in the US, Canada and Britain argued that the police, in adopting unsympathetic if not hostile attitudes, further victimized women (Brown 1984, Chambers & Millar 1983, Clark & Lewis 1977, Dutton 1988, Hanmer & Maynard 1987, Holstrom & Burgess 1978, MacLeod 1987, Martin 1976, Minch 1987, Pizzey 1974, Walker 1984). Such criticisms, which were clearly not confined to the Anglo-American police (Hanmer *et al.* 1989, Korn *et al.* 1996, Soetenhurst 1985), led to the emergence of Women's Refuges and Rape Crisis Centres.

However almost immediately divisions arose in the ways in which these institutions operated, with consequential implications for their relations with the police. One notable difference emerged between the US and Britain (Mawby & Gill 1987). In Britain the women's movement defined its position in *opposition* to the police, worked independently of the police, and in many cases discouraged women from reporting these crimes, on the grounds that the police were unlikely to effect an arrest (or gain a conviction) and that the main results of police intervention were to increase the victims' distress. In contrast in the USA the availability of LEAA money in the 1970s encouraged a degree of co-operation with the police and a scaling down of radical feminist rhetoric. As a result, while services for women victims of rape and violence featured as central to the victims movement of the time, in Britain they have tended to be peripheral.

This point should not be overstated. In the US (Gornick *et al.* 1985) and Canada (Amir & Amir 1979) a range of services exist with varying levels of co-operation with the police. In England, while the majority of services are in the radical feminist tradition, some women's refuges – like the original one in Chiswick (Horley 1990, Pizzey 1974) – have much better relationships with the police, and Blair's (1985) review of police response to rape revealed marked differences in police relationships with Rape Crisis Centres in different parts of the country. Moreover, while Mawby and Gill (1987) found that police in Devon and Cornwall were fairly critical of the refuge movement, they none the less referred women to refuges, if only as a means of 'dumping' the 'problem' on someone else! It is also evident that where English police forces have been reluctant to co-operate with Women's Refuges and Rape Crisis Centres, the government has, in recent years, encouraged and enticed closer relationships between the police and both Women's' Aid (Home Office and Welsh Office 1995) and Victim Support, and many local victim support schemes now take considerable numbers of referrals from the police. Referral is however only one course of police action. In the face of intense and repeated criticism the police have improved both the service they provide victims and the ways in which they deal with the offence itself and the offender concerned. In some cases this is the result of legal changes, giving the police more powers to arrest and detain; in other cases it is the result of changes in police policy. In England and Wales, for example, circular instructions are a mechanism whereby central government, through the Home

Office, can influence local policy. Circular 60, published in 1990 (Home Office 1990a), provides a clear statement of purpose, with individual forces being directed to treat domestic violence in the same way as other violent crime. The circular also incorporates recommendations on the types of facility, including specialist units, that the police should establish to enable them to respond both more effectively and with more compassion.

How then have the police in different countries improved their service to victims of rape and domestic violence? The evidence from Britain and North America suggests that there are at least four responses that have been adopted, singly or jointly.

The first of these, associated very much with the early theories of Milton Bard (1969, ibid. 1975), involved rejection of a punitive response in favour of intervention based around mediation or arbitration. This required training the police as mediators and encouraging them to develop a role in neighbourhood conflict resolution. While there is little evidence that this form of intervention was any more effective in preventing future victimization, it lost favour, at least as the *sole* strategy, as the women's movement argued that it involved a reluctance to take the crime seriously. That is, while mediation might have been, as Wright (1985) argued, a constructive alternative and an improvement on the 'do nothing' approach that preceded it, feminists argued that by seeing mediation as an appropriate response police were effectively accepting that domestic violence was 'not a real crime'.

Hostile rejection of the non-punitive approach led to an emphasis upon punishment. That is, it was argued, offenders will only be deterred if they are arrested and prosecuted; police informal action is equated with a police failure to act, as an encouragement to offenders to think they have 'got away with it'. In England and Wales, this increased emphasis on prosecution featured through the 1980s, culminating in Circular 60. However it was most clearly expressed in Canada and the USA in the 1980s with a series of policies advocating the deterrent effects of arrest as opposed to non-arrest alternatives (Berk & Newton 1985, Breci 1987, Buel 1988, Burris & Jaffe 1983, Buzawa & Buzawa 1990, Jaffe *et al.* 1986, Sheptycki 1993, Sherman 1992, Sherman & Berk 1984, Ursel & Farough 1986). Whether or not such practices do act as a successful deterrent is a moot point. For example Sherman's (1992) review of five US initiatives suggests that the effects are by no means that clear-cut, (see also Dunford 1992, Hirschel & Hutchinson 1992, Klinger 1995) although he himself remains an advocate of arrest-practices. It is also notable that such practices may be rendered ineffectual if the courts fail to add their support.

Nevertheless, it is important that police response is such as to emphasize that rape and domestic violence *are* real crimes, indeed that they are very serious ones. Alternative approaches, therefore, are ones that combine a service-based orientation with an arrest-focus. One model here is that which sees the provision of improved services to rape and domestic violence victims as both desirable in its own right and a means to an end, namely the collection of better quality evidence. This is evident in a number of early initiatives in the US. For example in Tampa, Florida, the police operate in conjunction with a health-based rape response team where the non-police team personnel are involved in the collection of evidence, allegedly because victims are less likely to freeze up in a non-threatening situation and may remember more pertinent details. More recent British initiatives to provide separate rape and child abuse suites and domestic violence units (DVUs) are examples of a similar approach (Grace 1995; Home Office 1990a). A somewhat different approach, whereby women at extreme risk are loaned 'quick response pendant alarms' has been introduced in Merseyside (Lloyd *et al.* 1994). A fourth approach, which may be an extension of this model, again emphasizes the integration of service and sanction criteria, but particularly within an interagency framework. One example of this is the Duluth model, originating in Duluth, Minnesota in 1980 and involving a range of health and welfare agencies working alongside the police, and is based on the premise that different offences may require different solutions based on the skills of a variety of agencies. Within a multi-agency framework, policies may be discussed by police, probation, Women's Aid, Victim Support etc. that address the need to provide support for the woman and an appropriate response to the perpetrator. In the former case, this may involve practical and pyschological help. In the latter, it may involve cautioning the perpetrator (Buchan & Edwards 1991) or recommendation to the court to impose a probation order with conditions (Dobash *et al.* 1996), as opposed to a more punitive sentence. While these last alternatives are not necessary elements of a multi-agency strategy, it is clear that in Britain at least a co-ordinated response has gained critical approval.

> Co-ordinated CJS responses may, in fact, have two effects. First, they may bring offenders under further control and offer victims protection and support. Second, they may change the nature of the initial police intervention itself, since in jurisdictions with good CJS/community co-ordination the police often demonstrate a commitment to tackling domestic violence (Morley & Mullender 1994: 16).

The same authors go on to conclude:

> The international evidence shows that effective policing requires more than policy change. It requires, above all, *co-ordination* between the police and other criminal justice and community agencies, *police accountability to women victims* through continued internal and independent monitoring, and well-funded *independent victim advocacy and support* services which work closely with the police (ibid.: 26).

A review of the international literature thus reveals that the police approach to domestic violence and rape has improved markedly in recent years. Nevertheless, there is still room for considerable improvement. As Belknap (1995) notes many individual officers still operate within traditional frameworks where mediation is seen as more desirable than legal sanctions. Similarly, in evaluating DVUs, Grace (1995) notes that whereas specialist police are appreciated and supportive many front-line officers seem unaware of policy changes and operate much as before.

Police Response to Victims of Conventional Crime

Compared with rape and domestic violence, police response to victims of conventional crime differs at least in emphasis. For example the police are less likely to perceive the accounts given by victims as problematic, except perhaps in the context of loss estimation and insurance, and the trauma suffered by victims is less. On the other hand, where victims of burglary, for example, draw analogies with rape and argue that their private space has been invaded and that their property feels unclean, the need for sympathetic support is obvious. But whereas Van Dijk (1985) implied that the police fail victims in all societies, it is plausible to suggest that different policing traditions will vary in their 'victim-proneness'. For example, the welfare and service orientation of the Japanese police (see Leishman in this volume) might lead one to hypothesize that Japanese victims would find their police more sympathetic and helpful. Conversely, there is little about continental European policing traditions (Mawby 1990) or colonial policing (see Cole in this volume) to suggest that the police would be supportive of victims, and equally the more militaristic, order-oriented police of Eastern Bloc countries (Fogel 1994, see also Shelley in this volume) reveal little evidence of 'victim-proneness'.

The only large-scale international data currently available come from the second and third international crime surveys (ICSs) (Del Frate *et al.* 1993, Mayhew and Van Dijk 1997), where victims were asked if they were satisfied with the way the police handled their crime. Data from the second survey shows that overall respondents in countries in the Anglo-American tradition – New Zealand (79 per cent), Australia (77 per cent), Canada (75 per cent), England and Wales (71 per cent), USA (65 per cent) – and those from less militaristic European countries – Sweden (75 per cent), Netherlands (73 per cent), Finland (72 per cent) – were most likely to express satisfaction. Less victims in more centralized, militaristic policing systems – France (49 per cent), Spain (47 per cent) and Italy (41 per cent) – responded positively, and victims in developing societies, many with a colonial past, were generally negative, as were victims from Czechoslovakia (43 per cent) and Poland (16 per cent). However, perhaps unexpectedly, German victims (68 per cent) were relatively satisfied with police action while Japanese (54 per cent) and Norwegian (33 per cent) victims were less so. Unfortunately victims were only asked the one question about satisfaction. However, further data are available from the third survey, albeit only for 11 industrialized societies (Mayhew and Van Dijk 1997). This reveals a broadly similar pattern, for example with Finnish, Scottish and Swedish victims more satisfied and Austrian and French victims least so. Dissatisfied victims were subsequently asked the reasons for their dissatisfaction. The most common complaints noted were that the police 'did not do enough' and 'were not interested'. Rather less were dissatisfied because the police failed to clear up the offence or recover stolen property, or gave no information, were impolite or slow to arrive. However, it is difficult to draw too many inferences from this, since replies cover a range of offence types and other research suggests that victims of different crimes may have very different expectations and perceptions of police response (Bunt and Mawby 1994). In a separate analysis of the third ICS, focusing on burglary victims' views of the police in societies in transition, Zvekic (1996) shows: first, that in general victims in societies in transition were less satisfied than those in Western industrial societies; secondly, that within societies in transition considerable differences emerged, with victims from the Czech Republic and Hungary, for example, less critical than those from Poland and Romania; and thirdly, that the sources of dissatisfaction, while also varying between countries, were much broader than in the West.

Rather more detailed evidence comes from a smaller, more focused comparison of victims in six European cities. This research, conducted during 1993–94 in two English cities (Plymouth and Salford), two Polish cities (Warsaw and Lublin), one German city (Monchengladbach) and one Hungarian city (Miskolc), involved interviewing over 1,000 victims of burglary who reported their offences to the police. Victims were asked a series of questions about the crime and its impact on them and their household and about their contact with and views of the police and other relevant agencies. While on one level we could contrast the views of victims from three Western European cities and three cities in post-communist societies, we also expected each country to have its own distinctive profile. Notably we expected victims in England, with its image of the police as 'citizens in uniform', to be more satisfied with police services than victims from countries with more militaristic policing traditions, including here Germany as well as Poland and Hungary. The results however were more complex than that.

To disentangle them, we can distinguish victims' perceptions of the police on three levels: general attitudes towards the police, evaluation of police action regarding 'their' crime, and the extent to which the police were perceived as 'victim-prone'. In the following analysis the data have been reweighted to produce equal numbers of men and women in each city.

On a general level, respondents were given a list of 12 occupations and asked to choose up to three that they themselves particularly admired. Here clearly respondents from Western Europe were more positive about their police: 27 per cent of Plymouth victims, 25 per cent of Salford victims and 24 per cent from Monchengladbach chose the police from the list, compared with 15 per cent from Miskolc, 11 per cent from Warsaw and 7 per cent from Lublin. Responses to questions on the way the police handled their particular burglary produced a rather different picture. In Table 11.1 replies to four questions, on speed of response, whether victims were kept sufficiently well informed, the effort the police put into the case, and overall satisfaction have been included. Victims from Hungary and Germany were generally more positive in their responses, victims from Poland clearly least so. This is also evident when we scale scores, where criticism of the police on all four items scores 4 and no criticisms scores 0.

Where victims expressed some dissatisfaction with the police response they were asked to specify their criticisms from a prompt card on which eight complaints were listed. The percentage of *all* victims citing different criticisms is included in Table 11.2, in order of frequency.

Again it seems that Polish victims were most critical of the police, Hungarian victims least so, although here Monchengladbach victims voiced slightly more criticisms than did Plymouth victims. What is most striking about Table 11.2 though is that while lack of feedback is a common complaint, this apart Polish victims were particularly critical of the police on traditional 'crime fighting' grounds, namely because the police failed to make an arrest or recover the stolen goods. Levels of

Table 11.1 Percentage of victims expressing criticisms of police action in response to specific questions and mean score on scale of dissatisfaction

	Plymouth	Salford	Monchengladbach	Warsaw	Lublin	Miskolc
Police should have been quicker	25	26	16	37	33	16
Police should have kept victim better informed	40	52	28	65	73	29
Police efforts were insufficient	28	37	28	54	62	22
Victim dissatisfied with overall police response	22	31	19	65	59	16
Mean no. of criticisms	1.18	1.53	0.96	2.47	2.61	0.79

Table 11.2 Percentage of all victims citing each criticism

	Plymouth	Salford	Monchengladbach	Warsaw	Lublin	Miskolc
Lack of feedback	11	21	11	44	48	6
Crime undetected	4	16	10	44	52	5
Property not recovered	2	15	8	42	55	5
Police did too little	11	13	10	17	26	8
Police appeared disinterested	8	21	8	22	17	3
Police too slow to attend	7	10	5	11	11	2
Mistakes made	1	0	6	6	8	0
Police impolite	3	1	3	5	3	3

satisfaction with police action thus reflect much wider assessments of policework than merely 'victim-proneness'.

This is evident if we consider respondents' views on police attitudes towards victims. On the one hand, they were asked how sympathetic the police were in dealing with the victims of, respectively, burglary, 'disasters like flood and fires' and 'rape and sexual assaults'. On the other hand they were asked whether they thought the police had got better or worse at handling the victims of crime over the last few years. In terms of responses to the three hypothetical situations, English victims appeared most likely to view the police as sympathetic, German victims least so (see also Mawby & Kirchhoff 1996). Amalgamating answers on a scale of 3–12, where a low score reflects police sympathy and a high score police lack of sympathy, mean scores were: Salford 6.48, Plymouth 6.65, Warsaw 6.95, Miskolc 7.14, Lublin 7.34 and Monchengladbach 7.96. But when asked how the police had changed, respondents from all three post-communist cities were highly likely to feel that the police had improved rather than got worse, while English and German victims were more ambivalent in their replies. Comparing these more detailed findings from four countries with those from the ICS two important points can be stressed. First, victims' perceptions of the police as helpful or supportive towards victims are not necessarily related to their overall evaluations of the police. For example in Monchengladbach respondents were very positive about the police generally but did not see the police as 'victim-prone'. There are any number of reasons why this relationship should be so tenuous. For example, overall evaluation of police action may be based on victims' prior expectations: if victims expected little from their police they might be less critical than those with higher initial expectations. Alternatively it may be, as has been suggested for Poland (Mawby *et al.* 1997), that criticisms of the police are based on perceptions of the crime problem as rising and out of control. Second, as we might have expected, the English police, with a very different tradition, were generally seen as more 'victim-prone' than their German counterparts. Equally, while the Polish and Hungarian police were rated somewhat in between it was here that victims perceived the most improvement in recent years. As a result, in Hungary the police were seen as providing a broadly-satisfactory response in terms of both crime control and service to victims; in contrast in Poland the police were seen as becoming more 'victim-prone' but at the same time were heavily criticized for their alleged inability to deal with crime.

Improving Police Services for Victims

The aforementioned research suggests that the 'victim-proneness' of the police may be improving in former Eastern Bloc countries. Equally in the West as victim issues have forced their way centre-stage so international and national pressures have tended to effect changes aimed at improving police services. At an international level, for example, the Council of Europe and the United Nations have each issued directives urging a more sympathetic police approach (Joutsen 1987). At a national level, governmental and police policies have deployed changes in the law, policy statements, training programmes etc. to improve services. This section focuses on four Western societies – England and Wales, the USA, Canada and the Netherlands – in which policies have been adopted in at least some parts of the country, and evaluates the policies involved.

England and Wales

There are two alternative accounts of police services to crime victims in England and Wales. One is that, at least until recently, the police focused on detection and ignored victims' other practical and emotional needs. The other, illustrated in an address by the then Commissioner of the Metropolitan Police, argues that by the 1980s pressure of work meant that the police were reluctantly forced to scale down their attention to victims' needs:

> As the demands on the Police Service have grown, it has become increasingly difficult for the Service to meet the needs of all victims of crime . . . There are enormous pressures on the young men and women who police large cities and their reluctance to spend much time with the victims of crime often results from their heavy workloads, not from any lack of sympathy or understanding (Newman 1983: 23–4).

Whatever the truth, it is clear that the establishment of victim support in the early 1970s reflected a lack of concern for the needs of crime victims among a host of criminal justice agencies, including the police. While the police were involved in the creation of the first scheme in Bristol and police membership was required on the management committee of each scheme, research indicated that police officers in general continued to underestimate the impact of crime on victims and where referral of victims to victim support was left to the police comparatively few victims were referred, the archetype victim considered in need of help being an elderly woman living alone (Mawby & Gill 1987). In Scotland victims continued to be referred by the police (Moody 1989) – and in consequence referral levels remained low – but in England and Wales close co-operation between police and victim support was reflected in a shift to direct referral, whereby personnel from victim support work directly from police crime reports and themselves decide which victims to contact and in which way. And despite a hiccup in the early 1990s when the police were criticized on the grounds that this threatened client confidentiality, with added safeguards this practice continues.

It could, of course, be argued that the growth of victim support allowed the police to opt out of providing direct support for victims. On the other hand, a number of other initiatives have ensured that victim-related issues remain to the fore. Two initiatives stem from government policy. One is the Victims' Charter, published by the government in 1990 (Home Office 1990b) and reintroduced in modified form in 1996 (Home Office 1996), which provides an integrated package of good practice standards regarding the relationship between the criminal justice system and victims. Thus with regard to the police it suggests appropriate police action *vis à vis* dealing with victims at the reporting stage, in contact with victim support, through court proceedings and in providing feedback to victims (Home Office 1990b: 8–21). It concludes with a series of checklists, including one for the police service, to ensure that the police are fully aware of their obligations (ibid.: 22–3). The other initiative following the Citizen's Charter and government attempts to enhance police accountability to the public as consumers, combines Police Force Charters with performance indicators, some of which may relate to victims' evaluations of police action (Bunt & Mawby 1994).

These initiatives have had some positive benefits, at least in some areas of the country. For example, victim issues now feature regularly in police initial training, and – as in Devon and Cornwall – victims of burglary and non-familial violent offences are regularly surveyed to ensure that individual officers follow force procedures (for example by giving victims a contact name and number and supplying information on victim support) (Bunt & Mawby 1994). In this context the Devon and Cornwall police provide victims with a handbook which includes information and advice on victim support, compensation, court procedure, and crime prevention. Nevertheless many of these policies aimed at improving police service to victims are the result of local initiatives rather than national requirements. Feedback through interviews with victims is not a compulsory performance indicator (see Davidoff 1993) and the Victims' Charter is a catalogue of best practice, best understood as a political and ideological document, which does not enhance victims' *rights* (Mawby & Walklate 1994: 164–75). Thus while police services to victims have improved in England and Wales, there are considerable regional variations as individual forces choose the extent to and ways in which they will interpret Home Office advice.

The Netherlands

Victim assistance programmes also emerged in the Netherlands in the 1970s, although unlike in England and Wales there was a deliberate attempt to experiment with different organizational forms. With regard to the role of the police, this was characterized by distinctions between schemes such as those in Alkmaer and the Hague that were run by the police from police stations, others – including schemes in Rotterdam and Breda – which were established as separate entities but with close co-operation with the police, and those like the Amsterdam scheme which were quite independent of the police and relied on self-referrals (Van Dijk 1989).

The fact that the police were not routinely referring victims to victim support, however, caused concern even in those schemes operated by the police. Hauber and Zandbergen (1991) for example reported on the situation in the Hague, where victim support was police-based but located centrally rather than in local stations, resulting in low rates of referral and poor knowledge of victim support among police officers. Rehousing victim support in local police stations resulted in improvements in police relationships and in police 'victim-mindedness'. The importance of improving police service to victims was recognized by two committees: the Beaufort Committee of 1981 which addressed sex offences and the wider ranging Vaillant Committee of 1983 (Wemmers & Zeilstra 1991). As a result a series of guidelines for police and prosecutors, what Penders (1989) calls 'pseudo-laws', was issued for sex offences

(1986) and victims in general (1987). The guidelines required the police to treat victims sympathetically, provide all the relevant information and, where necessary, refer them to other agencies, and victims have a right to cite the guidelines should they subsequently take legal action against the police. In this sense then, these circulars provide victims with legal rights that the British government's Victims' Charter does not. Nevertheless, in a meticulous evaluation of the subsequent operation of the police Wemmers and Zeilstra (1991) argue that improvements were limited, on the one hand because victims were unaware of their rights, on the other hand because the vagueness of the guidelines allowed the police considerable discretion in their interpretation.

Somewhat more positive conclusions were drawn from an evaluation of changes in police procedure and training in Zaarstrad (Winkel 1989, ibid. 1991). Improved police training in victim awareness was followed by an experimental programme whereby some crime victims were recontacted by the police some weeks after the crime and offered a range of additional support. The experimental group of victims were far more positive about police action than were a control group, and the author suggests that victims in general, and vulnerable victims in particular, drew tangible benefits from the extra service.

The commitment of the Dutch government to improving victim support is most illustrated in the 'Terwee law' of 1995 that requires both police and public prosecution service to liaise with relevant agencies in the adoption of policies that will improve the treatment of victims, enhance the information given to victims and encourage the development of restitution arrangements (Geveke & Verberk 1996). While little is known as yet of the effects of the new law, it does seem that there may be initial resistance, and interagency co-operation on a policy level is not always matched by co-operation at ground level. It thus seems that even in a system like the Dutch, where considerable emphasis has been placed on victim services, changing police practices is not always easy.

The United States and Canada

A wide range of victim services emerged in North America during the early 1970s (Mawby & Gill 1987, Mawby & Walklate 1994), aimed at different victim categories and different points of intervention, and with varying underpinning philosophies. Notably though, while both countries' police systems are diverse and generally decentralized (see Chapter 3 in this volume), with regard to victims, central government initiatives were crucial in the early phases (Rock 1986, Schneider & Schneider 1981).

As in England and Wales, victim assistance programmes owed much to the level of co-operation between the embryonic victim movement and the police. But while volunteers played a key role in victim assistance on both sides of the Atlantic (McClenahan 1987, Roberts 1990) in Northern America services were more likely to be based within a CJS agency rather than being independent. Services that targeted victims shortly after the offence was reported, consequently tended to be based within police stations. In Vancouver, for example, following the collapse of independent initiatives, victim assistance was eventually instituted as a separate body located within the police department (McClenahan 1987). As a result, in Vancouver, and also in many US schemes (Bolin 1980, Roberts 1990), volunteers worked from rapid response vehicles and often contacted victims as quickly as the police themselves; elsewhere though, services were based on follow-up (usually by telephone or letter) some time later.

Despite the apparently close relationship between police and victim assistance programmes, there is no evidence that services are any better co-ordinated than in England and Wales. For example in Minnesota, Chesney & Schneider (1981) noted a lack of police referrals to the in-house programme and also suggested that the police sometimes made unreasonable demands on the scheme. Equally there is no indication that in general the police in the US and Canada are any more 'victim-prone'. This is illustrated in two US studies of police services for crime victims. The first, in Houston, involved police following up a random sample of victims. Victims were phoned and asked whether they needed further assistance, and where necessary referred to support services or given additional advice. In their evaluation of the initiative, Skogan and Wycoff (1987) concluded that victims involved in the 'callback programme' were no more likely than a control group to voice satisfaction with the police or to improve their crime prevention measures. Moreover they were no more content with their neighbourhood and were *more* concerned about local crime and *more* afraid in general.

This rather pessimistic conclusion parallels Rosenbaum's (1987) research in Detroit, where a control group of police was compared with a group subjected to a three-day victim awareness training programme. Although the latter was clearly more victim-oriented at the end of the training period, four months later there was little difference between the two groups, with the experimental group rapidly losing its recently acquired 'victim-mindedness'. Furthermore, as in Houston there was no evidence that victims handled by the experimental group perceived themselves as receiving a better quality service *or* were more positive about police actions.

Summary

Ideally police response to crime victims should encompass a service approach along-side a concern to do everything possible to clear up the crime. However a traditional emphasis upon action, excitement and 'real' policework means that the police have often been criticized for their lack of concern for victims and – in the case of rape and domestic violence – an unwillingness to take the incident seriously.

While these criticisms have been directed at the police in a number of societies, there is some evidence of improvements in police response within recent years. With regard to domestic violence and rape, for example, changes in police procedure have meant that in many cases the police are now more willing both to treat complaints as 'real' crimes *and* to place more emphasis on the service they provide to victims. With regard to property crimes, increased concern to monitor and evaluate police performance has in part led to a greater willingness to prioritize police service. Training and legislative control provide partial means to effect changes in police response.

However this does not necessarily mean that victims' ratings of satisfaction with police response will improve. As is indicated in research in Eastern Europe, victims may appreciate the new service role adopted by the police but be highly critical of police failure to fulfil their more traditional functions. This at least serves as a warning against shifting the emphasis too far: the public do expect the police to investigate their crimes and make some effort to clear them up: indeed, not to do so is to undermine the notion that the police take victims' complaints seriously. But victims also expect the police to respond sympathetically, to treat them as people rather than crime numbers, to provide help or advice where necessary, and to keep them informed of any progress regarding 'their' crime. It is against these criteria, in addition to detection rates, that police services for crime victims need to be measured.

Bibliography

Amir, D. & M. Amir 1979. Rape Crisis Centres: an arena for ideological conflict. *Victimology* **4**, 247–57.

Bard, M. 1969. Family intervention police teams as a community mental health resource. *Journal of Criminal Law, Criminology and Police Science* **60**, 247–50.

Bard, M. 1975. *The function of the police in crisis intervention and conflict management.* Washington, DC: US Department of Justice.

Bayley, D.H. 1994. *Police for the future.* New York: Oxford University Press.

Belknap, J. 1995. Law enforcement officers' attitudes about the appropriate responses to woman battering. *International Review of Victimology* **4**, 47–62.

Berk, R.A. & P.J. Newton 1985. Does arrest really deter wife battery? An effort to replicate the findings of the Minneapolis spouse abuse experiment. *American Sociological Review* **50**, 254–62.

Blair, I. 1985. *Investigating rape.* Beckenham: Croom Helm.

Bolin, D.C. 1980. The Pima County victim witness program: analysing its success. *Evaluating Changes Special Issue*, 120–6.

Breci, M.G. 1987. Police officers' values on intervention in family fights. *Police Studies* **10.4**, 192–202.

Brown, S.E. 1984. Police responses to wife beating: neglect of a crime of violence. *Journal of Criminal Justice* **12**, 277–88.

Buchan, I. & S. Edwards 1991. *Adult cautioning for domestic violence*, London: Home Office.

Buel, S.M. 1988. Mandatory arrest for domestic violence. *Harvard Women's Law Journal*, **11**, 213–26.

Bunt, P. & R.I. Mawby 1994. Quality of policing: the consumer's perspective. *Public Policy Review* **2.3**, 58–60.

Burris, C.A. & P. Jaffe 1983. Wife abuse as a crime. *Canadian Journal of Criminology* **25.3**, 309–18.

Buzawa, E.S. & C.G. Buzawa 1990. *Domestic violence: the criminal justice response.* Newbury Park, Calif.: Sage.

Chambers, G. & A. Millar 1983. *Investigating sexual assault*. Edinburgh: HMSO Scottish Office.

Chesney, S. & C.S. Schneider 1981. Crime victim crisis centres: the Minnesota experience. In *Perspectives on crime victims*, B. Galaway & J. Hudson (eds). St Louis: C.V. Molsby.

Clark, L.M.G. & D.J. Lewis 1977. *Rape: the price of coercive sexuality*. Toronto: Women's Press.

Davidoff, L. 1993. Performance indicators for the police service. *Focus on Police Research and Development* **3**, 12–17.

Dijk, J.J.M. van, 1985. Regaining a sense of community and order. In *Research on crime victims*. Strasbourg: Council of Europe.

Dijk, J.J.M. van, 1989. The challenge of quality control: victim support in the Netherlands. Unpublished paper, The Hague: Ministry of Justice.

Dobash, R., R.E. Dobash, K. Cavanagh, R. Lewis 1996. *Research evaluation of programmes for violent men*. Edinburgh: HMSO.

Dunford, F.W. 1992. The measurement of recidivism in cases of spouse assault. *Journal of Criminal Law and Criminology* **83**, 120.

Dutton, D.G. 1988. *The domestic assault of women: psychological and criminal justice perspectives*. Boston: Allen and Bacon inc.

Fogel, D. 1994. *Policing in Central and Eastern Europe*. Helsinki: HEUNI.

Frate, A.A. del, U. Zvekic, J.J.M. van Dijk 1993. *Understanding crime: experiences of crime and crime control*. Rome: UNICRI.

Geveke, H. & M. Verberk 1996. *The organisation of victim support* (In Dutch). Den Haag: Ministry of Justice.

Grace, S. 1995. *Policing domestic violence in the 1990s*. London: Home Office (Home Office Research Study no 139).

Greenwood, P.W. & J. Chaiken 1977. *The criminal investigation process*. Lexington, MA.: D.C. Heath.

Gornick, J., M.R. Burt, K.J. Pittman 1985. Structure and activities of rape crisis centres in the early 1980s. *Crime and Delinquency* **31**, 247–68.

Hanmer, J. & M. Maynard 1987 (eds). *Women, violence and social control*. London: Macmillan.

Hanmer, J., J. Radford, E.A. Stanko 1989. *Women, policing and male violence*. London: Routledge.

Hauber, A.R. & A. Zandbergen 1991. Victim assistance in police stations on the move. An experiment of victim assistance in police stations. *International Review of Victimology* **2**, 1–13.

Hirschel, J.D. & I.W. Hutchinson 1992. Female spouse abuse and the police response: the Charlotte, North Carolina experiment. *Journal of Criminal Law and Criminology* **83**, 73.

Holstrom, L.L. & A.W. Burgess 1978. *The victim of rape: institutional reactions*. New York: Wiley.

Home Office, 1990a. *Domestic violence*. London: HMSO (HO Circular 60).

Home Office, 1990b. *Victims' Charter*. London: HMSO.

Home Office, 1996. *Victims' Charter*. London: HMSO.

Home Office and Welsh Office 1995. *Interagency circular: inter-agency co-ordination to tackle domestic violence*. London: Home Office.

Horley, S. 1990. No haven for battered women. *Police Review* (17 August), 1635–1636.

Jaffe, P., D.A. Wolfe, A. Telford, G. Austin 1986. The impact of police charges in incidents of wife abuse. *Journal of Family Violence* **1.1**, 37–49.

Joutsen, M. 1987. *The role of the victim of crime in European criminal justice systems*. Helsinki: HEUNI.

Klinger, D.A. 1995. Policing spousal assault. *Journal of Research in Crime and Deliquency* **32**, 308–24.

Korn, Y., J. Putt, M. James 1996. Preventing domestic violence, paper presented to National Domestic Violence Forum, Canberra.

Lloyd, S., G. Farrell, K. Pease 1994. *Preventing repeated domestic violence: a demonstration project on Merseyside*. London: Home Office (Crime Prevention Unit Series No 49).

MacLeod, L. 1987. *Battered but not beaten . . . : preventing wife battering in Canada*. Ottawa: Canadian Advisory Council on the Status of Women.

Martin, D. 1976. *Battered wives*. San Francisco: Glide.

Mawby, R.I. 1979. *Policing the city*. Aldershot: Gower.

Mawby, R.I. 1990. *Comparative policing issues: Britain and America in international perspective*. London: Unwin Hyman.

Mawby, R.I. & M.L. Gill 1987. *Crime victims: needs, service and the voluntary sector*. London: Tavistock.

Mawby, R.I. & G. Kirchhoff 1996. Coping with crime: a comparison of victims' experiences in England and Germany. In *Understanding victimisation: themes and perspectives*, P. Davies, P. Francis & V. Jupp (eds). Newcastle: University of Northumbria Press.

Mawby, R.I., Z. Ostrihanska, D. Wojcik 1997. Police response to crime: the perceptions of victims from two Polish cities. *Policing and Society* **7**, 235–52.

Mawby, R.I. & S. Walklate 1994. *Critical victimology*. London: Sage.

Mayhew, P. & J.J.M. van Dijk 1997. *Criminal Victimisation in Eleven Industrial Countries*. Amstelveen, the Netherlands: WODC.

McClenahan, C.A. 1987. Victim/witness services: Vancouver, British Columbia, Canada. Paper presented to American Criminological Association Annual Conference, Montreal.

Minch, C. 1987. Attrition in the processing of rape cases. *Canadian Journal of Criminology* **29**, 389–404.

Moody, S. 1989. Referral methods in victim support: implications for practice and philosophy. In *Guidelines for victim support in Europe*, First European Conference of Victim Support Workers. Utrecht, the Netherlands: VLOS.

Morley, R. & S. Mullender 1994. *Preventing domestic violence to women*. London: Home Office (Crime Prevention Unit Series No 48).

Newman, K. 1983. The police and victim support schemes. In *Third Annual Report*, NAVSS. London: Victim Support.

Penders, L. 1989. Guidelines for police and prosecutors: an interest of victims; a matter of justice. In *Guidelines for Victim Support in Europe*, op cit.

Pizzey, E. 1974. *Scream quietly or the neighbours will hear*. Harmondsworth: Penguin.

Reiss, A.J. 1971. *Police and public*. New Haven, Conn: Yale University Press.

Roberts, A.R. 1990. *Helping crime victims*. London: Sage.

Rock, P. 1986. *A view from the shadows*. Oxford: Clarendon Press.

Rosenbaum, D.P. 1987. Coping with victimization: the effects of police intervention on victims' psychological readjustment. *Crime and Delinquency* **33**, 502–19.

Schneider, A.L. & P.R. Schneider 1981. Victim assistance programs. In *Perspectives on crime victims*, B. Galaway & J. Hudson (eds). St Louis: C.V. Molsby.

Sheptycki, J.W.E. 1993. *Innovations in policing domestic violence*. Aldershot: Averbury.

Sherman, L.W. & R.A. Berk 1984. The specific deterrent effects of arrest for domestic assault. *American Sociological Review* **49**, 261–72.

Sherman, L.W. 1992. *Policing domestic violence: experiments and dilemmas*. New York: Free Press.

Skogan, W.G. & M.A. Wycoff 1987. Some unexpected effects of a police service for victims. *Crime and Delinquency* **33**, 490–501.

Soetenhurst, J. 1985. The victim issue in the political agenda. *Victimology* **10**, 687–98.

Terlouw, G.J., M. Kruissink, C.J. Wiebrens 1994. Measuring police performances. *Dutch Penal Law and Policy* **9**. The Hague: Ministry of Justice.

Ursel, E.J. & D. Farough 1986. The legal and public response to the new wife abuse directive in Manitoba. *Canadian Journal of Criminology* **28**, 171–83.

Walker, L.E. 1984. *The battered women syndrome*. New York: Springer.

Wemmers, J.M. & M.I. Zeilstra 1991. Victims services in the Netherlands. *Dutch Penal Law and Policy* **3**. The Hague: Ministry of Justice.

Winkel, F.W. 1989. Responses to criminal victimization: evaluating the impact of a police assistance programme and some social psychological characteristics. *Police Studies* **12.2**, 59–72.

Winkel, F.W. 1991. Police responses aimed at alleviating victims' psychological distress and at raising prevention-awareness: some grounded intervention programmes. Paper presented to annual conference of Law and Society Association, Amsterdam.

Wright, M. 1985. The impact of victim/offender mediation on the assumption and procedures of criminal justice. *Victimology* **10**, 631–45.

Zvekic, U. 1996. Policing and attitudes towards police in countries in transition. In *Policing in Central and Eastern Europe*, M. Pagon (ed.) Ljubljana, Slovenia; College of Police and Security Studies.

CHAPTER 12

Policewomen: an International Comparison

J. BROWN, A. HAZENBERG AND C. ORMISTON

Introduction

Policing has been characterized as being a quintessentially male occupation, into which women were reluctantly admitted and whose duties were strictly limited (Toch 1976, Martin 1979, Fielding 1994). Research into the history and experience of women officers seems to have been similarly marginalized with relatively little published material appearing until Susan Martin's ground breaking study of American policewomen (Martin 1979). In this chapter evidence is reviewed from various countries in response to the rather broad question: is the story of policewomen's histories the same or different cross-culturally? The goals of comparative studies are: a fuller understanding of the respective home environments; broadening of ideas by learning lessons from abroad; access to wider case material to develop theoretical ideas (Jones 1985). Das (1991) suggests that international reviews can identify themes and issues of concern whilst Bayley (1992) proposes that the comparative approach is an important benchmarking exercise in establishing what is known. The task of comparative analysis requires source materials, translatable concepts and a common framework (Heidensohn 1992). With regard to the development of women's roles and responsibilities in policing these tools are rather underdeveloped. Source materials are somewhat elusive and original material for the present chapter was collected during professional visits made by the second and third authors whilst working for the European Network of Policewomen (ENP). Additional papers and observations were collected by the first author when attending a number of conferences for policewomen held in Eastern Europe and Australia in 1995 and 1996. In addition, original language material was made available from the ENP's documentation centre and the Police Staff College library at Bramshill. The conceptual analysis was derived from Heidensohn's (1992) grounded theory study of American and British police women. Brown (1997) has previously demonstrated the translatability of Heidensohn's working concepts when providing a comparative analysis of European policewomen's experiences: unsuitable job for a woman; equal opportunities; the gentle touch; desperate remedies. Heidensohn's framework is adapted for use in the present chapter and consists of the following: 'pioneering' and 'mission' are used to review police women in their historical setting; 'working with partners', 'professionalism' and 'transformational scenes' allow comparison of working practices; 'soft cops', 'female cop culture' and 'top cops' are drawn together under the general heading of women's coping adaptations.

As with other chapters in this volume, it should be noted that the police must be considered against the wider frame of reference of social, cultural and political influences that affect the style of policing and rates of organizational change. Societal attitudes are an important factor when considering the role of policewomen and the speed of their full integration into the whole spectrum of policing activities.

Pioneering and Mission

Unsuitable job for a woman

Women's entry into the police post-dates the establishment of most countries' police forces. The idea of women officers appears to have been met with both incredulity and hostility wherever the suggestions were first made. Owings (1925: 70) notes in a contemporary review of the progress of women's entry into policing that the French public would not accept the appointment of women as guardians of the peace and the 'French mind refused to accept the possibility of a lady cop'. A French police captain, M. Faralieq, interviewed by *The Policewoman's Review* (June 1928) elaborates this notion as follows: 'What would happen in Paris if we put women policemen in the street? There would collect a jeering crowd of hobbledehoys, girls, men, women and children round every unfortunate policewoman. No it is not possible. It is utterly impossible in France. In France woman rules in one domain. She rules her husband (at home) her children her house. But there she ends.' Similar sentiments can be found in other countries. In India the notion of women police officers was thought to interfere with their mandatory role as home makers (Mahajan 1982). Examples from early attempts by African women to form a women's police corps were met with contempt and vilification of ugly man haters who would be unable to deal with criminals (Segrave 1995). Women did not enter policing in the African sub continent until the 1950s and 1960s. Igbinovia (1987: 32) notes that the women's branch of the police was first formed in Ghana in 1952, in Nigeria 1955 and in Kenya in 1965. By 1978, Egypt, Mauritania and Senegal still did not employ any policewomen. It is the contention of Igbinovia (1987) that Eurocentric prejudices were a factor in the late employment of women officers in police forces in Africa. Not only did African countries inherit sex discrimination from European models of law enforcement, but administrators in new African nations maintained bias against policewomen. This was especially the case in French Colonial Africa since policewomen in the home country were, according to Igbinovia (1987: 33) 'nothing better than meter maids without any police power or authority'.

The gentle touch

The agitation for women police officers arose in both the United Kingdom and United States as a consequence of the activities of moral rescue campaigners, the social hygiene movement of the late nineteenth and early twentieth centuries (Heidensohn 1992, Segrave 1995) and reformists who wished to see greater protection for women within criminal justice agencies (Radford 1989). It was thought that women could both reform the police culture and bring justice closer to all citizens including women. This is illustrated by Owings (1925: ix) who argued that 'women are acting as a socialising agency to the whole police force, resulting in a better and more intelligent attitude on the part of policemen towards men, women and children requiring their attention'. She also argued that the presence of women officers 'affects the attitudes of judges and prosecutors trained in the individualistic, unsocial theory of a legal system seldom taking into account the protection of women'. The rationale for developing a policewomen's brigade in Poland in 1925 owes much to the expectation of a gentler touch that 'policewomen would bring into police work new methods, at once more social and more humane' than policemen (Paleolog n.d:16). Similar sentiments were expressed by a senior Belgian police officer on the introduction of women into the Gendarmerie (reported in Brown 1997: 9).

Desperate remedies

However, the reality of the employment of policewomen probably owes less to the missionary zeal of agitation and more to Heidensohn's notion of the 'desperate remedy' in the light of labour shortages or some other prevailing crises, often around sexual mores and behaviour (Woodeson 1993, Levine 1994). Hazenberg & Ormiston (1995) report that the first policewoman employed in the Dutch police in 1911 followed pressure from women's groups because of changes in the law concerning sexual offences and the increasing number of prostitutes. Woodeson (1993) suggests that entry of women into the British police was not only due to the chronic shortages of civilians in the workforce following national conscription in the 1914–18 War but also a moral crisis occasioned by young women in receipt of married allowances or munitions factory pay who, unfettered by the presence of their menfolk who were serving at the front, might freely give or sell sex. *The Policewoman's Review* (May 1927) describes the invention of the 'Morals Police' or '*police des moeurs*' in several European countries. France's first policewoman appointed in Le Touquet was required to admonish bathers whose lack of clothing overstepped the 'bounds of decency' *(The Policewoman's Review 1930)*. The Polish Women's Police Brigade followed changes in the law concerning sexual offences and prostitution (Paleolog n.d.). In post-war Germany policewomen were recruited in Cologne in 1923 to combat the spreading of VD amongst the occupying troops.

Waugh (1994: 5) describes the employment of the first women police in New Zealand where 'true to form they were first employed as matrons dealing with lost children and the inspection of boarding-houses for orphaned or delinquent youth.' The first collective call for the recruitment of women officers had come from the New Zealand Young Women's Christian Association which, in 1916, had sought the appointment of women police because of changes in social conditions created by the War and the absence of men. The appointment of the first women officers in South Australia and New South Wales was in response to concerns about loss of labour due to conscription, increased prostitution, vagrant girls and women and lost or begging children (Prenzler 1993).

As in Britain, in New Zealand and to some extent Australia, opposition to women officers came from the police themselves and after the First World War there was a reduction in numbers or slow down in recruitment of women to accommodate the re-employment of returning soldiers.

The immediate pre- and post-Second World War period saw the advent of women police, albeit in a limited capacity, in Asia and Africa. The situation created by the fight for Independence in India saw the involvement of women in politics and the need for women offenders to be dealt with by women officers (*The Policewoman's Review*, December 1932). Independence in 1947 brought an influx of refugees as a result of Partition, established a measure of emancipation for women as a consequence of social legislation, and introduced a greater number of women into the labour market. Under these circumstances more women and children were drawn into a male dominated criminal justice system that could not cope. In Japan women were introduced into the police in 1946 to assist in the traffic and juvenile sections (Sherman 1977). Their limited job assignments according to Sherman were because it was believed that they were unable to cope with street fighting, would not be able to arrest armed robbers nor could they be expected to work after midnight. In March 1949, ten 'ladies' formed Singapore's Women's Special Constabulary (Ho 1974). Their employment arose out of the need to deal with ill or destitute children and homeless women. Calderwood (1974) records that the entry of women into the Hong Kong police in December 1949 was to undertake clerical and interpreter duties. In Hong Kong in 1962, an influx of illegal immigrants and in Singapore in 1970 acute shortages of manpower led to increased recruitment of women officers and extensions to their roles.

Post War reconstruction also saw the introduction of women into some Eastern European forces. Nineteen women began working in Budapest in 1946 and the women's tasks, in the main, was to collect and find homes for displaced children. Sarkozi (1994) notes that women police in Hungary today still tend to be involved in administrative rather than operational tasks.

Summary

There are a number of paradoxical features worth highlighting from this early period during which women sought to gain entry into the police services of their respective countries. Firstly, there emerged a number of single minded women pioneers who agitated for and/or became early policewomen. Several were viewed with a certain amount of ribaldry or hostility which fuelled the claims of detractors and supplied reasons for the discontinuance of the women patrols. Mary Allen was referred to in the *New York Times* of June 1926 as 'chief of the British Bobbyettes in full regalia with mannish haircut, military boots and monocle' (Segrave 1995). Lillian Wyles writes in her autobiography (Wyles 1952: 18) of being 'a lone woman in a camp of if not hostile at least indifferent men.' The police women's movement was decried as 'a farcical manifestation of feminist agitation' (*The Policewoman's Review*, June 1931). Other women became celebrities, such as Alice Stebbins Wells, the first sworn woman police officer in the United States, who lectured widely encouraging the employment of women police (Heidensohn 1989) or Kate Cocks who gained an outstanding reputation as one of the early women police officers to serve in Australia (Prenzler 1993). Such successes acted as a further justification for the extension of women and their roles within policing. British policewomen demonstrated their worth throughout 1914–18 by their 'good character and wealth of service [such that] the mouths of detractors may be closed (Carden n.d.). This notion of individual women's success or failure acting as a cypher for the competence of women officers has been observed in more recent times by Heidensohn (1992: 142) who describes how, both in the United States and the United Kingdom, respect is awarded as a statement of exceptionalism whilst contempt is a class action denigrating the abilities of all women. Currently women who achieve senior rank are treated as singular and find their appointments the subject of comment because of their gender: for example Christine Silverberg, when becoming the new chief of police in Calgary in October 1995 (Morton 1996), Pauline Clare, Britain's first woman chief constable (Graham 1995) and Koraiza Abdullah, who became the first woman police commander in Kuala Lumpur's 189-year police history (*Sarawak Tribune*, 9 August 1996). The first woman dog handler, authorized firearms user, diver, or specialist detective are heralded as the new pioneers (Lock 1987, Heidensohn 1992) with the attendant pressures of managing to perform well as a highly visible minority. Secondly, as Radford (1989) discusses, there was disagreement amongst the early pioneers as to the agenda for women police. The more radical feminists wished women police to protect other women from the violence of men. In contrast, and more dominant, were those policewomen who saw their role as public servants preserving the status quo by exercising the same controls over women as policemen. Friction occurred between Nina Boyle who saw the work of British policewomen as countering the injustices meted out to women and Margaret Damer Dawson who sought an accommodation with the establishment. A row ensued over the curfewing of women in Grantham in 1916. Boyle wrote that it was impossible to be associated with any work supported by Damer Dawson, no matter how useful, if it meant the coercion of women and girls and depriving them of their liberty (Levine 1994). Factions also occurred in Germany with an early pioneer policewoman Josefine Erkens being removed as head of the detective unit in Hamburg prior to it being disbanded in 1931.

Whilst attending a conference of policewomen in Poland in 1995, the first author observed friction between two schools of thought amongst the women officers: that which viewed the supporting role played by women officers as entirely appropriate and sought a 'softly softly' accommodation with male colleagues: the other viewed policewomen's treatment as discriminatory and wished for a more radical reformist agenda.

Thirdly, both resistance to and active promotion of women's entry into the police, their continuance and the extension of their roles was orchestrated by men. As illustrated above, a male view persisted that policing was an unsuitable job for a woman. However, men did play a key role in advancing the progress of women police. Whilst women had been used as typists in 1914 by the Prefet de Police in Paris, it was a later Prefet, Roger Langeron, who decided in 1935 to use women operationally to assist in the city's juvenile bureau (Dene 1992). The Marques de Fronda conceived the idea of creating a nucleus of women officers in the Vigilance Department of the Spanish Police, anticipating problems arising from the International Exhibition of Barcelona in 1929 (*The Policewoman's Review*, September 1930). Persuaded by the effectiveness of particular policewomen, the Commissioner for South Australia and later the Commissioner for Melbourne made public pronouncement of support, thereby officially sanctioning their usefulness. In 1938, a breakthrough for women wishing to join the police in New Zealand was made when the Minister of Justice, Peter Fraser, facilitated the amendment of the Police Act to include women (Waugh 1994). In Britain, in 1944, a conference supported by the Archbishop of Canterbury was instrumental in stimulating the Home Office to issue a circular to forces encouraging the appointment of more women (Radford 1989). This was to be a pattern repeated elsewhere after the war years. During the 1950s in the Netherlands, the chief constable of Heerlan initiated a programme of employing women officers and in Germany during the 1970s the Minister of the Interior authorized women to join the uniformed police service (Hazenberg & Ormiston 1995). The role of supportive male colleagues is a feature of modern-day career progression for women police officers. In a recent international survey Brown & Heidensohn (1996) showed that policewomen were more likely to need the support of senior male rather than senior female officers to further their career.

Working Practices

Unsuitable job for a woman

Duties of early women police officers involved working with women and children, dealing with female prisoners, runaways, shop lifters and 'cases of men who annoy or insult women' (*The Policewoman's Review* 1927). They were mostly organized within women's bureaux engaging in work 'not superseding but supplementing men's work'. As noted earlier, women were also engaged in clerical and administrative work. However women were used as 'agents provocateurs' or undercover to break into prostitution and drugs racketeering. A policewoman recounts her experiences in 1918 (Kerner 1955: 11) 'For sixteen weeks I stank. Joan smelt just as awful. She was a policewoman and, like myself, had not looked at soap or water for all of four months. Why were Joan and I there like that?' – because they were posing as cocaine users and were deployed to locate the dealers. Hutzel (1933) describes the undercover work of American women officers in liqueur cases and indecent proposals. Despite some reservations about the abilities of women officers in front-line operational duties, it is perhaps striking that both in Singapore and Hong Kong women were deployed as decoys in undercover operations.

However, it seems policemen's reservations about the capabilities of women on patrol are universal. Research studies in the United States (Vega & Silverman 1982), New Zealand (Love & Singer 1988), Sweden (Lindberg 1995), England (Fielding 1988), Scotland (Wilkie & Currie 1989), Northern Ireland (Brewer 1991), and India (Mahajan 1982) find hostile attitudes amongst men concerning the role of women officers as patrol partners. Martin (1980) and Hunt (1990) describe some American policemen's concerns about women officers: unreliability in situations requiring backup; potential for emotional entanglements; belief that women will blow the whistle on men's extramarital affairs or extra-legal activities. In contrast in India more concern seemed to be expressed about the state of women's morals! Mahajan's (1982) survey of police officers in the Punjab found 50 per cent of policemen thought women officers were of 'easy morals' (p. 146). Whilst in Japan, women's display attributes were thought to be a positive advantage: as Sherman (1977: 29) notes, Japanese policewomen 'form a particularly attractive aspect of the Tokyo landscape and are especially visible during the tourist season where their highly feminine appearance and extremely personable style enables them to relate most effectively to the public.'

Research data evaluating women's proficiency during training and patrol competency mostly derive from the United States (see review by Lunneborg 1989). Overall, findings show that women perform as well as men in academic tests and general patrol work. However as Balkin (1988) indicates, despite the accumulation of evidence that demonstrates women's capability to undertake patrol work competently, there is a reluctance by policemen to accept women on equal terms.

Brown and Sargent (1994) reported such reluctance in relation to women being trained in firearm use in one English force. In mainland Britain, firearms training is a specialist post since only about 5 per cent of officers are authorized to carry weapons. The policemen in the study tended to believe that women lacked appropriate tactical skills, doubted women's ability to fire when necessary and were reluctant to have a woman as back up. One male officer participating in the survey wrote: 'In my years of service I've come across very few women police officers whom I feel I could trust in dangerous/violent situations due to their lack of physical strength/courage. They all appear to want to talk the situation through rather than act. If the situation develops they are unable to deal with it; in firearms situations this is not good enough and could prove fatal.' Auten (1989) showed from research in the United States that women did score lower on firearms tests than men. Auten attributed women's lower scores to lack of experience with weapons and failure to tailor weapons to individual physical requirements. Through remedial classes, grip exercises and changes in gun stocks, Auten reports remarkable improvements in women's scores. On the second problem of women's supposed inadequacy in violent confrontations, Grennan (1987) analysed such encounters occurring within the New York Police Department. If women were inadequate in the face of physical force, it was hypothesized that women would be more likely to use their gun than men. Similarly, if policemen were protecting their women patrol partners or if women officers were staying in the background then male officers might be expected to sustain a higher injury rate. Results showed that in mixed gender patrol teams it was policemen who more often discharged their firearm and there were no significant differences in injury rates. It is Heidensohn's (1992) view that women officers seek approval from their fellow officers through high standards of work and thereby gain a measure of acceptance. From her interview data of women officers in both England and America she gathered 'war' stories of their exploits. Prenzler (1993: 6) reports similar experiences from Australian officers illustrated by the following examples: 'Once I had a couple of good pinches [arrests] under my belt [the male sergeant] started to boast to the other senior sergeants who had been giving him flak.' 'For the first few months I really had to prove myself to the men. They were very nervous until we had a high-speed pursuit one night with two blokes about to do an armed hold up and who put up quite a fight. Because I backed up the men, I was set.'

A breakthrough in attitudes towards women in the Singapore police came when they were first used in public order policing in 1962 and similarly in Hong Kong in 1967 when women were successfully deployed in defusing potential disorder in industrial disputes (Ho 1974: Calderwood 1974). The picture from Africa is a little harder to paint as there is a dearth of research recording the experiences of the early policewomen pioneers. Comments from a senior officer from one African country replying to Brown & Heidensohn's (1996) questionnaire survey provides some suggestive evidence that experiences were not dissimilar to elsewhere: 'Being one of the first policewomen there were times when senior officers did not know how to handle us (women) and we had to put up with a number of frustrating circumstances. To be accepted in the higher positions I had to work extra hard to prove myself that I am capable of doing as well as my male colleagues'. The breakthrough for her came when she defused a riotous situation thereby preventing a potential diplomatic incident.

Equal opportunities

A significant catalyst for the advancement of women in policing has been equal opportunities legislation. Again, dates and details vary but the principle of integrated policing being established by law is common. In the United States the 1972 Title VII Amendment to the Civil Rights Act of 1964 prohibited discrimination on grounds of race, colour, religion, sex or national origin. Implementation involved the setting of hiring quotas and affirmative action programmes (Prenzler 1992). Prenzler reports that in Australia, rapid expansion in numbers of women police followed the introduction of anti-discrimination legislation, although in the immediate aftermath, only some Australian states have introduced part time working and grievance procedures to handle sexual harassment. Little was initially done by way of affirmative action programmes. It was not until the introduction of such programmes, certainly in New South Wales police, that women police roles expanded (Sutton 1992). In Britain, the Sex Discrimination Act of 1975 and Race Relations Act of 1976 mean that selection for recruitment and promotion must be made on merit irrespective of gender or race. The law also allows for certain actions to be taken to redress the effects of previous inequality of opportunity. Jones (1987) and Wilkie & Currie (1989) reviewed the progress made by women officers subsequently in England and Wales and in Scotland respectively. It seems little was done to prepare for or evaluate integration which occurred virtually overnight. Jones (1987) noted that at that time, some ten years after sex discrimination legislation, no force in England and Wales had any written statement of equal opportunities policy. Women still tended to be deployed on the basis of stereotypical gender demarcations. Wilkie & Currie presented a similar picture in Scotland. (A similar response to the legislation ensued in Australia (Prenzler 1994)).

As elsewhere in the European Union, Britain is subject to European directives on equal pay and equal treatment. Gregory (1987) considers that appeals to European law have not been successful in improving women's position in the workforce in the various countries of the European Union. That may be so in the early years; for example the Minister of Defence in Belgium used European law to exclude women from the Gendarmerie (*Rijkswacht*) because it was believed that the work was 'too physically and morally risky' (Hazenberg & Ormiston 1995). However, the *Garda Siochana* was obliged to lift its exemption from the Employment Equality Act in 1985 because of European Directive SI331.

The use of litigation seems to have been a powerful stimulus enabling women to progress in the police. In 1961, one of the first civil actions was brought by Felicia Shpritzer of the New York Police Department because, although having served as an officer for over 20 years, she was held to be ineligible for promotion to sergeant (Heidensohn 1989). This opened the way for American women officers to challenge height requirements, and physical tests and selection criteria have also been successfully challenged. Shpritzer's pioneering efforts were recognized by a special award made to her at the 1996 International Association of Women Police Training Conference.

In Australia, Prenzler (1994) argues that whilst legislation did accelerate the recruitment of women into the police, litigation acted as a fillip to recalcitrant States. In 1980, a rejected woman applicant took the New South Wales Police to the Anti-discrimination Board on the grounds that an illegal quota system was in place. The quota system was subsequently removed, as was the marriage bar in 1981 after a woman applicant successfully challenged her rejection on the grounds that she was married. Use of litigation is limited within countries of the European Union although there has been some successful utilization of the European Court as in the case of Johnston versus the Royal Ulster Constabulary (RUC) (Equal Opportunities Commission 1990). Mrs Johnston, a part time reservist in the RUC, successfully claimed that she had been discriminated against when her contract was not renewed because she was unable to use a firearm. It was force policy not to arm women. The chief constable agreed to pay 30 former policewomen and one serving officer a total of £250,000 in compensation as settlement of their claim after which further claims totalling £900,000 were settled.

Civil litigation undertaken on behalf of women officers in the *Garda Siochana* resulted in agreement that women officers performed work of equal value to that of male counterparts in terms of demands, skill, physical and mental effort, responsibility and working conditions. In 1978, women sergeants received the same rate of pay as men. Recourse to litigation in Britain is rare but perhaps because of this when cases occur they attract considerable attention. Wendy de Launay brought an early successful case when a supervisor returned her to foot patrol duties, believing that her being partnered with a male colleague in a patrol car adversely affected morale. An incomplete case involving Assistant Chief Constable Alison Halford's claim that she had been passed over for promotion in favour of less able male candidates resulted in a review of the appointment of chief officers. More recently, policewomen have turned to civil law in order to seek remedies against sexual harassment.

The history of women's entry into policing in the United States was marked by open and widespread sexual harassment and discrimination. Prenzler (1992) notes that women were often denied back up, were the subject of jokes, pranks, sexual innuendo and propositions, were denied locker facilities and subject to capricious application of rules. Martin (1990) reports a diminution of such overt hostility with the passage of equal opportunities legislation and procedures for handling harassment. Within European countries, varying levels of harassment have been reported.

It seems from limited analysis conducted by the police themselves that women officers in the RUC and the eight Scottish police forces enjoy equality of treatment and do not suffer from sexual harassment (Cameron 1992, Her Majesty's Inspectorate of Constabulary 1993). Academic research however found evidence for discrimination and sexual harassment both in the RUC (Brewer 1991) and at least one Scottish force (Brown 1994). Sexual harassment of women officers by policemen has been established to be present in some degree (amongst at least 20 per cent of women) in the Belgian Police (Corryn 1994) and Danish police (Froslee Ibsen, cited in Hazenberg & Ormiston 1995). Sutton (1992: 85) reports results of a survey carried out amongst New South Wales policewomen in which 45 per cent had experienced some form of sexual harassment. This compared with 16 per cent of non sworn personnel who were harassed by policemen and 6 per cent of women ministerial employees who indicated they had suffered sexual harassment from male colleagues. Many of the incidents amongst policewomen however remained unreported as officers bowed to the 'evident truth that in policing male privilege is predominant' (Sutton 1992: 78). Eikenaar (1993) and Anderson *et al.* (1993) in studies of the Dutch and English police respectively found high levels of harassment reported by nine out of ten policewomen in their national samples.

The personal cost of undertaking litigation is high, with litigants reporting symptoms of stress associated with the legal process in addition to the experience they complain of (*Guardian*, 9 October 1996). The likelihood of success in sexual harassment claims for policewomen is low. In 1995 in Britain 50 women officers went to Industrial Tribunals to complain of sexual harassment, which were either settled before the hearing and agreements subjected to confidentiality clauses, or complaints were rejected. In either case, no public vindication of the complaints was possible. There is limited research evidence available on the presence of sexual harassment in police jurisdictions in Asia and Africa. 'Eve teasing' seems to be present within Indian forces (Mahajan 1982). Brown & Heidensohn's (1996) international survey of policewomen found that a third of the African women officers reported experiencing sexual harassment with a quarter indicating this happened sometimes or often.

Desperate remedies

Heidensohn notes that policing has a complex and colourful history beset from time to time by crises and scandal. The 1960s and 1970s was a particularly critical time in the United States when the first crime surveys revealed the incidence and fear of crime; riots occurred in several inner city areas and there was a spate of police scandals, notably in Chicago and New York. Heidensohn (1989: 4) remarks 'recruiting women, in a period when wages were low and morale poor, was seen as one solution to the crisis.' Jones (1987) suggests that during the 1970s in Britain there had been a downturn in recruitment to the police. This had been caused by resignations and early retirements and the period had been marked by a bitter pay dispute. In 1975 the Sex Discrimination Act was passed legislating for equal employment opportunities for women. Jones (1987: 295) argues that 'whilst examination of national and local data does show that immediately after the [Sex Discrimination] Act there was an unusual surge in the recruitment of women, it is clear that this had more to do with the need to make up for acute *man*power shortages' [original emphasis]. Jones proposes that the abolition of the separate women's police department, prompted by legislation, allowed forces to recruit women to compensate for the high rate of resignations and low recruitment numbers from men. Once the 'crisis' was over, male recruitment once again took precedence over that of women in spite of the legislation. Gregory (1995) proposes that recruitment for police forces in Eastern Europe is made especially difficult because officers are required to be untainted by association with the previous communist regimes and there are also problems of poor pay and lack of status, dimensions again associated with the encouragement of women to join the police. Gregory reports that in Hungary, for example, there are at least 1,200 unfilled posts out of 26,000 with the Government aiming to increase the numbers of police personnel by 20 per cent in 1996. It will be interesting to see if women have become the target of recruitment.

Summary

Insistence on the importance of physicality creates styles of policing that present difficulties for women and place limits on their professional options. Assumptions about the needs for physical strength related to fighting is embedded in myths about the essentials of policing (Bell 1982). Having a woman and presumably 'weaker' partner challenges male beliefs about the fundamentals of working practices. When women are in the minority it is argued that their behaviour tends to move between two extremes: defeminization or deprofessionalization. Hochschild (1973) describes defeminized women as distancing themselves from other women officers and identifying instead with men and adopting a pseudo masculinity. Deprofessionalized women appear to be satisfied with a subordinated role. Brewer (1991) discusses the social construction of gender identity in the occupational culture of the police. He writes (p. 232) . . . 'In an occupational culture that valorises masculinity Hippolyte and the Amazons are metaphorical descriptions for alternative role models which policewomen adopt at work in the face of the Hercules-like gender identity of their male colleagues. Some women officers become "one of the boys" emulating masculine models of unprofessional behaviour whilst others manage their gender identity by retaining as much of their femininity as the regime allows and seeking out desk jobs or support roles.' Concessions to employment of women officers seems to be done grudgingly and is more often prompted as a solution to crises of male recruitment shortfalls or scandals caused by the excessive uses of force or corruption rather than in response to matters of social justice.

Coping Adaptations

Unsuitable job for a woman

Despite much evidence to the contrary, a cherished myth held mostly by policemen is that policing is about violence and crime (Bell 1982; Reiner 1985; Jones 1987). Heidensohn (1992) points out that it is the very importance given to this myth, which is about the nature of policing itself, that both confirms men's legitimacy to maintain law and order and denies women an equal role in this enterprise. Heidensohn goes on to argue convincingly, that it is male officers' claim to both define control and to own the methods of control that give them their ascendancy. Women are only granted certain franchises to exercise control within limited domains such as dealing with victims, young people and women offenders. The organizational structures and cultural accoutrements are designed to maintain the domination of policing as a male preserve and these appear to be universal. A recent graphic example may be found with the Belgium Gendarmerie which, despite its change from a military to a police service, was reluctant to give up a lapel flash of an exploding hand grenade. Aleem (1989: 102) characterizes law enforcement officers in India whose task is deemed to be crime suppression in the following terms: 'a policeman with a club in his hand and a gun on his hip knocking down bad people'. From his survey of Indian police officers Mahajan (1982) notes that one of men's objections to policewomen was their ineffectiveness in chastizing prisoners.

Empirical studies show that policewomen believe themselves to be excluded from certain duties because of their gender: 83 per cent of a sample of New Zealand women police (Waugh 1994) agreed with this statement as did 70 per cent of a sample of English policewomen (Coffey et al. 1992). In comparing a national sample of men and women officers' assignments in the Canadian police, Walker (1993) found 60 per cent of men were engaged on patrol; 14 per cent in investigation duties and 3 per cent on crime prevention. This contrasted with 73 per cent of women who were patrol officers; 7 per cent detectives and 5 per cent were involved in crime prevention. In a more detailed analysis of gender differences in assignments in the Vancouver police women were not as readily assigned as their male counterparts to: planning and research; communications; criminal investigations; identification; internal affairs and gaoler duties. Brown & Campbell (1991) found from a study of officers serving in one English force that women officers were more likely to be deployed on foot or car patrol and less likely to be involved in specialist investigation departments, prisoner handling and traffic patrol, and were absent from dog, air support and marine sections. Differential assignments were still evident when controlling for length of service. This pattern is repeated nationally in England and Wales (Anderson et al. 1993).

The gentle touch

Considerable research effort has examined the occupational culture of the police and the status of women officers within it, notably in the United States (Martin 1979, 1980, 1989, 1990; Hunt 1990) and in Britain (Jones 1986, 1987; Brewer 1991, Young 1991, Heidensohn 1992, Fielding 1994, Walklate 1992, 1995). This body of work portrays a picture of an informal 'canteen' cop culture in which scatological humour, boasting about sexual exploits and feats of physical prowess dominate. Societal expectations about the role of women as caring, nurturing and being 'soft' become confused with occupational stereotyping of police as forceful, pragmatic and hard. In order to preserve the distinction, policewomen are pushed towards certain 'acceptable' roles within policing and 'controlled' through harassing behaviour by men. Thus women are much more likely to be found in support and administrative functions than men; are more likely than men to be engaged in community based work or crime prevention and less likely to be found in high prestige functions such as criminal investigations. Martin (1989: 7) expresses this pushes and pulls thesis thus: 'The pushes result from the persistence of the attitude held by many policemen that most women officers are unsuited for the danger of the street and cannot provide adequate back up for street officers. The pulls are due to the desire of women to escape from patrolmen's harassment, to use the clerical or administrative skill that many possess, and to obtain daytime hours more compatible with family life . . .'. This is manifested by the dearth or absence of women in the more elite investigative units.

There is some research evidence to suggest the emergence of a distinctive female cop culture. Martin (1979) reported a distinctiveness in policewomen and their policing style. Young (1991) finds examples of the 'new policewoman' amongst British women officers whom he estimates make up about 10 per cent of the female establishment. These women officers adopt a feminine competence which makes little concession to entrenched stereotypes. Interestingly Hunt's (1990) notion of women's cop culture is that it has a reforming alchemy, a theme which has resonance with the earlier history of women police.

Other observers of police occupational culture (Fielding 1994) argue that there is little evidence of an emergent female cop culture. Although some empirical findings (Lunneborg 1989) suggest that women officers place higher priority on domestic violence and their approach is different to that of male officers. Price (1989) concludes that policing appears to change the women rather than vice versa. From Price's analysis, women appear to be less aggressive and manage violent confrontations better than men, are more pleasant, respectful to and communicate better with citizens than men, but that none of this appears to influence men's style of policing.

Policewomen's management styles were found to differ from men's by Scharloo and Werkhoven (1989) in the Dutch police. Price (1974) had found that compared to men, American women police executives scored lower on scales of conservatism, sadism and insularity and higher on creativity and emotional independence. Martin (1990) noted that policewomen supervisors seek to convince rather than command when compared with equivalent males. Given the universally small numbers of senior women officers, it is difficult to see this difference in managerial approach having, as yet, much impact. In Canada, Walker (1993) comments that women officers are virtually excluded from upper management of the police. Of the male complement of police 23 per cent make up supervisory rank (that is from sergeant upward). The equivalent percentage for women is 0.34 per cent. In American police departments, on average 3.7 per cent of sergeants are women, 2.5 per cent lieutenants and 1.4 per cent hold higher rank (Adler 1990). Collectively, for the forces in England and Wales, Anderson et al. (1993) report that only 3 per cent of all supervisory staff are women. In England the first women to hold the ranks of Assistant Chief Constable (Alison Halford), Deputy Chief Constable (Susan Davies) and Chief Constable (Pauline Clare) have all been the subject of considerable media attention. A woman occupant of such senior posts is rare with Sweden amongst the few other countries in which women hold the most senior rank. In New Zealand the highest rank held by a woman officer is that of inspector (Waugh 1994) and in the Danish uniformed police it is chief inspector (Hazenberg & Ormiston 1995). In Holland and the Belgium Municipal police, women have reached the rank of *commissaris* (with only *hoofdcommissaris* being above). In Portugal's National Republican Guard women only entered in 1994 and have yet to achieve any significant rank. The issues of turnover rates, years of service, and experience have been used to explain women's absence from supervisory and senior ranks within the police (Jones 1986). These are however problematic. Adler (1990) points out that length of service per se does not necessary demonstrate suitability for promotion. Brown et al. (1993) suggest that differential deployment practices can limit women's policing experience as can male officers' overprotectiveness (Heidensohn 1992) which may disadvantage women when competing for higher rank. Marriage bars, lack of part time working arrangements or job share opportunities disadvantage women parents to a greater degree than men. Adler (1990) shows that in US police departments with affirmative action programmes, assessment centres and absence of length of service as an eligibility criteria, women achieve a higher proportional rate of success in promotion.

Conclusions

What do we know about the experiences of policewomen cross-culturally? The task of comparative analysis has only recently been undertaken with respect to police-women (Dene 1992, Heidensohn 1992, McKenzie 1993, Prenzler 1994). The absence of a gender dimension in Mawby's (1990:192) international comparison was due to the 'patchy' availability of materials. When Heidensohn undertook a comparative study of American and British policewomen's experiences she found few shared concepts and no analytical framework to guide the task. These were derived through the use of a grounded theory methodology in which concepts and a framework were derived from her interview material with police officers. Heidensohn's work-ing concepts and analytical framework were adapted for use in the present review which attempted an international comparison of women in policing. This enterprise, of applying more widely insights gained from intensive case studies, is suggested by Bayley (1992) to be a valuable outcome of comparative research.

Additional outcomes of comparative work are suggested by Mawby (1990: 4): enabling the discovery of constants and contrasts and helping to provide explana-tions for these. In addition, comparative analysis permits application to practice and some educated predictions. The research evidence and observations reviewed in the present chapter suggests several constants: the entry of women into policing was characterized by struggle and that once in, women continue to experience resistance from policemen. That resistance is manifest by limited job opportunities and sexual harassment of women officers. Researchers and commentators from whichever cul-tural tradition testify to the dominance of masculine values in policing and beliefs about its inherent unsuitability as a job for a woman. Women officers are demarcated into stereotypic gender role tasks. Differences in experiences seem to be more a matter of emphasis than substance.

In trying to assess the differences, comparative researchers tend to make two-way comparisons. Dene (1992: 242) for example, concludes that whilst the status of women in the French police has improved to a degree, 'it would appear that the level to which they are accepted both within the service and by the public still lags behind a number of their colleagues in England and Wales.' In her assessment of the achievements and rate of progress of women police officers in the United States and Britain, Heidensohn (1994a) concludes that there were significant differences in the reactions and awareness of the officers in the two countries. American women had a greater consciousness about gender issues in policing and generally a higher level of feminist awareness. They had been much more active too in pursuing law suits to gain admission and to progress their police careers (possibly because America more generally is a litigious country). American women had also been more active in forming and developing networks at informal as well as at national level. American legislation is quite interventionist with hiring quotas and affirmative action pro-grammes. There was considerable impact from the research that had demonstrated women's equal capacity to perform patrol duties. This together with the more ready availability of official statistics and the impetus of litigation in the United States pro-moted the adoption of equal opportunities policies by police departments. Amongst her British sample, Heidensohn observes that they were not only more circumspect but also less ebullient than the American officers. Women's entry into policing in Britain had been more protracted than in America and, from her research sample of British women officers, Heidensohn still found evidence of pioneering. Development and implementation of equal opportunities policies and practice is more voluntary in Britain. Yet despite these differences, Heidensohn (1992) had concluded that rate of progress and achievements of women police in both countries was about the same. The wave of feminism associated with suffrage campaigns did have an influence on agitation for women's entry into the police at the beginning of the twentieth century on both sides of the Atlantic. Martin (1990) argues that the growth of the Civil Rights and Women's Movements in America during the 1960s and 1970s was instrumental in policewomen's progress. Networking and the woman's movement in Britain, by and large seemed to by-pass policewomen, although lobbying by women's groups has been instrumental in changing practices related to the investigation of domestic violence and rape (Walklate 1995). Networking has been a more important factor in the awareness raising of Dutch policewomen's situation (Hazenberg and Ormiston 1995). Sarkozi (1994) reports that the Hungarian policewomen's exposure to a European Network of Policewomen's conference stimulated the formation of a support group in Hungary and the first research into the position of policewomen within the country.

Prenzler (1994: 87) suggests that overall the status of women in Australian policing is ahead of England and America. It is Scutt's view (Scutt 1988 quoted in Prenzler 1994) that in Australia gradual change occurring prior to the application of equal opportunity legislation is probably best attributed to increasing public acceptance of women in male occupations. The second wave feminism of the 1970s did not generate focused lobbying for more Australian policewomen, although the modern period has seen a continuation of the earlier feminist arguments that fair treatment for women by the police depends on greater representation of women within the police.

Various triggers can be identified as precursors of action facilitating the development of women's role in policing. It was to be the Revolution in Portugal in 1974 that was instrumental in changing attitudes to women's role in society and it became more widely accepted that women should enter previously male dominated occupations such as the police in an operational capacity. In Indonesia and India the fight for independence saw women in militant campaigns, a role which was to change their social status. A Government inspired initiative in the Netherlands for gender equity in the public sector resulted in an action plan for the Dutch police.

Development of the present analysis allows the proposing of a model for more general application to the examination of policewomen's experiences. This model, presented in Figure 12.1, suggests three axes; a time frame represented by developmental stages of women's progression entering and playing a role within policing (an extension of Heidensohn's analytical framework); areas of discriminatory treatment (application of Heidensohn's working concepts) and a cross cultural frame. This may be thought of as a matrix providing a model to analyse the progress of women police in a cross cultural context broadly divided into three traditions of policing: Anglo-American, colonial and European.

Figure 12.1   Framework for cross cultural comparison of roles and experiences of policewomen

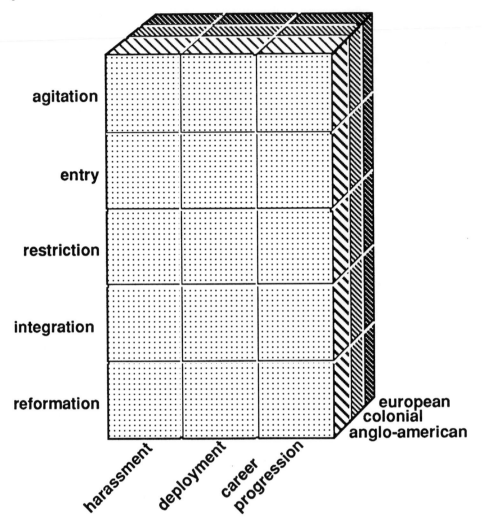

Stage one is marked by agitation to gain entry into the police. This is stimulated by demands, often from women themselves, to seek reform and redress for women against exploitation by men. Frequently agitation is met with initial resistance but this gives way in the light of some pragmatic need such as: shortages of labour; an inability of an exclusively male police to deal with problems generated by political, social and/or economic emergencies affecting women and children; or a crisis of confidence occasioned by scandals or malpractice from a largely male police force who turn to recruiting women in desperation as a remedy. Having gained entry, the effort involved in being highly visible and the energy needed simply to sustain their position seems to be associated with a quiescent stage of consolidation. Further progress is marked by the intervention of a few key individuals, often men, advocating the value of women police officers. Restriction of women's role in policing is frequently not lifted without the intervention of equal opportunities legislation. It is not just the legislation per se which is important but the willingness of a few courageous individuals who are prepared to litigate in order to establish precedent for change. It is through the legal process that often problems acting as impediments to women's progress are defined and challenged (for example height restrictions, marriage bars, illegal application of quotas). As the role and experiences of women police officers moves from the sidelines, academics, notably feminist scholars, begin to engage in research that removes gender from 'asides' (Heidensohn 1992: 80) to mainstream.

This assembly of empirical data helps to establish that the complaints of individuals are indeed generalized throughout the population of policewomen and brings to light new problems (such as sexual harassment). However it is not just the accessibility of statistical information that leads to an acceptance of the generality of problems, but it is the pressures caused by making such information publicly available that engenders debate, so adding some political impetus to finding solutions. Often, the police lack the skills or knowledge to develop solutions themselves. Part of the integration process is the stage of counter cultural willingness to admit outsiders into the organization to offer external scrutiny and develop procedures for training, grievance handling, open and fair recruitment and selection procedures. Finally, there appears to be a need to maintain external scrutiny through some watchdog mechanism to police the organization.

There are of course problems with developmental models: stages may not be progressed through an invariant sequence; there may be a regression rather than progression and return to an earlier stage; time frames may vary between countries. Further difficulties occur because of terminology. In the early phase of women's entry into policing, women varied considerably in terms of duties, skills and training. In Sweden nurses were recruited as pioneer policewomen and officers were known as police sisters. In some jurisdictions such as Britain, women engaged in uniformed street patrol, whereas others such as France employed women in largely clerical and administrative functions. This lack of equivalence may be applied to contemporary comparative research. In jurisdictions with longer histories of policewomen, they are more likely to be operationally deployed in ways similar to their male counterparts, whereas in policing organizations with relatively recent employment of women officers, such as Austria, women are more likely to provide operational support rather than be out on the street themselves.

Despite nearly a hundred years of women's involvement in policing in some countries, they are still a marginalized minority. Twenty-five per cent of a minority in the workforce is the suggested take off, at which point the members of the minority are seen as normal and have sufficient mutual support (Heidensohn 1989). Of the available statistics reviewed for this present chapter, no country was found to be close to this percentage. The next stage in development for women in the police then is likely to occur when numbers approach the tip-over stage when women play a full part in all aspects of policing and achieve higher rank in greater numbers. At such a point, women may actually have a greater impact on the character and style of policing. This then provides a clue to the predictive enterprise and the agenda for future research effort. Heidensohn (1992: 248) speculates that as the numbers of women officers increase then policing could be either less macho, having a more balanced service/enforcement orientation, or become more macho and diverge from its service commitments. Theoretical prediction from the work of Kanter (1977) on gender inequalities in organizations suggest that as numbers of women increase then inequalities will be 'bureaucratized out' (Halford *et al.* 1997: 9). However, some preliminary findings presented by Brown (1998) suggest that this is far too optimistic a prediction. These research results show there not to be a linear correlation between levels of sexual harassment experienced and gender ratio. Other factors such as the role in which women serve and organizational location play a crucial part in the levels of discriminatory treatment. The next phase of research might deconstruct further the dynamics of gender ratio within the police and evaluate the impacts on policing a different number of women officers.

Bibliography

Adler, Z. 1990. Hill street clues; the US record on promoting women. *Personnel Management* (August), 28–33.

Aleem, S. 1989. Women in policing in India. *Police Studies* **12**, 97–103.

Allen, M. 1925. *The pioneer policewoman.* London: Chatto & Windus.

Anderson, R., J. Brown, E.A. Campbell 1993. *Aspects of sex discrimination within the police service in England and Wales.* London: Home Office Police Research Group.

Auten, J. 1989. The relative firearms performance of male and female police officers. *Law and Order* (September), 48–53.

Balkin, J. 1988. Why policemen don't like policewomen. *Journal of Police Science and Administration* **16**, 29–38.

Bayley, D. 1992. Comparative organization of the police in English speaking countries. In *Modern Policing: Crime and Justice* **15**.

Bell, D.Z. 1982. Policewomen; myth and reality. *Journal of Police Science and Administration* **10**, 112–20.

Bloeyaert, M. 1990. *Vrouwen bij de politie, een onderzoek in opdracht van Merv. M. Smet.* Staatssecretaris voor Maatschappelijke Emancipatie.

Brewer, J. 1991. *Inside the RUC; policing in a divided community.* Oxford: Clarendon.

Brown, J. 1994. Equality environment in the Central Scotland Police. Paper presented to an equal opportunities seminar, Stirling: Central Scotland Police, 12–13 May.

Brown, J. 1997. European Policewomen: a comparative research perspective. In *International Journal of the Sociology of Law* **25**, 1–19.

Brown, J.M. 1998. Aspects of discriminatory treatment of women police officers serving in forces in England and Wales. *British Journal of Criminology* **38**, 265–83.

Brown J. & E.A. Campbell 1991. Less than equal. *Policing* **7**, 324–33.

Brown, J.M. & F. Heidensohn 1996. Exclusion orders. *Policing Today* **2** (4), 20–24.

Brown, J., A. Maidment, R. Bull 1993. Appropriate skill task matching or gender bias in deployment of male and female officers. *Policing and Society* **3**, 21–136.

Brown, J. & S. Sargent 1994. Police women and firearms in the British police service. *Police Studies* **18**, 2, 1–16.

Calderwood, A. 1974. *In service of the community*. Hong Kong: Liang Yo Printing.

Cameron, M. 1992. *Women in green*. Belfast: RUC Historical Society.

Carden, M.G. n.d. *Women Patrols*. London: National Union of Women Workers of Great Britain and Ireland.

Carrier, J. 1988. *The campaign for the employment of women as police officers*. Aldershot: Avebury/Gower.

Coffey. S., J. Brown, S. Savage 1992. Policewomen's career aspiration; some reflections on the role and capabilities of women in policing in Britain. *Police Studies* **15**, 13–19.

Corryn, S. 1994. *Ongewenst seksueel gedrag op het werk geprojecteerd binnen de entiteit van gemeentelijk politie*. Gentbrugge: Police Academy of East Flanders.

Das, D.K. 1991. Comparative police studies; an assessment. *Police Studies* **14**, 22–35.

Dene, E. 1992. A comparison of the history of entry of women into policing in France and England and Wales. *Police Journal* **65**, 236–42.

Eikenaar, L. 1993. *Dat hoort er nu eenmaal bij . . . Aard en omvang van ongewenste omgangs-vormen bij de Nederlandse politie*. Amersfoort: Landelijke Politie Emancipatie Commissie.

Equal Opportunities Commission 1990. *Managing to make progress; a report of a collaborative exercise between the Metropolitan Police and the Equal Opportunities Commission*. London: Receiver for the Metropolitan Police.

European Network for Policewomen 1994. Facts, figures and general information compiled and edited by A. Hazenberg and A. Kroeze for the European conference 1994 'Police=Wo/men=Quality=Service', Brussels: 21–24 November.

Fielding, N. 1988. *Joining forces; police training, socialization and occupational competence*. London: Routledge.

Fielding, N. 1994. Cop canteen culture, In T. Newburn & E. Stanko (eds), *Just boys doing the business; men, masculinity and crime*. London: Routledge.

Graham, V. 1995. The chief. *Police Review*, 7 July, 28–29.

Gregory, F. 1995. Trans-national crime and law enforcement cooperation: problems and processes between East and West in Europe. Paper prepared for the Mountbatten Centre for International Studies, University of Southampton, unpublished.

Gregory, J. 1987. *Sex role and law*. London: Sage.

Grennan, S.A. 1987. Findings on the role of officer gender in violent encounters with citizens. *Journal of Police Science and Administration* **15**, 78–85.

Halford, S., M. Savage, A. Witz 1997. *Gender, Careers and Organizations*. London: MacMillan.

Hazenberg, A. & C. Ormiston 1995. *Women in European policing; What's it all about?* Amersfoort: European Network of Policewomen.

Heidensohn, F. 1989. *Women in policing in the USA*. Police Foundation.

Heidensohn, F. 1992. *Women in control? The role of women in law enforcement*. Oxford: Clarendon.

Heidensohn, F. 1994. Gender and crime. In *The Oxford Handbook of Criminology*, M. Maguire, R. Morgan, & R. Reiner (eds), 997–1039. Oxford: Oxford University Press.

Heidensohn, F. 1994a. From being to knowing; some issues in the study of gender in contemporary society. *Women & Criminal Justice* **6**, 13–37.

Her Majesty's Inspectorate of Constabulary 1992. *Equal opportunities in the police service*. London: HMSO.

Her Majesty's Inspectorate of Constabulary 1993. *Thematic inspection on equal opportunities*. Edinburgh: Scottish Office.

Ho, Loon Geok, 1974. History of the women police in the Singapore police force. *Singapore Police Journal* (January), 48–52.

Hochschild, A.P. 1973. Making it, marginality and obstacles to minority consciousness. *Annals of the New York Academy of Sciences* **208**, 79–82.

Horne, P. 1980. *Women in law enforcement*, 2nd ed. Springfield Ill. Charles C. Thomas.

Hunt, J. 1990. Logic of sexism amongst police officers. *Women and Criminal Justice* **1**, 3–30.

Hutzel, E. 1933. *The policewoman's handbook*. New York: Columbia University Press.

Igbinovia, P.E. 1987. African women in contemporary law enforcement. *Police Studies* **10**, 31–5.

Intomart, 1991. *Emancipatie bij de politie, stand van zaken 1991*. Amersfoort: Landelijke politie Emancipatie Commissie.

Jermier, M.J., J. Gaines, N. McIntosh 1989. Reactions to physically dangerous work. *Organisational Behaviour* **10**, 15–33.

Jones, A. 1985. *Patterns of social policy; an introduction to comparative analysis*. London: Tavistock Press.

Jones, S. 1986. *Women and equality*. London: Macmillan.

Jones, S. 1987. Making it work; some reflections on the sex discrimination act. *Police Journal* **60**, 294–302.

Kanter, R.M. 1977. *Men and Women of the Corporation*. New York: Basic Books.

Kerner, A. 1955. *Further adventures of a woman detective*. London: Werner Laurie.

Levine, P. 1994. 'Walking the street in a way no decent woman should': women police in World War I. *Journal of Modern History* **66**, 34–78.

Lindberg, G. 1995. Professional policework turns on equal opportunities. Paper presented to Police Training College, Stockholm.

Lock, J. 1979. *The British policewoman; her story*. London: Hale.

Lock, J. 1987. Suitable job for a woman? *Police Review*, 24 April, 119–21.

Love, K. & M. Singer 1988. Self efficacy, psychological well-being, job satisfaction and job involvement; a comparison of male and female police officers. *Police Studies* **11**, 98–102.

Lunneborg, P.W. 1989. *Women police officers; current career profile*. Springfield. Ill.: Charles C. Thomas.

McKenzie, I. 1993. Equal opportunities in policing; a comparative examination of anti-discriminatory policy and practice in British policing. *International Journal of Sociology and Law* **21**, 159–74.

Mahajan, A. 1982. *Indian policewomen; a sociological study of a new role*. New Delhi. Deep & Deep publications.

Martin, S.E. 1979. Policewomen and policewomen; occupational role dilemmas and choices of female officers. *Journal of Police Science and Administration* **2**, 314–23.

Martin, S.E. 1980. *Breaking and entering*. Berkeley: University of California Press.

Martin, S.E. 1989. Women in policing; the 80s and beyond. In *Police and policing; contemporary issues*, D. Kenney (ed.), 3–16. New York: Praeger.

Martin, S.E. 1990. *On the move; the status of women in policing*. Washington: Police Foundation.

Mawby, R. 1990. *Comparative Policing Issues*. London: Unwin Hyman.

Morton, J. 1996. First among equals? *Police Review*, 11 October.

Owings, C. 1925. *Women police; a study of the development and status of the women police movement*. New York: Bureau of Social Hygiene.

Paleolog, S. n.d. *The Women Police of Poland: 1925 to 1939*. London: Association for Moral and Social Hygiene.

Prenzler, T. 1992. Women and policing; policy implications from the US experience. *Research and Policy Paper* 3, Griffith University Centre for Crime Policy and Public Safety.

Prenzler, T. 1993. *Women in Australian policing; an historical overview.* Griffith University. Centre for Crime Policy and Public Safety.

Prenzler, T. 1994. Women in Australian policing: an overview. *Journal of Australian Studies,* **42**, 78–88.

Price, B.R. 1974. A study of leadership strength of female police executives. *Journal of Police Science and Administration* **2**, 219–26.

Price, B.R. 1989. Is policework changing as a result of women's contribution. Paper presented to the International Conference on Police Women. Netherlands, 19–23 March.

Radford, J. 1989. Women and policing; contradictions old and new. In *Women, policing and male violence,* J Hanmer, J. Radford, & E. Stanko (eds), 12–45. London: Macmillan.

Reiner, R. 1985. *The politics of the police.* Oxford: Oxford University Press.

Sarkozi, I. 1994. *Policewomen in Hungary.* Budapest: Institute for Law Enforcement Management Training and Research.

Scharloo, A. & G. van Werkhoven 1989. *De (op) eigen wijze leidinggevende vrouw; een vergelijklkend onderzoek naar de leiderschapsstijlen van vrouwen en mannen binnen de Nederlande politie.* Apeldoorn: Dutch Police Academy.

Scutt, J. 1988. Women and the police. In I. Freckelton & H. Selby (eds), *Police in our society,* 32–41. Sydney: Butterworths.

Segrave, K. 1995. *Policewomen, a history.* Jefferson NC: McFarland.

Sherman, L. 1977. Policewomen around the world. *International Review of Criminal Policy* **33**, 25–33.

Sutton, J. 1992. Women on the job. In P. Moir & H. Eijkman (eds), *Policing Australia; old issues new perspectives.* Melbourne: Macmillan.

Toch, H. 1976. *Peace Keeping Police: Prison and Violence.* Lexington Books.

Vega, M. & I.J. Silverman 1982. Female police officers as viewed by their male counterparts. *Police Studies* **5**, 31–9.

Walker, S.G. 1993. *The status of women in Canadian policing.* Ottawa: Office of the Solicitor General.

Walklate, S. 1992. Jack and Jill join up at Sun Hill; public images of police officers. *Policing and Society* **2**, 219–32.

Walklate, S. 1995. Equal opportunities and the future of policing. In F. Leishman, B. Loveday & S. Savage (eds). London: Longman.

Water, van de, J. 1987. Wat gebeurt er met vrouwen in de opleiding en tijdens de stageperiode van diezelfde opleiding en de hoeverre heert dit aanknopingspunten met de theorie? Dissertation, University of Utrecht.

Waugh, A. 1994. A case study of policewomen's experience in New Zealand. Masters Dissertation, University of Wellington, Victoria.

Weigel, E. 1991. Schutzfrau in der mannerwelt. *Deutsche Polizei* (April).

Wilkie, R. & C. Currie 1989. *The effects of sex discrimination on the Scottish police service.* Strathclyde: University of Strathclyde Centre for Police Studies.

Woodeson, A. 1993. The first women police; a force for equality or infringement? *Women's History Review* **2**, 217–32.

Wurz, J. 1993. *Frauen in vollzugsdienst der schutzpolizia.* Europaische Hochschukschriften. Frankfurt am Main: Peter Lang.

Wyles, L. 1952. *A woman at Scotland Yard: reflections on the struggles and achievements of 30 years in the Metropolitan Police.* London: Faber and Faber.

Young, M. 1991. *An inside job; policing and police culture in Britain.* Oxford: Clarendon.

CHAPTER 13

Private Policing: Uniformity and Diversity

L. JOHNSTON

Introduction: Policing and Security

For over 200 years British policing has been regarded as the prerogative of a body of state functionaries – the police – whose role is determined by their location within the wider system of criminal justice. Yet, prior to the formation of public police forces, policing was defined much less narrowly. For one thing, it was by no means perceived as a state monopoly. For another, it referred to broad socio-political functions exercised throughout civil society – 'the general regulation of government, the morals or economy of a city or country' (Palmer 1988: 69) – rather than to narrow criminological ones exercised exclusively within the confines of the state. It was only in the mid-eighteenth century that the word police was used by reformers, such as Fielding, to describe a specific body of persons engaged in the prevention of crime, the protection of property and the maintenance of public order. After the formation of the 'new police' in 1829, however, this narrow definition of policing became the accepted one. Yet, this equation of police with policing was misleading, public policing never eradicating the private forms which preceded it. On the contrary, public and private modes of policing have co-existed with one another, in varying balance, from 1829 to the present day.

Policing may be defined as a complex of institutions and practices geared towards the regulation of a determinate social order. Far from being an exclusively criminological practice, policing is also a moral one. Colquhoun's demand that the emerging Metropolitan police should aim to 'give the minds of the People a right bias' (cited in Philips 1980: 177) was, after all, reflected in the policing of prostitution, truancy and contagious diseases during the Victorian era, just as it is in current attempts to reconstitute communities as moral entities through community policing. To equate policing with the moral order is, however, only part of the picture. The preservation of an 'established order' from internal or external threat involves not merely the presence of protection but also the absence of risk (Shearing 1992).

According to this view, policing may be regarded as synonymous with 'security', the key to which lies in the elimination of fear. (The Latin derivation of security, *se* ['without'] *cura* ['care'] confirms that point). Spitzer captures the essence of this relationship in his observation that '[s]ecurity is said to exist when something *does not* occur rather than when it does' (Spitzer 1987: 47). Policing consists, then, of those regulatory practices through which some guarantee of security is given to members of an established order.

Private policing

Private policing consists of two components. 'Commercial' policing involves the purchase and sale of security commodities in the market place. 'Civil' policing consists of those voluntary policing activities undertaken by individuals and groups in civil society. The history of commercial policing in Britain is a long one, McMullan's (1987) account of crime control in sixteenth and seventeenth century London pointing to the systematic recruitment of paid informers and thief-takers by a state unable to control unregulated areas. This is an early example of what South (1984) has referred to as 'the commercial compromise of the state', an invariable feature of all systems in which the commercial sector has a policing role, though one whose precise character varies with circumstances.

A comparison of the pattern of historical development in Britain and the USA confirms this point. In Britain, public policing emerged as an attempted political solution to two problems: the crime and social disorder associated with capitalist industrialization; and the corruption and inefficiency said to be associated with the old system of parish constables. Significantly, however, the germ of public police organization lay in the commercial sector (Bowden 1978). Colquhoun's Marine Police Establishment of 1798 received the bulk of its funding from the West India Company, while the privately funded Bow Street Runners were by no means averse to accepting rewards for services offered. Even after the formation of the 'new police', wealthy merchants continued to deploy private guards and subscription forces continued to be recruited in the localities (Emsley 1987).

The situation in the USA was somewhat different. The first public police force was established in New York in 1844, others being set up in Chicago and the major cities thereafter. However, the police were initially regarded as incompetent and politically untrustworthy. More than that, the same allegations of corruption which had been made about the old police in Britain were directed at the new American forces a century later (Spitzer & Scull 1977). The uneasy balance between state and federal power, together with the delay in the development of federal law enforcement, also placed demands on new forces which they found difficult to meet. The result was a different trajectory of development from that in Britain. British public policing was seen as the panacea for private graft and incompetence whereas, in the USA, commercial policing emerged to compensate for the perceived inadequacies of the new public police. Only a decade after the establishment of the Chicago police, Pinkerton set up his North West Police Agency in the city. By 1892 there were 15 commercial policing agencies in Chicago and 20 in New York.

For these reasons commercial policing developed more rapidly in the USA than in Britain. The American state's commercial compromise was also a more overt one. Private police forces – such as the notorious 'Pennsylvania Cossacks' – were recruited in the manufacturing, mining and railroad industries to discipline the workforce, some states handing over wholesale policing powers to company forces (Morn 1982). Commercial policing corporations, such as Pinkerton, Burns and Brinks also had close connections with the state from their inception, both Pinkerton and Burns having worked for the US Secret Service (Nalla & Newman 1990). So pervasive was the activity of the Pinkerton agency in the fields of political and industrial espionage that one commentator observed 'the Pinkerton law enforcement dynasty provided America with something we always boasted we didn't need and never had: a national police force' (O'Toole 1978: 28).

There is also a long history of civil policing in Britain and America. Prior to the establishment of a public justice system, victims of crime wishing to seek redress had to undertake private prosecutions. In England and Wales the expense of prosecution encouraged people of property to band together in 'felons associations' in order to share costs. Associations usually consisted of between 20 and 60 members operating in a geographical area of between 10 and 20 miles. Usually, they would offer rewards for information leading to arrest and conviction, assist members in prosecution and, in some cases, undertake posse and patrol activity. Though there is dispute about the precise number of felons associations – Shubert (1981) suggests between 750 and 1,000 while King (1989) estimates between 1,000 and 4,000 – by the 1830s their numbers were, undoubtedly, considerable. During the second quarter of the century some of these associations developed into commercial subscription forces, a number of these eventually merging into 'new' public police forces.

Felons associations were set up to deal with property crimes such as burglary, sheep stealing and, in particular, horse theft. The 'anti-horse thief' movement which appeared in America at the same time was part of what Brown (1975) has termed 'the American vigilante tradition'. The first vigilante movement appeared in 1767 and, from then until about 1900, vigilantism was a dominant factor in American life. At least 326 movements have been documented for this period, most containing a few hundred members whose leaders were drawn, primarily, from business, professional and farming elites. Like their English counterparts in felons associations, such local vigilante leaders had a desire to reduce the tax burden and saw merit in a system of justice which was 'cheaper, as well as quicker and more certain than regular justice' (Brown 1975: 117). Though vigilantism is popularly seen as a response to crime, a distinction has been drawn between 'classic' (or 'crime control') and 'neo' (or 'social control') vigilantism (Brown 1975: Rosenbaum & Sedeberg 1976). The former was directed at horse thieves, outlaws and the rural lower classes up to about 1900. The latter was directed at the control of urban Catholics, Jews, Negroes, radicals and labour leaders from the late nineteenth century onwards, as well as at moral transgressions such as drunkenness, gambling and prostitution.

There are both similarities and differences between the English felons associations and American vigilantes (Little & Sheffield 1983). In both cases, local elites engaged in civil policing in order to produce speedy and efficient justice. However, while American vigilantes often exceeded the law, felons associations retained a strong attachment to it. In both cases civil policing was a reaction to the disruption arising from rapid social change. Yet, the distinctness of each mode reflected different structural conditions. In England, felons associations operated in a paradoxical manner: autonomous of, yet dependent upon law and the courts. On the American frontier, the sparseness of settlement and the inadequate tax base arising from it, made the very idea of law enforcement problematic. Formal justice, where it existed, was fragile, outlaws bribing officials, packing juries and intimidating witnesses without compunction. In those circumstances, classic vigilantism consisted of organized, extra-legal movements whose members invariably took the law into their own hands (Brown 1975). Civil policing may arise, then, as a common adaptive form during times of social instability, though one which will have specific characteristics according to given social conditions.

Contemporary commercial policing
Though commercial security has had a significant role to play in American policing for much of the twentieth century, the industry's rapid expansion during the post war era attracted particular interest during the 1970s. Kakalik & Wildhorn (1972), having compared the rates of growth for public and private policing between 1950 and 1970, predicted that despite the significant expansion of contract guarding, public policing would continue to grow more rapidly than its commercial counterpart. In fact, by the end of the 1970s public police growth had stabilized. In the light of this, the first 'Hallcrest Report' (Cunningham & Taylor 1985) indicated that the number of uniformed guards alone exceeded the total of 580,000 sworn police officers then in post, and concluded that private police outnumbered public police by a ratio of 2:1. The second Hallcrest study (Cunningham *et al.* 1990) indicated that by 1990 a total of 965,300 personnel were employed in commercial security, 54 per cent of whom were contract guards. The same report predicted that by the year 2,000 total employment would number almost 1.5 million, half of whom would be employed in the guard sector. On that basis, the private/public policing ratio in the USA would be in the region of 3:1.

Whereas in the USA and Canada (Shearing & Stenning 1981; Stenning & Shearing 1980) there is a reliable body of empirical data on the size and structure of the commercial security sector, the position in other jurisdictions is less clear. A few companies operated between the wars in Britain, France, the Netherlands, Sweden and Finland (South 1988; de Waard & van der Hoek 1991; Johnston 1992) though often, as in Britain, consolidation only occurred after 1945. Elsewhere, development happened later. The first Japanese company was established in 1962, the industry being given impetus by the security demands of the 1964 Tokyo Olympic games (Miyazawa 1991). Since then, growth has been dramatic. Between 1989 and 1993 the number of Japanese security businesses grew from 5,248 to 7,062 and the number of guards from 232,617 to 321,721. By comparison, the combined authorized police strength for the Japanese national and Prefectural Police stood at 259,000 in 1993 (National Police Agency 1994). In Spain the industry emerged as a result of legislation passed in 1974 requiring security to be employed in the transportation of cash

(Gomez-Baeza 1988). Indeed, the most significant period of expansion in Europe occurred during the 1970s when 'fiscal crisis' came to be regarded as a key problem of government. In Italy, for example, no less than 50 per cent of companies were established between 1970 and 1975, the majority of others being formed after 1976 (Johnston 1992).

Estimates of the size of the industry in Britain have been notoriously inaccurate. However, recent research by Jones & Newburn (1998), based on data drawn from the Yellow Pages Business Classification and the Labour Force Survey, has produced far more reliable figures. Total employment in the British contract security industry now exceeds one third of a million (333,631), with employment in the 'services and equipment sector' (which includes guarding) standing at 182,596. This latter figure, alone, is equivalent to the total number of police and civilians employed in the 43 constabularies in England and Wales. As is the case in other countries, the most rapid area of expansion is in electronic security. Indeed, out of the total of 6,899 security companies identified in the research, no fewer than 2,547 are in the electronics sector, the remainder being in services and equipment (2,281), the provision of locks and safes (864), detective services (767) and bailiff services (440).

A comparative analysis of commercial security in ten European countries has recently been undertaken by the Dutch Ministry of Justice, though the authors' admission that 'international comparisons entail many problems' (de Waard & van der Hoek 1991: 3; see also de Waard 1993) should be noted. In order to consider commercial policing in its wider context, the study examines (i) numbers of police personnel (ii) numbers of private security personnel (iii) total security personnel (public plus private) and (iv) the ratio of public to private security for each country. According to the authors '[a] remarkable finding in this study is the high number of police personnel per 100,000 inhabitants for the Southern European countries like Portugal, Spain and France' (de Waard 1993: 62) compared to Northern ones. Thus, the highest ranked countries – Portugal (486 police per 100,000 inhabitants), Spain (422) and France (360) – contrast with Britain (ranked fifth at 317) and the Netherlands (ranked ninth at 195). The position with commercial security is, however, less geographically polarized, Germany (307 private security personnel per 100,000 inhabitants) being followed by Sweden (182) and Spain (165). When the two categories are combined it is concluded that Portugal (636 security personnel per 100,000), Germany (634) and Spain (587) 'are well in the lead in Europe as regards security services' (de Waard & van der Hoek 1991: 27).

Overall, this study suggests that despite the rapid expansion of the last 20 years, the private security sector in Europe – unlike its counterpart in the USA – remains the secondary, rather than the primary, protective resource, the highest ratio of private to public police (Germany at 0.94: 1) still falling well short of the 2:1 or 3:1 ratios cited for the USA. However, one has to be cautious about the figures used in this research – based mainly on police statistics and expert opinion – and about the conclusions drawn from their use. In the case of Britain, for example, the estimation of private security employees (70,000) appears to include only those working for member companies of the British Security Industry Association, the main trade body. On the basis of these figures, Britain ranks sixth in terms of private security employees (123 per 100,000 inhabitants) and has a private security to public police ratio of 0.39:1. By using Jones & Newburn's (1998) data, however, these estimates are transformed dramatically. This happens whether one bases calculations on guard numbers alone, or upon the total number of personnel employed in the security industry. In the first case, the figure of 182,596 guards identified in the research generates 321 security personnel per 100,000 inhabitants and a private security to public police ratio of 1:1. In the second case, 333,631 security employees generates a private security to public police ratio of 1.85: 1, a figure far in excess of the estimate for Germany, the highest ranked country in the sample. In effect, two conclusions can be drawn from Jones & Newburn's (1998) research: that Britain has roughly one private security guard for every public police officer, a figure comparable to that found in the USA during the early 1980s (see Cunningham & Taylor 1985: 106, Table 8–1); and that Britain has almost two private security employees for each police officer.

Inevitably, these conclusions cast doubt on the claim made by the Dutch researchers that commercial security remains subsidiary to public policing as a protective measure throughout Europe. Without detailed empirical studies of private security employment in the individual European countries it is impossible to draw definitive conclusions. However, it is almost certain that the Dutch research underestimates not just the numbers of British private security personnel but also those employed in other European countries. This intuitive conclusion is borne out by the continued rapid expansion of the European security market. Though considerably smaller than its counterpart in the USA – predicted to reach $103 billion by the year 2000 (Cunningham *et al.* (1990) – the European market is growing rapidly. Research carried out by McAlpine Thorpe and Warrior (Narayan 1994) indicated that the total market for security products and services in five European countries (Germany, Spain, Italy, France and the UK) stood at £11.2 billion in 1992, the largest market being in Germany (£3.7 billion) and the second largest in the UK (£2.4 billion). MTW predicted that the market would grow at an average rate of 6 per cent per annum with security services (including guarding) retaining the highest market share, the fastest annual growth rates being in CCTV, access control and integrated security systems.

Contemporary civil policing

The growth of commercial security is associated with a fragmentation of policing whose main effect is to disperse activity between multiple providers. Civil policing – defined here as voluntary activity undertaken in civil society rather than under the aegis of the state – contributes further to this dispersal. There are several ways of differentiating between the forms of civil policing. A crude categorization, beloved by British Home Secretaries, distinguishes 'vigilance' (the good citizen acting as the 'eyes and ears' of the police) from 'vigilantism' (the irresponsible citizen 'taking the law into his or her own hands'). An alternative view (Johnston 1992) distinguishes 'responsible citizenship' (voluntary policing sponsored by the state) from 'autonomous citizenship' (voluntary policing which lacks state support and may, in fact, receive state condemnation). This distinction implies that initiatives, such as the neighbourhood watch street patrols recently approved by the Home Office, lie on the margins of civil policing proper due to their reliance on state authority. According to that view the purest form of civil policing is the autonomous one. Since both responsible and autonomous modes of engagement contribute towards the fragmentation of policing, however, each should be considered.

Nowadays, virtually all states attempt to mobilize responsible citizens for policing purposes. These attempts take various forms. As this paragraph is being written the British Home Secretary has announced a £4 million initiative to increase the size of the volunteer Special Constabulary. In the Netherlands, a key element of crime prevention policy has been the attempt to maximize 'functional surveillance' of public space. This policy has led to various initiatives: the employment of uniformed staff to counteract fare dodging and vandalism on public transport; the appointment of 'social caretakers' to patrol housing estates; and the recruitment of long-term unemployed people as 'City Stewards' – unsworn persons, employed by the police or the local authority to prevent crime and to interact with the public (Van Andel 1989, Hesseling & van den Hul 1993). In North America a number of police forces are assisted by citizen patrol groups. One such group, in Baltimore, runs nightly patrols of a dozen men drawn from a pool of 500 volunteers. Members ride in their own marked cars and report suspicious incidents to the police by walkie-talkie (Johnston 1992).

These initiatives have developed for two reasons: first, as an attempt by the police to respond to escalating public demand for security – a factor related to its growing commodification (Spitzer 1987); secondly, as an attempt to re-exert police control over an increasingly fragmented policing system, a rationale which has been expressed in both Britain and the Netherlands (Davies 1989, Hesseling & van den Hul 1993). Neither of these objectives is, however, feasible. The expansion of commercial policing will ensure that the demand for security will continue to outstrip supply, a process which will result in further fragmentation of provision and greater dilution of police control over policing functions.

The growing significance of autonomous vigilante activity in the USA and Britain confirms this point. In America, violent vigilantism by 'organized, extra-legal movements, the members of which take the law into their own hands' (Brown 1975: 95–6) was a recurrent historical theme (Ayers 1984; Culberson 1990). In the 1960s a new wave of self-protection groups emerged, some to defend themselves against racism, riot and disorder; others to undertake anti-crime street patrols (Marx & Archer 1973). The most famous of these was, of course, the Guardian Angels. Recognition that citizen patrol groups, like the Angels, were neither illegal nor essentially violent, caused Brown to redefine vigilante organizations as 'associations in which citizens have joined together for self-protection under conditions of disorder' (Brown 1975: 130).

Vigilante activity has also been a significant development in Britain during recent years. Sometimes that activity conforms to Brown's (1975) original definition, the clearest example being the 'punishment shootings' inflicted by paramilitary groups in Northern Ireland (Munck 1988, McCorry and Morrisey 1989, Conway 1993). Yet vigilantism has taken a variety of different forms: singular acts of individual revenge directed at the alleged perpetrators of criminal acts; organized acts of group violence directed against drug pushers; preventive, non-violent anti-crime patrols; self-protective groups mobilized to protect the potential victims of racial or sexual violence; and groups of residents organized against the entry of travellers into their locality (Johnston forthcoming).

One question which arises is whether vigilante activity can be incorporated by the state and at what cost? After all, states engage not only in 'commercial compromises', but also in 'populist' ones: '[i]n the [American] South, the line between vigilante justice and official justice was scarcely discernible at all . . . until . . . the 1960s' (Skolnick and Fyfe 1993: 29). On occasions, however, compromise may be less malignant. The 'Civil Guard' movement which emerged in Israel out of a growing fear of terrorism was successfully co-opted by a national police force, fearful of its continued autonomy: 'What began as a neighbourhood-based, self-help initiative was molded into a quasi-governmental, police-oriented voluntary organization' (Yanay 1993: 381). In this case, the state's capacity to transform autonomous acts into responsible ones owed much to the collective sensibilities of a population faced with external threat. Yet, this example raises an important question. If fragmented policing is to be managed, is the state the most appropriate agency to manage it?

Conclusion: Uniformity and Diversity

Though the history and character of private policing vary from society to society, its current expansion is linked to structural changes whose impact is global. First, while the majority of security companies are small and medium-sized operations, the most significant ones are multinational enterprises operating in diverse fields (including policing, corrections, electronic surveillance and defence) whose influence and connections have led some to label them a new 'military-industrial complex' (Lilley & Knepper 1992). The Pinkerton organization employs 45,000 security personnel in 250 different offices throughout the USA, Canada, Mexico, Asia and Europe. Pinkerton's American rival, the Wackenhut Corporation, employs 39,000 staff in a range of activities: from executive protection to airline security; and from the management of correctional facilities to the provision of security at nuclear installations. Similarly, the UK-based Securicor Group of companies employs 41,000 personnel in a bewildering range of activities: electronic surveillance and alarms, immigration services, the finance, design and construction of prisons, electronic monitoring, mobile and static guarding, hotels, recruitment services, vehicle fleet servicing and mobile communications to name but a few. The transnational character of these huge security enterprises makes (national) comparative analysis of their structure and function problematical. After all, one of their principal aims is to operate, more and more, across national jurisdictions. Wackenhut is now actively involved in British private prisons. Securicor International has recently developed joint ventures in South Africa, Hong Kong, Malaysia, Macau, Indonesia, Thailand and the Caribbean. The pattern of transnational activity can also change quickly. Though functional diversification is commonplace, some companies may choose to consolidate in the light of market assessment. In 1995 the Australian-based Mayne Nickless Group, one of the leading guard firms in North America, announced the sale of its general security operations to the UK-based Rentokil Group as part of a wider strategy of rationalization. Activities also may be affected by political circumstances. British security firms have penetrated the post-apartheid security market in South Africa to the tune of £20 million per annum. Chubb, one of the top five security providers in South Africa, now supplies its customers with 'armed reaction teams' – private SWAT squads which race to the locations of suspected crimes (Woolf 1996).

Secondly, the expansion of private policing has been influenced by two global factors, 'fiscal crisis' and 'mass private property'. As to the first, it has been argued that the state's shrinking tax base has led to an imbalance between the public's demand for security and the public police's capacity to meet it. Under those conditions, the commercial security sector rushes in to 'fill the vacuum'. In Britain, more and more security companies offer preventive patrol services to local authorities and to groups of residents wishing to protect their property. In North America special Business Improvement Districts (BIDs) have been set up to facilitate co-operation between public police and commercial security companies in the resuscitation of urban areas. Since the first initiative in New Orleans in 1975, more than 1,200 cities in the United States and Canada have implemented such schemes, New York City alone having 24 BIDs (Puente 1997, Seamon 1995). Commercial policing has also expanded as a direct consequence of the spatial transformation of private property in late modern societies. 'Mass private property' (Shearing & Stenning 1981), whose archetypal form is the shopping mall, combines private ownership with relatively unlimited public access. Private policing resolves the tension within that relationship: maximizing consumption by restricting access to those who might undermine the commercial imperative – drunks, beggars and the like. In most western societies – though particularly in North America – there is an increased tendency for residential space to adopt the form of mass private property, people living in private apartment blocks and gated communities, rather than in traditional streets. Though this is undoubtedly a global tendency, however, there may be variations in the speed and scope of its development. Jones & Newburn (1998) note that, in Britain, locations which would be archetypal forms of mass private property in North America (such as educational institutions, leisure complexes and hospital sites) have either been owned and run by the state or by non-market 'hybrid' organizations (Johnston 1992). For that reason, they suggest, 'mass hybrid property', rather than mass private property, may be of greater relevance to the future development of commercial policing in Britain.

This observation raises a third point, that global tendencies are mediated by social specifics. In any society, the pace of change in the public/private policing ratio will be affected by specific factors of culture, history and politics. Nevertheless, indications are that commercial policing will gradually become the primary form of protection in most jurisdictions. In Britain, that likelihood has already provoked debate about the 'loss' of police functions (Johnston 1992, Independent Committee 1994, Home Office 1995). Though that debate is important, it tends to obscure a more fundamental point: that, irrespective of how functions are 'parcelled out' between the sectors, police practice in many countries is *already* moulded by the same 'actuarial' philosophy which underpins commercial security. The underlying objective of commercial policing – the prevention of client loss – is premised upon two things: the anticipation of risk and the development of strategies to calculate its level of acceptability: 'Risk management is the anticipation, recognition and appraisal of a risk and the initiation of some action to remove the risk or reduce the potential loss from it to an acceptable level' (Broder: cited in Nalla & Newman 1990: 92). Yet, more and more, public police also prioritize *anticipatory* strategies: the 'targeting' of potential offenders; the surveillance (through CCTV) of locations where crimes might occur; the use of informants for the collection of information which can facilitate intelligence-led policing; the establishment of formal and informal links between police, commercial and military security; and the deployment of dedicated inter-agency teams to nip offending in the bud (Johnston forthcoming). One consequence of that process is that police organizations become part of a network of information-based expert systems seeking to produce knowledge for – and to collect reciprocal knowledge from – other security agencies (Ericson 1994). In effect all police – both public and private – become knowledge brokers.

Fourthly, the increased fragmentation of policing has to be located within a wider pattern of social diversity. In many societies social divisions are more complex and heterogeneous than hitherto, conflicts being spread along plural lines rather than polarized across singular ones. This begs the question of whether multiple bases of conflict generate correspondingly plural modes of policing. Social diversity is, moreover, accompanied by the dispersal and devolution of state power. Such dispersal is not merely due to the contraction of the public sphere through privatization. Globalizing tendencies, such as the internationalization of capital and the process of 'Europeanization', compromise the sovereignty of the nation state. Yet, these processes also have an uneven impact. Globalization not only produces uniformity across social formations, it leads to diverse forms of local resistance being mobilized around national, regional and cultural issues. In those circumstances the state is pulled, simultaneously, in different directions, statehood being 'stretched' (Bottoms and Wiles 1994) or even 'unravelled' (Crook *et al.* 1993) in the process.

The globalizing and restructuring tendencies which shape late modern societies have important implications for comparative analysis, since the trajectory of change which they predict is one in which structural uniformity leads to social diversity. This paradox is evident in the case of policing. On the one hand, the expansion of mass private property, the commodification of security, the dispersal of state authority, the development of actuarial modes of calculation, the push towards inter-agency and community policing strategies and the drive to make citizens more and more responsible for their own security are uniform tendencies in all late modern societies. On the other hand, the effect of those tendencies is to disperse policing amongst a diverse multiplicity of alternative providers. What, then, will determine the specificity of such 'uniformly diverse' policing systems in the future?

The answer to this question lies in politics, though no longer only in the state. The key issue for policing in the twenty-first century will be about 'governing diversity'.

How, in other words, are fragmented policing systems to be governed so as to maximize democratic accountability, justice and effectiveness? Failure to address that question might have serious consequences. Davis's (1992) analysis of Los Angeles describes a post-modern nightmare in which public space is eradicated, vigilantism is rife, private armies dominate and those who can afford to do so retreat behind walled enclaves. Yet, there are signs that a debate is developing. In Britain the re-emergence of municipal policing (Johnston 1993) has begun to raise questions about the management of relations between commercial, civil, public and municipal police at local levels (Independent Committee 1994). Brogden & Shearing's (1993) analysis of the situation in South Africa addresses the same issue, proposing a 'dual model' in which policing – perceived as a series of local networks – is grounded primarily in (local) civil society and only secondarily in the (central) state. As that analysis proposes, any solution to the problem of governing diversity will require a fundamental re-assessment of relations between civil society and the state. That is not to suggest a single solution to the problem. The way in which diversity is managed in any society will reflect the exact pattern of policing found there, the distinctive culture and structure of that society and the specific manner in which politics is deployed to mediate between the locality and the centre. It is these issues which provide the agenda for comparative policing in the next century.

Bibliography

Ayers, E.L. 1984. *Vengeance and justice.* New York: Oxford University Press.

Bottoms, A.E. & P. Wiles 1994. Understanding crime prevention in late modern Societies. Paper presented at 22nd Cropwood Round Table Conference: Preventing Crime and Disorder: Targeting Strategies and Community Responsibilities, Institute of Criminology, Cambridge, England.

Bowden, T. 1978. *Beyond the limits of the law.* Harmondsworth: Penguin.

Brogden, M. & C.D. Shearing 1993. *Policing for a new South Africa.* London: Routledge.

Brown, R.M. 1975. *Strain of violence.* New York: Oxford University Press.

Conway, P. 1993. The informal justice system in Northern Ireland. Paper presented at British Criminology Conference, Cardiff: Wales.

Crook, S., J. Pakulski, M. Waters 1993. *Postmodernization: change in advanced society.* London: Sage

Culberson, W.C. 1990. *Vigilantism: political history and private power in America.* New York: Greenwood Press.

Cunningham, W.C. & T. Taylor 1985. *Private security and police in America*, Portland: Chancellor Press.

Cunningham, W.C., J.J. Strauchs, C.W. Van Meter 1990. *Private Security Trends 1970–2000.* Boston: Butterworth-Heinemann.

Davies, S. 1989. Streets ahead. *Police Review* (10 November), 2277.

Davis, M. 1992. *Beyond blade runner: urban control: the ecology of fear.* Westfield, New Jersey: Open Magazine Pamphlet Series.

de Waard, J. 1993. The private security sector in fifteen European countries: size, rules and legislation. *Security Journal* **4** (2), 58–63.

de Waard, J.J. & J. van der Hoek 1991. *Private security: size of sector and legislation in the Netherlands and Europe.* Ministry of Justice: The Hague.

Emsley, C. 1987. *Crime and society in England 1750–1900.* London: Longman.

Ericson, R. 1994. The division of expert knowledge in policing and security. *British Journal of Sociology* **45** (2), 149–75.

Gomez-Baeza, R. 1988. Spain – too fast too soon? *International Security Review*, September/October, 45–7.

Hesseling, R. & H. van den Hul 1993. Surveillance – a public or private concern? In *Policing . . . private or public? proceedings of a conference.* Manchester: Metropolitan University.

Home Office 1995. *Review of police core and ancillary tasks.* London: Home Office.

Independent Committee of Inquiry into the Role and Responsibilities of the Police 1994. *Discussion document.* London: Police Foundation/Policy Studies Institute.

Johnston, L. 1992. *The rebirth of private policing.* London: Routledge.

Johnston, L. 1993. Privatisation and protection: spatial and sectoral ideologies in British policing and crime prevention. *Modern Law Review* **56** (6), 771–92.

Johnston, L. 1996. What is vigilantism? *British Journal of Criminology* **36** (2), 220–36.

Johnston, L. forthcoming *Policing Britain.* London: Longman.

Jones, T. & T. Newburn 1998. *Private security and public policing*, Oxford: Clarendon Press.

Kakalik, J.S. & S. Wildhorn 1972. *Private police in the United States, 5 vols.* National Institute of Law Enforcement and Criminal Justice, Washington: US Dept. of Justice.

King, P. 1989. Prosecution associations and their impact in eighteenth century Essex. In *Policing and prosecution in Britain 1750–1850*, D. Hay & F. Snyder (eds), 171–207. Oxford: Clarendon Press.

Lilley, J.R. & P. Knepper 1992. An international perspective on the privatization of corrections. *Howard Journal* **31** (3), 174–91.

Little, C.B. & C.P. Sheffield 1983. Frontiers and criminal justice: English private prosecution associations and American vigilantism in the eighteenth and nineteenth centuries. *American Sociological Review* **48**, 796–808.

McCorry, J. & M. Morrisey 1989. Community, crime and punishment in West Belfast. *The Howard Journal of Criminal Justice* **28** (4), 282–90.

McMullan, J.L. 1987. Policing the criminal underworld: state power and decentralized social control in London 1550–1700. In *Transcarceration: essays in the sociology of social control*, J. Lowman, R.J. Menzies & T.S. Palys (eds), 119–38. Aldershot: Gower.

Marx, G. & D. Archer 1973. The urban vigilate. *Psychology Today* (January), 45–50.

Miyazawa, S. 1991. The private sector and law enforcement in Japan. In *Privatization and its alternative*, W.T. Gormley (ed.), 241–57. Madison: University of Wisconsin Press.

Morn, F. 1982. *The eye that never sleeps.* Bloomington, Indiana: Indiana University Press.

Munck, R. 1988. The lads and the hoods: alternative justice in an Irish context. In *Whose law and order? aspects of crime and scoial control in Irish society*, M. Tomlinson, T. Varley & C. McCullagh (eds), 41–53. Belfast: Sociological Association of Ireland.

Nalla, M. & G. Newman 1990. *A primer in private security.* New York: Harrow & Heston.

Narayan, S. 1994. The West European market for security products and services. *International Security Review*, Spring, 43–4.

National Police Agency Government of Japan. 1994 *White paper on police 1994 (Excerpt)*, Tokyo: Police Association.

O'Toole, G. 1978. *The private sector: private spies, rent-a-cops and the police–industrial complex*, New York: Norton.

Palmer, S.H. 1988. *Police and protest in England and Ireland 1780–1850.* Cambridge: Cambridge University Press.

Philips, D. 1980. 'A new engine of power and authority': the institutionalisation of law enforcement in England 1780–1830. In *Crime and the law: the social history of crime in Western Europe since 1500*, V.A.C. Gatrell, B. Lenman &. G. Parker (eds), 155–89. London: Europa.

Puente, M. 1997. Public-private teaming is revitalizing downtowns. *US Today*, 18 November.

Rosenbaum, H.J. & P.C. Sedeberg (eds) 1976. *Vigilante politics.* Pennsylvania: Pennsylvania University Press.

Seamon, T.M. 1995. Private forces for public good. *Security Management*, September, 92–3.

Shearing, C.D. 1992. The relation between public and private policing. In *Modern policing: crime and justice: a review of research vol. 15*, M. Tonry and N. Morris (eds), 399–434. Chicago: University of Chicago.

Shearing, C.D. & P.C. Stenning 1981. Modern private security: its growth and implications. In *Crime and justice: an annual review of research, vol. 3.* Chicago: University of Chicago Press.

Shubert, A. 1981. Private initiative in law enforcement: associations for the prosecution of felons. In *Policing and punishment in nineteenth century England*, V. Bailey (ed.), 25–41. London: Croom Helm.

Skolnick, J.H. & J.J. Fyfe 1993. *Above the Law: police and the excessive use of force.* New York: Free Press.

South, N. 1984. Private security, the division of policing labour and the commercial compromise of the state. *Research in Law, Deviance and Social Control* **6**, 171–98.

South, N. 1988. *Policing for profit.* London: Sage.

Spitzer, S. 1987. Security and control in capitalist societies: the fetishism of security and the secret thereof. In *Transcarceration: essays in the sociology of social control*, J. Lowman, R.J. Menzies & T.S. Palys (eds), 43–58. Aldershot: Gower.

Spitzer, S. & A. Scull 1977. Privatization and capitalist development: the case of the private police. *Social Problems* **25** (1), 18–29.

Stenning, P.C. & C.D. Shearing 1980. The quiet revolution: the nature, development and general legal implications of private security in Canada. *Criminal Law Quarterly* **22**, 220–48.

Van Andel, H. 1989. Crime prevention that works: the case of public transport in the Netherlands. *British Journal of Criminology* **29** (1), 47–56.

Woolf, M. 1996. British firms cash in on crime. *The Observer*, 14 July.

Yanay, U. 1993. Co-opting vigilantism: Government response to community action for personal safety. *Journal of Public Policy*, Oct–Dec, 381–96.

Index